Why C++? Why The Beginner's C

D0608088

The natural successor to C, in driving the development community is C++. This new 'customized' version of C, has all the right elements for 21st century programs. Portability across machine types, thinking in modules and speed of execution. As a beginner with C++, you have chosen the fastest route to a professional language skill. Beginner's C++ will step you through all the aspects of this worldwide language, including the challenging area of Object Oriented programming. Examples all the way will give you the best grounding in programming techniques using C++. If you have the requisite starting material - a PC and a willingness to experiment, then the Wrox learning system in this book will give you a painless entry into C++.

What is Wrox Press?

Wrox Press is a computer book publisher which promotes a brand new concept - clear, jargon-free programming and database titles that fulfill your real demands. We publish for everyone, from the novice through to the experienced programmer. To ensure our books meet your needs, we carry out continuous research on all our titles. Through our dialog with you we can craft the book you really need.

We welcome suggestions and take all of them to heart - your input is paramount in creating the next great Wrox title. Use the reply card inside this book or mail us at:

feedback@wrox.demon.co.uk
or
Compuserve 100063, 2152

Wrox Press Ltd.
2710 W. Touhy
Chicago
IL 60645
USA

Tel: **0101 312 465 3559**
Fax: **0101 312 465 4063**

The Beginner's Guide to
C++

Oleg Yaroshenko

Wrox Press Ltd.®

The Beginner's Guide to C++

© 1994 Oleg Yaroshenko

Published by Wrox Press Ltd. 1334 Warwick Road, Birmingham, B27 6PR UK
Library of Congress Catalog Number: 94-78390

ISBN 1-874416-26-5

Trademark Acknowledgements

Wrox has endeavored to provide trademark information about all the companies and products mentioned in this book by the appropriate use of capitals. However, Wrox cannot guarantee the accuracy of this information.

Credits

Author
Oleg Yaroshenko

Technical Editors
Ivor Horton
Ian Wilks

Series Editor
Nina Barnsley

Technical Reviewers
David Bolton
Julian Templeman

Production Manager
Gina Mance

Book Layout
Ewart Liburd
Eddie Fisher
Greg Powell
Joanne Wheeler

Proof Readers
James Hare
Pam Brand

Additional Material
Ian Wilks

Cover Design
Third Wave

For more information on Third Wave, contact Ross Alderson on 44-21 456 1400

cover photograph supplied by Pictor International

About the Author

Oleg Yaroshenko is a programmer and head of department at the Scientific Research Institute of Automated Systems which is part of the research and production association Agat. He has 20 years programming experience and is the author of 24 publications. In his spare time, Oleg enjoys sports, especiallly skiing and cycling.

Thank You

Thanks must go to my wife Galina, my sons Jan and Alexander, and my mother and sister for their invaluable help and support during the writing of this book. Thanks also to my colleagues Galina Chernovetz, Galina Kuzmenok and Ludmila Grigorieva for their typing skills!

SUMMARY OF CONTENTS

CONTENTS

Chapter 15 - Using Preprocessing Directives 597

Why The Beginner's Guide?

This book is going to teach you C++ easily and painlessly. The book has been designed to include a mixture of carefully designed example programs that illustrate the subject, and useful programs that demonstrate the tools you learn in action.

We have designed the book like this because we know that people don't learn for the sake of learning. Most people want to learn to program so they can achieve something with their programs. So learning C++ isn't an aim in itself, you want to be able to really use the language. For this reason, wherever possible, each chapter in the book ends with a real life application of what you have learnt. This takes you through a problem and finds its solution in a C++ program. This shows you how the language works - not just the language constructs.

The programs in the book aren't trivial and can be quite tough. The reward is that their effectiveness in teaching you how C++ is applied in practice is much greater than the average example.

The book is based on the principle that you learn best by doing. If we promised to teach you French just by teaching you the grammar, you might find it dubious if we claimed you would be fluent by the end. The only way you can become fluent is if you use what you learn in a real life way. We make extensive use of complete working examples throughout the book, together with clear and thorough explanations.

How to Use This Book

Because we believe in the hands-on approach, you will write your first programs in the very first chapter. Every chapter has several programs to put the theory into practice and these examples are key to the book. We would advise you to type in as many as possible. You won't always find it easy or get it right, but the very act of typing programs in is a tremendous aid to remembering the language elements. When you do get a program to work for the first time, particularly when you are trying to solve your own problems, the sense of excitement and satisfaction will make it all worthwhile.

Each chapter covers a lot of ground. Don't expect to be able to digest it all in a few hours. Take your time and experiment with your own ideas. Try modifying the programs and see what you can do, that's when it gets really interesting. Don't be afraid of trying anything out. If you don't understand how something works, just type in a few variations and see what happens. Making mistakes is usually very educational (unless you are a highwire walker!) A good approach is to read a chapter through, and once you have a good idea of its scope, go back to the beginning and work through all the examples. For some topics you will almost certainly need to go through the material a couple of times before it really sticks.

You may find the end of chapter programs quite hard. Don't worry if it isn't all completely clear on the first try. There are bound to be bits that you find difficult to understand at first because they often apply what you have learnt to quite complicated problems, so persevere. Some programs take time to understand because they are doing complicated things. If you really get stuck, all the end of chapter programs are designed so that you can skip them, carry on with the next chapter and come back to them at a later date. You can even go through the book right to the end without worrying about them. The point of these programs is that they are useful, even after you finish the book.

Who is This Book For?

This book is for both beginners to programming and beginners to C++. If you are a complete novice then this book will teach you programming, using C++ as the vehicle. If you already know another language, but want to learn C++, this book will teach you all you need to know. It assumes no knowledge, but moves quickly and easily from the basics to the real meat of the subject. By the end of the book you will have a thorough grounding in C++, and provided you have used, understood and exercised all the examples, you should have little trouble in writing programs for yourself.

What You Need To Use This Book

The only personal attributes you need to tackle programming in C++ is a basic knowledge of high school math, and the enthusiasm to get through a 500+ page book. You will also need a computer with a C++ compiler installed on it, so you can run the examples.

Conventions Used

To enable you to find your way around this book easily, we have used various different styles to highlight different references.

Program Code

All programs in the book are highlighted with a blue background so you can find them easily.

When we use extracts from this code we also shade it so you can spot it quickly.

When we have shown general examples of code or the output from a program we have put it in this style:

```
The is how general code and output will look.
```

When code features in the middle of sentences, we write it in **this_style**.

When for the sake of brevity we haven't printed some lines of code we'll use three periods
...
to indicate a missing fragment.

In the end of chapter programs we repeat a lot of the code. This is deliberate, so that you can see the flow of the program develop. We have shaded lines which are new additions to the program, and left the lines that are repeated unshaded. This will enable you to see immediately where new stuff has been added.

```
This is repeated code.
This is new code.
This is repeated code.
This is new code.
This is new code.
```

Important Bits, Interesting Bits

Bits that you really must read are in this type of box.

Things that are interesting but not essential are in this type of box.

- Important words are in **this style**. These are significant words that we are meeting for the first time. Subsequently they will appear as normal test.

- File names are in **THIS_STYLE**. All file names appear like this in the text, even when they are conventionally written in lower case inside a program.

- Keys that you press are in *this style*, such as *Enter* or *Ctrl*.

Tell Us What You Think

One last thing. We've tried to make the book enjoyable and accurate. The programming community is what we're here to serve, so if you have any queries or suggestions, or comments about this book, let us know, we will be delighted to hear from you. You can help us ensure that our future books are even better. Return the reply card at the back of the book, or contact us direct at Wrox. You can also use e-mail:

feedback@wrox.demon.co.uk
Compuserve: 100062,2152

Thanks for your support.

CHAPTER 1

Your First Programs

This book is going to take you on an exciting journey into the world of C++. This journey is going to be a bit like learning a sport, like skiing or horse riding. It can be hard work, but when things go well it can also be exhilarating.

If this is your first language, or you are new to C++ we are going to teach you all the fundamentals of C++ programming in an enjoyable and easy-to-understand way. By the end of this first chapter you will have written your first few C++ programs and will have had an exciting taste of controlling your computer.

We are going to have to cover a few basic ideas about computers, but the hands-on approach means you will be writing your own programs as soon as possible. Don't worry if you don't understand everything. The main thing is to get your fingers on the key board and start typing. You will make mistakes, we all do, but that's the quickest way to learn.

In this chapter you will:

> Understand what a program is

> Understand what a programming language is and does

> Write and run your first programs

What is a Program?

A computer program is a series of simple instructions that tell your computer to do some particular task. The instructions a computer is able to execute have to be of a very specific kind. Give a computer something that isn't one of the instructions it understands and it won't do anything.

Computer Instructions

Computers don't speak English. They don't even speak C++. They are so simple that the only things they understand are ones (1s) and zeros (0s) like:

        1011 0100 0000 1001 ....

Does this mean anything to you? All programs look like the example above, and are collections of numbers, known as **binary** numbers because the only digits involved are 0 and 1. The numbers instruct your computer to perform an action, and tell it where the data it needs can be found. Don't worry though, you won't have to produce thousands of binary digits like these. Nowadays there is a better way.

Early on in computing, some bright, or possibly lazy, individuals cottoned on to a revolutionary idea: instead of all these 1s and 0s, if you had a program that could read instructions that were a bit closer to what the average human was happy to deal with, and then translate them into the weird stuff, then computers might be a whole lot easier to use - and could conceivably be quite useful.

This was a brilliant idea and it produced various languages which people could use to communicate with their computers more easily and which could then convert that communication into something the computer was happy with. C++ is one of those intermediaries and is one of the most versatile and widely used.

There are now many such programs which let humans give instructions to computers. They are generally called **compilers**, which translate - or rather compile - a program written in a high-level programming language into binary machine instructions. Since in reality, your computer only understands binary numbers, this process is an essential part of producing a computer program.

In the programming world there are high-level and low-level languages. This simply means that since the native language of a computer is machine code, a single instruction in a low-level language corresponds closely to a single instruction in machine code. In a high-level language, one statement or instruction could correspond to many more lines of machine code. Languages such as Assembler are low-level, and languages like BASIC, Lisp and Prolog are high-level languages. High-level languages are much closer to English, and therefore much easier to understand. C++ is an odd ball: it is really a medium-level language because it has some features of both types of language.

The Ideas Behind a Programming Language

You are now ready to create your first C++ program. The program is going to demonstrate how you can output information to your screen and it will give you your first taste at really controlling your computer. This kind of output is an important part of the majority of professional programs.

Once you have written this first program, you'll be able to program the computer to output a copyright message, stating that you are the author of the program, or modify the program to display other information.

Of course, you have enough experience of life to understand the difficulties that can face the novice horse-rider, cyclist or skier. You will realize that while creating your first program you will have to overcome obstacles that have no direct connection with programming or with C++.

If you decide to go skiing, you need a lot of things other than skis: ski-bindings, boots, sticks, a ski-suit, sun-glasses, gloves etc. It is the same with programming. You'll need the right equipment (a computer) and programming tools (such as an operating system, text editor, compiler etc.).

Your First Program

Let's start putting what we have learnt into practice. In the places where the action is specific to either DOS or UNIX, we have described both alternatives, just look for the heading that covers your operating system.

Try It Out!

Try It Out - Your First C++ Program

For this first program we are going to get you to type in something that probably won't mean much to you and then show you how to compile and run it. We are going to explain a little about what is happening in your computer, using a real example.

1 Switch on your computer.

2 In DOS

Load your compiler. To do this from the **c:** prompt you need to change the directory to the one where the compiler commands are found. This is normally a sub-directory such as **c:\tc\bin.** (This is for Turbo C++ but the exact subdirectory will depend on what product you use and where on your fixed disk you install it. The easiest thing is to check your manual.)

Next type the command to start your compiler, the command will again depend on which product you are using, but would typically be **tc.exe** or something similar. This process can be summarized as follows:

```
c:\>

c:\>cd   tc\bin

c:\tc\bin>

c:\tc\bin>tc.exe
```

You will now be in the editing screen where you can type and edit your program.

Using the file menu of your compiler select a **New** file. This will then open up an editing screen where you will be able to write your code (refer to your product manual for a full description of how to use your editor). If you are using a command line compiler then you may have to use the DOS edit program to write and edit the program. To do this from the **c:** prompt, type **edit**. If you have already created a file and you want to edit it, you simply add the file name. For example, to edit the file **prog1.cpp,** you would type **edit prog1.cpp**.

In UNIX

Load your editor. There are many text editors available for UNIX, a common one would be the **vi** editor. To use this type **vi prog1.cpp** and then type your code. For more information on how to use the editor for UNIX, refer to your manual. You need to give the file the extension **.cpp** (for example, **example.cpp**) as this is important for when the computer actually compiles the code.

3   Type in the following program exactly as written below. Be careful to use the punctuation exactly as you see here.

```
//        Program 1.1

#include <iostream.h>

void main()
{
  cout <<  "Hello! "
          "Congratulations on your first"
          " C++ program";
}
```

It consists of a few lines of text which you will understand, and some characters which you may not. Be careful when typing in the program. The punctuation is very important. Check you use the right kinds of brackets and braces, and don't forget the semi-colon. Can you guess what output you get from the program?

4   Save the file (call it **PROG1.CPP** for example).

In DOS

In a DOS environment go to the **File** menu and then select the **Save** option. Type the name you want to use (remember the **.CPP** extension) and **OK**.

In UNIX

In a UNIX environment using **vi** simply quit from the editor, and the file that you have just produced can be found in your current working directory.

5   Now that you have created your file containing your program code it is time to produce a program you can run on the computer. This is the process of compiling, and linking your file. **Compiling** the file is the process of translating all the code you have written in C++ into the 1s and 0s of machine instructions. **Linking** is the process of

putting all the pieces of program together when there is more than one part to your program. C++ is designed to enable you to develop your programs in pieces (it is a **modular language**, which means you can break your code into **modules**, or **functions**). The final stage is to run the program. You should get the following output on the screen.

```
Hello! Congratulations on your first C++ program
```

In DOS

In Borland compilers, to compile the code you must select the main menu **C**ompile, and then choose the **C**ompile option. Alternatively you can use the keyboard and press *Alt + F9*. If this is successful you will get a message to tell you.

The next stage is to link all your compiled code modules (we only have one here as it is a very small program). To link, you again use the **C**ompile menu, but now choose the **L**ink option. If you have any errors you must return to the editing stage, find where the incorrect code is and change it. If, however, you have completed both these stages without any errors then you can run your program. There are 2 ways to do this.

One way is to use the menu item called **R**un in the **R**un menu. This means you can compile, link and execute the program in one go. To see the results (the output), you need to use the **W**indow menu to change to an **O**utput window.

The other way is to leave the compiler environment and move to the output directory (you can check where this is by looking in the **O**ptions menu and choosing the directories option). From this directory, simply type the name of the executable file (**prog1.exe**) and the program will run. For other types of compiler you will have to check your manual.

In UNIX

The command supplied to compile C++ source code is **cc**. To compile the code you must type:

```
cc prog1.cpp
```

This will also link the compiled code, if it can, and produce a file called **A.OUT** which is the executable version of your program. We recommend that you change the name of this as soon as you have produced it because each time you use the compiler, the same name is used and the old program is always replaced by the new.

You've done it! This is your first program, which displayed the word **Hello** on the screen. You could try altering the same program to display your name on the screen. For example, if your name is Anthony, try editing the program to read like this:

```
//        Program 1.1 Modified

#include <iostream.h>

void main()
{
   cout << "Hello Anthony! "
           "Congratulations on your first"
           " C++ program";
}
```

Which gives the output:

```
Hello Anthony! Congratulations on your first C++ program
```

You now have written a program using the editor, edited it and then compiled, linked and executed it. You have told the computer to do something and it did it. Let's look again at what happens during each of these phases. At the end of our analysis we have included a figure that links them together visually.

> Execution sounds nasty, but in computer jargon executing a program simply means running it.

Editing

This is the process of creating, or later modifying your **source code** - the name given to the program code you have written, for example in the "Hello" program above. The result of this process is a file containing the source code for your program.

> By convention your C++ source file has the extension **.CPP**, so you should use names such as **PROG1.CPP** or **TEST.CPP** or some other useful name. Most compilers will expect the source file to be named in this way.

Many C++ compilers will have a specific editor with them which can provide a lot of assistance in managing your programs. Indeed, products from both Microsoft and Borland provide a complete environment for writing, managing, developing and testing your programs. This is called the **Integrated Development Environment**, or IDE. You can also use other editors such as the DOS editor. If you are working in a UNIX environment, then you should have the **vi** editor or something similar.

> You could use a word processor, such as Word or WordPerfect, though they aren't very suitable for producing program code. They have no special facilities to help you in this and normally create a lot of hidden codes that will cause havoc in the next phase if you don't ensure they are omitted. They generally provide a function to save as ASCII DOS text which eliminates these codes, but it isn't the easiest method to produce your source code.

Compiling

This is the process of translating your original C++ program into machine language. The input to this phase is the file you produced in the editing phase which is usually referred to as a **source module**. The actual lines of C++ programming are the **source code**. The translation program, called the compiler, will first send the file to a preprocessing stage which prepares the text for translation into computer language.

The preprocessor carries out instructions in the source file to insert text and replace text. These instruction start with a hash (#) symbol. You'll have seen one of these in the program above.

The next stage is where actual compilation into machine instructions takes place (remember we talked about translating your file from C++ into a language the computer can understand). The compiler can detect many different kinds of errors during the translation process, and most of these will prevent the machine language module, usually called an **object module**, from being generated. Various messages are generated by the compiler to tell you what sort of error has been detected.

Try typing in the example again, but miss off the semicolon (;) as shown on the next page.

```
//        Program 1.1

#include <iostream.h>

void main()
{
   cout << "Hello! "
          "Congratulations on your first"
          " C++ program"


}
```

You will see an error message, which may vary depending on which compiler you are using. A typical example is shown below:

```
error C2143: syntax error : missing ';' before '}'
  CL returned error code 2.
HELLO.CPP - 1 error(s), 0 warning(s)
```

It's hard to believe that all this could be caused by the absence of just one little semi-colon! When you start programming, you will probably get lots of errors in compilation that are caused by simple punctuation mistakes. It's so easy to forget a little comma or a bracket - but don't worry, lots of experienced programmers make the same mistake.

A common cause of confusion, initially, is that just one error can result in a whole stream of abuse from your compiler, referring to a large number of different errors, as you can see in the example above. The basic approach is, after considering the messages carefully, to fix those you know you can, and have another go at compiling. You may find other errors have been fixed too. All errors, at this and later stages, usually mean you have to go back to square one and re-edit the source code. When you finally succeed in compiling your program, you will have the object module in a file ready to be input to the next phase.

The steps that you must actually take to compile a program depend on what sort of compiler you are using. In a DOS compiler such as Borland, you simply have to select the compile option from the drop-down menu. The compiler package will then do the rest of the work for you. Under a UNIX based system, you would use the **cc** command with the name of the file you have produced, for example:

```
cc myprog.cpp
```

The result of a successful compilation stage also depends on what system you are using. A DOS based system will produce a file with the same name as you used, but the extension will have changed to **.OBJ** and a UNIX system will produce the file **A.OUT** by default. It will be left to you to change the name here to something specific if you want to.

Linking

This process links together all the pieces necessary to make your program complete. The pieces include the object file (generated during the previous phase from the C++ code you have written), and any **library routines** your programs use. Library routines are standard functions you include in your program to carry out a specific task to save you having to write the code for it yourself. All C++ compilers have an extensive library of functions covering a wide range of facilities, from getting information into and out of your program, to mathematical functions. Pre-processor directives will have told the compiler which of these library files to use. We will discuss these in a moment. Also, your program may be built up from a large number of parts you have produced separately. These parts are called modules, which we mentioned earlier.

By programming in pieces you can break up a large program which is difficult to write and modify into many smaller, simpler ones. The **linker**, or **link editor,** as it is sometimes called, will bring in the required library functions and modules automatically. A failure during this phase again means you have to go back to square one and modify the source code. Success will result in a file containing an executable program.

Often you will be working with programs that are made up of a lot of modules. In this case, to use the linker on a DOS based system you should use the **Project** menu option. This tells the linker which modules the program needs to link together to produce an executable module. To start the linking process there is a menu option in the drop-down **Compile** menu. If linking has been successful, a message will be displayed.

In UNIX the required modules are all given together with the **cc** command. For example:

```
cc myprog.cpp firstmod.cpp secondmod.o
```

These 3 modules will be linked together. Notice that two of them have the **.cpp** extension and the last one has **.o**. This is because the final module has previously been compiled to produce the **A.OUT** which has been renamed. The **.o** extension tells the compiler that the module is only waiting to be linked with the others and doesn't need to be compiled.

Execution

This phase is where you run your program, having completed all the previous phases successfully. Unfortunately, this phase also commonly generates a wide variety of error conditions, from producing the wrong output, through sitting there and doing nothing, to crashing your computer. In all cases, it's back to square one.

The process described is, in practice, essentially the same for developing programs in any environment with any compiled high-level language. Once you are experienced in writing and testing C++ programs successfully, you will find it relatively easy to try another language. The whole process of editing, compiling, linking and executing your program is shown in the figure below.

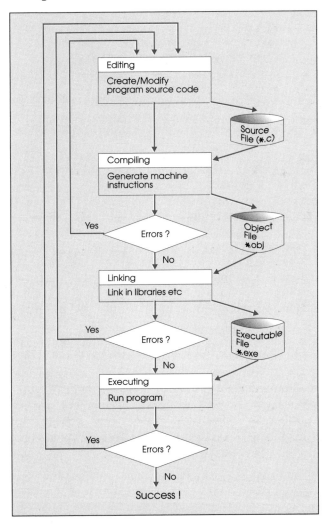

What Do the Program Parts Mean?

Now that you have run your first program, and have received encouraging words from the computer, we can start to discuss the program. We can look at what all the parts mean and how they work.

Try It Out - Another Simple Example

Let's look at another program and go through it step-by-step analyzing what each line means.

```
//        Program 1.2

#include <iostream.h>

void main()
{
   cout << "Hello! "
          "This is another program. "
          "It's very similar to the first.";
}
```

The output you get when you run the program looks like this:

```
Hello! This is another program. It's very similar to the first.
```

How It Works

We can analyze this line by line.

Comments

```
//        Program 1.2
```

This first line is a comment. It doesn't actually affect the program's running at all. It's purpose is to explain in normal language what the programming is doing. Here our comment is very simple. We are just reminding ourselves that this is a simple program.

The first two backslashes // let the compiler know that the text is just a comment and doesn't need any action. They must be the right way round and there shouldn't be any blanks between them (if you try to insert a space, you'll get a compilation error). A comment doesn't have to start from the first position in a line, as it does in this program. You can place a comment anywhere you like in a line. The end of a comment is the end of the line.

In C++ you can also write comments using the symbols /* and */, but we will discuss this in the next chapter.

Comments don't affect compilation. The compiler will ignore all characters from // to the end of the line. Therefore, you can remove this line or change the text after the // in the above program, and the result will remain the same.

Comments are very useful as your programs get larger. You know how hard it is to remember things you did a few days, maybe hours, ago. Well the same applies to programs. What might be clear now, probably won't be when you look at the program again, or when another programmer looks at it and tries to understand what you were doing and why.

The Preprocessor Directive

```
#include <iostream.h>
```

The file **IOSTREAM.H** is a header file. The whole line is what is known as a preprocessor directive. We will discuss this directive in more detail in Chapter 15, where the preprocessor and its directives will be considered. For now you just need to know that this directive must be placed above the function **main()** (which we will explain in a moment) and that it's necessary if you want to use the << operator in a program for us to be able to write text to the screen.

The main() Function

```
void main()
{
...
}
```

The first line here is a definition of the function **main()**. The opening and closing braces {} tell the compiler that the word **main** is the name of the function. The word **void** is there to explain that the function doesn't return a value. This will become clearer as we go through the book.

In C++ the word **main** is a keyword. There are several dozens of keywords in this language. Keywords are words that are reserved for a specific purpose, and shouldn't be used for anything else (see Appendix A for a full list of keywords). As you will have noticed when you compared Program 1.1 and Program 1.2, C++ isn't too strict about the use of spaces between program elements, about transferring text to a new line or about the use of empty lines. These features can be used to improve the legibility of a program (we'll return to this at the end of the chapter).

In Chapter 6 you'll learn how to execute programs that contain more than one function. However, one **main()** function is sufficient for writing simple programs.

Brackets, Braces and Parentheses

You may have noticed different types of 'brackets' used in the program. The difference is important. We will refer to the symbols ( ) as parentheses, the symbols { } as braces and the symbols [ ] as brackets.

The Body of the main() Function

Any text that is written between the **{** and **}** symbols forms the function body. In the simple program above, the function body isn't divided into other functions, and only consists of some instructions (or in C++ terminology - **statements**).

The function **main()** is always present in C++ programs. A C++ program consists of functions just as a house consists of rooms. The function **main()** serves as the entrance hall - this is where program execution begins. The opening brace **{** is the entrance to the house and the closing brace **}** means that the door is closed and you are outside. The word **main** can only be used in C++ programs as the name of the sole main function.

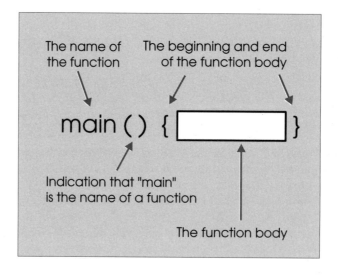

Statements

```
cout << "Hello! "
        "This is another program. "
        "It's very similar to the first.";
```

These lines are the only statement in our function **main()**. The semi-colon serves to mark the end of a statement. The word **cout** (Console OUTput) is the name of what is known as a **stream**. It designates where the text should be output, in this case to the console (screen). The pair of consecutive symbols **<<** designates the output operation. To be exact, this is the C++ operator called "put to" or the insertion operator. The text to be output is placed in double quotes (the quotes themselves will not be output).

The compiler won't check anything written inside the quotes. Therefore, you can include keywords, such as the word **main** here (as we did in Program 1.1). Outside the quotes, the word **main** may only be used as described earlier.

Analyzing Your Program Structure In More Detail

We can see more easily how the structure works if we mess about with our program a little. You have already seen that we can edit the text inside the quote marks, adding our name. In the same way we can add additional lines of code to display more text.

The simplest (and least useful) C++ program you could write and compile would be:

```
void main(){}
```

The body of this program doesn't contain any statements. Try typing it in to check whether or not this can be compiled without error, in other words whether C++ allows functions that don't do anything.

Splitting Lines

Try placing the text on several lines and recompiling, for example:

```
void main(){
}
```

or

```
void main()
{
}
```

or

```
void main
()
{}
```

You can see that sometimes the compiler will let you split things onto separate lines and sometimes it won't. You can't divide keywords into parts and split them over two lines. For example, if you split the word **main** as follows:

```
void
ma
in(){}
```

you will get an error during compilation.

Obvious Errors to Avoid

Try modifying the programs we have written by inserting one or more spaces in various locations, for example, before or after the word **main**, between () and {}. You will see that spaces aren't allowed if they divide a keyword or operator. For example, the following programs would result in errors at compilation:

```
ma in(){}
```

```
main(){co ut << "Hello, Programmer!";}
```

```
main(){cout <   < "Hello, Programmer!";}
```

See what happens if you use the name **Main** instead of **main**. Your program won't compile because C++ is case-sensitive, which means that upper and lower-case letters are considered to be different.

According to the ANSI C++ standard, all symbols in the name of the function **main()**, as well as all characters in keywords, should be in lower-case.

Try leaving the word **main** out. The message output by the compiler will show that you can't do without the function **main**.

Try removing one or both of the round brackets () or curly braces {} and see what error messages the compiler outputs. You can see that you must always have pairs of parentheses or braces in C++.

Remove the semi-colon from the end of the statement, you will get an error on compilation.

All the above are extremely common mistakes that people, especially beginners, make. If you have errors when you compile your programs first of all check that all your punctuation is correct. It is so easy to forget a comma, or use the wrong kind of brackets.

Your Next Program

When you ran Program 1.1 you checked it was correct by looking at the result on the screen, comparing it with what you expected to be output. If you don't get to see the results of your program, you won't be able to tell whether it's right or not. Did it get your name right, for example? In the majority of programs, you have to output information to the screen in order to display the results of an operation. We are therefore going to consider some programs that perform this task.

Program 1.3 shows how several statements are executed one after another.

```
//   Program 1.3
//   Seven statements

#include <iostream.h>

void main () {

cout << "Statement 1.";
cout << "Statement 2.";
cout << "Statement 3.";

cout << "Statement 4."; cout << "Statement 5.";
cout << "Statement 6."; cout << "Statement 7.";
}
```

This program outputs the following text to the screen:

```
Statement 1.Statement 2.Statement 3.Statement 4.Statement 5.Statement
6.Statement 7.
```

Comment Lines

```
//   Program 1.3
//   Seven statements
```

These first lines contain comments which, as we have already explained, are there just to explain what is happening in the program.

Empty Lines

This next line is empty. The compiler will ignore any spaces (or tabs) in it.

Empty lines are used to improve the appearance of a program and to make it easier to read. You can insert or remove as many empty lines as you like in a program, it won't influence the result (you can check this).

The Natural Sequence of Statement Exec

Have a look at the body of the **main()** function. Its first three statements are as follows:

```
void main () {

  cout << "Statement 1.";
  cout << "Statement 2.";
  cout << "Statement 3.";
  . . .
}
```

These lines are executed from top to bottom. This sequence is called a natural one because it corresponds to the way in which we read - line by line, top to bottom (we in the western world, at least).

Placing Several Statements in One Line

```
  cout << "Statement 4."; cout << "Statement 5.";
  cout << "Statement 6."; cout << "Statement 7.";
```

With C++, you don't have to place each new statement on a new line, as you can see. These two lines contain two statements, each of which is terminated by a semi-colon. You aren't limited to two statements per line, but you have to be careful not to reduce the legibility of the program. It isn't a good idea for a line to go off the screen, or for the line to be too long to fit on a sheet of paper when printed. Good style dictates that lines will be kept relatively short, and contain only one statement.

The statements in each line are executed from left to right. According to the natural sequence, the last line will be executed last. However, there are some special statements that can change the natural sequence of statement execution. These will be discussed in the following chapters.

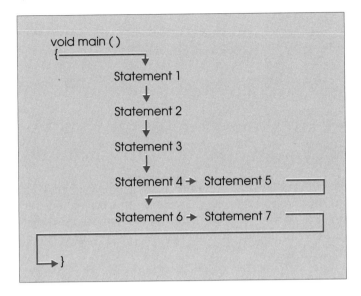

Unless you want to return a value to the operating system, it is usual to include the keyword **void** in front of **main()**. This will be explained later.

The Sequential << Operators

Note that the text you want to output (included in double quotes) isn't always output in the way that it appears in the source code.

```
cout << "Statement 1.";
cout << "Statement 2.";
cout << "Statement 3.";
```

These three statements will output text in one line, from left to right:

```
Statement 1.Statement 2.Statement 3.
```

No matter where it is located in the program text, each statement

```
cout << "...";
```

will begin outputting text immediately after the text that was output by the previous statement.

In order to output dividing spaces, you have to include them in the text that is included in quotes, for example:

```
"Hello, programmer!"
```

and

```
"        Hello,        programmer!        "
```

will output differently:

```
Hello, programmer!
      Hello,        programmer!
```

Placing Output on a New Line

Sometimes it's necessary to output a long string of text onto the screen. There are normally up to 80 characters on a screen line. If output starts from the first column and contains more than 80 characters, then the 81st character will be output at the beginning of the next line.

If the output text reaches the 80th column of the last screen line, the contents of the whole screen will be shifted upwards 1 line - the upper line will disappear and a new, empty line will be created at the bottom. The next symbol will be output here. This is called scrolling.

It would of course be very annoying (not to say fraught with errors), if you had to insert spaces in order for text to be placed on a new line. In C++ you can easily move to a new line as Program 1.4 will show:

```cpp
//   Program 1.4
//   Seven lines

#include <iostream.h>

void main () {

cout << endl;

cout << "Line 1.";
cout << endl;

cout << "Line 2."; cout << endl;
cout << endl;

cout << "Line 4." << endl << endl;
cout << "Line 6." << endl << "Line 7." << endl;
}
```

The results of this program will be seven lines on the screen:

```
Line 1.
Line 2.

Line 4.

Line 6.
Line 7.
```

How It Works

The program contains a new name - **endl** (**end** of line). If you look at the different ways it's used, you will see how it works.

```
cout << endl;
```

This statement causes movement to a new line, irrespective of where the previous output terminated on the screen. This statement is one more example of what should be used for a good programming style.

```
cout << "Line 1.";
```

This statement outputs the following text:

```
Line 1.
```

starting from the beginning of the line.

```
cout << endl;
```

This statement then again causes movement to the beginning of the next line.

If, at this point, text had been output up to the last screen line, then the contents of the screen would be scrolled up one line. You can check this by inserting several occurrences of the following line:

```
cout << endl;
```

into the program.

The next line shows that you can combine two of the operators << in one statement. Therefore, this:

```
cout << "Line 2."; cout << endl;
```

Can become this:

```
cout << "Line 2." << endl;
```

We don't have to repeat the word **cout**. This line contains one statement but gives the same result as the following two lines:

```
cout << "Line 2.";
cout << endl;
```

in other words, it moves the cursor to a new line after the output.

The next lines have an even longer statement that contains even more occurrences of the operator **<<**. These are executed from left to right.

Program 1.4 is terminated by the **endl** operator:

```
... << endl;
```

This will move the cursor to a new line and so allow the next program to start from the first position of the next line. Good tourists take their rubbish with them after a picnic so that future visitors aren't reminded that other people have been there. Good programmers do the same.

Statements on Multiple Lines

The statement that you wrote in the previous exercise will have been too long to place on the screen, or on a standard sheet of paper. However, this problem is easily solved. In C++ you can place one statement on several consecutive lines. You saw this in Program 1.1.

Try It Out - Long Strings

Program 1.5 shows three ways in which a statement can be carried over onto the next line.

```
//   Program 1.5
//   Long strings

#include <iostream.h>

void main () {

cout << "Long ................ string" << endl;

cout << "Long ............... "
   "string 1."        << endl;
```

```
cout << "Long ............... "
     << "string 2."        << endl;

cout << "Long .............. \
string 3."          << endl;
}
```

How It Works

Imagine there were a lot more dots in the line. We have had to reduce the number in order to fit the string on the page.

```
cout << "Long .............. string"  << endl;
```

This is an obvious, but not very satisfactory way of outputting a long line of text. In the following lines though, there are three quite satisfactory ways. No doubt you have done puzzles of the kind where you are given two very similar pictures and have to find the differences between them. Let's look at the other ways we have used to handle long output text strings:

```
cout << "Long ............... "
     "string 1."          << endl;
```

The first method divides the text string into two substrings, which are included in double quotes. The second substring is placed on a new line. Note that in this and the following cases, spaces have been inserted outside the quotes in the initial text. This are just to align the code; they aren't included in the text that is output on the screen.

```
cout << "Long ............... "
     << "string 2."        << endl;
```

The second method shows how the second line is output by repeating the operator <<.

```
cout << "Long .............. \
string 3."          << endl;
```

The third method shows that the text string between double quotes can be carried over onto the next line. Note that the last character of the first line is a backslash and you need to start the string from the first character on the continuation line. This performs approximately the same function as a hyphen at the end of a line in a book. If the backslash is followed by another character, you will get an error during compilation.

The first method is the shortest as the operator `<<` is absent from the second line. For this reason (and because we are lazy by nature), we prefer this one.

Try It Out - Different Ways of Displaying Strings

Program 1.6 includes shorter text strings and will enable you to see different ways of displaying essentially the same string.

```
//   Program 1.6
//   Output of a series of strings

#include <iostream.h>

void main () {

cout << "1"  "2"   "3"  << endl;

cout << "1"
   "2"  "3"     << endl;

cout << "1"  << "2"   << "3"  << endl;

cout << "1"
      << "2"  << "3"     << endl;

cout << "123"      << endl;

cout << "12\
3"        << endl;
}
```

The output from this program looks like this:

```
123
123
123
123
123
123
```

How It Works

In this program we are demonstrating how you can display strings on the screen from within your program.

```
cout << "1"  "2"   "3"  << endl;
```

The strings between the quotes could have contained much longer strings -
like a welcome message or a list of instructions.

```
cout << "1"
      "2"  "3"    << endl;
```

These lines show that your strings can be spread over several lines in your
program. The output is the same.

```
   cout << "1"  << "2"   << "3"  << endl;
```

You could rewrite the first **cout** statement like this. It gives the same
output and is simply a matter of choice. As before, you could split these
over several lines.

```
   cout << "123"      << endl;

   cout << "12\
   3"          << endl;
```

These statements are demonstrating that you can split the string itself by
using the backslash (\) provided the next character of the string is the first
character on the next line.

Designing Your Programs

So far we have described the programs themselves. Obviously, there is a lot
of preparation that is needed to actually design your programs. This will
become more and more important as your programs get more complex.
Each chapter in the book ends with a full program that we describe in
detail. What we will do is go through the process of solving a problem
using a computer program. Let's have a closer look at this process.

The Process of Writing a Program

Writing programs is an activity like any other. The best way of explaining
the process is to use an analogy. Imagine you decide to bake some bread
and let's compare the process to creating a simple program.

```
//      Program 1.1

#include <iostream.h>

void main()
{
   cout << "Hello! ";
}
```

1   You have probably decided to do some baking because you are hungry and you want some fresh bread to eat. You write a program because you want a result. In our first program the result we wanted was to display the text on the screen. This, like the bread, is the output.

2   Next you need to think about what you need to use to get the result. This is your input. To bake bread you need flour, water, yeast, salt and a bowl. For the program you need, among other things, keywords (**void**), functions (**main()**), an editor and a compiler. The process of baking the bread is to transform these items into a tasty loaf. The art of the program is to successfully transform the input data into output.

3   This leads to the actual design of the process. How do you get from input to output? From flour and yeast to bread? You might do the following:

Mix flour, yeast and salt	Include the C++ library **IOSTREAM.H**
Knead dough	Call the **main()** function
Leave to rise	Let it know that it doesn't return a value (use **void**)
Knead again	Use **cout <<**
Bake	Display the words "Hello"

4   Now that we know where we are going and how to get there, we can write the program using the design to get the computer to do the task. Computer instructions are written in a programming language, in this case C++. In effect, the program becomes the recipe for making the bread. Now that the recipe isn't just in your head, you can pass it to anyone, and whenever you are hungry get them to bake the bread. Now that's useful!

5   Next we need to prepare the input data. This involves deciding what flour to use, and whether to use fresh or dried yeast. We would also need to make sure the utensils (like the mixing bowl) are on hand.

6   OK. So you have a recipe. Unfortunately though, you wanted to bake a French baguette and this recipe is in French. You will either have to try to remember your high school French, or call a friendly neighbor to translate it for you. The same applies to the program. The program is in C++ but the computer doesn't speak C++. That's right, your computer doesn't speak either English or C++. For the computer to understand it, it needs to be translated into **machine code** which is the language all computers speak. This is where compiling comes in. Compiling translates your programs from C++ into machine code.

7   Once you have it in a form the computer can understand, you can actually run it. Running it means performing all the *doing* processes, so you mix the ingredients, bake and eat the bread. With the program, when you run it, you compile, link and execute the program.

8   You might think the process ends there, but not a bit of it. Imagine you sit down, finally, to eat your delicious baguette and horror of horrors it tastes awful. Is it burnt? Didn't it rise? Does it have too much salt, or not enough yeast?? What can you do?

The simple way is to **debug** your program. Although this term originated from the time a machine wasn't working and a real bug was discovered to be the culprit, it now refers to any error in a program. The process of debugging is a powerful way of assessing what went wrong and where.

Functions

The word function, with reference to the `main()` function, has appeared a few times so far in this chapter. We need to explain a little about what this means. Most programming languages, including C++, provide a means of breaking a program up into segments which can be written more or less independently of one another, like splitting a recipe up into steps. In C++ these segments are called functions. Each segment, or function, will be designed with a specific interface to other functions in terms of how information is transferred to it, and how results generated by the function are transmitted back from it.

To continue our previous analogy, if we wrote three separate functions, one that bakes bread, one that makes apple pie and one that makes lemonade, we could then use the **main()** function to call all of them (one at a time) and end up with a program that prepares a whole picnic. Great!! When confronted with a tricky task, like making a picnic, the easiest thing to do is to break it down into small chunks and tackle those individually. It makes life much easier and means that if you do run into problems, you can quickly locate the problem area without having to check the whole program. This is vital when your programs get bigger. This is called modular programming and is what we were referring to when we talked about modules and source modules earlier.

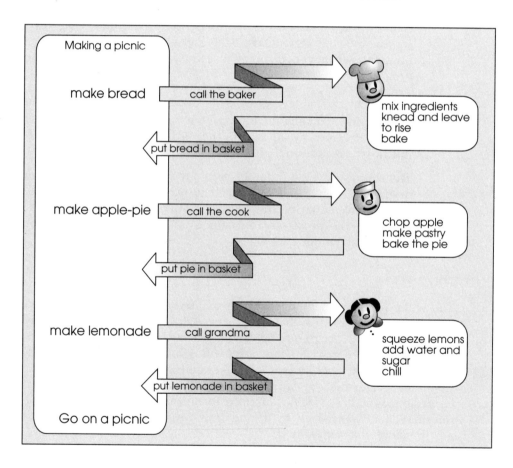

Let's go over the reasons again for designing a language to allow the segmentation of programs in this way.

> Dividing the program into a lot of separate functions allows each piece to be written and tested separately. This greatly simplifies the process of getting the total program to work.

> Several separate functions are easier to handle and understand than one huge function.

> Libraries are basically just sets of functions that people tend to use all the time. As they have been pre-written and pre-tested, you don't have to go to all that trouble. You know they will work and you don't need to bother typing them in. This will obviously accelerate program development and leaves you to cope with your own code problems. This is a fundamental part of the philosophy of C++. The richness of the libraries greatly amplifies the power of the language.

> You can accumulate your own standard libraries applicable to the sort of programs you are concerned with and interested in. If you find yourself using a function all the time (if you are really fond of home-made bread and bake it every day), you can build this into your own library.

> In the development of very large programs, which can be from a few thousand to millions of lines of code, development can be undertaken by teams of programmers, each team working with a defined sub-group of the functions comprising the whole program.

We will be covering C++ functions in great detail in Chapter 6. However, because the structure of a C++ program is inherently functional, you have met standard functions in the very first example.

Summary

In this chapter we have given you an outline of how C++ works. We have shown you the framework of a C++ program and you have written your first programs. You have used your programs to do display text on the screen and have had a taste of the potential for your programs.

We have really just given you a rough overview of a C++ program. We can now summarize the program structure in the following figure.

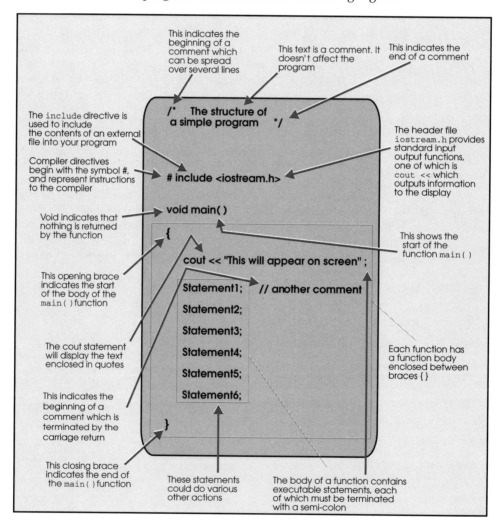

CHAPTER 2

Basic Ideas

Now that we have examined the outline and structure of a simple C++ program we can get on to more exciting uses. In this chapter we are going to build on what we learnt in Chapter 1 and start to actually manipulate the data in the program. By the end of the chapter you will be able to use C++ to do simple calculations. We will also explain a little about computer memory so you get a better picture of what is happening.

In this chapter you will:

- Learn about simple calculations in C++
- Understand what a variable is
- Understand how to use variables
- Learn about some different variable types

Performing Simple Calculations

You have already dealt with text lines, which are also called string literals or string constants. We will now move on to another type of literal - numeric constants. In C++ these are the ordinary numbers. The C++ language permits decimal, octal and hexadecimal integer constants, and decimal floating point constants. We will start with decimal integer constants.

In C++, decimal integer constants are written quite normally:

```
  - 123
  + 123
    123
```

You can omit the "+" sign as it is implied by default. Integer constants are always limited by a highest and lowest possible value. If you write a constant that is out of this range, the compiler will either inform you of the mistake, or will do the calculation and give you an answer that's wrong. Of course, it won't tell you it's wrong.

The arithmetic operations that can be performed with integer constants are:

Operator symbol	Operation
+	Addition
-	Subtraction
*	Multiplication
/	Division
%	The remainder after division

The Order of Operation

In complex formulas that contain more than one operation, you can use brackets () as you do in mathematics. This enables you to explicitly control the sequence in which calculations are made. For example, take the formula:

```
4/2*2
```

If you first divide 4 by 2, and then multiply the result by 2, you get 4. If, however, you first multiply 2 by 2, and then divide 4 by the result, you'll get 1. In mathematics, division (/) and multiplication (*) are considered of equal importance, and are performed in a "natural" sequence, i.e. from left to right. The same rule applies to the compiler and so the formula 4/2*2 will produce the result 4. If you want to obtain the answer 1, you will have to add parentheses:

4/(2*2)

The operation in parentheses is always calculated first. If you have parentheses within parentheses (nested parentheses) then the innermost ones are calculated first. For example:

4*(5/(4+6))

equals 2. First 4+6 is calculated. Then 5 is divided by the result, and the result of that calculation is multiplied by 4.

Try It Out - Parentheses in Action

Program 2.1 demonstrates the use of parentheses.

```
//    Program 2.1
//    Integer constants

#include <iostream.h>

void main ()
{                                  // Output
   cout << 1 + 2      << endl;     //    3
   cout << 1 - 2      << endl;     //    -1
   cout << 2 * 2      << endl;     //    4
   cout << 5 / 3      << endl;     //    1 !!!
   cout << 5 % 3      << endl;     //    Remainder 2

   cout << 4/ 2*2     << endl;     //    4
   cout << 4/(2*2)    << endl;     //    1

   cout << (1+1) *2   << endl;     //    4
   cout << 1+ (1*2)   << endl;     //    3
   cout << 1+ 1*2     << endl;     //    3
}
```

Try It Out!

The output from this program looks like this:

```
3
-1
4
1
2
4
1
4
3
3
```

How It Works

In this program the comments aren't just located at the beginning of the program.

```
cout << 5 % 3          << endl;      //    Remainder 2
```

Look at this line, for example. Here we have included a comment to remind us that **%** gives us the remainder and let's us know what this remainder will be.

```
cout << 1 + 2     << endl;      //    3
cout << 1 - 2     << endl;      //    -1
cout << 2 * 2     << endl;      //    4
cout << 5 / 3     << endl;      //    1 !!!
cout << 5 % 3     << endl;      //    Remainder 2
```

In the first line here the addition operation is performed, the result is output to the screen and the cursor moves to the next line. The subsequent lines do other operations. They all output the result to the screen and move the cursor to the next line. To improve the appearance of the program, we have aligned all the **<<** operators, **endl** statements and comments (but this is not a requirement).

Have a look at the division operation **5/3**. When you perform division with two integer constants, the result will always be an integer number. Any fractional part of a result will be discarded.

```
cout << 4/ 2*2     << endl;      //    4
cout << 4/(2*2)    << endl;      //    1

cout << (1+1) *2   << endl;      //    4
cout <<  1+ (1*2)  << endl;      //    3
cout <<  1+  1*2   << endl;      //    3
```

These next lines perform slightly more complicated calculations. Look at the first two. 4/2*2 gives a result of 4, whereas if we add parentheses 4/(2*2) gives a different result 1. This is because, without parentheses, operations that are of equal precedence are executed left to right. In the first example, 4 is divided by 2 and then the result is multiplied by 2. In the second example, 2 is first multiplied by 2. Then 4 is divided by the result.

If you compare the result of the next lines, you'll see that in C++, just as in arithmetic, if there are no parentheses, multiplication is performed before addition. The seniority of an operation is called its precedence. The same rules of precedence apply to all operations in C++. On the whole these coincide with the mathematical rules you will have learnt at school. As a reminder, multiplication, division and modulus (the operation to obtain the remainder) are equal in rights, and take precedence over addition and subtraction, which are also equal in rights. Operations that are equal in rights are performed from left to right.

If you use parentheses (), you can get away without knowing anything about an operation's precedence. Operations inside parentheses always happen first. However, if you use a lot of parentheses, they can clutter up the program text and make it difficult to understand. In that case, splitting the calculation into a number of simpler calculations would probably be better.

Outputting Numbers and Strings

In the previous program we didn't output the numbers themselves, but the results of the different arithmetic operations.

It's obvious what will happen if you write the statement:

```
cout << 1;
```

In general, the item after the operator << is typically an expression, but here it is a very simple one: the statement will output the number 1 to the screen.

Let's compare the output of a number with that of a string. Have a look at the following two statements:

```
cout << "1";
cout <<  1 ;
```

In both cases 1 will be displayed on the screen. However, the string constant "1" and the integer constant 1 are completely different objects in C++. They will be represented differently in the computer's memory. This will be discussed in more detail later on.

Overloading Operators

In spite of the distinction between the operands "1" and 1, the operator `<<` will process both objects successfully. This feature, performing the same operation on different types of objects, is called overloading, and is an important difference between C++ and its predecessor C. Overloading greatly simplifies output programming, and therefore makes life easier for everybody.

Program 2.1 is really a simple calculator. You can write a few lines with different complex expressions and then compile the program and obtain the results. The drawback is that compilation is a time-consuming process. Using a computer as a calculator like this is a bit like trying to crush a fly with a steam-roller.

Before proceeding, we should draw your attention to the fact that in Program 2.1 we used spaces round the operators `+ - * /` randomly - sometimes we put spaces on both sides of the operator, sometimes just on one side, sometimes we omitted them altogether. The compiler accepts all versions and you can use spaces to make the text easier to read.

Using Large Numbers

So far the numbers we have used in our examples have been fairly small and simple. What happens when the numbers get bigger?

Try It Out - Using Large Integer Constants

Type in the next program and see what results you get when you run it.

```
//   Program 2.2
//   Large integer constants

#include <iostream.h>

void main ()
{
  cout << 10000        << endl;
  cout << 100000       << endl;
```

```
    cout << 1000000        << endl;
    cout << 10000000       << endl;
    cout << 100000000      << endl;
    cout << 1000000000     << endl;
    cout << 10000000000    << endl;   // ???
    cout << 100000000000   << endl;   // ???
}
```

The output from this program on our computer looks like this:

```
10000
100000
1000000
10000000
100000000
1000000000
1410065408
1215752192
```

Our computer gives an incorrect result for values of 10^{10} and higher. To understand how it works we need to understand a bit more about how your computer deals with the information you give it.

Memory In Your Computer

The program of instructions your computer executes, and the data they act upon, have to be kept somewhere while your computer is making its way through them one at a time. The place they are kept at this time is called the machine's memory. It is also referred to as **main memory** and **Random Access Memory** (or **RAM**).

Your PC also contains another kind of memory called Read Only Memory, or ROM. As its name suggests ROM cannot be changed by you, you can only read its contents or have your machine execute instructions contained within it. The information contained in ROM was put there when the machine was manufactured. This information is mainly programs which control the operation of the various devices attached to your PC, such as the display, the hard disk drive, the keyboard, and the floppy disk drive. These programs are called the Basic Input Output System or BIOS for your computer. (If you are using a UNIX machine, BIOS doesn't apply.)

You can think of the memory of your computer as an ordered line of boxes. Each of these boxes is one of two states, either the box is full (let's call this state 1), or the box is empty (this is state 0). Already you see that we are talking binary here (1s and 0s). The computer thinks of these in terms of **True** and **False**: 1 is True and 0 is False. Let's stress that we are talking about computer memory not the C++ language.

Even though we're talking about memory, if you can't remember about binary, don't worry. It's computer memory we're talking about, not yours. The important point here is that the computer can only deal with 1s and 0s, Trues and Falses. These can be grouped into sets of 1s and 0s (for example, 10010011) but they are made up of the same building blocks.

For convenience we group our boxes in sets of 8. To get to the contents we label each of the groups of 8 boxes with a number, starting from 0 and going up to whatever number of groups of boxes you have. To return to the real world situation, each box is a **bit** and each of these groups of boxes is a **byte** of storage. To summarize we have our building blocks (called bits), in groups of eight (called bytes). A bit can only be either 1 or 0.

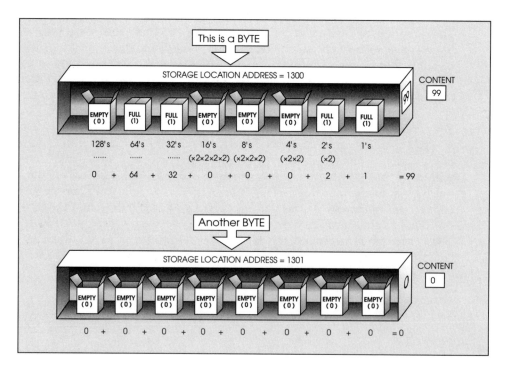

This storage is the computer's memory. But, you may think, how does the computer know where each byte is? The information is there somewhere, but where? Surely you end up with all the information in the computer but you can never find it again (not much use). The way the computer solves this problem can be compared to the way the post office deals with your mail (only the computer should be a lot more efficient). When you post your letter, you don't just abandon it in the mailbox and hope it will arrive safely, you use an address. This means the post office will be able to find where the letter should be delivered without any problems.

Similarly, in your computer each byte of memory has a number which is used to reference it, this is called its address.

Memory is often expressed in terms of so many kilobytes, megabytes, or even gigabytes. But just what do these terms mean? Simple.

- 1 kilobyte (or 1K bytes) is 1024 bytes

- 1 megabyte (or 1M bytes) is 1024 kilobytes which is 1,048,576 bytes

- 1 gigabyte (or 1G bytes) 1024 megabytes which is 1,073,741,841 bytes

Wait a minute, I hear a strangled cry - why all these weird values rather than simply one thousand or one million or one billion? Once again it's very simple. There are 1024 numbers from 0 to 1023, and 1023 happens to be 10 bits in binary - 11 1111 1111, so this is a very convenient binary value. On the other hand, 1000 is a very convenient decimal value, but it tends to be inconvenient in a binary machine. The kilobyte is defined in a manner that's convenient for your computer, rather than for you. Similarly, for a megabyte we need 20 bits, and for a gigabyte we need 30 bits.

Types of Numbers

So far we've only looked at integer numbers without considering how much space they take up in memory. Different types of numbers take up different amounts of memory. The bigger the space allocated, the more memory it takes up. Memory is an important consideration in programming as it is such a valuable part of a computer. As your programs get longer you need to be able to create programs that are efficient with their use of memory.

Your computer's memory is organized into bytes. So, how many bytes are needed to store our integers? Well, one byte can store 256 different values. This would be enough for the numbers we've seen so far, but what if we wanted to store a count of the average number of stitches in a pair of knee length socks - one byte wouldn't be anywhere near enough. This is where integer types come into play.

An integer requires two bytes of memory to store a range of values from -32,768 to 32,767. There are a number of different modifiers that can change the range of values. Some of these modifiers require additional memory to store the increased values. Don't worry about this now - we'll return to this subject in a little while.

Floating Point Constants

As you have seen, the result of the division applied to integer constants in Program 2.1 is an integer constant, and the fractional part is discarded: the result of 5/2 was given as 2, whereas it should really be 2.5.

In C++, you can work with floating point constants as well as with integer constants. These numbers include a decimal point, for example:

```
+123.
 123.
  12.3
  -1.23
   0.123
```

You use integers to count numbers of items, like the number of oranges in a box. Floating point numbers are used to represent inexact quantities, like a temperature of 38.4 degrees.

As with integer constants, you can omit the + sign. Note that floating point constants are very different from integer constants as far as the computer is concerned. For example, the integer constant 123 and the floating point constant 123. are completely different and will act differently in a program.

Floating point numbers should be used if you want a result with a fractional part. Floating point constants contain both the integer and the fractional parts of a number, so 5./2. will give the expected result of 2.5. To use floating point values all you need to do is include a decimal point with the number. For example, if you write 123. the compiler understands that this is a floating point value even though there is nothing after the decimal point.

Try It Out - Using Floating Point Constants

Program 2.3 gives some examples of floating point constants and operations on them.

```
//   Program 2.3
//   Floating point constants

#include <iostream.h>

void main ()
{                                     // Output
  cout << 1.          << endl;  // 1
  cout << -1.         << endl;  // -1

  cout << 123.        << endl;  // 123
  cout << 0.123       << endl;  // 0.123

  cout << 1.e3        << endl;  // 1000
  cout << 1.e-3       << endl;  // 0.001

  cout << 1.23e2      << endl;  // 123
  cout << 123.e-2     << endl;  // 1.23

  cout << 0.123456789 << endl;  // 0.123457
  cout << 123456789.  << endl;  // 1.234567e+8

  cout << 1./2.       << endl;  // 0.5
  cout << 1./2        << endl;  // 0.5
  cout << 1 /2.       << endl;  // 0.5
  cout << 1 /2        << endl;  // 0
}
```

Typical output from this would be:

```
1
-1
123
0.123
1000
0.001
123
1.23
0.123457
1.234567e+08
0.5
0.5
0.5
0
```

How It Works

```
cout << 1.e3      << endl;  // 1000
cout << 1.e-3     << endl;  // 0.001

cout << 1.23e2    << endl;  // 123
cout << 123.e-2   << endl;  // 1.23
```

These lines demonstrate how to write numbers in exponential (scientific) form. As you can see, 1.E3 means one multiplied by 10^3, in other words 1000, and 1.E-3 means one multiplied by 10^{-3}, in other words 0.001.

You can experiment with different power indices. Remember that in C++, you can have very large numbers with a power index of several hundred or even thousands. The specific limit depends on the version of C++, and may be different for different computers and compilers.

```
cout << 0.123456789  << endl;  // 0.123457
```

Here we have too many digits written after the decimal point in a fractional floating point constant, so the number is rounded off when output.

```
cout << 123456789.   << endl;  // 1.234567e+8
```

In this line where the value of the constant is too large, the compiler converts it to exponential representation.

```
cout << 1./2.    << endl;  // 0.5
cout << 1./2     << endl;  // 0.5
cout << 1 /2.    << endl;  // 0.5
cout << 1 /2     << endl;  // 0
```

These lines show different combinations of integer and floating point constants in one expression. There are some rules of conversion for these cases. However, for now it is better to avoid mixing constants of different types in one expression.

Repeated Constants

We now combine the information from the previous sections about the output of text and digits. At the same time, we'll introduce you to the **#define** directive.

In 1994, the Winter Olympic Games took place in Norway. As you may have already realised, we are sports fans - in fact we spend quite a lot of time watching both the computer and TV screen (at the same time). As a result, some of the examples in this book are based on sport or the Olympic games.

Our next example displays the results of the Olympic champion, Permila Wiberg from Norway, in alpine skiing (combined slalom, which consists of three phases: downhill and two slalom attempts). The combined times were as follows:

> 88.70 Downhill
> 138.05 Slalom, 1st attempt
> 185.16 Slalom, 2nd attempt

Try It Out - Using Constants

The following program outputs the results of each separate competition.

```
//   Program 2.4
//   Ski combination

#include <iostream.h>

void main ()
{

  cout << endl
       << "The Olympic Games, Lillehammer, Norway"  << endl
       << "ALPINE SKIING - Combined Slalom Women"   << endl
       << "21-feb-94" << endl

       << "P. Wiberg, NOR" << endl
       << "Downhill            " <<    88.71          << " sec." << endl
       << "Slalom, 1st attempt " << (138.05 - 88.71)  << " sec." << endl
       << "Slalom, 2nd attempt " << (185.16 - 138.05) << " sec." << endl;

}
```

The output of this program is:

```
The Olympic Games, Lillehammer, Norway
ALPINE SKIING - Combined Slalom Women
21-feb-94
P. Wiberg, NOR
Downhill            88.71 sec.
Slalom, 1st attempt 49.34 sec.
Slalom, 2nd attempt 47.11 sec.
```

How It Works

The insert operator `<<` allows you to combine strings, digits and expressions in one statement.

Suppose you wanted to change the data to give the times for another competitor, or else correct an error (this is what we must do, as we have output a downhill time of 88.71 instead of 88.70). To alter the program, you have to replace the number 88.71 twice. This is time-consuming and means there is room for error - you may change the wrong constant or make a mistake when typing it in the second time. If the program was large (dozens or even hundreds of lines), it would be even harder to alter.

So what should you do? The solution is to use the `#define` preprocessor directive.

Try It Out - Using the #define Directive

In Program 2.5 there are five occurrences of this directive.

```
//   Program 2.5
//   Ski combination with #define directive

#include <iostream.h>

#define  TIME1   88.71     // Downhill
#define  TIME2   138.05    // ... + slalom, 1st att.
#define  TIME3   185.16    // ... + slalom, two att.

#define  NAME  "P. Wiberg, NOR"
#define  SE  " sec." << endl

void main ()
{
    cout << endl
         << "The Olympic Games, Lillehammer, Norway" << endl
         << "ALPINE SKIING - Combined Slalom Women"   << endl
         << "21-feb-94" << endl

         << NAME << endl
         << "Downhill                " << TIME1          << SE
         << "Slalom, 1st attempt " << (TIME2 - TIME1) << SE
         << "Slalom, 2nd attempt " << (TIME3 - TIME2) << SE;
}
```

The output from this program is exactly the same as the first example. The difference is how the program is constructed.

How It Works

```
#define  TIME1   88.71    // Downhill
#define  TIME2  138.05    // ... + slalom, 1st att.
#define  TIME3  185.16    // ... + slalom, two att.

#define  NAME  "P. Wiberg, NOR"
#define  SE  " sec." << endl
```

The **#define** directive enables you to replace a part of the program code that occurs more than once with a designation (name). In this program the name **TIME1** replaces the constant 88.71, and the name **TIME2** replaces the constant 138.05.

Each preprocessor directive must be placed on a separate line. The name should be written after the word **#define**, separated from it by a space. This name can consist of letters or letters and digits, but the first must be a letter. Traditionally, names specified in **#define** directives are written in capital letters, but this isn't obligatory. The value which is to be used instead of the name should be written after the name, again separated from it by a space. So here **TIME1** is used instead of 88.71, and the name **NAME** is used instead of the string:

```
"P. Wiberg, NOR"
```

(note that **NAME** replaces the quotes too). The name **SE** is used instead of the fragment:

```
"sec." << endl
```

The **#define** directive doesn't need a semi-colon after it. Adding a semi-colon is a common error to watch out for.

Using Directives

So what is the advantage of using directives? If you need to change a constant, you need only alter the code in one place, in the **#define** directive. The compiler will automatically alter the whole program text. They can also help to make the program text clearer.

At this point we should warn you that this program (and other programs in this book) were written to illustrate a point and shouldn't be interpreted necessarily as normal usage of the directive. Program 2.5 has a somewhat artificial nature which in practice would be solved differently. You'll see how later on.

The use of the **#define** directive does have some disadvantages. If it is used instead of a particular part of the source code, for example, an expression, then you may get unexpected side-effects (we'll discuss this further in Chapter 15). Therefore, for now we suggest that you should only use the **#define** directive to define constants.

The Changeable World of Variables

So far you have only dealt with constants and operations on constants. Constants can be strings, integers or floating point values. They remain unchanged throughout program execution. The elements of computer memory that hold constants are simply read by the processor, never written.

However, even back in Ancient times, the Greeks noticed that everything moves, everything changes. This is also evident in programming - in languages such as C++. There are **variables** (in other words objects which, unlike constants, can change their value during a program); these are much more important and widespread than constants.

Declaring a Variable and Using It

In order to use variables, you need to understand how to declare one. The easiest way to explain it is to show you a variable in action.

Try It Out - Declaring Variables

The next program contains an example of how a variable is declared and used. We have assigned the name **x** (a traditional name in algebra) to the variable.

```
//   Program 2.6
//   Declaring variable and using it

#include <iostream.h>

main()
{
  int x;          // Declaring
```

Try It Out!

```
    x = 1;          // Assigning
    cout << x;      // Using
}
```

This program outputs the number 1 on the screen.

How It Works

```
    int x;          // Declaring
```

This line contains the declaration of a variable **x** of type **int**. The type of the variable defines its characteristics. The type **int** (abbreviated from of the word integer) means that the variable will be used to store integers (both positive and negative).

The structure of the declaration statement is illustrated in the following figure, albeit in a somewhat simplified form. The semi-colon serves to mark the end of the statement. In C++, there are several standard types: **char** (character), **int**, **float** and others. The type defines the amount of memory that the variable will occupy, as well as the sort of values it can assume.

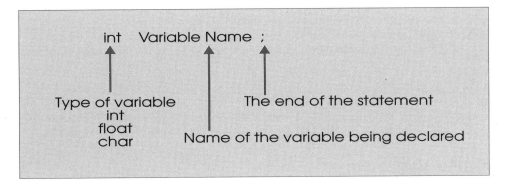

All C++ variables must be declared; the declaration for a variable must be placed before it's used. Declarations of all the variables in a program are usually grouped together and placed at the beginning of the function body, just after the opening curly brace **{**, though this isn't obligatory. An empty line is often used to separate declarations from the executable statements. This isn't compulsory, but can help make a large program easier to understand.

Assigning a Value to a Variable

To change the value of a variable you should use the **=** sign, which will be familiar to you from mathematics. However, in programming this sign means something different to the sign used in math.

Have a look at this statement:

```
x = 1;
```

This means that the value 1 will be stored in the memory area allocated for the variable **x**. Once this statement has been executed, you can say that:

variable **x** has the value **1**

The expression:

```
x = 1
```

reads as:

assign the value **1** to the variable **x**

The **=** sign is called the assignment operator. In mathematics, the expression:

```
x = 1
```

means something different. Here the point isn't that the value **1** is *assigned* to the variable **x**, but that **x** *already* has the value **1**.

Using Variables

The following line from the above program shows how the value of the variable is used. The statement:

```
cout << x;        // Using
```

outputs the value 1 onto the screen, which is the value that the variable **x** has at the present moment.

The program we have looked at so far doesn't really show you what you can do with a variable. Let's look at an example where we use a single variable to store the results of several simple calculations.

Try It Out - Using Variables

The next program shows how the value of a variable can change in the course of the program.

```
//   Program 2.7
//   Changing variable's value

#include <iostream.h>

void main ()
{
  int  x;
                                 // Output

  x = 1;
  cout          << endl;
  cout << x;               // 1
  cout << x  << endl;      // 1

  x = 2;
  cout << x  << endl;      // 2

  x = 1 + 2;
  cout << x;               // 3
}
```

Typical output from this program would be:

```
11
2
3
```

How It Works

```
  int  x;
                                 // Output
  x = 1;
  cout          << endl;
  cout << x;               // 1
```

These lines are the same as in Program 2.6. First we declare an integer variable called **x**. We then assign the value of 1 to the variable **x** and output that value onto the screen. Just because the value of the variable is output from the memory doesn't mean that **x** loses this value though. The value of **x** doesn't change. Therefore, the next statement:

```
cout << x << endl;      // 1
```

outputs 1 again. You can use the values from it time and again, and yet the values remain there.

```
x = 2;
cout << x  << endl;     // 2
```

Here a new value **2** is assigned to variable **x**. The old value of **x** is now lost. The new value is output to the screen.

```
x = 1 + 2;
cout << x;              // 3
```

This time there is an arithmetic expression on the right of the **=** sign. This is calculated and the result 3 obtained. This result is then assigned to the variable **x** and this value is output to the screen.

When using the operator **=**, you can write any expression which includes names of variables on the right of the **=** sign.

Initializing Variables

You can supply an initial value to any variable at the same time as you declare it. For example, in the previous program we could have written:

```
int  x = 1;
```

which would have both declared variable **x** of type **int**, and also initialized it to 1.

Initializing variables as you declare them is a good idea in general. It avoids any doubt about what their initial values are, and if the program doesn't work as it should, it can help track down where the errors reside. If you experience errors where a variable seems to have a different value to what you expect, look to see if it's initialized.

Until they are assigned a value, uninitialized variables have whatever value happened to be in the memory location concerned when the program was loaded. This will be whatever was left by the previous program or action. It's a good habit to always initialize variables in your programs, even if just to 0.

Try It Out - Using Expressions With Variables

Let's see how this works in action.

```
// Program 2.8
// Initializing variables and using expressions

#include <iostream.h>

void main()
{
  int  x=1;
  int  y;
                          // Output
  cout << y << endl;      // ?
  cout << x << endl;      // 1

  y = x;
  cout << y << endl;      // 1

  y = x*x + x;
  cout << y << endl;      // 2

  y = y + 1;
  cout << y << endl;      // 3

  y++;
  cout << y << endl;      // 4
}
```

The output from this program looks like this:

```
1008
1
1
2
3
4
```

How It Works

The declaration:

```
int  x=1;
```

initializes the variable **x** to 1 when it is declared.

```
int  y;
                            // Output
cout << y << endl;    // ?
```

In the program, the variable **y** isn't initialized during its declaration. Therefore, the output of its value to the screen is marked by a comment with a question mark. The result will be uncertain and will change randomly when the program is run under different conditions. Its value will depend on the contents of the memory location allotted to the variable.

```
cout << x << endl;    // 1
```

The output of the variable **x**, which was initialized to 1, gives the expected result.

```
y = x;
cout << y << endl;    // 1
```

Here we have an elementary assignment statement. The value of the variable **x** (which is equal to 1) is copied into the area of memory allocated to the variable **y** (the initial value of **x** doesn't change, as we mentioned above, but any value in **y** would be overwritten by this assignment).

```
y = x*x + x;
cout << y << endl;    // 2

y = y + 1;
cout << y << endl;    // 3

y++;
cout << y << endl;    // 4
```

Here we have 3 more complicated expressions that alter the value in **y**. We output the new value in **y** each time. Although we use the value of **x** in some of these expressions, its value isn't altered. For example, using the variable **x** in operations such as:

```
y = x*x + x;
```

won't affect its value, which remains equal to 1.

Let's look at the other 2 expressions in more detail. They will help explain why the language is called C++.

Why C++?

Look at the following statement:

```
y = y + 1;
```

This means that 1 is added to the value of **y**, which up till now was equal to 2; the result 3 is then stored in the variable **y**. In other words, this operation increments the value of **y** by 1. This kind of operation is often used in programming, which is why there is a special increment operator (**++**). This is present in the next line. The statement

```
y++;
```

is an abbreviated way of writing the statement **y = y + 1**, and means exactly the same, in other words increment the value **y** by 1. You will now understand why the new, incremented version of C was given the name C++ (with two plus signs rather than just one).

The Limits of the Possible

There is a maximum value for all integer variables. Let's see how you can apply what you have learnt so far to find out what this value is.

Try It Out - Calculating the Limits of Variables

The expression **x = x * 2**, which appears a lot in this program, increases the value of **x** by 2. The program calculates 2^N.

```
//   Program 2.9
//   Calculating the limit of int

#include <iostream.h>

void main()
{
  int  x=1;                       // Power of 2     Output

    cout << (x=x*2) << endl;      //      1          2
    cout << (x=x*2) << endl;      //      2          4
    cout << (x=x*2) << endl;      //      3          8
    cout << (x=x*2) << endl;      //      4          16
    cout << (x=x*2) << endl;      //      5          32
    cout << (x=x*2) << endl;      //      6          64
    cout << (x=x*2) << endl;      //      7          128
```

Try It Out!

```
    cout << (x=x*2) << endl;     //    8        256
    cout << (x=x*2) << endl;     //    9        512
    cout << (x=x*2) << endl;     //   10        1024
    cout << (x=x*2) << endl;     //   11        2048
    cout << (x=x*2) << endl;     //   12        4096
    cout << (x=x*2) << endl;     //   13        8192
    cout << (x=x*2) << endl;     //   14        16384
    cout << (x=x*2) << endl;     //   15        -32768 !!!
    cout << (x=x*2) << endl;     //   16        0
}
```

The program's output should look like the list in the comments of the program.

How It Works

Here you can see that in the expression:

```
cout << (x=x*2)
```

the output value is an assignment expression, not a constant or arithmetic expression. This demonstrates a general rule of the C++ language: you can use an assignment expression just about anywhere that you can use a single variable. It means that you can simultaneously calculate the next power of the number 2 and output it onto the screen.

The exact results of Program 2.9 will depend on the type of computer you run it on. On our computer the results are as shown in the comments. As you can see, 2^{15} power is displayed as a negative value. This illustrates the fact that in our computer exactly 15 bits are used to represent the numeric values of the type **int**. In our case, the highest permitted numeric value of the type **int** is 2^{15} -1, i.e. 32767, and the lowest permitted (negative) value is -32768.

So, we know that 15 bits are used to represent an integer number but earlier we told you that an integer variable occupies 2 bytes (16 bits) of memory. Well, what's happened to the missing bit? The other bit is the sign bit. For a positive integer, say 100, the sign bit will be 0. For a negative number, say -50, the sign bit will be 1. Setting the sign bit to 1 makes the number negative.

Named Constants

The last program showed that to obtain correct results, the value of the variable must remain within the permitted range of values. Otherwise, as you can see from the results in the comments, the sign of the value that is out of range will be changed and therefore the operation itself is altered.

Try It Out - Using a const Modifier

Let's look at another program that uses named constants to give us another option in our programs.

```
//   Program 2.10
//   const modifier

#include <iostream.h>

void main()
{
  const  int  Max = +32767;
  const  int  Min = -(Max+1);      // -32768
    int  x;

                                   // Output
  x = Max;
  cout << x << endl;               // 32767

  x = Max + 1;
  cout << x << endl;               // -32768

  x = Max + 2;
  cout << x << endl;               // -32767

  x = Min;
  cout << x << endl;               // -32768

  x = Min - 1;
  cout << x << endl;               // 32767

  x = Min - 2;
  cout << x << endl;               // 32766
}
```

The output from this program is again shown in the comments of the program.

How It Works

```
const  int  Max = +32767;
const  int  Min = -(Max+1);      // -32768
```

These lines demonstrate how to declare named constants. You do this by writing the keyword **const** (which is a type modifier) in front of the type of the variable. This keyword converts the named object to a constant.

It's important to remember that any constant declared like this must be initialized straight away. This is because you can't subsequently use it on the left side of the assignment operator. For example, the compiler will give an error message if you write:

```
Max = 1;
```

Because you have given **Max** a value and made it a fixed value that can't change.

The advantage of using named constants is the same as with the **#define** directive: you need only write a numeric value once to be able to use it many times in a program. To change a constant, you need only change it in one place. For example, if, on your computer, **Max** has a different value than that in the program, all you have to do is substitute the value in the declaration, **const int Max = +32767**. Therefore, **const**s should be used instead of **#define**.

```
const  int  Min = -(Max+1);      // -32768
```

Note that in this line the value **Max** (which was defined earlier) is used to initialize **Min**. You can use any name as long as you first declare it.

The Problem of Names

When you declare a new variable, you encounter the problem of naming your creation. This isn't easy as any parent, including those unfamiliar with programming, will confirm. First of all you have to take the rules into account. Some names are forbidden by rules of politeness or criminal legislation, others are simply reserved by the developers of C++ (for example, the keywords **main**, **int** and so on - see Appendix A).

A name should not be too short (the names **x** and **y** may be suitable in algebra, but they don't tell you much about what the variable is for when used in real programs). However, at the same time, a name shouldn't be too long (remember that you have to input and read them yourselves). C++ does define the maximum size of a name, but this is large enough not to worry about it.

It is important to choose a name that will describe the contents of the variable, for example, **street** or **ZIPcode**, etc. If you want to create a name from several words, you can use a number of styles but the most common ones are:

```
variableName
variable_name
```

The first name is slightly shorter than the second, but you have to make an extra keystroke when typing it, as you have to press the *Shift* key twice. The first type of name is generally used in Pascal, the second type - in C++. However, it's up to you which type you choose.

Rules For Naming Variables

There are some rules which have to be followed when choosing the names of variables. You can only use:

▶ The letters a...z, A...Z

▶ The underscore symbol "_"

▶ The digits 0...9 (but not as the first symbol in a name)

As we have said, C++ is case-sensitive, so the words

```
main    Main    MAIN
```

are different: the first is a keyword and it cannot be used as a variable name, the others can be variable names. All C++ keywords are in lower case.

Inputting Data

The programs you have met so far have all contained whatever data they need. This data took the form of constants, variables, and named constants. Programs that contain all the data they need only execute an algorithm once. If you want to obtain different results you have to input new data into the initial text and recompile the program.

Try It Out - Inputting Data

We are now going to show you how to write a program that will accept data that is input while it's running. We have been moving backwards through the chain of events "input-processing-output" and so are almost at the end. This program demonstrates how numbers can be input from the keyboard.

```
//   Program 2.11
//   Keyboard input of number

#include <iostream.h>

void main()
{
int   Number=0;

cout << "Type any integer number and then press key ENTER: ";

cin  >> Number;    // Will wait until Enter is pressed

cout << "You entered " << Number << endl;
}
```

The output from this program looks like this:

```
Type any integer number and then press key ENTER: 8
You entered 8
```

How It Works

The program doesn't process the input data - it just outputs the number that was input.

```
int   Number=0;
```

First we declare and initialize our variable.

```
cout << "Type any integer number and then press key ENTER: ";
```

We then display a message on screen to ask the user to type in a number. Notice that we haven't used **endl** so that the response will appear on the same line.

```
cin >> Number;    // Will wait until Enter is pressed
```

The input is performed by this statement. The program will wait until *Enter* is pressed before completing this operation.

Note the new operator **>>** (don't confuse this with **<<**). The operator **>>** is called a "get-from" or extractor operator. In the above program, it accepts the input data from the keyboard, converts the digits into a numeric value and stores this value in the integer variable **Number** (in other words, it assigns the input value to the variable **Number**).

The word **cin** (Console **IN**put) designates the input stream associated with the keyboard. The following figure shows how the **>>** operator works.

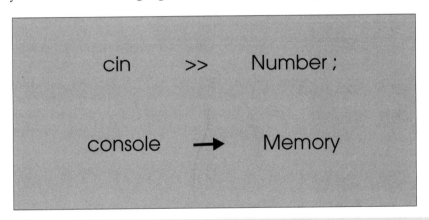

```
cout << "You entered " << Number << endl;
```

This final statement displays the text "You entered" and then displays the value the user typed in.

When you compile and run the program it will output the message:

```
Type any integer number and then press ENTER:
```

and then pause. This is because the `>>` operator waits for you to press a key. Press any digit key and this digit will appear on the screen. Again there is a pause. You can input more digits, or delete a digit using the *BkSp* key.

To inform the `>>` operator that input is complete, press *Enter*. The `>>` operator will process the input digits and then write them into the variable **Number**.

Execution of the statement `cin >> number` then terminates and the next statement is executed. This outputs the text telling the user what they entered.

You may wonder what would happen if you entered a letter instead of a digit. Try it - you will get the message:

```
You entered 0
```

This is because the variable **Number** was initialized to 0 originally.

Checking What is Happening

Try replacing the constant 0 in the program with another number. Now run the program and enter a letter - watch what's output.

Why is no value assigned to the variable? The answer is simple. The `>>` operator checks the characters entered, and if any non-numeric character is keyed as part of a numeric input value, it stops processing immediately and no value is assigned to the variable.

When working with the `>>` operator you should remember that it will ignore all initial spaces. If there is a space in the middle of the characters entered, it will ignore all characters to the right of the space.

Try running the program and enter some digits with a space between them, for example:

```
1 2
```

Only the first value is assigned to the variable **Number**.

You will see that the input of data causes problems that didn't occur when using the `<<` operator. The above problem is actually quite serious. It is to do with the validity of the input data. For example, if you were entering a price, but some of the digits were invalid or there are too many of them, someone, either the customer or the supplier, isn't going to be happy.

There are many stories about enormous losses incurred by companies because of a mistake in the input data. When any real-world program is written, a lot of attention has to be paid to the control of input data.

Multiplication Tables

We can now use variables to perform some simple arithmetic calculations.

Try It Out - Multiplying Integer Numbers

The next number calculates the product of a pair of integers.

```
//  Program 2.12
//  Multiplying integer numbers

#include <iostream.h>

void main()
{
  int  Number1 = 0;
  int  Number2 = 0;

  cout << "Multiplication of two numbers." << endl << endl;

  cout << "Enter the first integer number: ";
  cin  >> Number1;

  cout << "Enter the second integer number: ";
  cin  >> Number2;

  cout << "Result is " << Number1 * Number2 << endl;
}
```

The output from the program is:

```
Multiplication of two numbers.

Enter the first integer number: 7
Enter the second integer number: 13
Result is: 91
```

Try It Out!

How It Works

```
int   Number1 = 0;
int   Number2 = 0;
```

We declare and initialize 2 variables.

```
cout << "Multiplication of two numbers." << endl << endl;
```

It starts by outputting a message about what the program does, so that the user knows what to input.

```
cout << "Enter the first integer number: ";
cin  >> Number1;
```

A prompt is then output and the program will wait until you input a number.

```
cout << "Enter the second integer number: ";
cin  >> Number2;
cout << "Result is " << Number1 * Number2 << endl;
```

A second number is then entered in the same way and the result of the multiplication operation is output to the screen. If one or both of the numbers are entered incorrectly, for example, if a non-numeric character or a decimal point is input, then the result of the program will be zero (you can check this). This is because both **Number1** and **Number2** were initialized to zero. If they hadn't been initialized, incorrect input would result in an unpredictable value (you can check this too).

Analyzing What's Happening

You can check the accuracy of the output from this program by trying different input values. Try inputting an invalid number (one that includes letters, the decimal point, or spaces) and check the results.

Try multiplying large numbers (for example, 1000 * 1000). Is the result correct? If so try even larger numbers. Sooner or later the program will output an incorrect result, because you are still using **int**s. To get around this problem you need to use different types of variables.

Floating Point Variables

You can improve the last program by changing the type of the variable from **int** to **float** (a number with a floating decimal point).

Try It Out - Using Floating Point Variables

Using floating point variables means our programs can be more flexible. We can input and output decimal numbers. This is especially important for division.

```
//  Program 2.13
//  Multiplying floating point numbers

#include <iostream.h>

void main ()
{
  float  Number1 = 0;
  float  Number2 = 0;

  cout << "Multiplication of two numbers." << endl << endl;

  cout << "Enter the first number: ";
  cin  >> Number1;

  cout << "Enter the second number: ";
  cin  >> Number2;

  cout << "Result is " << Number1 * Number2 << endl;
}
```

The output from this program looks like this:

```
Multiplication of two numbers.

Enter the first number: 3.45
Enter the second number: 17.9

Result is: 61.755001
```

How It Works

The program works in the same way, except we have declared our variables as type floating point.

```
float  Number1 = 0;
float  Number2 = 0;
```

Try inputting the same floating point values in the first version of the program, you won't get the right result.

If you use the floating point type, rather than the integer type variables, the numbers you will be able to multiply without mistake will be much larger.

Writing Programs

At the end of this chapter, we'll discuss the rules of good style that apply to writing and commenting a C++ program. We have already mentioned some of these rules (for example, that each statement should start on a new line), others you may have realized intuitively.

However, we are going to begin by showing that these rules don't affect the actions of the C++ compiler, but do affect the person who is working with the program and their ability to understand the source code.

Have a look at the next two programs. These programs give identical results. Their source code differs only in the number of whitespace characters. However, at first sight they don't look similar at all. The first program looks a lot easier to understand and far more accessible than the second. The programs calculate the circumference and area of a circle of a given radius.

Try It Out - A Good-looking Example

```
//   Program 2.14
//   The length and area of a circle

#include <iostream.h>

void main()
{
  const  float  Pi = 3.141593;
  float  Radius;          // of circle
  float  Circumference;
  float  Area;

  cout << "Enter the radius of circle: ";
  cin  >> Radius;

  Circumference  = 2. * Pi * Radius;
  Area  = Pi * Radius * Radius;

  cout << "The circumference of circle is " << Circumference << endl;
  cout << "The area   of circle is " << Area    << endl;
}
```

Try It Out!

Try It Out - A Bad-looking Example

```
// Program 2.15
// Bad style
#include <iostream.h>
void main() {const float Pi = 3.141593;
float Radius,Circumference,Area;
  cout<<"Enter the radius of circle: ";cin>>
Radius;Circumference=2.*Pi*Radius;Area=Pi*Radius*Radius;
  cout<<"The circumference of \
circle is "<<Circumference<<endl;cout<<"The area    \
of circle is "
  <<Area<<endl;}
```

The layout of the first example follows several rules:

1   There is just one statement in each line.

2   The operators are surrounded by spaces.

3   Tabs or spaces are used in variable declarations to align the variable names.

4   Empty lines separate groups of associated statements.

A program that looks good is actually more likely to be good, in essence as well as form. The reason for this is simple - programmers who don't worry about the form of a program will probably not have thought about the design of their program as clearly. However don't be taken in by the dangerous thought that the main thing is for a program to work, and that its design or the way it is written isn't important. Your slogan should be: "Simplicity plus beauty".

Whitespace Characters

Thanks to a C++ language rule which allows you to insert any number of whitespace characters wherever a space is permitted, means that you have quite a degree of freedom in program lay-out.

The word "whitespace" covers all of the following characters (which aren't usually displayed by text editors though they may be present in the text): space, new line, vertical and horizontal tab, form feed, and carriage return.

Try It Out!

Spaces are permitted anywhere as long as their presence won't change the division of the source code into elements. Spaces aren't allowed in keywords, names, integer or floating point constants, or operators defined by more than one character, as a space serves to mark the beginning and end of these objects.

Within a character string that is included in quotes, spaces are interpreted in the same way as all other characters in the string.

The following examples show where whitespaces can be inserted:

Without whitespace	With whitespace
`main(){}`	`main   (   )   {   }`
`x++;`	`x    ++   ;`
`cout<<x;`	`cout    <<    x   ;`
`x=1;`	`x    =    1   ;`
`y=x*x+1;`	`y    =    x    *    x    +    1    ;`

Comments

We have already mentioned comments in Chapter 1, but they are so important that we are going to quickly look at them again. Comments are necessary, mainly so that programs can be understood in the future, when the time comes to update them. If a program has no comments, it may well be that it is easier to write it all over again than to try to decipher the code. This is true for both your own and for other's programs.

The examples in this chapter contain very few comments, because explanations are provided in the book. However, if the source code is the only source of information about a program, then comments are necessary.

In C++, comments can be written in two ways. As we have seen, you can write two consecutive slashes `//`, without any whitespace characters between them. This defines the rest of the line as a comment. The compiler will ignore all characters from the `//` onwards.

Alternatively, you can write comments using the following symbols:

```
/* ... */
```

There must not be any spaces between the / and * at each end of the comment. The symbols /* open a comment and */ close it. The closing pair can be placed on another line (as long as this isn't above the line with the opening pair). Therefore, you can define several lines as one comment, for example:

```
/* This is a permitted comment
   in C++
*/
```

This method of writing comments is often used in program headings. It is convenient when you want several lines to be interpreted as one comment.

Note that the ANSI standard doesn't permit comments of this type to be nested, for example:

```
/*  ... /* ... */ ... */
```

isn't allowed. However, the // style of comment can be nested in /* ... */ and vice versa.

Summary

This chapter has introduced you to some important concepts of programming and of C++. You have learnt about variables and how they are used in your programs. You have seen how different types of variables are needed in different situations. You have written some programs that input, process and output data, and have learnt how to lay out your programs clearly. So that your programs can do more interesting things you now need to learn about the C++ control structures that enable you to organize branching and loops in programs. This is what we are going to move on to in the next chapters.

CHAPTER
3

Making Selections -
Choosing Ways

In this chapter we will take a great leap forward in the range of programs we can write, and the flexibility we can build into them. You will meet some of the more complicated elements of C++, including the selection and jump statements. These allow you to write more elaborate programs to perform actions that depend on variables, such as the program menus and the validation of input data. We will add one of the most powerful programming tools, the ability to compare variables with other variables and constants and, based on the outcome, choose to execute one set of statements or another.

What this means is we will be able to control the flow of the program more. Up until now, once you have set your program running you can't actually control what is happening. You simply type in information and the computer displays a result. In this chapter we will change all that.

In this chapter you will:

- Make decisions based on arithmetic comparisons
- Use logical operators
- Understand more about reading characters from the keyboard
- Write a program that will analyze the digits and characters you enter

The Decision-Making Process

We will start with the essentials of decision-making in a program. Making decisions in a program is concerned with choosing to execute one set of program statements rather than another. In everyday life you do this kind of thing all the time. Each time you wake up you have to decide whether it's a good idea to go to work or school. You may go through these questions:

Do I feel well?   If the answer is no, stay in bed.
                   If the answer is yes, go to work.

You could rewrite this as:

If I feel well I will go to work.
Otherwise I will stay in bed.

That was a straightforward decision. Later, as you are having breakfast you notice it's raining, so you think:

If it's raining as hard as it did yesterday, I will take the bus. If it's raining harder than yesterday, I will drive to work. Otherwise, I will risk it and walk.

This is more complex. It's a decision based on comparing the value of the rain and can have any of three different results.

As the day goes on you are presented with more of these decisions. Without them you would be stuck with only one course of action. Until now in this book you have had exactly this problem with your programs. All the programs will run a straight course, without making any decisions, to a defined end. This is a severe hindrance, and one that we will rectify now. First let's set up some basic building blocks of knowledge to enable us to do this.

Arithmetic Comparisons

In order to make a decision, we need a mechanism for comparing things. This involves some new operators. Since we are dealing with numbers, one way or another, comparing numerical values is basic to decision-making. We have three fundamental operators:

<	is less than
==	is equal to
>	is greater than

The "equal to" operator has *two* successive equals signs. You will almost certainly use one equals sign on occasions by mistake. If you type `my_weight = your_weight` it is an assignment statement that puts the value in the variable `your_weight` into the variable `my_weight`. If you type the expression `my_weight == your_weight` you are comparing the two values. You are asking *whether* they are exactly the same, not telling them to *be* the same.

Logical Expressions

Have a look at these examples:

```
5 < 4      1 == 2      5 > 4
```

These expressions are called logical expressions and each of them can result in just one of two values, **True** or **False**. The value **True** is represented by a non-zero value and **False** is represented by 0. The first expression is **False** since 5 is patently not less than 4. The second expression is also **False** since 1 isn't equal to 2. The third expression is **True** since 5 is greater than 4.

The if Statement

A very useful statement in the C++ language is the `if` statement. This statement allows you to affect what happens depending on whether certain conditions are met or not.

Try It Out - Using the if Statement

Let's get straight to an example of using the **if** statement. Programs 3.1 and 3.2 will show you how you can change direction and how you can alter the flow of control in a C++ program.

```
//   Program 3.1
//   if statement

#include <iostream.h>

void main()
{
  int  x = -1;

  cout << "Enter 0 or 1: ";
  cin  >> x;

  if ( x )
    cout << x;
}
```

The output from the program looks something like this:

```
Enter 0 or 1: 1
1
```

How It Works

```
int  x = - 1;
cout << "Enter 0 or 1: ";
cin  >> x;
```

First we declare and initialize our variable and ask the user to enter a number. This number is then stored in the variable **x**. If something other than a number was input, **x** simply keeps the value with which we initialized it (i.e. -1).

```
if ( x )
  cout << x;
```

This is the **if** statement, and operates as follows. If variable **x** has a value not equal to zero, then the following statement (located underneath and indented to the right of **if(x)**), in other words:

```
cout << x;
```

is executed and the value of the variable x is displayed on the screen (or

-1, if you input a letter or another non-numeric character by mistake).

If the value of variable **x** is equal to 0, then the following statement isn't executed, and the program doesn't output anything. Try running this program several times, using different input values, including 0.

Try It Out - Using the if Statement Again

We can look at another example:

```
//   Program 3.2
//   Choosing the right direction with an if statement

#include <iostream.h>

void main ()
{
  int  Right = 1;

  cout << endl << endl
       << "Which way?" << endl
       << "Enter 0 to go straight" << endl
       << "or" << endl
       << "enter any other number to go to the right "
       << "and then go down: " << endl;
  cin  >> Right;

  cout << "I ";

  if ( Right )
    cout << "go to the right and then ";

  cout << "go down." << endl;
}
```

Typical output would be:

```
Which way?
Enter 0 to go straight
or
enter any other number to go to the right and then go down: 5
I go to the right and then go down.
```

Try It Out!

How It Works

Again the program starts by asking you to input a number. The action the program performs next depends upon the number input by you. There are two possibilities. Either the number you enter is zero, or it isn't.

```
cout << "I ";

if ( Right )
   cout << "go to the right and then ";

cout << "go down." << endl;
```

If you input 0, then it will give you the message:

```
I go down.
```

If you input any other value, then the program output will be:

```
I go to the right and then go down.
```

You can see how the phrases are made up of several parts defined by the operators `<<`.

You now know how to choose different routes within a program.

The Sequence of Statement Execution

The execution of an **if** statement is illustrated in the figure opposite. We are assuming that the source code contains the following sequence of statements:

```
previous-statement
if (expression)
   not0-statement
next-statement
```

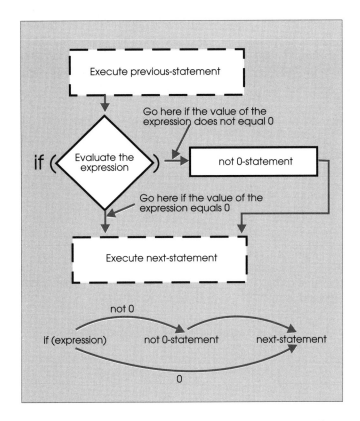

Here the words **previous-statement**, **next-statement**, and **not0-statement** stand for any C++ statement, and the word **expression** means an expression, the value of which can be converted into an integer. In the previous two programs, **expression** was an integer variable. A statement finishes with a semi-colon, an expression doesn't have one.

So the following:

```
cout << 1;
```

is a statement, but:

```
cout << 1
```

isn't a statement, but is an expression.

You can see from the figure that the value of the expression in parentheses following **if** is calculated first. If the resulting value of the expression isn't equal to 0 then the **not0-statement** is executed, followed by the **next-statement**. If the resulting value is equal to 0 then the **next-statement** is executed and the **not0-statement** is ignored.

So the **if** statement simply represents a way of skipping over a statement. You could make the figure easier to understand by substituting the following question for the diamond in the figure:

Is it true that the value of the expression is not equal to 0?

If the answer is "yes" then we go to the **not0-statement**, whereas if the answer is no, we go down to the **next-statement**.

This is an important topic and you should try to ensure that you understand it as you will then find the other control statements are quite straightforward.

The general form or syntax of the **if** statement is as follows:

```
if (expression)

    Statement1;

Next_statement;
```

You will see that the condition (or the question part) of the **if** statement is enclosed in parentheses and doesn't have a semi-colon at the end. The second line could be written following straight on from the first but, for clarity, people tend to put it on a new line. That's why there is no need for a semi-colon after the expression. Your compiler carries on reading to the end of the first statement - the end of the line. The second and last lines both end with a semi-colon.

The test condition can be any expression that gives a result of **True** or **False**. If the expression has the value **True**, then **Statement1** is executed after which the program continues with **Next_statement**. If the expression is **False** then **Statement1** is skipped and execution continues immediately with **Next_statement**. This is illustrated in the following figure.

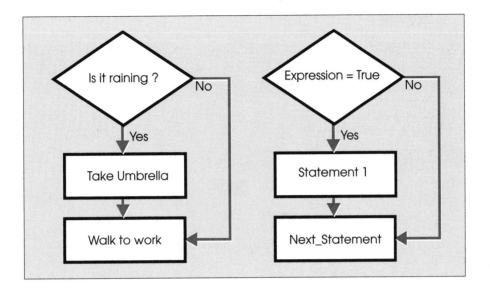

Try It Out - More Uses of if

Look once again how the **if** statement operates in Program 3.3. This program is purely for illustration, as it uses constants for the **if** expression, rather than variables as would normally be the case.

```
//  Program 3.3
//  Test of the if statement

#include <iostream.h>

void main()
{
  if ( 1 )
    cout << 1;
  cout << 2;
  if ( 0 )
    cout << 3;
  cout << 4;
}
```

This program will output to the screen

124

How It Works

We can follow the course of the program execution in the following figure.

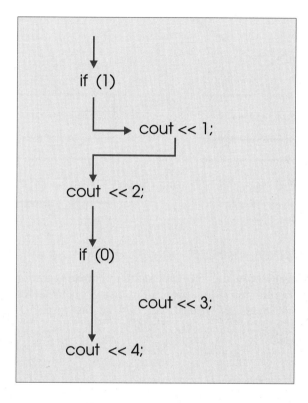

Let's go through the program.

```
if ( 1 )
    cout << 1;
```

You see that here the expression in parentheses is non-zero which is why the statement:

```
cout << 1;
```

is executed.

```
cout << 2;
```

Then the above statement is executed.

```
if ( 0 )
   cout << 3;
```

Here the expression in parentheses is equal to 0, so the statement:

```
cout << 3;
```

won't be executed and the next statement:

```
cout << 4;
```

is executed.

You can only write one statement following the test condition. If, for example, you wrote the code like this:

```
if ( 0 ) cout << 3; cout << 4;
```

it won't make any difference to the operation of the **if**. The decision is always about whether to execute the statement following the test condition:

```
cout << 3;
```

More Than One Statement to Execute

As you have seen before now, there can only be one statement that will be executed if an **if** statement evaluates to **True**. So what should we do if we wanted to execute several statements if the expression in the **if** statement isn't equal to 0? The answer is the following construction:

```
if (expression)
{
  statement 1;
  statement 2;
  ....;
}
```

As is shown in the following figure, opening and closing braces {} are used to group statements together into a block. One block is equivalent to one statement.

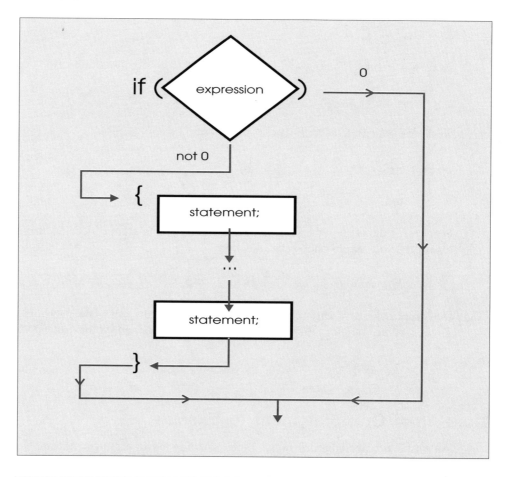

A block may be written in any place where you can write a statement.

Note that after the closing brace of the block, there isn't a semi-colon. Sometimes its presence is harmless, but sometimes it is a mistake.

Don't place ";" after the closing brace of a block.

Indention in an if Statement with a Block

An **if** statement with a block is usually written as follows:

```
if (expression)
{
  statement;
  statement;
  ...
}
```

Indentation in the body of a block isn't obligatory, but it's recommended for improving the readability of the program. Programmers generally will make up their own mind as to the indentation they prefer, but usually it's from two to four characters. You may prefer an alternative form of writing the **if** statement with a block:

```
if (expression) {
    statement;
    statement;
    ...
}
```

Try It Out - Forgetting Your Braces

Be careful not to forget the **{}** surrounding the block following an **if** statement. The next program demonstrates the problem which arises if you do forget.

```
//   Program 3.4
//   if statement with block

#include <iostream.h>

void main()
{
  if ( 0 )
  {
    cout << "This is ";
    cout << "never printed text.";
  }

  if ( 0 )
    cout << "This is ";
  cout <<        "Printed text.";
}
```

Try It Out!

The output from this program looks like this:

```
Printed text.
```

How It Works

```
if ( 0 )
{
  cout << "This is ";
  cout << "never printed text.";
}

if ( 0 )
   cout << "This is ";
cout << "Printed text.";
```

These are the interesting statements. In the first statement there are braces { } delimiting the block consisting of two statements, and in the second statement they are absent. Since the value of the expression in the **if** is equal to 0, the block isn't executed and the text:

```
This is never printed text.
```

isn't output.

As for the next statement, we have already considered this case when discussing Program 3.3. The statement

```
cout << "This is";
```

will be skipped, but the next statement

```
cout <<  "Printed text.";
```

will be executed, which is why we get the output shown above.

Everything Is Learnt by Comparison

Very often in **if** statements, you use algebraic expressions like:

```
x > 1
```

This is an example of one more type of statement in C++ - a relational expression, also known as a conditional expression, or simply as a condition. The result of evaluating such expressions is either integer 0, if the condition is false, or integer 1, if the condition is true. The following table shows the full list of relational operators available in C++.

Operator	Meaning
<	Less than
<=	Less than or equal to
==	Equal to
>=	Greater than or equal to
>	Greater than
!=	Not equal to

As we have already said, in C++, the condition testing for *is equal to* is written with the help of two equals signs **==** standing side by side. The expression:

```
x == 1
```

tests whether the value of **x** is equal to 1.

> Remember, **==** asks the question whether the two things are equal (the answer is either True of False), **=** actively assigns the value of the expression on the right to the variable on the left.

Try It Out - Using Relational Expressions

The next program demonstrates relational expressions in action.

```
//   Program 3.5
//   Relational expressions

#include <iostream.h>

void main()
{                          // Output
  cout << (0 <  2);        // 1
  cout << (2 >  0);        // 1
  cout << (2 == 2);        // 1

  cout << (0 >= 2);        // 0
  cout << (2 <= 0);        // 0
  cout << (2 != 2);        // 0
}
```

The result output is:

111000

Try It Out!

How It Works

```
cout << (0 <  2);    // 1
cout << (2 >  0);    // 1
cout << (2 == 2);    // 1
```

Here the relational expressions in parentheses are true, in other words their values are equal to 1.

```
cout << (0 >= 2);    // 0
cout << (2 <= 0);    // 0
cout << (2 != 2);    // 0
```

Here the expressions are false and their values are equal to 0.

Try It Out - Using Relational Expressions

This next program takes us a little further. This time we are not just going to evaluate expressions, we are going to assign values to variables and compare them.

```
//   Program 3.6
//   Relational expressions

#include <iostream.h>

void main()
{
  int  x = 1;
  int  y = 2;
  int  YesOrNo;

                            // Output
  YesOrNo = ((x+1) == y);
  cout << YesOrNo;          // 1

  YesOrNo = ((x+1) == y/2);
  cout << YesOrNo;          // 0
}
```

Program 3.6 shows the assignment of the value of a relational expression to an integer variable. It's output is:

10

How It Works

```
int  x = 1;
int  y = 2;
int  YesOrNo;
```

First we declare 3 variables and initialize 2 of them. We are going to use the integer variable **YesOrNo** to store the integer result of the evaluation of the logical expressions.

```
YesOrNo = ((x+1) == y);
```

In this line **YesOrNo** is assigned the value of the logical expression. Let's look at this in a bit more detail.

```
(x+1) == y
```

Since the value of **x** is equal to 1, and the value of **y** is equal to 2, this expression gives **2==2**, so the condition is true. Therefore, the variable **YesOrNo** assumes the value 1 which is output to the screen.

```
YesOrNo = ((x+1) == y/2);
cout << YesOrNo;         // 0
```

The same principle works for the next two statements. **YesOrNo** is assigned a value depending on the evaluation of the expression:

```
(x+1) == y/2
```

This is false and, therefore, 0 is output.

Making Choices from a Menu

We can now apply the **if** statement and the relational operators we have learnt about to write programs that give us menu choices. This means we can offer the user several options and display different results depending on what they select.

Try It Out - A Simple Menu

Let's see how this works in action. To keep our program simple, the menu contains only two items.

```
//   Program 3.7
//   Simple Menu

#include <iostream.h>

void main ()
{
  int  Choice = 0;

  cout << endl
       << "Make your choice, please."
       << endl << endl;

  cout << "Choice 1." << endl
       << "Choice 2." << endl << endl
       << "Input 1 or 2 and then press Enter" << endl;

  cin  >> Choice;

  if ( Choice == 1 )
    cout << "Your choice is 1." << endl;
  if ( Choice == 2 )
    cout << "Your choice is 2." << endl;
}
```

Typical output from the program would be:

```
Make your choice, please.

Choice 1.
Choice 2.

Input 1 or 2 and then press Enter
1
Your choice is 1.
```

How It Works

When you run this program it outputs the menu, and will be waiting for the input of the number 1 or 2 - the numbers of the menu items. For instance, if you enter 1 then the variable **Choice** will be set to 1, and the condition:

```
Choice == 1
```

will be true, in other words the expression in the **if** statement is equal to 1, and this statement will output:

```
Your choice is 1.
```

In the next **if** statement the condition:

```
Choice == 2
```

will be false and the statement to the right of the **if** won't be executed.

To Be or Not to Be

Very often you have to choose between two options, for example, to answer "Yes" or "No". In C++ we have the **if else** statement to allow a choice between two alternatives. It has the following syntax:

```
if(expression_is_not_zero)
   do_this_statement
else
   do_this_instead
```

This statement may be read as follows:

"If the value of the expression is not equal to 0, then execute **do_this_statement**
otherwise, execute **do_this_instead**".

This is illustrated in the following figure.

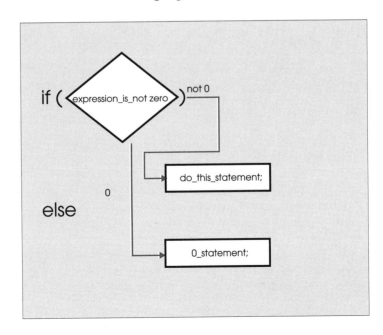

Try It Out - The if else Statement

The next program is going to test how the **if else** operation works. This program also demonstrates the use of blocks containing several statements. If you enter Yes (1) in answer to the question, one series of statements will be executed, if you answer No, a different set of statements will be executed.

```
//   Program 3.8
//   if else with blocks

#include <iostream.h>

void main()
{
  const  int  Yes = 1;
  const  int  No  = 0;
    int  YesOrNo = No;

  cout << "Do you like C++?" << endl;
  cout << "(Enter 1 for 'Yes' or any other for 'No'.)"
       << endl;
  cin  >> YesOrNo;

  if ( YesOrNo == Yes )
  {
    cout << "Your choice is 'Yes'" << endl;
    cout << "You had only one key for the right answer, ";
    cout << "and you have pressed it.";
  }
  else
  {
    cout << "Your choice is 'No'" << endl;
    cout << "May be you didn't understand my question. ";
    cout << "Re-run the program, and try again, please.";
  }
}
```

Typical output from this program might be:

```
Do you like C++?
(Enter 1 for 'Yes' or any other for 'No'.)
2
Your choice is 'No'
Maybe you didn't understand my question.
Re-run the program, and try again, please.
```

How It Works

```
  const  int  Yes = 1;
  const  int  No  = 0;
    int  YesOrNo = No;
```

In the above program the constants **Yes** and **No** can be initialized with values of 1 and 0, respectively. These help make the program easier to read.

In a program that contains blocks for the **if else** statement, it isn't always as easy as it is here to see which statement will be executed afterwards, for example:

```
cout << "and you have pressed it.";
```

You can use indention to help here. The following figure illustrates **if else** with blocks.

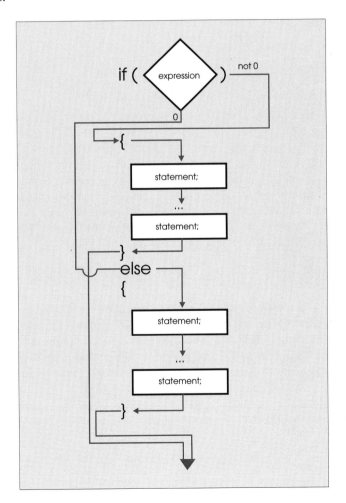

If you forget the braces for the block after an **if** which also has an **else** clause, the compiler will output an error message (you can check this). If you forget the braces for a block after **else**, compilation will proceed without error, but it won't give you the result you expect.

Don't forget the braces for a block after `else`.

This is similar to the situation that we saw earlier with **if**. C++ language rules mean that the **0-statement** must either be a single statement, or else a block of statements enclosed within braces. Therefore, the program fragment:

```
if (1)
   cout << 1;
else
   cout << 2;
cout << 3;
```

will output the digits 1 and 3, and discard the 2.

You can try removing the closing brace from either the **if** block or the **else** block in Program 3.8 and get an error message. Now remove both braces after the **if**. Again you will get an error message. Remove both braces after **else**. You'll see that the compiler doesn't give an error message. However, if you run the program and input 1 the output is incorrect.

In the Labyrinth of Questions

If, from a philosophical and artistic point of view, the answer to the question "To be or not to be?" is complicated, for a programmer it is a simple matter of choosing between two options using **if else**. However, in programs, just like in life, at every turn you have to deal with a large number of different conditions and complicated combinations of conditions.

We'll now show you how you can use **if else** statements to find the exit from this labyrinth of conditions in a C++ program.

Nested ifs

Have another look at the form of the **if else** statement:

```
if (expression)
  not0-statement
else
  0-statement
```

First of all, you can see that the whole **if else** is a statement itself. Therefore, you can use another **if else** instead of **not0-statement** or **0-statement**. In other words, **if else** statements can be nested inside each other like Russian matryoshkas, the wooden dolls that contain another doll, that contain another doll, that contain another doll....

Try It Out - Nested ifs

The next program contains four simple formal examples of nested **if** statements.

```cpp
// Program 3.9
// Nested if else

#include <iostream.h>

void main()
{
  int  x = 0;
  int  y = 0;

  cout << "Enter a pair of integer numbers." << endl
       << "Note that only the combination 1 1 makes "
          "the program work." << endl;

  cout << "Enter first  number: " << endl;
  cin  >> x;
  cout << "Enter second number: " << endl;
  cin  >> y;

  if (x==1)
  {
    if (y==1)
      cout << 1;
  }

  if (x==1)
  {
    if (y!=1)
      x=x;
```

```
     else
        cout << 2;
   }

   if (x!=1) ;
   else
   {
     if (y==1)
        cout << 3;
   }

   if (x!=1) ;
   else
   {
     if (y!=1) ;
     else
        cout << 4;
   }
}
```

This program outputs the numbers 1, 2, 3, 4 one by one. It will only output:

```
1234
```

if the user enters 1 in answer to both questions. In other cases the program won't output anything.

How It Works

Let's have a look at how each nested **if** statement works.

```
   if (x==1)
   {
     if (y==1)
        cout << 1;
   }
```

In this line there is an **if** statement where the **not0-statement** is another **if** statement. We have added braces to the only **not0-statement** to indicate that there is only one statement here after the previous **if** (the braces can be omitted):

```
   if (y==1)
        cout << 1;
```

This statement will only be executed when **x** is equal to 1. In its turn

```
        cout << 1;
```

will only be executed, and 1 output to the screen, when **y** is equal to 1.

```
if (x==1)
{
  if (y!=1)
    x=x;
else
  cout << 2;
}
```

In this line the **not0-statement** for the first **if** is replaced by the **if else** statement:

```
if (y!=1)
  x=x;
else
  cout << 2;
```

Here we wrote the formal statement

```
    x=x;
```

to show that when **y** isn't equal to 1, nothing is done. If you discard the expression **x=x** and just retain the semi-colon, you will have a "null statement" which means that nothing will be done. We are only using this code as a demonstration and don't suggest you write code like this that does nothing. The null statement is used in subsequent lines of the program.

In our program you can see that when **y** isn't equal to 1, the empty statement is "executed", otherwise (when **y** is equal to 1) 2 is output to the screen.

```
if (x!=1) ;
else
{
  if (y==1)
    cout << 3; }

if (x!=1) ;
  else
  {
    if (y!=1) ;
    else
      cout << 4;
  }
```

Here a nested **if** and an **if else** (in braces) replace the **0-statement** for the first **if**. The **not0-statement** is empty as there is only a semi-colon. In the first line, if **x** isn't equal to 1, then the null statement is executed, otherwise the **0-statement**:

```
if (y==1)
   cout << 3;
```

is executed, and if **y** is equal to 1, the number 3 is output. The second line here works in much the same way.

Nested if else Without Braces

In Program 3.9, we deliberately wrote each nested **if** statement on a separate line and put the nested **if** statement in braces. If you discard the braces in the line:

```
if (x==1)
{
   if (y==1)
      cout << 1;
}
```

you'll get:

```
if (x==1)
   if (y==1)
      cout << 1;
```

Be careful not to confuse nested **if** constructions like this with several consecutive constructions written on one line. Compare this line with the following:

```
if (x==1)
   cout << 0;
if (y==1)
   cout << 1;
```

This line contains two **if** statements (note the two semi-colons) whereas the first line only contains one semi-colon. It should be clear that these lines operate in different ways.

Remember that **else** is associated with the nearest preceding **if**.

Choosing Between Three Options

If you return to the problem of the menu (Program 3.7), you'll see that there is an obvious drawback in it, which we will now eliminate. As it stands, the program doesn't react to a wrong choice, in other words to a choice of something that doesn't exist. If a waiter gives a customer a menu that includes two dishes but the customer orders a third dish that isn't on the menu, then you need an option for the waiter to tactfully suggest that the customer reads the menu again and make a different choice.

Try It Out - Different Options

We can write a program that follows this behavior. To do this, we will use nested **if** statements. This next program is a modification of Program 3.7. In this new version, a third case is added, when any value that is absent in the menu (in other words, not 1 or 2) is entered.

```cpp
//   Program 3.10
//   Menu with nested if statements

#include <iostream.h>

void main()
{
  int  Choice = 0;

  cout << "Make your choice, please." << endl
       << "Press 1 or 2 and then press Enter." << endl;

  cout << "Choice 1." << endl;
  cout << "Choice 2." << endl;

  cin  >> Choice;

  if ( Choice == 1 )
    cout << "Your choice is 1." << endl;
  else
  {
    if ( Choice == 2 )
      cout << "Your choice is 2." << endl;
    else
      cout << "Your choice is incorrect. Try again." << endl;
  }
}
```

The program's output will look something like this:

```
Make your choice, please.
Press 1 or 2 and then press Enter.
Choice 1.
Choice 2.
4
Your choice is incorrect. Try again.
```

How It Works

As you can see, the program is now harder to understand, because the natural sequence of statement execution has been violated. To analyze and test the program's validity we need the flow of control to be clearer in the **if else** statements.

The input value is analyzed in the following way.

```
if ( Choice == 1 )
   cout << "Your choice is 1." << endl;
```

In this line the value of the variable **Choice** is checked. If it is equal to 1 then the program outputs:

```
Your Choice is 1.
```

```
else
{
  if ( Choice == 2 )
    cout << "Your choice is 2." << endl;
  else
    cout << "Your choice is incorrect. Try again." << endl;
}
```

If the value of **Choice** isn't equal to 1, then the nested **if else** (we have put it in braces) is executed. If the value of the variable **Choice** is equal to 2 then the program outputs:

```
Your Choice is 2.
```

and control passes to the next statement after the **if else**. This line doesn't contain any executable statements and is followed by the end of the program.

However, if the value of **Choice** isn't equal to either 1 or 2, the **else** is executed. Again, after this line the program ends.

The Problem of Abundance

It's now quite simple to prepare a program that enables the user to choose one option from many. In fact it's so easy that we haven't even included a separate program for it. We'll just show you how to modify Program 3.10 for a menu with 3 choices:

```
if ( Choice == 1 )
{
  ...
}
else
  if ( Choice == 2 )
  {
    ...
  }

  else
    if ( Choice == 3 )
    {
      ...
    }

    else
      if ( Choice == ... )
      {
        ...
      }

      else
      {
        ...
      }
```

In the braces, you should write any statements that should be executed when the corresponding value of the variable **Choice** is entered. The final else will apply to all values of the variable not covered previously.

Jumps

We are now going to look at a statement in C++ that allows us to move to parts of the code, skipping other parts.

The goto Statement

The **goto** statement can transfer control to the beginning of any statement in the program. All you have to do is write a label before this statement.

To use the **goto** statement you must insert a label in your code at the desired location. The label is terminated by a colon. The keyword **goto** followed by the label's name takes you to the label. For example:

```
void main()
{
  label:
    cout << "Example of the use of goto\n";
  goto label;
}
```

This example causes an infinite loop that repeatedly displays:

```
Example of the use of goto
```

on your screen.

The label must be unique. You can't have more than one label with the same name in a function.

So, the **goto** statement is a simple means of moving between blocks of code. However you shouldn't abuse it. Many people feel it's better to manage without the **goto** statement at all. There are many reasons for this. Use of the **goto** statement produces code that is harder to understand and follow. Some programmers feel that the **goto** statement should never be used at all, ever, but this is an extreme point of view. It's more reasonable to say that the use of **goto** is occasionally justified, for example, in emergency situations. Consider the situation where you have an error condition in the middle loop of several nested loops and need to jump right out of all the loops. In this situation, a **goto** statement provides the quickest and neatest solution but otherwise it is best avoided.

However, in this kind of situation it's still advisable to avoid passing control upwards. We'll use **goto** very rarely in this book and only for educational purposes. You should remember that any program can be written without **goto**s.

Spaghetti

As we have said, the **goto** statement can make programs difficult to understand. A program in which control is constantly passed backwards and forwards is commonly called "spaghetti" code. The next program is an example of this spaghetti.

Run the following program and then try to analyze the code and find out why it operated as it did. If you can't understand it, just take it as a good example of why you shouldn't write programs like it.

```
//   Program 3.11
//   Spaghetti

#include <iostream.h>

int main()
{
  int x=1;
  goto S;
  F:
    return 0;
  E:
    if (x!=6)
      if (x<9)
      {
        cout<<"t";
        x++;
        goto E;
      }
      else
      {
        cout<<"i"; x++;
        goto F;
      }
    else
    {
      cout<<"e";
      x++;
      goto E;
    }
  G:
    if (x==5)
    {
      cout<<"h";
      x++;
      goto E;
    }
```

```
    else
    {
      cout<<"g";
      x++;
      goto G;
    }
  S:
    if (x==1)
    {
      cout<<"S";
      x++;
      goto S;
    }
    else
      if (x==3)
      {
        cout<<"a";
        x++;
        goto G;
      }
      else
      {
        cout<<"p";
        x++;
        goto S;
      }
}
```

The return Statement

```
return 0;
```

In this line we used a jump statement that you haven't met yet:

Here, control will be returned from the function **main()** to the operating system program. This is because the statement **return** was absent, and for the **main()** function it's desirable but not obligatory. The **return** statement is usually placed at the end of the program, before the closing brace of the main function body, although it can be almost anywhere.

An alternative syntax is:

```
return(0);
```

Selecting From a Menu - The switch Statement

The ladder-shaped **else if** construction, based on the value of the same variable in all **else-if**s, is often found in programs. In C++ there is a special selection statement for it, called **switch**.

Try It Out - Using the switch Statement

This next program works in the same way as Program 3.10, but uses this **switch** statement instead of a nested **if else**.

```
//   Program 3.12
//   Menu with switch statement

#include <iostream.h>

void main()
{
  int  Choice = 0;

  cout << "Make your choice, please." << endl
       << "Press 1 or 2 and then press Enter." << endl;

  cout << "Choice 1." << endl;
  cout << "Choice 2." << endl;

  cin  >> Choice;

  switch (Choice)
  {
    case 1 :
      cout << "Your choice is 1.";
      break;
    case 2 :
      cout << "Your choice is 2.";
      break;
    default:
      cout << "Your choice is incorrect. Try again.";
  }
}
```

The output from this program looks like this:

```
Make your choice, please.
Press 1 or 2 and then press Enter.
Choice 1.
Choice 2.
2
Your choice is 2.
```

Try It Out!

How It Works

The new features in this program are:

The keyword **switch**
The keyword **case**
The keyword **break**
The keyword **default**

Let's look at how the **switch** statement operates.

```
switch (Choice)
{
```

Here the value of the variable **Choice** is calculated.

```
case 1 :
  cout << "Your choice is 1.";
  break;
case 2 :
  cout << "Your choice is 2.";
  break;
default:
  cout << "Your choice is incorrect. Try again.";
```

If it is equal to 1, control is passed to the statement with the case label **case 1**. If it's equal to 2, then control is passed to the statement labeled **case 2**, and so on.

```
case 1 :
  cout << "Your choice is 1.";
  break;
```

In this first line the word **case** is a keyword. The number 1 means that if the value of the variable **Choice** is equal to 1, control will be passed to here. The colon (:) indicates that the text **case 1** is only a label, a mark to show the point in the program to where **switch** should pass control. Following the colon, you write the statements which should be executed. At the end of the line, there is a jump statement:

```
break;
```

This breaks the natural sequence of statements and passes control to the statement following **switch**, (the statement after the brace which marks the end of the switch block of statements). If there was no **break** statement then each of the following lines would be executed. A typical mistake when programming **switch** statements is to forget the **break** statement.

> Don't forget the **break** statement in a **switch** statement.

The label with the keyword **default** in the line:

```
default:
```

marks the point to which control is passed for all values of the variable **Choice**, that weren't covered by the above case labels, in this case for all values except 1 or 2 (including negative values and 0). The word **default** isn't obligatory. If it's omitted, then for all other values nothing will be done.

Designing a Program

We have almost reached the end of this chapter. We now have enough tools in C++ to do something really useful and interesting. We will now go through a final implementation of some of the topics we have covered.

What we will do is set a task that a programmer might be asked to complete. We will go through the problem, analyzing what is needed and how we can get the result we want. We will then give the complete code for you to try.

The Problem

When you start writing larger programs you will have to consider various things, such as the layout of the screen, the amount of help to be given to the user, and what kind(s) of checks will you make to see if the user enters information correctly. For example, if the user is meant to enter a number, can you check that a number was entered?

The program that we will write is one that checks the character entered by the user and reports whether it's a digit, an upper-case letter, or a lower-case letter.

The Analysis

1   Output a message asking the user to input a keyboard character and store the character in a suitable variable.

2   Check the character entered to see whether it is a digit, an upper-case character, a lower-case character, or any other printable character.

3   Output the result to the screen.

The Solution

1   The first thing is to output a suitable message asking the user to enter a character and store the character in a suitable variable. Therefore, we will have to include the header file **IOSTREAM.H**. The obvious variable type to use is a character variable.

```
#include <iostream.h>

void main()
{
  char ch;

  cout << "\n\n\tPlease enter a character:  ";
  cin >> ch;

}
```

2&3 The character must be checked to see what type of character it is. An **if** statement can be used to test whether the character is a digit. Characters are stored using a numeric code (the ASCII code) and it is possible to see whether the ASCII code is greater than or equal to the ASCII code of the character 0. We could do this using a statement like **if(ch >= '0')**. Similarly, we can check to see whether the ASCII code of the character is less than or equal to the ASCII code of the character 9 using a similar statement.

However, by making use of the logical AND operator, **&&**, it's possible to combine the statements. If the character is a digit we will issue an appropriate message. If it's not a digit we will have to perform another test. Here, the **if else** statement is suitable.

```
#include <iostream.h>

void main()
{
  char ch;

  cout << "\n\n\tPlease enter a character:  ";
  cin >> ch;

  if(ch >= '0' && ch <= '9')
    cout << "\n\tThe character " << ch << " is a digit.\n";
  else

}
```

We can use similar methods to check whether the character is an upper-case letter or a lower-case letter.

```
#include <iostream.h>

void main()
{
  char ch;

  cout << "\n\n\tPlease enter a character:  ";
  cin >> ch;

  if(ch >= '0' && ch <= '9')
    cout << "\n\tThe character " << ch << " is a digit.\n";
  else
    if(ch >= 'A' && ch <= 'Z')
      cout << "\n\tThe character " << ch
           << " is upper case.\n";
    else
      if(ch >= 'a' && ch <= 'z')
        cout << "\n\tThe character " << ch
             << " is lower case.\n";
      else
        cout << "\n\tOther printable character - "
             << ch << endl;
}
```

Library Functions

Although this chapter isn't about functions, it is worth mentioning that there are several functions in the header file **CTYPE.H** which perform tests of this nature.

These functions include:

isdigit	which tests if a digit was entered
isalpha	which tests if a letter - lower or upper-case - was entered
islower	which tests if a lower-case letter was entered
isupper	which tests if an upper-case letter was entered
isspace	which tests if a space was entered
isgraph	which test if a printable character was entered

There are other functions and you should refer to your compiler documentation for further details.

To use these functions you have to pass an integer value (the ASCII value) to the function. As our program saves the character to a **char** variable we have to cast the variable to an **int**. This is done by putting the keyword **int** in parentheses. For example:

```
isdigit( (int) ch);
```

The functions return a non-zero value if the test is successful. Therefore, the functions can be used with the **if** statement.

To use these functions in our program would mean that we have to include the header file **CTYPE.H** in our code.

You can alter the program to test these functions.

```
#include <iostream.h>
#include <ctype.h>

void main()
{
  char ch;

  cout << "\n\n\tPlease enter a character:   ";
  cin >> ch;

  if(isdigit((int) ch))
    cout << "\n\tThe character " << ch << " is a digit.\n";
  else
    if(isupper((int) ch))
      cout << "\n\tThe character " << ch
           << " is upper case.\n";
    else
```

```
if(islower((int) ch))
   cout << "\n\tThe character " << ch
        << " is lower case.\n";
else
   cout << "\n\tOther printable character - "
        << ch << endl;
}
```

Summary

In this chapter you've learnt how to make decisions using **if**, **if else**, **switch** statements and unconditional transfers using **goto**. You have seen how to develop programs that select one of several options, analyze the values of variables and have learnt how to program different sequences of statements depending on these values. You are now able to combine statements into blocks, and know that in C++, one block is the same as one statement.

In the programs we've looked at so far, each variable has been associated with a single data value. In the next chapter we will be looking at a way of handling large amounts of data of the same type, which is a powerful tool when used with some of the other flow of control statements.

CHAPTER 4

Working With Large
Amounts Of Data

In this chapter you will become acquainted with two features of the C++ language: arrays, and the loop or iteration statement. Arrays allow you to handle large amounts of data in a very compact manner. The loop statement enables you to describe, in a few lines of code, long repetitive actions which load the computer with a large amount of work. In the chapter you will also hear about new data types: **long int**, **double**, **long double** and **char**.

In this chapter you will:

▶ Learn about arrays and how to use these in your programs

▶ Look at problems that can occur regarding the boundaries of arrays

▶ Use some of the other C++ data types

▶ Use the powerful iteration statement - **do**

▶ Write a program that calculates the average and sum of any numbers you enter

Data Mountains - Arrays

The speed of modern computers is as impressive as the size of memory they now offer. They can process large quantities of data in fractions of a second. Let's work out, for example, how much time a computer would need to process a million bank accounts. Suppose that the processing of one account takes one millionth of a second (ten computer instructions). Then processing a million accounts will take only one second.

But now you might wonder how long it would take for a programmer to describe such a quantity of data. If you use the method shown in previous chapters, then simply to describe the balance of each account you'll need nearly a year! The balance of each account will be denoted by a statement of the type.

```
int Acnt000001;
```

This contains 15 characters (including a blank). So, to describe a million accounts it will be necessary to input 15 million characters. If you input 2 characters per second, it will take 7.5 million seconds or more that 2000 hours. Working a 40-hour week, means more than 50 weeks, or about a year.

Fortunately, you don't need to spend so much time on such an unrewarding activity, as the C++ language provides a simple feature for the description of large amounts of data. This feature is called an **array** of data.

The Highest Mountains

Let's first consider the description of multiple data elements using the method we have already seen in previous chapters. Then we'll see how to simplify this description using the array concept.

Try It Out - Not Using Arrays

This program shows the height in meters of the highest mountain peaks of seven continents: America (North and South), Europe, Asia, Africa, Australia and the Antarctic. To keep the program free from unnecessary details, we deliberately avoided outputting the names of the peaks and continents to the screen. This first program shows how we could do this given what we already know. Even with just seven continents you can see how cumbersome the program is.

```
// Program 4.1
// The highest mountains of 7 continents

#include <iostream.h>

void main()
{
  int  Mountain0;
  int  Mountain1;
  int  Mountain2;
  int  Mountain3;
  int  Mountain4;
  int  Mountain5;
  int  Mountain6;

  Mountain0 = 2228;    // Kosciusko         Australia
  Mountain1 = 5140;    // Vinson Massif  Antarctica
  Mountain2 = 5642;    // El'brus           Europe
  Mountain3 = 5895;    // Kilimanjaro    Africa
  Mountain4 = 6193;    // McKinley       North America
  Mountain5 = 6960;    // Aconcagua      South America
  Mountain6 = 8848;    // Everest        Asia

  cout << Mountain0  << endl  << Mountain1  << endl  << Mountain2  << endl
       << Mountain3  << endl  << Mountain4  << endl  << Mountain5  << endl
       << Mountain6  << endl;
}
```

The output from the program looks like this:

```
2228
5140
5642
5895
6193
6960
8848
```

How It Works

The program works in the same way as the programs we have already
seen. For the declaration of each data element (the height of a mountain in
meters) you can use a statement of the type:

```
int  Mountain0;
```

Alternatively, you could use the names of the peaks, for example:

```
int  Everest;
```

or possibly:

```
int   EverestHeight;
```

We have used digits to distinguish the names and will use these digits again later on.

If you wanted to write the same program to include all of the peaks with heights in excess of 1000m, then the height data would have occupied a significantly larger space.

Try It Out - Using Arrays

In this program, we are going to use something new called an **array**. It describes the same data, but in a more structured and compact way. Compile and run the program to verify that it outputs the same results as the previous program.

```
//   Program 4.2
//   Array of 7 mountains

#include <iostream.h>

void main()
{
  int  Mountain[7];

  Mountain[0] = 2228;    // Kosciusko       Australia
  Mountain[1] = 5140;    // Vinson Massif   Antarctica
  Mountain[2] = 5642;    // El'brus         Europe
  Mountain[3] = 5895;    // Kilimanjaro     Africa
  Mountain[4] = 6193;    // McKinley        N. America
  Mountain[5] = 6960;    // Aconcagua       S. America
  Mountain[6] = 8848;    // Everest         Asia

  cout << Mountain[0] << endl << Mountain[1] << endl << Mountain[2] << endl
       << Mountain[3] << endl << Mountain[4] << endl << Mountain[5] << endl
       << Mountain[6] << endl;
}
```

How It Works

The main advantage of this program over the previous one is the reduction in the number of names and declarations. In Program 4.1 seven objects were declared with the names **Mountain0, Mountain1, ... Mountain6**. In Program

4.2 only one object was declared:

```
int  Mountain[7];
```

This is an array of integer numbers. Its name is **Mountain**. It consists of 7 elements. The number of elements is indicated in brackets **[ ]** just after the name (spaces are admissible before and after the bracket). The square brackets are called a subscript operator. The keyword **int**, before the array name, indicates the type of the array elements. All elements in an array are of the same type. Instead of an integer constant for the number of elements, you could also write an expression resulting in a positive integer.

The next figure shows the structure of an array declaration statement. Here the word **type** means the name of an admissible type of data, for example, **int**, or **float**. The name of an array is defined with the same rules as the name of a variable.

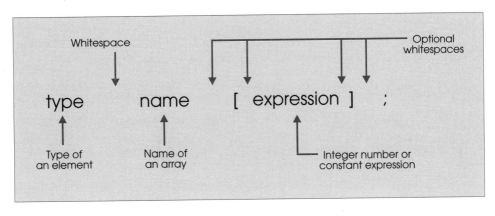

To really understand what is going on we need to look at arrays in more detail.

Addressing Array Elements

An array provides a compact description of a set of variables which are to be processed in the same way. So in Program 4.2 we combined 7 variables into one array. How can we reference particular elements of the array? The following form is used to address the first element of the **Mountain** array:

```
Mountain[0]
```

The second element is specified by `Mountain[1]` and so on. The array elements referenced in such a way, may be used as ordinary variables: they may be assigned values:

```
Mountain[0] = 2228;    // Kosciusko      Australia
Mountain[1] = 5140;    // Vinson Massif  Antarctica
Mountain[2] = 5642;    // El'brus        Europe
Mountain[3] = 5895;    // Kilimanjaro    Africa
Mountain[4] = 6193;    // McKinley       N. America
Mountain[5] = 6960;    // Aconcagua      S. America
Mountain[6] = 8848;    // Everest        Asia
```

Their values may be output to your display:

```
cout << Mountain[0] << endl << Mountain[1] << endl << Mountain[2] << endl
     << Mountain[3] << endl << Mountain[4] << endl << Mountain[5] << endl
     << Mountain[6] << endl;
```

or used in arithmetic expressions.

Note the difference between using `[]` in a declaration, and referencing a particular element name. For example, the declaration:

```
int  Mountain[7];
```

defines an array of 7 elements, with the name `Mountain`. The statement:

```
Mountain[0] = 2228;
```

assigns a value to the first element of the array.

For example, the number `i` in brackets in a reference to an array element:

```
Mountain[i]
```

is called the index of the element of the array. In C++, an index has a value which is one less than the position of the element in the array. An index of an array composed of N elements has the values from 0 to N-1.

To sum up, an array is a contiguous object, consisting of ordered and numbered elements of the same type. Elements are addressed by an index which is one less than the ordinal number of the element. The figure opposite illustrates this point with the example of an array of mountain peak heights.

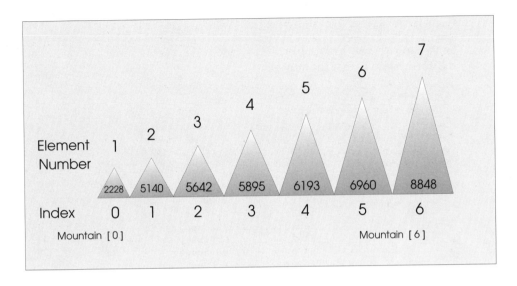

The Index and the Number of an Element

There is a potential ambiguity in the use of the term "number of an array element". The i-th element of an array shouldn't be confused with the element with index **i**. For example, `Mountain[1]` didn't refer to the first but to the second mountain, and `Mountain[7]` isn't present at all in an array of seven elements.

Confusion arises because we start labeling array elements at 0, and not at 1. The array index is the offset from the start of the array, so the first element is 0 because it isn't offset at all.

Be careful if you come across an expression of the type "i-th element of an array". We shall use "i-th element" to indicate the element number of an element, and not the index.

> The individual elements of an array have index values starting at zero.
> This can cause confusion at first because the fifth element of an array
> (called `array` for example) will have an index of 4 (`array[4]`).
> Remember, the last element always has an index value of one less than
> the number of elements.

Try It Out - An Expression as an Index

Since we can use a variable as an index, we can rewrite our last example in the form shown in Program 4.3.

```
//   Program 4.3
//   Indexing array elements

#include <iostream.h>

void main()
{
  int Mountain[7] = { 2228,        // Kosciusko
                      5140,        // Vinson Massif
                      5642,        // El'brus
                      5895,        // Kilimanjaro
                      6193,        // McKinley
                      6960,        // Aconcagua
                      8848         // Everest
                    };
  int  i=0;         // Index of array

  cout << Mountain[i]  << endl;
  i++;
  cout << Mountain[i]  << endl;
  i++;
  cout << Mountain[i]  << endl;
  i++;
  cout << Mountain[i]  << endl;
  i++;
  cout << Mountain[i]  << endl;
  i++;
  cout << Mountain[i]  << endl;
  i++;
  cout << Mountain[i]  << endl;
  i++;
}
```

The output from the program is the same as the first example.

How It Works

```
int  i=0;         // Index of array

cout << Mountain[i]  << endl;
```

Here, we declare and initialize a variable **i**. Then an element of the array, **Mountain[i]**, is referred to where the integer variable **i** is the index. Since the current value of **i** is 0, we get **Mountain[0]**. The value of this element will be output to the screen.

```
i++;
```

Here we have the operator **++**. It increases the value of the index **i** by 1. So in the next line:

```
cout << Mountain[i]  << endl;
```

Mountain[i] is **Mountain[1]** and the height of the second mountain is output. The heights of the remaining mountains are output in exactly the same way with **i** being incremented by 1 each time.

Initializing Arrays

A new facility is introduced in Program 4.3.

```
int  Mountain[7] = { 2228,      // Kosciusko
                     5140,      // Vinson Massif
                     5642,      // El'brus
                     5895,      // Kilimanjaro
                     6193,      // McKinley
                     6960,      // Aconcagua
                     8848       // Everest
                   };
```

This is the initializer list. It is used to assign initial values to the array elements. The characteristics of the list are shown in the following figure.

121

The elements of the initializer list may be separated by spaces and carried over onto a new line. They are separated by commas, but there is no comma before the closing brace. Don't confuse the use of {} here with a block. Unlike the block, a semi-colon is obligatory after the closing brace.

Difference Between Array Elements and Initializer Lists

The number of array elements and the number of elements in the initializer list may differ. The following three cases are possible:

1   There is no initializer list. For example:

```
int  Mountain[7];
```

In this case no initial values for the elements are defined, and they are to be assigned values within the program itself.

2   The number of array elements exceeds the number of elements in the list. For example:

```
int  Mountain[7] = {5029,5140};
```

In this statement, out of 7 array elements, the first two will be assigned the values shown. The rest will be set to zero.

3   The number of array elements isn't indicated, and there is an initializer list. For example:

```
int  Mountain[] = {5029,5140};
```

Since the number of array elements isn't specified, the compiler will set the number of array elements to be equal to the number of elements in the list, so 2 in this example.

If you try to specify more initializing values than there are elements in the array, then the compiler will treat it as an error.

More About Data

There is a potential problem of space shortage when creating arrays. If you define an array of an exceptionally large size, it may require more memory than you have available in your PC.

C++ has a special operator which can tell you how much memory is required for the allocation of this or that object. This is the **sizeof** operator.

Try It Out - Using the sizeof Operator

We can see the **sizeof** operator in action in the following program.

```
//  Program 4.4
//  Size of Mountain

#include <iostream.h>

void main()
{
  int  Mountain [7];
                                              // Output
    cout  << sizeof Mountain      << "/"      // 14/2=7
          << sizeof Mountain[0] << "="
          << sizeof Mountain / sizeof Mountain[0]
          << endl;

  char  Char;
  int   Int;
  long  int  LongInt;

  float   Float;
  double  Double;
  long    double  LongDouble;

    cout  << sizeof (char)              // 1   Type
          << sizeof Char                // 1   Variable
          << sizeof '1'                 // 1   Constant
          << endl
          << sizeof (int)               // 2
          << sizeof Int                 // 2
          << sizeof 1                   // 2
          << endl
          << sizeof (long  int)         // 4
          << sizeof LongInt             // 4
          << sizeof 1L                  // 4
          << endl
          << sizeof (float)             // 4
          << sizeof Float               // 4
          << sizeof 1.F                 // 4
          << endl
          << sizeof (double)            // 8
          << sizeof Double              // 8
          << sizeof 1.                  // 8
          << endl
          << sizeof (long  double) << " "  // 10
```

Try It Out!

123

```
            << sizeof LongDouble << " "        // 10
            << sizeof 1.L                      // 10
            << endl;

        char CA[7];     // Character Array
        int IA[7];      // Int Array
   long int LIA[7];     // Long Int Array
        float FA[7];    // Float Array
        double DA[7];   // Double Array
   long double LDA[7];  // Long Double Array

    cout  << sizeof  CA / sizeof  CA [0]     // 7
          << sizeof  IA / sizeof  IA [0]     // 7
          << sizeof LIA / sizeof LIA [0]     // 7
          << sizeof  FA / sizeof  FA [0]     // 7
          << sizeof  DA / sizeof  DA [0]     // 7
          << sizeof LDA / sizeof LDA [0];    // 7
}
```

The output from the program looks like this:

```
14/2=7
111
222
444
444
888
10 10 10
777777
```

How It Works

```
    cout << sizeof Mountain     << "/"        // 14/2=7
         << sizeof Mountain[0] << "="
         << sizeof Mountain / sizeof Mountain[0]
```

In the first line here, the **sizeof** operator gives the size of the whole array, and in the second, the size of the first element of the array. On our computer we get 14 and 2 bytes respectively. However, it's possible that you may get different values on your computer, but the ratio:

```
sizeof Mountain / sizeof Mountain[0]
```

will be the same on any computer, and will be equal to the number of array elements specified in its declaration in the array:

```
int Mountain[7];
```

You could check this by changing the number of array elements in this line.

You could also try to discover the approximate maximum size of **int** array which can be declared on your computer, by gradually incrementing the number of array elements, and repeating the compilation until it fails.

New Types of Data

The previous program also demonstrates some new data types. These are **char**, **long**, **double**, and **long double**. We will now briefly describe each of them. Remember, the information about the memory size given in the comments of Program 4.4 applies to our computer. On other computers the memory requirement may be different.

The Shortest Data Type

Data of type **char** (from character) are just 1 byte long. From the name, you may have guessed that variables of this type are used mainly for storing characters. However, they can be used in arithmetic operations as well. Data of the type **char** will be described in more detail later in this chapter.

```
char Char;
```

In this line there is a declaration of the variable **Char** of a **char** type. Note that the first letter of variable **Char** is upper-case. This makes it possible to distinguish this variable from the lower-case keyword **char**. This is essential as variables mustn't be given the same name as keywords.

```
cout << sizeof (char)        // 1  Type
     << sizeof Char          // 1  Variable
```

This line shows that the **sizeof** operator may be applied to the name of a data type (in this case - **char**). Here it's necessary to place the data type name between parentheses. The next line gives the memory size occupied by the variable **Char**.

```
<< sizeof '1'              // 1  Constant
```

Here you see a constant, '1', which is of type **char**. There should be exactly one character between the quotes (and no extra spaces).

Long Modifier

```
long int LongInt;
```

In this line a variable of type **long int** is declared. The length of a variable of this type on our computer is 4 bytes. This extra length means that variables of the **long int** type may store significantly larger values than variables of type **int**. Later in this chapter you will see how to calculate the maximum value of a **long int** with the help of a program.

Instead of **long int**, you can write just **long**, omitting **int** (you can check this by changing the program).

Integer constants of the **long int** type are written with the letter **l** or **L** at the end. If you write a particularly large constant without **L** at the end (for example, 100000) the compiler will issue a warning.

Floating Types

```
<< sizeof (double)          // 8
```

```
<< sizeof (long  double) << " "  // 10
```

To represent fractional numbers more exactly, with a larger number of significant digits and a wider range, C++ uses the types **double** and **long double**. The lengths of variables of these types on our computer are 8 and 10 bytes respectively.

```
<< sizeof 1.F          // 4
```

```
<< sizeof 1.          // 8
```

```
<< sizeof 1.L          // 10
```

Constants with a decimal point have the type **double** by default, and occupy 8 bytes (see above). In order to define a constant of the type **float** it is necessary to write **F** or **f** at the end (see above). Constants of the type **long double** are written with a decimal point, and with **L** or **l** at the end. They occupy 10 bytes.

```
     char CA[7];       // Character Array
     int  IA[7];       // Int Array
long int  LIA[7];      // Long Int Array
     float FA[7];      // Float Array
     double DA[7];     // Double Array
long double LDA[7];    // Long Double Array
```

In the last section of the program arrays of different types are declared, starting with **char** and ending with **long double**.

Problem With Array Bounds

There is a very common mistake made when using arrays. Most C++ compilers do not prevent the use of an array index above the maximum value defined by the array declaration. For example:

```
int array[10];      //define an array of integers holding 10 elements
array[15] = 99;
```

Since the array only contains ten elements, then the index **array[15]** can't exist. The compiler won't report an error and will allow the program to run. The data will be stored in memory reserved for another variable or even the program code. This will lead to run time errors or may even cause the program to crash.

The responsibility for ensuring the use of valid index values of array elements in C++ lies wholly with you, the programmer. Using index values outside the range of a given array may cause a whole range of problems, from data loss, to crashing the operating system.

Incrementing Array Indexes

When processing arrays, it's often necessary to perform the operation "pass on to the next element". You saw this in Program 4.3, where the **++** operator was used for this purpose.

You already know that **i++** means increment the value of the variable **i** by 1. But the increment operator **++** has some unusual features which are constantly used in C++ programs.

Try It Out - Using the ++ Operator

Let's consider these features shown in simple examples in the following program.

```
//  Program 4.5
//  Postfix and prefix increment

#include <iostream.h>
```

Try It Out!

```
void main()
{                          // Output
  int  i;

// Postfix increment
  i=1;
  cout << i;               // 1
  cout << i++;             // 1
  cout << i++;             // 2
  cout << i;               // 3
  cout << endl;

// Prefix increment
  i=1;
  cout << i;               // 1
  cout << ++i;             // 2
  cout << ++i;             // 3
  cout << i;               // 3
  cout << endl;

// May be suprising results !?
  i=1;
  cout << i                // 3211   !!!
       << i++
       << i++
       << i
       << endl;
}
```

The program output looks like this:

```
1123
1233
3211
```

How It Works

This program shows that the **++** operator may be placed either to the right of a variable (**postfix increment**), or to the left (**prefix increment**). In each case it behaves differently.

```
  i=1;
  cout << i;               // 1
  cout << i++;             // 1
  cout << i++;             // 2
  cout << i;               // 3
```

At the start **i** equals 1. The postfix increment, adds 1 after the **<<** operator outputs the value of **i**, so the value 1 is displayed. In the next line the new value **i** is output, which is now 2, and again after the output it is incremented by 1.

```
i=1;
cout << i;        // 1
cout << ++i;      // 2
cout << ++i;      // 3
cout << i;        // 3
```

The prefix increment, first adds 1 to **i**, so that **i** is equal to 2, and then this new value of **i** is output.

It's better not to use the **++** operator for more than one instance of a variable in the same expression. You might think that these lines:

```
i=1;
cout << i         // 3211  !!!
     << i++
     << i++
     << i
     << endl;
```

will produce the same output as the first block:

```
i=1;
cout << i;        // 1
cout << i++;      // 1
cout << i++;      // 2
cout << i;        // 3
```

But the result will surprise you.

```
i=1;
cout << i         // 3211  !!!
     << i++
     << i++
     << i
     << endl;
```

So why does this happen? The **++** operator, positioned after the variable, known as the postfix increment uses the value of the variable in the expression and then increments its value. In a complex expression, like this one, the **++** operator associates from the right. Therefore, when the statement is executed the values are as shown in the next diagram.

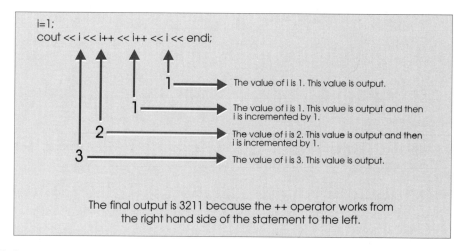

```
i=1;
cout << i << i++ << i++ << i << endl;
```

1 — The value of i is 1. This value is output.

1 — The value of i is 1. This value is output and then i is incremented by 1.

2 — The value of i is 2. This value is output and then i is incremented by 1.

3 — The value of i is 3. This value is output.

The final output is 3211 because the ++ operator works from the right hand side of the statement to the left.

If the operator is positioned before the variable, the variable is incremented and then the operation is carried out.

Try It Out - Using the Increment Operator

Using the increment operator we can simplify Program 4.3:

```
//   Program 4.6
//   Incrementing an array index

#include <iostream.h>

void main()
{
  int Mountain[7] = { 2228,       // Kosciusko
                      5140,       // Vinson Massif
                      5642,       // El'brus
                      5895,       // Kilimanjaro
                      6193,       // McKinley
                      6960,       // Aconcagua
                      8848        // Everest
                    };
  int  i=0;       // Index of array

  cout << Mountain [i++]  << endl;
  cout << Mountain [i++]  << endl;
  cout << Mountain [i++]  << endl;
  cout << Mountain [i++]  << endl;
  cout << Mountain [i++]  << endl;
  cout << Mountain [i++]  << endl;
  cout << Mountain [i++]  << endl;
}
```

The output is the same but the program structure is different.

How It Works

We have integrated the incrementing of the index value, **i**, into the output statement for each mountain.

```
int  Mountain [7] = {
```

We declare our array.

Then we use the increment operator to display the values of each different array element one-by-one.

```
int  i=0;        // Index of array

cout << Mountain [i++]  << endl;
cout << Mountain [i++]  << endl;
cout << Mountain [i++]  << endl;
cout << Mountain [i++]  << endl;
cout << Mountain [i++]  << endl;
cout << Mountain [i++]  << endl;
cout << Mountain [i++]  << endl;
```

Repeating a Block of Statements

You can now see the need for statements that will do things like repeat an action 7 times. The statements to do this in C++ have the collective name of **iteration**, or **loop** statements and are:

▶ The **do** statement

▶ The **while** statement

▶ The **for** statement

Loop statements allow the computer to be programmed to repeat the same actions many times on different data, without the need to write out instructions explicitly each time.

Do It Again and Again

Now you'll see how to repeat the same statement as many times as required using the **do while** statement. This will repeat an action until certain conditions that you specify are met.

Try It Out - Using the do Statement

Compare this next program with the first program (Program 4.1), in which the array wasn't used and there was no iteration statement. You can see how much shorter the program is now.

We have also improved the program by making the compiler responsible for determining the number of elements in the array from the number of values in the initializer list. We determine the array dimension **NM** by using the **sizeof** operator so effectively making the compiler responsible for this too.

```
//   Program 4.7
//   Do while ...

#include <iostream.h>

void main()
{
   int Mountain[] =   {2228,5140,5642,5895,6193,6960,8848};
   int NM;                          // Number of Mountains
   int i = 0;

   NM = sizeof Mountain / sizeof Mountain[0];

   i = 0;
   do cout << Mountain[i++] << endl; while (i < NM);

   // Output in reverse order
   i = NM;

   do
      cout << Mountain[--i] << endl;
   while (i > 0);
}
```

The program output looks like this:

```
2228
5140
5642
5895
6193
6960
8848
8848
6960
6193
5895
5642
5140
2228
```

How It Works

In order to change the number of array elements in this program, it's enough to only change the initializer list. This avoids the potential errors inherent in explicit specification of the array size.

```
i = 0;
do
   cout << Mountain[i++] << endl;
while (i < NM);
```

After the initialization of **NM**, the program outputs the height of each mountain in the first **do** loop.

```
do
   cout << Mountain[--i] << endl;
while (i > 0);
```

In the second **do** loop, you see the prefix decrement operator used to output the heights of mountains in reverse order. The **--** operator is similar to the **++** operator except that the variable is decremented by 1. As with the **++** operator, if the **--** operator is in front of the variable, the variable is decremented before being used. If the **--** operator is after the variable, the existing value is used and then the variable is decremented.

How Does the do Statement Work?

We can illustrate how the **do** statement works with the help of another program.

Try It Out - The do Statement

Here, the **do** statement is simulated with the help of **goto** and **if** statements already familiar to you.

```
//   Program 4.8
//   How does the do statement work ?

#include <iostream.h>

void main()
{
   const int N = 2;   // Number of cycles
   int  i;

   // do statement
   i = 1;
```

133

```
    do             // Keyword (lower-case)
      cout << i++;
    while (i <= N);

    cout << endl;

    // goto model of do statement
    i = 1;
    DO:            // Label (upper-case)
      cout << i++;
      if (i <= N) goto DO;
}
```

This program outputs two similar lines:

```
12
12
```

How It Works

```
i = 1;
do             // Keyword (lower-case)
  cout << i++;
while (i <= N);
```

The first line is output by the **do** statement.

```
i = 1;
DO:            // Label (upper-case)
  cout << i++;
  if (i <= N) goto DO;
```

The second line is output in a loop defined using the **goto**. You can see a label **DO**. This is in upper-case in order to avoid a conflict with the keyword **do**. Instead of label **DO** we could have chosen any other legal name. The value of **i** is output and then **i** is incremented by 1. Finally, the condition **i<=N** is checked. Since **N** is equal to 2 it's true. Therefore, the statement:

```
goto DO:
```

is executed and the jump to the label **DO** takes place. Here **i** is output again (now equal to 2), and then **i** is incremented by 1, so that it equals 3.

Now the expression **i<=N** proves to be false and the statement that follows the **if** statement, is executed and the program exits from the loop. In this case the next statement is the closing **}** of **main()**.

```
i = 1;
do          // Keyword (lower-case)
  cout << i++;
while (i <= N);
```

The **do** statement operates in exactly the same way. Here the keyword **do** (written as all other keywords of C++, in lowercase) stands for a label to which a jump is performed if the expression in parentheses after **while** isn't 0.

The **do** statement has the general form:

```
do statement while (expression);
```

Its operation with a single statement is illustrated in the following figure.

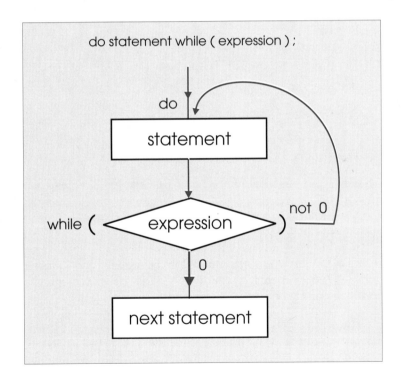

In the next figure there is an illustration of flow control for the **do** statement using a block of statements inside curly braces. This follows the general rule you already know: a block may be located anywhere that a single statement can.

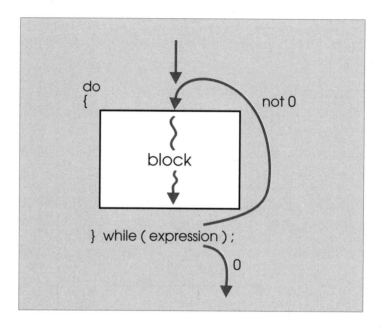

You have already seen similar charts in Chapter 2, so we won't discuss them in detail.

The Dangerous goto

Since the action of a **do** statement can be exactly replicated with a label, an **if** and a **goto**, you might wonder why the **do** statement is needed if a **goto** statement can be used successfully to replace it.

The disadvantage of a **goto** statement is the necessity to use a label. A **do** statement doesn't require this label. While using **goto**, every subsequent loop in the program will need a label with a new name, since the names of all labels in a program must be different. This makes programming errors more likely, because if a **goto** statement refers to the wrong label the program will jump to the wrong statement. Rectifying such errors can cost the programmer valuable time.

Such errors are especially probable because programs are often written by copying existing lines of code and then modifying them. You can easily forget to correct a label in a **goto** statement after copying it to a new position, as in the last line of the program fragment given below:

```
Label1:
...
if (...) goto Label1;
...
Label2:
...
if (...) goto Label1;
```

Here the last line is incorrect. It should read:

```
goto Label2;
```

As far as the compiler is concerned, this isn't an error. It just doesn't do what was intended. If we rewrite this fragment with the help of the **do** statement

```
do
{
  ...
} while (...);
...
do
{
  ...
} while (...);
```

then such an error will never arise.

There are other grounds for preferring the **do** statement. They are connected with the statements **continue** and **break**, which we'll consider below. We can compare the **do** with **goto** as follows. Using the **goto** statement to define a loop is a potential source of errors which can be difficult to detect. It's easier to read loops and they express the problem more exactly than **goto**s and labels. Therefore, you shouldn't use the **goto** statement to organize loops.

Checking Characters Input

Let's return briefly to the program we designed and wrote at the end of the last chapter. You will recall that this program checked a character the user entered via the keyboard and reported whether the character was a digit, an upper-case letter, a lower-case letter, or one of the other printable characters.

Unfortunately, this program had to be executed separately for every character that the user wanted to check. Wouldn't it be simpler if the program continued until a terminating character was input.

Try It Out - Improving the Last Chapter's Final Program

We can achieve this by using a **do while** loop. The entire program is put inside a **do while** loop which continues to loop until a termination character is input.

```
#include <iostream.h>
void main()
{
  char ch;

  do
  {
    cout << "\n\n\tPlease enter a character:   ";
    cin >> ch;

    if(ch >= '0' && ch <= '9')
      cout << "\n\tThe character " << ch << " is a digit.\n";
    else
      if(ch >= 'A' && ch <= 'Z')
        cout << "\n\tThe character " << ch << " is upper case.\n";
      else
        if(ch >= 'a' && ch <= 'z')
          cout << "\n\tThe character " << ch << " is lower case.\n";
        else
          cout << "\n\tOther printable character - " << ch << endl;
  } while(ch != 'q' && ch != 'Q');
}
```

The program will now run until either **q** or **Q** is entered.

Flow Control Within Loops

Whether you are in a **for** loop, a **while** loop, or a **do** loop you can control the flow of execution of the statements in the loop by the use of the keywords **break** and **continue**.

The **break** statement is a safe jump (recommended in C++) unlike the dangerous **goto**. The **break** statement may be used only to exit from loops and **switch** statements. Elsewhere it isn't permitted.

Try It Out - Using the break Statement

You can check the operation of the **break** statement in the next program.

```
// Program 4.9
// Break statement in a do loop

#include <iostream.h>

void main()
{                       // Output
  cout << 1;            // 1

  do
  {
    cout << 2;          // 2
    break;
    cout << 3;                          // Never executed
  } while (0);
  cout << 4;            // 4
}
```

It outputs onto the screen:

```
124
```

How It Works

```
    break;
    cout << 3;                          // Never executed
  } while (0);
  cout << 4;            // 4
```

Here the **break** statement causes the loop to terminate and control passes to the line that follows the end of the loop. As a result, one line in this program is never executed. The compiler can see this and will output a warning.

Note that we put 0 as the expression in **while**. This means that the loop body, will be executed only once.

Try It Out!

This next figure shows the operation of the **break** statement within a loop.

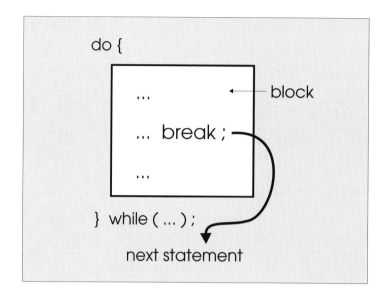

Jump From a Nested Loop

When loops are nested within one another as in the next program, then the **break** statement exits the innermost loop in which it's enclosed.

Try It Out - Jumping From a Nested Loop

Let's look at an example.

```
//   Program 4.10
//   Break from nested loops

#include <iostream.h>

void main()
{                        // Output
   cout << 1;            // 1

   do
   {
      cout << 2;         // 2
```

```
  do
  {
    cout << 3;        // 3
    break;
    cout << 4;      // Never executed
  } while (0);

  cout << 5;      // 5
  break;
  cout << 6;      // Never executed
  } while (0);

  cout << 7;      // 7
}
```

How It Works

```
do
{
  cout << 2;      // 2

  do
  {
    cout << 3;        // 3
    break;
    cout << 4;  // Never executed
  } while (0);

  cout << 5;      // 5
  break;
  cout << 6;  // Never executed
  } while (0);

  cout << 7;      // 7
```

Here, the first **break** statement exits from the inner loop, where it resides, to the statement:

```
cout << 4;
```

The second **break** statement exits from the outer loop. That's why the output of this program is:

```
12357
```

Perpetual Motion

A more realistic illustration of the use of the **break** statement is in the next program, which shows how the **break** statement is used together with an **if** statement for exiting the loop. The condition:

```
while(1)
```

is of special interest. This loop will continue indefinitely, since the conditional expression is always 1, and the jump to the beginning of the loop body will always take place. There is, of course, an exit out of the cycle provided by the **break** statement.

Try It Out - Using break With if

Let's see this in action.

```
//   Program 4.11
//   Using break with if

#include <iostream.h>

void main()
{
  int  x;

  cout << "Start" << endl;

  do
  {
    cout << "Break ? (0 - no, all other - yes) ";
    x = 1;
    cin >> x;
    if ( x )
      break;
    cout << "Go" << endl;
  } while (1);

  cout << "Finish";
}
```

How It Works

Using **break**, it is easy to exit from the loop at different points of the loop body, and under different conditions.

```
if ( x )
   break;
```

Try It Out!

Exit out of the loop will take place if **x** isn't equal to 0, even if letters are keyed in instead of numbers, because here:

```
x = 1;
cin >> x;
```

x is initialized to 1 and because the **>>** operator leaves the value of **x** unchanged if erroneous input is detected.

Eliminating break

It is quite possible to write the last program without the **break** statement.

Try It Out - Eliminating the break

This is shown in the following example.

```
//  Program 4.12
//  Eliminating break

#include <iostream.h>

void main()
{
  int  x;
                                        // Output
  cout << !2 << !-2 << !0 << endl;      // 001

  cout << "Start" << endl;
  do
  {
    cout << "Break ? (0 - no, all other - yes) ";
    x = 1;
    cin >> x;
    if ( ! x )
      cout << "Go" << endl;
  } while (!x);

  cout << "Finish";
}
```

How It Works

```
    if ( ! x )
      cout << "Go" << endl;
  } while (!x);
```

Here the negation, or "not" operator (**!**), is used.

143

```
cout << !2 << !-2 << !0 << endl;      // 001
```

The above statement demonstrates its operation. This operator converts any integer number or expression not equal to zero into zero, and any equal to zero into one. Taking this into consideration you see that the statement **cout << "Go" << endl;** will be executed only if **x** is equal to 0. The cycle will be continued in the same way until **!x** isn't equal to 0 (in other words, **x** is equal to 1). Therefore, this program operates like the previous one with **break**.

This makes it seem that the **break** statement is unnecessary. However, programs would becomes much more bulky and difficult to read. You can do without the **break** statement, but the simplicity and clarity of the program may suffer.

The continue Statement

Let us now consider the **continue** statement. The following figure shows that in a **do** statement, **continue** performs a jump to the expression in

```
while (expression)
```

after which the expression is analyzed as usual, and the loop is executed or bypassed accordingly. The **continue** statement may be used only in iteration statements. It serves to bypass a portion of the loop body within an iteration.

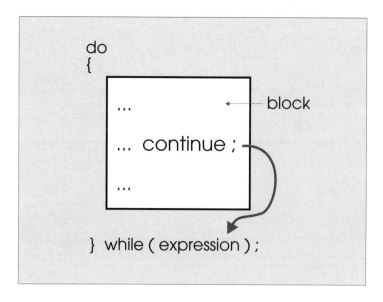

Try It Out - Using continue

The **continue** statement in the next program bypasses the last statement in the loop, and passes control to the **while** expression.

```
//   Program 4.13
//   The continue jump

#include <iostream.h>

void main()
{                      // Output
  cout << 1;           // 1

  do
  {
    cout << 2;         // 2
    continue;
    cout << 3;   // Never executed
  } while (0);
  cout << 4;           // 4
}
```

The output of the program will be:

    124

The **break** and **continue** statements are useful tools in C++. As we have seen, the **break** statement causes an exit from a loop and can be used where a test has been made, and, as a result of the test results, the loop is no longer needed. However, most programmers would probably use a **while** or a **do** loop. It's most useful feature, however, is for exiting from the **switch** statement.

The **continue** statement exits from the current cycle of the loop and then goes back into it. This is useful when something unexpected happens and you want to go back to the top of the loop. For example, you may have a program that is dividing one number by another. If the user entered a 0 for the divisor then a divide by zero error may result. As programmers, we should guard against this. We could put the input routine into a loop and check the divisor before performing any calculations - if the divisor was equal to zero, **continue** could take us back to the top of the loop.

Try It Out!

Inputting Data into Arrays

Now that we have a good grasp of arrays, we can write a program to handle an arbitrary number of mountains of arbitrary height. What this means is that we can declare an array, but leave the values uninitialized. The user can enter values, which will be stored as the elements of the array.

Try It Out - Using Arrays

The following program calculates the height of mountains (input in meters) in feet.

```
//   Program 4.14
//   Any number of mountains

#include <iostream.h>

void main()
{
  const  int   MaxN=7;                // Maximum number of mountains
  const  float   Feet=1./0.3048;      // Number of feet in a meter

  float  Mountain[MaxN] = {0.};       // Array  of mountain
  int  N = MaxN;                      // Number of mountains
  float  Height = 0;                  // Height of mountain
  int  i = 0;                         // Index  of array

  cout  << "Enter height of mountain in meters "
        << "not less than 1000." << endl
        << "Enter 0 or any negative value for end." << endl;
  i = 0;
  do
  {
    Height = 1;                       // For test of error input
    cin >> Height;                    // Input height
    if (Height <= 0)
      break;                          // Exit
    if (Height == 1)
      break;                          // Error input
    if (Height <  1000)
      continue;                       // Ignore invalid input
    Mountain [i++] = Height;          // Fill array
  } while (i < MaxN);

  N = i; i = 0;
  do
  {
    cout << Mountain [i++] * Feet << endl;
  } while (i < N);
}
```

The output from this program looks like this:

```
Enter height in meters not less than 1000.
Enter 0 or any negative value to end.
1290
3807
5412
0
4232.283691
12490.157227
17755.90625
```

How It Works

The main idea of this example, is that the user can input data themselves into an array, **Mountain**, and then display the data entered.

```
const int MaxN=7;                 // Maximum number of mountains
```

Here a constant is initialized which determines the maximum possible number of array elements. You could substitute another value for 7. We chose a small number in order to simplify the testing of the condition for exiting from the loop when the array is full.

```
const float Feet=1./0.3048;     // Number of feet in a meter
```

We declare another constant to work out the conversion from meters to feet.

```
float Mountain[MaxN] = {0.};    // Array of mountain
int  N = MaxN;                  // Number of mountains
float Height = 0;               // Height of mountain
int  i = 0;                     // Index of array
```

Here an array of type **float** is declared. Only the first array element is initialized, but all the rest will be set to 0. In general, it's a good idea to initialize all variables, even though this isn't obligatory. Initializing declared variables is good programming practice.

The program consists of two loops.

```
i = 0;
do
{
  Height = 1;                   // For test of error input
  cin >> Height;                // Input height
  if (Height <= 0)
```

```
        break;                        // Exit
    if (Height == 1)
        break;                        // Error input
    if (Height <  1000)
        continue;                     // Ignore error input
    Mountain [i++] = Height;          // Fill array
} while (i < MaxN);
```

Here we have the loop for data input. Heights entered that are less than 1000 meters are ignored (we only want to deal with serious mountains!). Input of 0 or a negative number results in the termination of the loop. If a character other than a digit is entered, the input process is halted, although it would be logical to ignore the error and to continue the main input loop.

```
if (Height <= 0)
    break;                           // Exit
if (Height == 1)
    break;                           // Error input
if (Height <  1000)
    continue;                        // Ignore error input
```

The sequence of these lines is important. If, for example, we rearrange them to:

```
if (Height <  1000)
    continue;
if (Height <= 0)
    break;
if (Height == 1)
    break;
```

then you will be trapped in an infinite loop, as there would be no way to exit from the program. Any value you enter will first be checked whether it's less than 1000. If it is then you continue and never get to test whether it equals 1 or is less than 0.

```
Mountain [i++] = Height;             // Fill array
```

In this line the height entered is stored in the next array element and then the index is incremented. It's important to set a correct condition for exiting the loop. In this line:

```
} while (i < MaxN);
```

you see that after filling the last element of the array (**Mountain[6]**), the index is equal to 7 and the condition **i<MaxN** is false, so the exit from the loop takes place.

```
N = i; i = 0;
```

In this line, **N** is the number of elements entered. It equals the value of index **i**, after exiting from the previous loop. This is true regardless of whether the exit was made, or the condition in this line is met.

```
N = i; i = 0;
do
{
   cout << Mountain [i++] * Feet << endl;
} while (i < N);
```

Finally, we have the loop for data output.

Boundaries of the Possible

Using a **do** statement let's determine the maximum possible values for the integer types: **char** and **long int**. But first we'll do this for variables of the type **int**, having modified one of the programs from Chapter 2.

Limits of int

In Chapter 2 we worked out on our computer the maximum possible value of variables of the **int** type. This is equal to 32767 or 215 - 1. The number 15 indicates how many bits are assigned to represent a number of **int** type in computer memory. Add here one more bit for a sign, and you get 16 bits, or 2 bytes. And this is exactly the value of **sizeof(int)**.

Try It Out - Using sizeof

We can now look at an example that shows how we can use what we have learnt to warn us if we are going past the limits of the variable type we have declared.

```
// Program 4.15
// Powers of 2 and limit of int type

#include <iostream.h>

void main()
{
  int  x=1;

  do
    cout << (x*=2) << endl;
  while (x>0);
}
```

The output of the program has the form (on our computer):

```
2
4
8
16
32
64
128
256
512
1024
2048
4096
8192
163844
-32768
```

How It Works

If you compute successive powers of 2, at some value (in our example it is 15), 2 to that power suddenly happens to be negative, and 2 raised to higher powers are in general equal to 0. This feature serves as a condition for exiting from a loop.

```
do
    cout << (x*=2) << endl;
while (x>0);
```

The loop continues as long as **x>0**. Because the program uses the **do** statement, it's very short and neat. There is also something new here. Let's see what the program is really doing.

Operator *= and Others

In the last program we used the expression:

```
x *= 2
```

This is the same as the expression:

```
x = x * 2
```

In C++, there are similar assignment operators for other arithmetic operations, for example:

```
+=    -=    /=    %=
```

In all cases the pair of operator symbols must be written without intervening spaces.

You may ask why we need these extra operators, which don't add any new capabilities to the language. In order to answer this question look at the statements:

```
Identifier0WithLongName = Identifier0WithLongName * 2;
IdentifierOWithLongName = IdentifierOWithLongName * 2;
```

Using the *= operator one can write the first line in a shorter way:

```
Identifier0WithLongName *= 2;
```

The advantage of the *= operator is that the program becomes more concise and easier to input, change and understand.

You won't be able to shorten the second line, as in the right and left parts of the assignment operation there are different identifiers. Can you see this difference? We hid it deliberately, demonstrating very bad style in naming variables. The identifiers differ by just one character. In addition, we used characters that look very similar to each other, the letter "O" in the left identifier, and the digit "0" in the one on the right. You should never do this, as we hope this example demonstrates.

Limits of Integer Types

If we go back to the last example (Program 4.15), try changing the variable definition to:

```
long int x=1;
```

Now the same program will compute the maximum values permitted for variables of the **long int** type.

Try It Out - The Limits of Different Types

Now let's look at another program that outputs the minimum and maximum values for variables of the types, **char**, **int**, and **long**, as well as types with the modifier **unsigned** which are new to you.

```
//   Program 4.16
//   Limits of integer types

#include <iostream.h>
#include <iomanip.h>

void main()
{
  signed   char      SChar = 1;
           char       Char = 1;
  unsigned char      UChar = 1;
           int         Int = 1;
  unsigned int        UInt = 1;
     long  int        LInt = 1;
  unsigned long int  ULInt = 1;

  do Char *= 2;   while ( Char>0);
  do SChar *= 2;  while (SChar>0);
  do UChar *= 2;  while (UChar>0);
  do    Int *= 2; while (  Int>0);
  do   UInt *= 2; while ( UInt>0);
  do   LInt *= 2; while ( LInt>0);
  do  ULInt *= 2; while (ULInt>0);

  cout<< "Minimum and maximum values for integer types"
      << endl << endl;

  cout  << setw (20) << "Type"
        << setw (12) << "Minimum"
        << setw (12) << "Maximum" << endl << endl;

  cout  << setw (20) << "signed char"
        << setw (12) << (int)SChar
        << setw (12) << (int)(char)(SChar-1) << endl;

  cout  << setw (20) << "char"
        << setw (12) << (int)Char
        << setw (12) << (int)(char)(Char-1) << endl;

  cout  << setw (20) << "unsigned char"
        << setw (12) << (int)UChar
        << setw (12) << (int)(unsigned char)(UChar-1) << endl;

  cout  << setw (20) << "int"
        << setw (12) << Int
        << setw (12) << Int-1 << endl;
```

```
    cout   << setw (20) << "unsigned int"
           << setw (12) << UInt
           << setw (12) << UInt-1 << endl;

    cout   << setw (20) << "long int"
           << setw (12) << LInt
           << setw (12) << LInt-1 << endl;

    cout   << setw (20) << "unsigned long int"
           << setw (12) << ULInt
           << setw (12) << ULInt-1 << endl;
}
```

The output of this program is as follows:

```
Minimum and maximum values for integer types

                    Type      Minimum      Maximum

        signed char            -128          127
               char            -128          127
      unsigned char               0          255
                int          -32768        32767
       unsigned int               0        65535
           long int     -2147483648   2147483647
  unsigned long int               0   4294967295
```

Some values in the table may be different on your computer.

How It Works

As we have seen the minimum possible number is generated at the exit from a loop of the type:

```
do cout << (x*=2) << endl; while (x>0);
```

The maximum possible number may be calculated by the subtraction (!) of one from the minimum number. This curious feature we found out as long ago as Chapter 2. Therefore, in lines:

```
do Char *= 2;  while ( Char>0);
do  SChar *= 2;  while (SChar>0);
do  UChar *= 2;  while (UChar>0);
do   Int *= 2;  while (  Int>0);
do   UInt *= 2;  while ( UInt>0);
do   LInt *= 2;  while ( LInt>0);
do  ULInt *= 2;  while (ULInt>0);
```

the minimum values are computed, which are then output together with the maximum values. Let's go over what else is new in the program.

Unsigned Integer Numbers

```
signed    char SChar = 1;
          char  Char = 1;
unsigned  char UChar = 1;
          int   Int = 1;
```

Here you encounter the specifiers **signed**, and **unsigned**. These specifiers are applicable to any of the types **int**, **long**, and **char**. But for **int** and **long** types the **signed** specifier is implied by default, in other words **signed int** means the same as simply **int**.

Look at the results from the program for **unsigned int**. You see that numbers of this type don't have a sign and, therefore, can't have negative values. The lack of a sign bit means that all 16 bits can be taken up with the number, so the maximum value is almost twice as large as their signed counterparts. Their minimum value is equal to zero. The same also applies to other types with the **unsigned** modifier.

Type Casting

```
cout  << setw (20) << "signed char"
      << setw (12) << (int)SChar
      << setw (12) << (int)(char)(SChar-1) << endl;

cout  << setw (20) << "char"
      << setw (12) << (int)Char
      << setw (12) << (int)(char)(Char-1) << endl;

cout  << setw (20) << "unsigned char"
      << setw (12) << (int)UChar
      << setw (12) << (int)(unsigned char)(UChar-1) << endl;
```

In these lines we should explain the use of expressions of the form:

```
(int) Char
```

or, in the general case:

```
(Type) Variable
```

Here the type of the data is in parentheses, and to the right of it there is a variable name. This is an explicit type conversion. It means that the variable **Char** of type **char** is to be converted into type **int**. If we don't include such a conversion then:

```
cout << Char;
```

will output characters rather than numbers.

The Manipulator setw()

For output formatting we use the manipulator **setw()**. This sets the width of column at which the next **<<** operator will output a value. The use of this manipulator requires another header file to be included, which you can see in the line:

```
#include <iomanip.h>
```

Designing a Program

The end of this chapter is in sight. Let's construct a final example of some of the topics we have covered.

The Problem

Arrays are sets of variables all with the same name but with different identifying indices which offer a compact method of handling blocks of data. This program enters data into an array and manipulates it.

We will write a program to sum a set of numbers entered into the computer via the keyboard and report the sum of the data entered and the average of the data. The program will accept an unknown quantity of data items, limited only by the size of the array.

This type of problem is quite common. Programs have to be able to handle different quantities of data on a regular basis.

The Analysis

1 Enter the data into the computer via the keyboard and count the number of data items entered.

2 Sum the data.

3 Calculate the average.

4 Output the results.

The Solution

1 We want to write a routine that allows us to enter an unlimited amount of data. We could ask the user to specify the number of data items and enter this information via the keyboard. This number could be saved as an integer variable and used to control a **for** loop. However, the disadvantage with this approach is that the user may have to count the number of data items and if they miscounted they would have to start again.

The easiest method is to use a **while** loop and ask the user after each entry if they wish to enter more data. If they want to enter further data the loop continues.

```
#include <iostream.h>

void main()
{
  const int MAX = 50;   //MAX size of array - this could be larger
  int count = 0;    //count number of items input
  int index = 0;    //loop variable
  float numbers[MAX];   //array to store numbers
  char ch = 'Y';    //input check

  //input data
  while(ch == 'Y' || ch == 'y') //the || is the symbol meaning OR
  {
    cout << "Please enter number: ";
    cin >> numbers[index++];
    count++;
    cout << "Do you want to enter another number? (Y/N)  ";
    cin >> ch;
  }

}
```

```
while(ch == 'Y' || ch == 'y') //the || is the symbol meaning OR
```

The || operator is the logical OR operator. The statement reads, **while ch is equal to Y execute the block, or while ch is equal to y execute the block**. This operator allows us to combine conditions when testing for true or false conditions. Similarly, **&&** is the logical AND operator and is used in a similar way.

2   Once the data has been entered, the data can be summed. This is a reasonably simple matter as we have counted the number of data items entered. A simple **for** loop can be used.

```cpp
#include <iostream.h>

void main()
{
  const int MAX = 50;   //MAX size of array - this could be larger
  int count = 0;     //count number of items input
  int index = 0;     //loop variable
  float numbers[MAX];  //array to store numbers
  float sum = 0.0;     //variable to sum array elements
  char ch = 'Y';     //input check

  //input data
  while(ch == 'Y' || ch == 'y')
  {
    cout << "Please enter number: ";
    cin >> numbers[index++];
    count++;
    cout << "Do you want to enter another number? (Y/N)  ";
    cin >> ch;
  }

  //sum the elements
  for(index = 0; index < count; index++)
    sum += numbers[index];
}
```

3&4 The average can now be calculated by dividing the sum by the number of data items and the results can be displayed on the user's screen.

```cpp
#include <iostream.h>

void main()
{
```

```
const int MAX = 50;   //MAX size of array - this could be larger
int count = 0;     //count number of items input
int index = 0;     //loop variable
float numbers[MAX];   //array to store numbers
float sum = 0.0;    //variable to sum array elements
float average = 0.0;     //variable to store average
char ch = 'Y';    //input check

//input data
while(ch == 'Y' || ch == 'y')
{
  cout << "Please enter number: ";
  cin >> numbers[index++];
  count++;
  cout << "Do you want to enter another number? (Y/N)   ";
  cin >> ch;
}

//sum the elements
for(index = 0; index < count; index++)
  sum += numbers[index];

//calculate average
average = sum / count;

cout << "\n\tYou entered " << count << " numbers.  The sum is " << sum
     << endl << "\tThe average is " << average << endl;
}
```

Summary

In this chapter we have covered a variety of new topics. We have introduced arrays and shown you how you can group data of the same type together. We have discussed some new variable types and looked at how you can work out the size of these types using the **sizeof** operator. You have seen how to use the **do** loop to repeat actions.

In the next chapter we will continue to look at arrays and see how they apply to character strings and we will look at the other powerful loop statements.

CHAPTER 5

Arrays And Strings

In this chapter we are going to continue to work with the array and loop statement. As we have seen, the array allows us to handle large amounts of data in a very compact manner. We will now look at character arrays, or strings. You have already met strings - characters between double quotes.

We will also look at the logical operators **&&** and **||** and see how these can be used to combine relational expressions.

We have also looked at the **do** loop statement, which enables us to describe, in a few lines of code, long repetitive actions which load the computer with a large amount of work. We will look at the other two loops - the **for** loop and the **while** loop.

In this chapter you will:

▶ Apply your knowledge of arrays to arrays of characters (strings)

▶ Look at the logical operators

▶ Understand how these operators can be used to combine relational expressions

▶ Use the powerful iteration statements - **while** and **for**

▶ Write a program that can be used as a calculator

Representing Characters

From the very first program you have been familiar with the presentation of characters in the form of literal strings. This is text between double quotes, which was used to output a message to the computer screen.

For operations with single characters, C++ provides the **char** data type. Variables and constants of **char** type occupy 1 byte of memory. In the last chapter, we saw that the variables of **char** type can store one number with a value ranging from -128 to +127 or from 0 to 255. One character constant corresponds to each number. Therefore, there are only 256 different character constants.

ABC of Character Constants

Now we are going to go into the world of characters. The majority of single character constants in C++, are written as one symbol placed between a pair of single quotes.

Here are some examples of character constants:

```
'A'    '1'    '.'
```

For most of these ordinary character constants, there is a corresponding key on your computer keyboard in upper or lower-case (in other words, while *Shift* key is pressed or released).

Try It Out - Character Constants

The next program shows an example of using character constants.

```
//   Program 5.1
//   Character constants

#include <iostream.h>

void main()
{                                          // Output
    cout << 'A' << 'B' << 'C' << ' '       // ABC
         << 'a' << 'b' << 'c' << ' '       // abc
         << '1' << '2' << '3' << ' '       // 123
         << '<' << '.' << '>'              // <.>
         << endl;
    cout << (int) '0'    << ' '            // 48
         << (int) ' '    << ' '            // 32
         << (int) 'A'    << ' '            // 65
```

```
                   << (char) 48    << ' '              // 0
                   << (char) 65    << ' '              // A
                   << endl;

// ASCII table for 32-127 codes

   const int NRows = 32;               // Number of rows
   const int NCols =  3;               // Number of columns
   const int StartCode = 32;           // Code of blank
         int i =  0;                   // Row index
         char AnyChar;

   do
   {
     int  j = 0;                                   // Column index
     do
     {
       int Code = StartCode + i + NRows*j;    // Character code

       cout << (char) 9 << Code << '\t' << (char) Code;
     } while ( ++j < NCols );

     cout << endl;
     if ( i == NRows/2 - 1 )
     {
       cout << "Enter any character to continue: ";
       cin  >> AnyChar;                 // Pause
     }
   } while ( ++i < NRows );

   cout << "Enter any character to continue: ";
   cin >> AnyChar;                     // Pause

// Tabs
   cout << 0                      << endl    // 0
        << '\t' << 1              << endl    //          1
        << '\t' << '\t' << 2      << endl;   //          2
   cout << "1"        <<'\t'<< 9 << endl    // 1        9
        << "123"      <<'\t'<< 9 << endl    // 123      9
        << "1234567"  <<'\t'<< 9 << endl    // 1234567 9
        << "12345678" <<'\t'<< 9 << endl;   // 12345678      9
   cout << "1"        <<'.'<< 9 << endl    // 1.9
        << "123"      <<'.' << 9 << endl    // 123.9
        << "1234567"  <<'.' << 9 << endl    // 1234567.9
        << "12345678" <<'.' << 9 << endl;   // 12345678.9

   cout << "Column1\t\tColumn2"  << endl;

   cout << "\aEnter any character to continue: ";
   cin  >> AnyChar;                        // Pause
```

161

```
// New line and carriage return

  cout << "123"           << '_'   << endl      // 123_
       << "123" << '\n' << '_'   << endl      // 123
                                              // _
       << "123" << '\r' << '_'   << endl;     // _23

  cout << "Line1\nLine2\n";

// Null character

  cout << 1 << '\0' << 2          << endl      // 1 2
       << sizeof ("123")          << endl;     // 4

// 4 special characters ' " ? \

  cout <<'\''<<'\"'<<'\?'<<'\\' << endl      // '"?\
       << "\' \" \? \\ "          << endl;     // ' " ? \
}
```

The output from this program is:

```
ABC abc 123 <.>
48 32 65 0 A
  32      64 @ 96  `
  33  ! 65  A 97  a
  34  " 66  B 98  b
  35  # 67  C 99  c
  36  $ 68  D 100 d
  37  % 69  E 101 e
  38  & 70  F 102 f
  39  ' 71  G 103 g
  40  ( 72  H 104 h
  41  ) 73  I 105 i
  42  * 74  J 106 j
  43  + 75  K 107 k
  44  , 76  L 108 l
  45  - 77  M 109 m
  46  . 78  N 110 n
  47  / 79  O 111 o
Enter any character to continue: a
  48  0 80  P 112 p
  49  1 81  Q 113 q
  50  2 82  R 114 r
  51  3 83  S 115 s
  52  4 84  T 116 t
  53  5 85  U 117 u
  54  6 86  V 118 v
  55  7 87  W 119 w
  56  8 88  X 120 x
  57  9 89  Y 121 y
  58  : 90  Z 122 z
  59  ; 91  [ 123 {
```

```
   60  < 92  \ 124 |
   61  = 93  ] 125 }
   62  > 94  ^ 126 ~
   63  ? 95  _ 127 •
Enter any character to continue: b
0
      1
            2
1 9
123 9
12345679
12345678 9
1.9
123.9
1234567.9
12345678.9
Column1  Column2
Enter any character to continue: c
123_
123

_
123

_
Line1
Line2
14
'"?\
'  "  ?  \
```

How It Works

Quotes to the left and right of a character are used so that the compiler can distinguish it from other contexts, such as the name of a variable, or an integer constant.

Don't confuse character constants with string literals. The latter are written between double quotes. For example, the string literal **"A"** isn't the same as the character constant **'A'**, though the output of both the constants to the screen gives the same result. We will see more about string literals later in this chapter.

Let's go through the previous program step by step.

Ordinary Characters

```
cout << 'A' << 'B' << 'C' << ' '              // ABC
     << 'a' << 'b' << 'c' << ' '              // abc
     << '1' << '2' << '3' << ' '              // 123
     << '<' << '.' << '>'                     // <.>
```

These lines demonstrate the output of character constants onto the screen. The quoted characters appear, but the quotes themselves aren't displayed. The quotes indicate the beginning and the end of a character constant description.

Blanks

Note that the last character being output in each line is a blank, and is written as ' '. Unlike all other spaces in the program text, the character constant ' ', and spaces within literal strings, aren't ignored by the compiler.

Thanks to the space in each output statement, the output to the screen of each of the above lines is separated by a space, and has the form:

```
ABC abc 123 <.>
```

Character Code

You know that all data in a computer is represented by a number. Therefore, a character constant is only a mask, it's a convenient and obvious designation which hides the true character face - the number, or character code. We can discard these masks with the help of the type conversion operator in the following lines.

```
cout << (int) '0'    << ' '              // 48
     << (int) ' '    << ' '              // 32
     << (int) 'A'    << ' '              // 65
     << (char) 48    << ' '              // 0
     << (char) 65    << ' '              // A
```

It serves to convert a character to the underlying number, which is then displayed by the << operator.

In the comments to the lines you see that the mask of the '0' character hides the number 48, and codes 32 and 65 correspond to blank (space), and 'A'. Then you see the inverse conversion of numbers into characters (putting on a mask) with the help of a type conversion to **char**. Numbers 48 and 65 are converted into characters and are displayed on the screen as '0' and 'A'.

The output looks like this:

32 65 0 A

The ASCII Table

Standardized graphical images of characters on the computer screen correspond to numbers in the range of 0 - 127. This standard table is known as the ASCII Table. It's shown in the following table for codes from 32 to 127. ASCII is an abbreviation for American Standard Code for Information Interchange.

ASCII Code	Character	ASCII Code	Character	ASCII Code	Character
32	<space>	64	@	96	`
33	!	65	A	97	a
34	"	66	B	98	b
35	#	67	C	99	c
36	$	68	D	100	d
37	%	69	E	101	e
38	&	70	F	102	f
39	'	71	G	103	g
40	(	72	H	104	h
41	)	73	I	105	i
42	*	74	J	106	j
43	+	75	K	107	k
44	,	76	L	108	l
45	-	77	M	109	m
46	.	78	N	110	n
47	/	79	O	111	o
48	0	80	P	112	p
49	1	81	Q	113	q
50	2	82	R	114	r
51	3	83	S	115	s
52	4	84	T	116	t
53	5	85	U	117	u
54	6	86	V	118	v
55	7	87	W	119	w
56	8	88	X	120	x
57	9	89	Y	121	y
58	:	90	Z	122	z
59	;	91	[	123	{
60	<	92	\	124		
61	=	93	]	125	}
62	>	94	^	126	~
63	?	95	_	127	•

Certain characters do not appear to display anything on the screen. The most obvious character is the space (ASCII code 32) which moves the cursor to the right. What about the horizontal tab (ASCII code 9) which moves the cursor to the right 4 spaces? There is a 'symbol' having the ASCII code of 0 (it's called the null character) which doesn't display anything on the screen.

Numbers in the range of 128-255 are used for coding special characters and the symbols of the national alphabets of different countries. We won't consider these here.

We have omitted showing 'symbols' having ASCII codes from 0 to 31 in the table. These 'symbols' all have a special meaning and some of them, when output, affect the output device, be it the cursor on the screen, or a printer. These 'symbols' are called control characters.

Control Characters

The first half of the code displays symbols with codes from 32 to 127 in the same form as in the table.

```
const int NRows = 32;          // Number of rows
const int NCols =  3;          // Number of columns
const int StartCode = 32;      // Code of blank
```

As with the table, we have deliberately omitted the output of symbols with codes from 0 to 31.

```
do           //do loop - the code in this block is executed repeatedly
{            //    until the condition in the while test is false
   int Code = StartCode + i + NRows*j;      // Character code

   cout << (char) 9 << Code << '\t' << (char) Code; // display to screen
} while ( ++j < NCols );                            //condition in ( .. )

   cout << endl;                            //output newline character
   if ( i == NRows/2 - 1 )                  //generates a pause
   {
      cout << "Enter any character to continue: ";
      cin >> AnyChar;                // Pause
   }
} while ( ++i < NRows );
```

Note that on the keyboard there are no keys bearing the images of such symbols. As an example, this line:

```
cout << (char) 9 << Code << '\t' << (char) Code;
```

166

uses the control character with code 9. The output of this symbol to the screen results, not in the display on the screen of a corresponding symbol, but moves the cursor 4 spaces to the right. This is called tabulation character or tab.

To write a tab character in the form of a character constant in C++, rather than as **(char)9**, we use a pair of symbols enclosed in quotes:

```
'\t'
```

Here the backslash (\) serves as an indication that the following symbol is special. The letter 't' is taken from the first letter of the word "tab" and reminds us about the assignment of the symbol **'\t'**. Note that 't' here must be written in lower-case.

We'll now go into the part of the program that outputs the ASCII table. Here the code of the next output character is computed. Note the declaration of the variable **k** directly in the block. This method reflects the general approach of declaring data as close as possible to the location of their application.

```
cout << (char) 9 << Code << '\t' << (char) Code;
```

In this line the tab character **(char) 9** is output, then - the value of the variable **Code** (the code of a character in the table), then again the tab character in the form **'\t'** and, finally, the image of the character by:

```
(char) Code
```

which moves the cursor to the right to the next predetermined tab column.

```
cout << 0                      << endl   // 0
     << '\t' << 1              << endl   //          1
     << '\t' << '\t' << 2      << endl;  //          2
cout << "1"        <<'\t'<< 9 << endl   // 1        9
     << "123"      <<'\t'<< 9 << endl   // 123      9
     << "1234567"  <<'\t'<< 9 << endl   // 1234567 9
     << "12345678" <<'\t'<< 9 << endl;  // 12345678         9
```

These lines demonstrate the action of the tab character. Compare the output with the output of the lines that follow:

```
cout << "1"        <<'.'<< 9 << endl   // 1.9
     << "123"      <<'.'<< 9 << endl   // 123.9
     << "1234567"  <<'.'<< 9 << endl   // 1234567.9
     << "12345678" <<'.'<< 9 << endl;  // 12345678.9
```

In the latter, instead of a tab control character, an ordinary symbol, '.', is output.

Without using the tabulation symbol we couldn't format the output of the table so easily. Try putting a line of several spaces into each line instead of a tab, and see how uneven the table is.

The tabulation symbol may be inserted into literal strings along with ordinary characters. For example, with the aim of properly formatting the headings of the columns, we have:

```
cout << "Column1\t\tColumn2";
```

Since we have chosen a table with 32 lines it won't all fit on a screen with 25 lines. That's why we put a pause after the display of the first 16 lines, with the help of the >> operator in lines:

```
cout << "Enter any character to continue: ";
cin  >> AnyChar;                // Pause
```

We could use an initial value of 0 for **StartCode** instead of 32, and the number of columns could be equal to 4 to try to print the full ASCII table. However, this doesn't give the required result (try it). The program output will be spoiled. This happens because some symbols with codes from 0 to 31 have special meanings when output to the screen and aren't simply displayed.

Alarms

The action of one of the control characters is particularly interesting. When it's output to the screen it sounds an alarm, which on the PC usually takes the form of a beep or a bell. This symbol has code 7 and is represented in C++ by '\a'. One may insert the symbol '\a' into literal strings when it's necessary to draw attention to something, as in this statement, for example:

```
cout << "Press any key to continue ...\a";
```

New Line and Carriage Return

Two more special control symbols assist cursor control; these are the newline character '\n' with code 10, and the carriage return '\r' with code 13.

Symbol '\n' moves the cursor to the beginning of the next line. This is shown in the comments to the lines in the program:

```
cout << "123"            << '_'   << endl      // 123_
       << "123" << '\n' << '_'   << endl      // 123
                                              // _
```

where the underline symbol '_' indicates the cursor position without, and with the '\n' output.

```
       << "123" << '\r' << '_'   << endl;     // _23
```

Here, outputting the '\r' character, moves the cursor to the beginning of the current line. As a result, the symbol "1" output earlier is overwritten by the symbol '_'.

The output of the '\n' symbol

```
cout << '\n';
```

is similar to the application of **endl**:

```
cout << endl;
```

Like other special symbols one may insert the symbol '\n' into literal strings for moving to a new line.

The Null Character

As is generally known the number 0 is very important: it's sufficient to add it to the right of a decimal value for an income, and it increases by tenfold. The symbol with a numeric value 0 also plays an important (though not such an impressive) role in the world of C++. It's written like this:

```
'\0'
```

This symbol doesn't have any graphical representation and at its output, nothing is displayed. Character '\0' is used in C++ as an indication of the end of a string literal.

```
       << sizeof ("123")        << endl;     // 4
```

Its presence results in the **sizeof** operator giving the value 4 when applied to the string **"123"**. Here '\0' is the fourth character. The compiler adds it automatically. It should be noted that all literal strings have a null character added by the compiler.

Four Special Symbols

Four character constants available on the keyboard are written in the same way as for special characters, with the use of a backslash. These are the characters:

```
'  "  ?  \
```

They are written as follows:

```
cout <<'\''<<'\"'<<'\?'<<'\\' << endl      // '"?\
```

Note that writing these without a backslash can be erroneous because these characters are used for special purposes in C++, for example:

```
'''   '"'   '?'   '\'
```

Here we conclude our discussion on character constants. Remember that you can get any symbol if you knows its numerical value, by a type conversion:

```
(char) value
```

Now you are familiar with all types of C++ constants: character constants, integer constants, floating constants, string literals.

Entering Single Characters

We will now consider character arrays. On the way, you'll overcome two obstacles. The first is a character keyboard input, and the second is logical operators.

Try It Out - Entering Single Characters

The next program shows how to read a single character from the keyboard. For each symbol entered, it outputs the decimal numerical value of its ASCII code.

```
//   Program 5.2
//   Entering single characters

#include <iostream.h>

void main()
{
```

```
   cout << "\aType any letter to get its numerical value, "
        "then press Enter.\n"
        "Enter letter Q to Quit.\n\n"
        "Letter\t\tASCII code\n\n";

   char  Letter;

   do
   {
     cin >> Letter;
     cout << "\t" << (int) Letter << endl;
     if (Letter == 'q' || Letter == 'Q')
       break;
   } while (1);
}
```

The output from the program looks like this:

```
Type any letter to get its numerical value, then press Enter.
Enter letter Q to Quit.

Letter          ASCII code

a               97
A               65
c               99
C               67
q               113
```

How It Works

Character input into the variable **Letter** of type **char**, is performed by the statement in the following line:

```
  cin >> Letter;
```

We have already used the **>>** operator for input of a single character in Program 5.1. This provided a pause during output to the screen of a large number of lines. You can see that the **>>** operator is as good at character input as it is at inputting integers.

```
cout << "\aType any letter to get its numerical value, "
        "then press Enter.\n"
        "Enter letter Q to Quit.\n\n"
        "Letter\t\tASCII code\n\n"
```

When you compile and run this program, you'll first hear a beep as a result of the `'\a'` symbol output. In the information message above the `'\n'` symbol is used several times. Its use within a literal string is somewhat more compact than the use of **endl** so it is often used instead. The final line in the above block contains the `'\t'` character to space the table heading.

```
cin >> Letter;
```

The program will wait for a keystroke. Press any character key and the corresponding character will appear on the screen due to the `>>` operator. Now press the *Enter* key. The input operation will terminate, and the line to display the ASCII code will be executed. You can enter upper or lower-case characters.

Improving the Program

Having established that the program works, you might like to look at some peculiarities in its operation. For example, it would be better if just after a keystroke, its code could be displayed without you having to press *Enter*. You'll see also that the code of the "space" symbol isn't displayed, since the `>>` operator ignores all spaces that precede the first non-whitespace character. For the sake of curiosity try to enter not one letter but several, with spaces between them. Check that pressing the *BkSp* key removes the previous character to the left.

Try pressing a function or character key while holding down the *Ctrl* key. The combination of *Ctrl* with *C* (usually written as *Ctrl-C*) is interesting. This combination results in program termination, provided the program has been called from the DOS prompt and not through the integrated environment supplied with several compilers. This is a standard feature of the input operation to this key combination. It's provided to permit emergency termination of the program.

All these problems can be overcome, but you need a deeper knowledge of keyboard input methods to achieve this.

```
    cout << "\t" << (int) Letter << endl;
    if (Letter == 'q' || Letter == 'Q')
       break;
 } while (1);
}
```

To provide a means of exiting from the endless loop, a test is made for an upper or lower-case Q being entered.

Logical Operators

Here you meet with another operator, which we mentioned briefly before, called the logical OR. It's written as two symbols following one another without intervening spaces:

||

The symbols are two vertical bar symbols - ASCII code 124. The operator results in 1 if either of its operands is non-zero, and 0 otherwise. This operand provides an alternative to nested **if else** statements:

In our program it gave us:

```
if (Letter == 'q' || Letter == 'Q')
   break;
```

instead of:

```
if (Letter == 'q')
   break;
else
   if (Letter == 'Q')
      break;
```

or

```
if  (Letter == 'q')
   break;
if (Letter == 'Q')
   break;
```

In this example the improvement as a result of using the || operator isn't so obvious. But imagine that instead of **break** in both cases, there is a complex block with multiple lines. Then, without the || operator, you would need to write this block twice.

There is another logical operator, the logical AND:

&&

It results in 1 if both its operands are non-zero, and 0 otherwise. The expression

```
if ( x && y ) ...
```

is used instead of nested `if` statements:

```
if ( x )
  if ( y ) ...
```

Try It Out - Using Logical Operators

The next program shows the use of both logical operators, and also the unary logical negation operator, `!`, which we have already seen used in the last chapter. Its value is 1 if the value of its operand is 0 and 0 otherwise.

```
//   Program 5.3
//   Logical operators

#include <iostream.h>

void main()
{
  cout << "\n\n\t Logical negation operator - !"
       <<    "\n\t x \t !x\n"
       <<    "\n\t 0 \t "        <<    ! 0
       <<    "\n\t not0 \t "      << ! (! 0);

  cout << "\n\n\t Logical OR operator - ||"
       <<    "\n\t x \t y \t x || y\n"
       <<    "\n\t 0 \t 0 \t "      << ( 0 ||  0)
       <<    "\n\t 0 \t not0 \t "   << ( 0 || !0)
       <<    "\n\t not0 \t 0 \t "   << (!0 ||  0)
       <<    "\n\t not0 \t not0 \t " << (!0 || !0);

  cout << "\n\n\t Logical AND operator - &&"
       <<    "\n\t x \t y \t x && y\n"
       <<    "\n\t 0 \t 0 \t "      << ( 0 &&  0)
       <<    "\n\t 0 \t not0 \t "   << ( 0 && !0)
       <<    "\n\t not0 \t 0 \t "   << (!0 &&  0)
       <<    "\n\t not0 \t not0 \t " << (!0 && !0);
}
```

This program outputs three tables that show the action of all three logical operators:

```
Logical negation operator - !
x       !x

0       1
not0     0
```

```
Logical OR operator - ||
x    y     x || y

0    0     0
0    not0      1
not0   0    1
not0   not0      1

Logical AND operator - &&
x    y     x && y

0    0      0
0    not0       0
not0   0    0
not0   not0      1
```

How It Works

In these tables **x** represents any integer expression. This may be a constant, an integer variable or a complex expression. In the table, "not0" indicates an expression having a non-zero value (either positive or negative), and "0" indicates an expression having a zero value. For example, the first line in the table for the logical negation operator means that if the value of expression **x** is equal to zero, then the value of **!x** is equal to 1. The second line means that if the value of expression **x** isn't equal to zero, than the value of **!x** is 0.

Try It Out - Testing Logical Operators

The use of logical operations in the last program with the help of !0 and 0 constants, instead of expressions, appears somewhat formal. Therefore, in this next program you can test the results of the logical operations on arbitrary operand values.

```
//  Program 5.4
//  Testing logical operators

#include <iostream.h>

void main()
{
  int  x = 0, y = 0;

  cout << "\nTesting logical operators\n";
  cout << "Enter integer x: "; cin >> x;
  cout << "Enter integer y: "; cin >> y;

  cout << "\n x          "  <<  x
```

```
            << "\n y         "  << y

            << "\n ! x        "  << !x
            << "\n ! y        "  << !y
            << "\n x || y      "  << (x || y)
            << "\n x && y      "  << (x && y);
    }
```

The program invites you to enter any two integers: **x** and **y**. Its output looks like this:

```
Testing logical operators
Enter integer x: 111
Enter integer y: 222

    x                111
    y                222
    ! x                0
    ! y                0
    x || y             1
    x && y             1
```

How It Works

Let's go through what is going on.

Declaration List

In this line you have an unusual variable declaration:

```
    int  x = 0, y = 0;
```

Here, in one statement two variables are declared at once. The comma serves as a delimiter in a list of variables being declared. The type **int** is written once and applies to all variables in the list.

It's good programming style to comment each variable declared. If the variables are declared in a list, then this rule of good style is most likely to be violated. Nevertheless, for the declaration of additional variables (such as array indexes, loop counters) that don't need any explanatory comments, a list is sometimes used, making the program a bit shorter.

Using Blanks For Output Formatting

In formatting the tabular output in the last program, we didn't use `setw()`, or tab characters, but simply used blanks to space the text. The deficiency of this approach is that all these spare blanks occupy memory locations within the program code, making it longer and occupying more space on disk.

Combining Relational Expressions

Logical operators are most often used with comparison operators in the `if` statement as for example:

```
if ( ( x != 0) && ( y != 0) ) ...
```

Note that the same condition can be written shorter, like this:

```
if ( x && y ) ...
```

When writing complex logical expressions, or complex arithmetic expressions, the rules of precedence play an important role. But as we saw with arithmetic expressions, you can compose the required logical expressions using parentheses. You often need to supply parentheses, because `&&` and `||` have the same precedence, and will be executed left-to-right, unless you specify otherwise. For example the next expression:

```
0 && 0 || 1
```

you can write in two ways, giving different results:

```
(0 && 0) || 1
```

and

```
0 && (0 || 1)
```

The first gives 1, the second 0. If you omit the parentheses, then it's necessary to know which operation is executed first.

Character Arrays

We have seen how integers can be stored in arrays and how useful this can be. Now let's see how characters are stored in an array.

Try It Out - An Array of Characters

Look at the following example.

```
//   Program 5.5
//   Array of characters

#include <iostream.h>

void main()
{
  char ABC [] = {'A', 'B', 'C'};

  cout << sizeof ABC                      << endl;    // 3
  cout << ABC[0] << ABC[1] << ABC[2]      << endl;    // ABC

  ABC[0] = 'a';

  int i = 0;
  do
     cout << ABC [i++];
  while ( i < sizeof ABC );                           // aBC
}
```

The output from the program looks like this:

```
3
ABC
aBC
```

How It Works

Let's see how the program works.

ABC as a Character Array

Compare the declaration of the **ABC** character array in this program:

```
char  ABC[] = {'A', 'B', 'C'};
```

with the declaration of the array of integers **Mountain** in Program 4.3. You see that the declaration of the character array follows the same rules already well known to you. The only difference is that the entries in the initializer list aren't integer constants as in the **Mountain** array declaration, but character constants.

The number of **ABC** array elements isn't indicated, so this number is equal to the number of elements in the initializer list, 3. Since each element occupies 1 byte, the length of the whole array is 3 bytes, so this value is returned by the **sizeof** operator:

```
cout << sizeof ABC          << endl;        // 3
```

Allocation of Memory

The next figure shows the layout of the **ABC** array elements in computer memory.

They occupy adjacent memory bytes. The first element of the **ABC** array, **ABC[0]**, contains the character **'A'**. The second element, **ABC[1]**, contains the character **'B'**, and the last element, **ABC[2]**, contains the character **'C'**.

```
cout << ABC[0] << ABC[1] << ABC[2]   << endl;     // ABC
```

Here, the elements of the **ABC** array are output to the screen.

```
ABC [0] = 'a';

int i = 0;
do
   cout << ABC [i++];
while ( i < sizeof ABC );                         // aBC
```

After modifying the first element of the array, the complete array is output to the screen again in the loop.

Special Form of an Initializer List

Arrays of characters are used in programs for storing and displaying textual information. However, it would be very inconvenient if we had to initialize arrays in the way used in the last program. Fortunately, the developers of C++ included in the language a special form for specifying initializer lists for an array of characters.

Try It Out - Character Strings

This form is shown in the next program, where a string literal is written as the initializer list.

```
// Program 5.6
// Character strings

#include <iostream.h>

void main()
{
  char  ABC[] = "ABC";                    // Null terminated

   cout << sizeof ABC                      // 4 0
        <<          ABC [3]
        << (int)  ABC [3]   << endl;

   char  ABC0 [ ] = {'A','B','C','\0'};
   char  abc0 [4] = {'a','b','c'};         // Null terminated

   cout << (int)  ABC0 [3]                 // 00
        << (int)  abc0 [3]   << endl;

   char  A [4] = "A";

   cout << sizeof ("")   << endl;          // 1

   int  i = 0;
   do
     cout << (int) A [i++] << ' ';         // 65 0 0
   while ( i < sizeof A);

   cout << endl;

   char  Z [4] = "";                       // Zero filled

   i = 0;
   do
     cout << (int) Z [i++] << ' ';         // 0 0 0 0
   while ( i < sizeof Z);

   cout << endl;

   char  N [4];                            // Not initialized
```

```
                                    // Not null terminated
    i = 0;
    do
        cout << (int) N [i++] << ' ';      // ? ? ? ?
    while ( i < sizeof N);
}
```

The output from this program looks like this:

```
4 0
00
1
65 0 0 0
0 0 0 0
4 4 22 4
```

How It Works

Let's go through each part of the program.

Character Strings

Because a character string is terminated by the character `'\0'`, the array
ABC will have 4 elements rather than 3.

```
    cout << sizeof ABC                  // 4 0
         <<          ABC [3]
         << (int)    ABC [3]  << endl;
```

The attempt to output the fourth element **ABC[3]**, results in a blank on the
screen, but the output of the numerical value of the fourth element
produces zero, since this is the ASCII code for `'\0'`.

The next figure illustrates the layout of **ABC** array elements in memory.

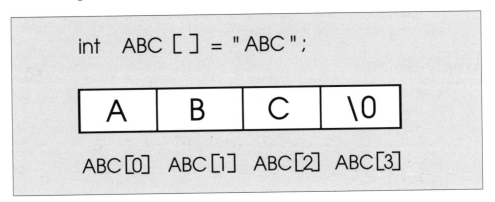

The availability of a null character at the end of a character string is a necessary condition for the `>>` operator, and other facilities for processing strings in C++, to work correctly. The null character marks the end of the string and signals where processing of the string should stop.

Incomplete Initialization

Compare the next two declarations of character strings.

```
char   ABC0 [ ] = {'A','B','C','\0'};
char   abc0 [4] = {'a','b','c'};          // Null terminated
```

The `ABC0` array contains 4 elements, including null character, and its initialization is identical to:

```
char   ABC [] = "ABC";                    // Null terminated
```

which is the initialization at the start.

But the array `abc0` is declared and the number of elements is indicated explicitly - 4. At the same time only three elements are recorded in the initializer list. How will the fourth element look? According to the output it will be a null character.

This is the result of a general rule for arrays of any type. The rule is that if the length of an array is indicated explicitly in brackets and the initializer list contains fewer elements, then the additional elements will be initialized by zeros. You can verify this once again in the line, where the numerical values of the elements of an array declared as:

```
char   A[4] = "A";
```

are output. String `"A"` contains only 2 characters: `'A'` and `'\0'`. The two remaining elements of `A` are filled with 0.

Empty Strings

A special case of initializing a character array only by zeros is presented in the line:

```
char   Z [4] = "";
```

Here you meet the empty string written as two double quotes following each other. It contains the single character `'\0'`.

Therefore, all characters of the array **z** are 0 (see the output).

Un-initialized Arrays

This is a good point to remind you once again that the use of un-initialized variables may result in errors that are difficult to find. Therefore, you should initialize all variables as you declare them, arrays included.

```
char  N [4];                        // Not initialized
```

Here is an example of the declaration of an un-initialized array. All its elements will contain random characters. Since the array will typically not contain a terminating null character, using it in its un-initialized state can cause serious errors.

Using << with Strings

You know that outputting an empty string:

```
cout << '\0';
```

produces a "blank" onto the screen. Hence you would probably think that output from the statement:

```
cout << "A" << "B";
```

must result in:

```
A   B
```

with a blank space between A and B. But this isn't the case in the previous program. Therefore, it's clear that null characters aren't output to the screen from a string literal by the `<<` operator.

Try It Out - Using << With Strings

Let's see how this works in practice.

```
//   Program 5.7
//   How does << operator work with strings ?

#include <iostream.h>

void main()
{
  cout << 'A' << '\0' << 'B'  << endl      // A B
       << "A"          << "B"  << endl      // AB
       << "A\0BC"       << 'D'  << endl;     // AD

  char  ABC[] = "ABC";

  int i = 0;
  do
    cout << ABC [i++];                       // ABC D
  while ( i < sizeof ABC );
  cout << 'D' << endl;

  i = 0;
  do
    cout << ABC [i++];                       // ABCD
  while ( i < sizeof ABC - 1 );
  cout << 'D' << endl;

  i = 0;
  do
    cout << ABC [i];                         // ABC D
  while ( ABC [i++] );
  cout << 'D' << endl;

  i = 0;
  while ( ABC [i] )
    cout << ABC [i++];                       // ABCD
  cout << 'D' << endl;

  ABC [1] = '\0';
  i = 0;
  while ( ABC [i] )
    cout << ABC [i++];                       // AD
  cout << 'D' << endl;
}
```

The output from the program looks like this:

```
A B
AB
AD
ABC  D
ABCD
ABC  D
ABCD
AD
```

How It Works

This program demonstrates the role of the null character as an indicator to stop processing a string. See how the output of the string **"A\0BC"** is carried out. Only the first character **'A'** is output. The **<<** operator processes the characters from the beginning of the string until it meets the null character.

The do Statement Model of << Operator for Strings

We tried to simulate the operation of the **<<** operator with the help of a **do** statement:

```
do
    cout << ABC [i++];                    // ABC D
while ( i < sizeof ABC );
```

However, this loop (as is evident from the comment) outputs an additional "blank" after **ABC** (which is the null character, in fact).

```
do
    cout << ABC [i++];                    // ABCD
while ( i < sizeof ABC - 1 );
```

For our next try we changed the exit condition for the loop, where the number of characters in the condition is decreased by 1. This produces the correct result, but isn't a valid algorithm for the case of the string **"A\0BC"**. All four symbols will be output and not just the first as is done by the **<<** operator.

```
do
    cout << ABC [i];                 // ABC D
while ( ABC [i++] );
```

Another approach is shown in these lines. Here the exit from the loop takes place if the next array element contains 0. You would think this is what's needed, but no. The null character itself is also output, but it shouldn't be.

It would be better to check first whether the array elements are equal to 0 or not, and only then to decide whether to exit or not. For problems of this kind, C++ has a special **while** iteration statement.

The while Loop

```
while ( ABC[i] )
    cout << ABC [i++];               // ABCD
```

See how the **while** statement solves the problem. The loop terminates when the null character is found because the null character has the value of 0 and acts as a false in the loop expression. You should bear in mind, that if for some reason the null character isn't on the end of the string, you could be in trouble as the loop will continue to output until a null character is found. The character itself isn't output. The following figure shows how the **while** statement operates. It has the following general form:

```
while (expression) statement
```

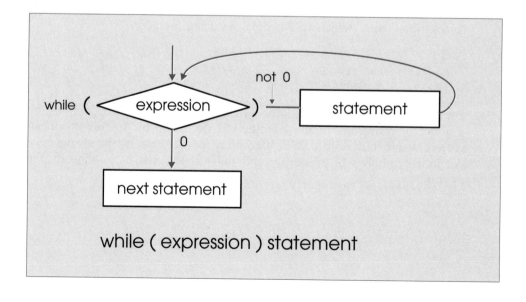

First the value of the expression is checked. If it isn't equal to 0, then the statement (or block) following **while** is executed. If the value of the expression isn't equal to 0, then control passes to the next statement. This is shown in the following figure.

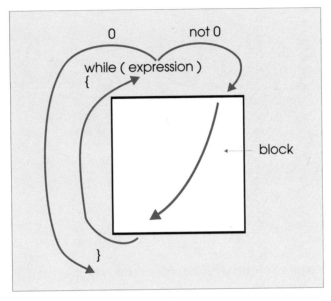

The statements **break** and **continue** act like the **do** statement. This should be obvious from the next figure.

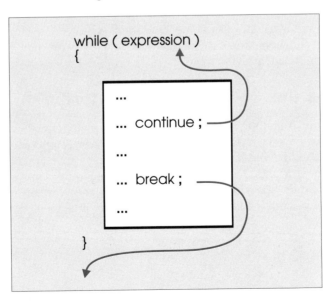

Using do or while

With the help of the **while** statement, you can simulate the **do** statement. However, you will need to write the statement or block within the loop twice. Therefore, the loop:

```
do
{
   block
} while (expression);
```

is equivalent to

```
{
   block
}
while (expression)
{
   block
}
```

You should use the **do** statement if the decision about the termination of a loop should be made *after* the execution of a block, and the **while** statement should be used if the decision about the execution of a block is to be made *before* its execution.

Manipulating Strings

In this part we'll discuss some operations with strings: output, input, copying and comparison. They all are based on the fact that a string is a null terminated array of characters.

How Does the << Operator Work for an Array?

You know from our first program that the << operator will output a string literal, in other words, a constant array of characters. Moreover, you understood the mechanism of its operation: to output symbols until a null character is found. The << operator will also output an array of characters, but, generally speaking, can it output any array, for example, an array of **int**? Why wouldn't it, if it can output each integer element separately?

Try It Out - The << Operator With Arrays

You can get answers to these questions with the help of the next program. You'll see that in an expression of the type:

```
cout << ABC
```

where the << operator copes very well with the output of a null terminated string. The terminating 0 character isn't output (there is no space between 'C' and '!').

```
// Program 5.8
// << operator for strings

#include <iostream.h>

void main()
{
  char  ABC[] = "ABC";      // declare and initialize array (string)
  cout << ABC               // ABC!
       << '!' << endl;

  char  ab[] = {'a','b'};   // note absence of null character in this array!
  cout << ab                // abABC?
       << '?' << endl;

  int  Int[] = {1,2,3,0};   //integer array
  cout << Int
       << '?' << endl;      // Strange output
}
```

On our computer the output from this program looks like this:

```
ABC!
abABC?
0x8ea7ffe8?
```

How It Works

Here we can see what happens if an array of characters isn't terminated by null, as in:

```
  char  ab[] = {'a','b'};
  cout << ab                // abABC?
       << '?' << endl;
```

On our computer, the output had the form:

```
abABC?
```

But on your computer it may be different. You are unlikely to be lucky enough to get the "true output":

```
ab?
```

The `<<` operator will begin output from the character `'a'`, then will output `'b'`, and then will continue byte after byte until the next byte happens to be null. It isn't difficult to guess that on our computer the compiler stores the characters `'a'` and `'b'` first in memory, and then the `"ABC"` string terminated by zero.

Generally, the output of a line not terminated by null is unpredictable. The output may be thousands of characters which will fill the screen, and perhaps force the computer to beep miserably (the result of the output of a byte that contains 7, which is the `'\a'` character). There is also the possibility that the program will crash, Windows will crash, or even that your machine will lock up.

```
int  Int[] = {1,2,3,0};
cout << Int
     << '?' << endl;        // Strange output
```

As for the output of the array of `int` defined here, this idea will fail in spite of our futile efforts to create a null-terminated array. Instead of the output of digits 123 you'll get a different sequence of digits and letters. This result can be quite reasonably explained as we'll see in the next chapter, but the fact remains that the `<<` operator didn't output the elements of the `int` array, number after number, as it did it for the ABC array.

In other words, the overloaded `<<` operator acts differently for arrays of various types. At the moment, the `char` type is the only type for which `<<` operator performs an element by element output until the nearest null byte.

Communicating With a Computer

Since you got acquainted with character strings, not so long ago, it has been possible to interact with your computer, inputting words and phrases.

Try It Out - Entering Your Name

In the next program this possibility is realized by the use of the `>>` operator. This operator provides for input of a sentence consisting of a sequence of characters including blanks.

```
// Program 5.9
// Enter your name

#include <iostream.h>

void main()
{
  char  Hello[] = "Hello, ";
  char  Programmer[256] = ""; //declaration of array, initialized to 0

  cout << "Enter your name, please: ";
  cin  >> Programmer;
  cout << Hello << Programmer;
}
```

The output from this program looks like this:

```
Enter your name, please: John
Hello, John
```

How It Works

Note the declaration of the 256-element array, initialized to zeros.

```
cin >> Programmer;
```

Here, the `>>` operator waits for a keystroke. On pressing the key it inputs a character from the keyboard and displays it on the screen waiting for you to press *Enter*. You may enter spaces, tab characters (by pressing the *Tab* key), or remove characters that were previously entered (by pressing the *BkSp* key). Only after pressing *Enter* does the `>>` operator begin to analyze the text entered, and to locate it in the array **Programmer** declared.

In response to the prompt, enter first several blanks and tabs, and then enter your name and press *Enter*. You'll find that none of blanks entered by you will be output by the statement:

```
cout << Hello << Programmer;
```

which means that the `>>` operator didn't copy these blanks into the **Programmer** array.

191

Another feature of the operation of the >> operator, is that it copies only the first word from the data you enter into the **Programmer** array. If you input your first name, then a blank (or some blanks), and then your surname and press *Enter*, in the response from your computer you'll find only your first name. Your surname and the blanks that preceded it weren't copied into the **Programmer** array.

The >> operator will automatically add '\0' to each string entered, so that outputting the **Programmer** array works correctly.

This is a standard mechanism for entering a character array using the >> operator. However, the input algorithm can be modified as you'll see later on.

Copying Strings

On acquiring a program, you'll almost certainly find in the instructions the advice to make a copy of the diskettes. This reduces the possibility of damage to the original diskettes.

Copying is often carried out while working with strings. Therefore, it would be a good idea to try to program this process. This is necessary because you can't use strings in an assignment. For example:

```
char From[ ] = "ABC";
char To[4] = "";
To = From;
```

will cause the compiler to display a message about an error. The essence of the error is that in C++, strange as it may seem, the array name isn't a variable that can be assigned a value.

In C++ there are standard facilities for copying strings which we'll consider in the next chapter. In the meantime, the next program shows how to copy one string into another.

Try It Out - Copying Strings

In this program you will see that it's important that the destination string isn't shorter than the source. At the same time the terminating `'\0'` in the source string must also be copied, and an additional byte must be allowed for it in the destination string. The **sizeof** operator takes into account the `'\0'`. With its help we can make the length of strings **To1** and **To2**, equal to the length of the string **From**.

```
//   Program 5.10
//   Copying strings

#include <iostream.h>

void main()
{
  char  From[]          = "I want to be copied.\n";
  char  To1[sizeof From] = "I want to get a copy\n";
  char  To2[sizeof From] = "I want to, too.\n";
  int  i;

  cout << From << To1 << To2;

  i = 0;
  do
    To1[i] = From[i];
  while ( From[i++] );
  cout << "To1 now contains: " << To1;

  i = 0;
  while ( (To2[i] = From[i]) != 0 )
    i++;
  cout << "To2 now contains: " << To2;
}
```

Typical output would be:

```
I want to be copied.
I want to get a copy
I want to, too.
To1 now contains: I want to be copied.
To2 now contains: I want to be copied.
```

How It Works

Two variants of a loop organization are shown in the program.

```
i = 0;
do
   To1 [i] = From[i];
while ( From[i++] );
cout << "To1 now contains: " << To1;
```

In the first, a byte is copied, then tested. When `'\0'` is copied, the loop terminates leaving the required result.

```
i = 0;
while ( (To2[i] = From[i]) != 0 )
   i++;
cout << "To2 now contains: " << To2;
```

In the second variant, the copy operation is part of the loop condition. As soon as the byte copied is null, the loop terminates.

```
(To2[i] = From[i])
```

This expression returns the value of `To2[i]`, so when the terminating null character is copied, it causes the loop to fail.

It's interesting that if you remove `!= 0`, you will get the same result in:

```
while ( To2[i] = From[i] )
   i++;
```

but the compiler may issue a warning, thinking you may have intended to write:

```
while ( To2[i] == From[i] )
   i++;
```

This is because this form of expression is used in a **while** statement more often. Although we only need the `=` sign, it's probably better to include the comparison as we have in the program, if only to avoid the compiler diagnostic.

Comparing Strings

While processing textual information, when using a text processor for example, an operation that is often needed is finding a particular word or piece of text. To do this requires the ability to compare two strings for equality.

Try It Out - Comparing Strings

This next program asks you to enter your name twice, and then verifies that both strings entered are identical.

```
//   Program 5.11
//   Testing input of a name

#include <iostream.h>

void main()
{
  const  int  Yes = 1;
  const  int  No  = 0;

  char  Name1[128] = "";
  char  Name2[128] = "";

  cout << "Enter your name, please: ";
  cin  >> Name1;
  cout << "Enter your name once more, please: ";
  cin  >> Name2;

  int  NamesEqual = Yes;
  int  i = 0;

  while (Name1[i])
  {
    if (Name1[i] != Name2[i])
    {
      NamesEqual = No;
      break;
    }
    i++;
  }
  if(Name2[i] != '\0')
    NamesEqual = No;

  if (NamesEqual)
    cout << "You entered two identical names.";
  else
    cout << "You entered two different names.";
}
```

Typical output would be:

```
Enter your name, please: Elizabeth
Enter your name once more, please: Elisabeth
You entered two different names.
```

How It Works

```
while (Name1[i])
{
  if (Name1[i] != Name2[i])
  {
    NamesEqual = No;
    break;
  }
  i++;
}
if(Name2[i] != '\0')
  NamesEqual = No;
```

The **while** statement loops until **Name1[i]** is equal to null (the end of the string).

```
if (Name1[i] != Name2[i])
{
  NamesEqual = No;
  break;
}
```

The code in the block of the **if** statement will be executed if the character in **Name1** does not equal the character in **Name2**. If the characters are not equal, **NamesEqual** is assigned the value **No** and the **break** statement terminates the loop. If the characters are equal the code in the block is not executed and

```
i++;
```

the variable **i** is incremented and the loop will repeat.

On the termination of the **while** loop

```
if(Name2[i] != '\0')
  NamesEqual = No;
```

Name2[i] is checked and if it does not equal the null character **NamesEqual** is assigned the value **No**.

```
if (NamesEqual)
   cout << "You entered two identical names.";
else
   cout << "You entered two different names.";
```

The variable **NamesEqual** is initialized by the value **Yes** (1). If both lines are identical then the line:

```
{
   NamesEqual = No;
   break;
}
```

in the loop will never be executed and the initially set value of the variable **NamesEqual** will be left unchanged.

The procedure presented in the program could be used during the input of a password in order to make certain it's valid. Of course, the password wouldn't be displayed on input.

Joining Strings Into an Array

Let's go back to the high mountains from which we began this chapter and see how we can join strings into an array.

Try It Out - Joining Strings Into an Array

We'll change a program from the last chapter so that we output the names of the mountains, rather than their heights.

```
//   Program 5.12
//   Names of the highest mountains of 7 continents

#include <iostream.h>

void main()
{
   char  Mountain0[] = "Kosciusko";
   char  Mountain1[] = "Vinson Massif";
   char  Mountain2[] = "El'brus";
   char  Mountain3[] = "Kilimanjaro";
   char  Mountain4[] = "McKinley";
   char  Mountain5[] = "Aconcagua";
   char  Mountain6[] = "Everest";
```

```
     cout << Mountain0  << endl
          << Mountain1  << endl
          << Mountain2  << endl
          << Mountain3  << endl
          << Mountain4  << endl
          << Mountain5  << endl
          << Mountain6  << endl;
}
```

The output will be:

```
Kosciusko
Vinson Massif
El'brus
Kilimanjaro
McKinley
Aconcagua
Everest
```

How It Works

You will notice the obvious similarity of this program to Program 4.1.
Where in Program 4.1 the integer variables were:

```
int  Mountain0;
```

now there are arrays of characters:

```
char  Mountain0[] = "Kosciusko";
```

This similarity may suggest an idea. Why not join the 7 arrays of characters
into one array, where each element is a string, similar to Program 4.2 where
we combined 7 integer variables into one array?

Try It Out - Arrays of Strings

The next program does just that and demonstrates that it's possible. In the
declaration of the array **Mountain**, the length of each name cannot exceed
20 characters including the terminating null.

```
//   Program 5.13
//   Array of strings

#include <iostream.h>

void main()
{
  const  int  N = 7;
```

```
    char  Mountain [N] [20] = {   "Kosciusko",
                                  "Vinson Massif",
                                  "El'brus",
                                  "Kilimanjaro",
                                  "McKinley",
                                  "Aconcagua",
                                  "Everest"
                              };
  int  i;

  for ( i=0; i < N; i++ )
    cout << Mountain[i] << endl;
}
```

The output from this program is the same as the previous one.

How It Works

C++ provides for multi-dimensional arrays.

```
    char  Mountain [N] [20] = {   "Kosciusko",
                                  "Vinson Massif",
                                  "El'brus",
                                  "Kilimanjaro",
                                  "McKinley",
                                  "Aconcagua",
                                  "Everest"
                              };
```

Mountain is declared as a two dimensional array being of size 7 by 20. This corresponds to the seven strings that are used to initialize the array with each string having a maximum length of 20 (19 plus the null character).

You can imagine a two-dimensional array as being an array of one dimensional arrays. C++ actually treats a two-dimensional array as a one-dimensional array, each of whose elements is itself an array. You can imagine a two-dimensional array as having rows and columns like a spreadsheet or sheet of graph paper.

```
  for ( i=0; i < N; i++ )
    cout << Mountain [i] << endl;
```

In this program **Mountain[i]** means the **(i+1)**-th array of characters (string) in the array **Mountain**. Index **i** has values from 0 for the first string, to 6 (**N-1**) for the last string. This code introduces something completely new - the **for** loop.

The for Loop

The **for** loop is the final loop to be discussed. In its simplified form:

```
for (i=0; i<N; i++) statement
```

it's encountered often and means execute the statement N times.

Its action is identical to the following construction with the **while** statement:

```
i = 0;
while ( i < N )
{
   statement
   i++;
}
```

As you see this is more bulky, which provides the rationale for the **for** loop.

There is one divergence between the **for** statement and our derived model in the form of the **while** statement. It occurs when you use a block with a **continue** statement. This is shown in the following figure.

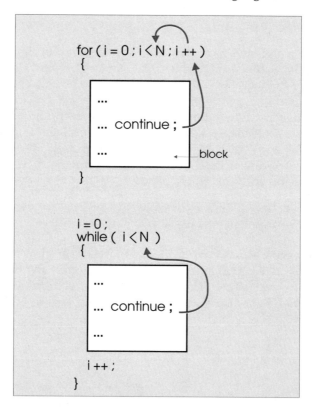

As you see, the **while** model doesn't reflect the operation of the **for** statement correctly. The **continue** in the **while** model of the **for** statement, doesn't execute **i++**, but passes control immediately to the condition **i<N**.

Try It Out - Using the for Loop

We can illustrate how the **for** statement works with another program.

```
//   Program 5.14
//   How does the for statement work?

#include <iostream.h>

void main()
{
  const  int  N = 3;  // Number of iteration
  int  i;  // Iteration variable

  cout << "Begin\n";

  for ( cout << "A ", i = 0; cout << "B ", i < N; cout << "C ", i++)
    cout << i << endl;

  cout << "\nEnd";
}
```

The output of this program has the form:

```
Begin
A B 0
C B 1
C B 2
C B
End
```

How It Works

```
for ( cout << "A ", i = 0; cout << "B ", i < N; cout << "C ", i++)
```

Within the parentheses of the **for,** there are three expressions containing the comma operator. The first:

```
cout << "A ", i = 0
```

outputs the symbol **"A"** to the screen, and then initializes the iteration variable **i**. It's apparent from the output of the program that this statement is executed once during the input to the loop.

Then the second expression:

```
cout << "B ", i < N
```

is executed. It outputs the symbol `'B'` and then tests the condition `i < N`. If this condition is true the loop body:

```
cout << i << endl;
```

outputs the value of the variable `i`.

After this, as you see from the output of the program, `'C'` is displayed. This means that the third expression is evaluated:

```
cout << "C ", i++
```

Here `i` is incremented by 1. And again the second expression is executed, in which the incremented value of `i` is compared with `N`. The loop process is continued until `i` becomes equal to 3. Then after the test of the condition `i<N` gives 0, the loop body isn't executed, but the statement that follows the **for** loop is executed.

The general form of the **for** statement may be written:

```
for (init-statement; condition; increment) statement
```

The following figure shows how control is passed in the **for** statement.

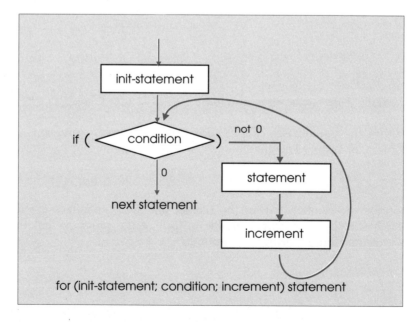

for (init-statement; condition; increment) statement

Designing a Program

Before we reach the end of the chapter we'll write another program, that links together what we have learnt so far.

The Problem

The problem we have to solve is to write a program that can add, subtract, multiply and divide two numbers entered via the keyboard.

The Analysis

1   Invite the user to enter the calculation.

2   Check the input to see if the user has asked for addition, subtraction, multiplication or division. Also check to see that the user hasn't asked to divide a number by zero.

3   Perform the calculation.

4   Print the results to the screen.

The Solution

1   If we use **cin**, the user will be able to enter the calculation. You will notice that we are using **cin** in a slightly different way

```
cin >> first >> op >> second;
```

but this allows the user to enter the calculation in a natural way because you can enter each input on the same line with a space between each item. For example:

9 / 2

We also have to create the memory space by declaring variables of the appropriate type.

```
// calc.cpp
// a program to add, subtract, multiply and divide
// two numbers

#include <iostream.h>

void main()
{
  float first, second;
  char op;

  cout << "\n\t\t A SIMPLE CALCULATOR "
    << "\n\t\t ++++++++++++++++++ \n\n";

  cout << "\tTo use the program enter your calculation as follows:\n"
       << "\tFIRST_NUMBER op SECOND_NUMBER\n\twhere op is +, -, *, or /"
       << "\n\n\tEnter your calculation: ";

  cin >> first >> op >> second;

}
```

2-4   We need to make sure that the user has entered +, -, *, or /.

How will we perform the calculations? The easiest method is to use the arithmetical operators but we have to ensure that, if the operation is to be a division, the divisor isn't zero because we will generate an error if you divide by zero. The simplest way to prevent this possible error is to use an **if else** statement.

We could also use nested **if else** statements to check that the correct operator has been input and then perform the calculations. However, as we have seen, the **switch** statement will be more efficient.

We need to display the results on the screen. We can perform the actual calculation in the **cout** statement.

```
// calc.cpp
// a program to add, subtract, multiply and divide
// two numbers

#include <iostream.h>

void main()
{
  float first, second;
  char op;
```

```
cout << "\n\t\t A SIMPLE CALCULATOR "
    << "\n\t\t +++++++++++++++++ \n\n";

cout << "\tTo use the program enter your calculation as follows:\n"
        << "\tFIRST_NUMBER op SECOND_NUMBER\n\twhere op is +, -, *, or /"
        << "\n\n\tEnter your calculation: ";

cin >> first >> op >> second;
```

```
switch(op)
{
  case '*':
    cout << endl << first << " * " << second << " = "
        << first * second;
    break;

  case '/':
    if (second == 0)
      cout << endl << "Unable to perform calculation."
          << "\nDivide by zero error";
    else
      cout << endl << first << " / " << second << " = "
          << first / second;
    break;

  case '+':
    cout << endl << first << " + " << second << " = "
        << first + second;
    break;

  case '-':
    cout << endl << first << " - " << second << " = "
        << first - second;
    break;

  default:
    cout << "Internal error.";
}
}
```

We can now try the program.

```
    A SIMPLE CALCULATOR
    +++++++++++++++++++

To use the program enter your calculation as follows:
FIRST_NUMBER op SECOND_NUMBER
where op is +, -, *, or /

Enter your calculation: 3.5 * 3.25

3.5 * 3.25 = 11.375
```

```
A SIMPLE CALCULATOR
+++++++++++++++++++

To use the program enter your calculation as follows:
FIRST_NUMBER op SECOND_NUMBER
where op is +, -, *, or /

Enter your calculation: 6.5 / 0

Unable to perform calculation.
Divide by zero error
```

Summary

So, you've conquered the peaks of arrays and strings. You have coped with jumps from iteration statements and although there is still a lot to learn, you have enough knowledge to write reasonably complex interactive programs.

We have re-invented a few wheels in this chapter, for example, the programs for copying and comparing strings. But these wheels were invented long ago using techniques and capabilities we are going to introduce next. These are called functions, and there are warehouses full of them called libraries. In the next chapter we'll begin assimilating these powerful methods that have been distilled from the knowledge of thousands of people.

CHAPTER 6

Using And Creating Functions

In the majority of our example programs we've only used one function - the function **main()**. However, in Chapter 3, you will recall that we discussed the use of some of the functions from the header file **CTYPE.H**. In this chapter we'll move another step up the ladder and show you how you can use functions developed and perfected by others. The sorts of functions we'll look at are the accumulation of much effort and experience and will allow you to do much more.

We'll also show you how to create functions which you'll be able to use as off-the-shelf building blocks to create your own programs, and introduce you to the concept of a pointer.

In this chapter you will:

> Use functions developed by other people

> Create your own functions

> Look at the scope of variables in functions

> See how the addresses of variables can be used

> Write a program that will manipulate a sentence you type in

Using Functions

First, we'll look at some simple examples which illustrate how you can use ANSI standard functions in your C++ programs. You've already dealt with complex algebraic formulae using the addition, subtraction, multiplication, and division operations in C++, but what would you do if you wanted to calculate the square root of a number or use another mathematical function? Although there is no operator to calculate square roots in C++, a set of standard functions (known as a library) can be added to any C++ compiler. These functions can number several hundreds. They aren't part of the C++ language as such, but are nevertheless an important and useful addition.

Try It Out - Using Functions

Program 6.1 shows how easy it is to use the standard function from the C++ library to calculate a square root. As you can see, all you need to do is write the name of the function, and then the value of **x** in parentheses, and, hey presto, up comes the answer:

```
y = sqrt( x );
```

On the surface this doesn't seem to differ from an ordinary math equation. However, don't forget that in C++ the sign **=** assigns the value of the function **sqrt(x)** to the variable **y**. In C++, this way of addressing the function is called calling the function.

```cpp
//   Program 6.1
//   Square Root function
#include <iostream.h>
#include <math.h>

void main()
{
  double x = 25, y = 0;

  y = sqrt(x);

  cout << "The square root of " << x << " is " << y << endl;
  cout << sqrt(x) << " * " << sqrt(x) << " = "
       << sqrt(x) * sqrt(x) << endl;
  cout << "The square root of 36 is " << sqrt(x + 11) << endl;
}
```

The output from the program is:

```
The square root of 25 is 5
5 * 5 = 25
The square root of 36 is 6
```

How It Works

You may have noticed that we've used another preprocessor directive in this program:

```
#include <math.h>
```

As you can guess from the name, the header file, **MATH.H**, contains information about mathematical functions, such as **sqrt()**. So, to use a function from the standard compiler library you need to:

▶ Include a line with the directive **#include** followed by the name of the header file in your program.

▶ Call a required function by its name indicating the value of the argument, or arguments if there are several of them.

You can find the lists of standard functions and their descriptions (including a reference to the required header file) in your compiler documentation.

```
y = sqrt(x);
```

the variable **x** is passed as an argument to the function **sqrt()**. The function calculates the answer and returns this value which is assigned to the variable **y**.

```
cout << sqrt(x) << " * " << sqrt(x) << " = "
     << sqrt(x) * sqrt(x) << endl;
```

From this statement, you can see that you don't have to use an assignment operator, as we did in the statement **y = sqrt(x);** to derive the value of a function. All you have to do is write the name of the function and give the argument in parentheses. The result of the function calculation is returned in the location where the function is written. Here we say the function returns the value. The value was used four times in the statement - the last two occasions the values were multiplied together.

```
cout << "The square root of 36 is " << sqrt(x + 11) << endl;
```

You can see that an expression can also be a function argument. First the value of the expression is calculated, and then the calculation result serves as the function argument.

Try It Out - Using sqrt()

Program 6.2 is a more useful example. It calculates **sqrt(x)** for any value **x**, entered via the keyboard.

```
//   Program 6.2
//   using sqrt()
#include <iostream.h>
#include <math.h>

void main()
{
  double x;
  cout << "\n\n\tSquare Root Calculator\n"
       << "\tEnter number:   ";
  cin >> x;
  cout << "\t√" << x << " = " << sqrt(x) << endl;
  //  Note - √ is inserted by typing alt - 251
}
```

Try running the program using several different values for **x**.

As an aside, you will see that the square root symbol was typed into the source code by holding down the *Alt* key and typing 251 (this only works with DOS).

Tables

In the age before computers were invented and calculators were common place, even in the class room, people had a book of mathematical tables. We can use a program to do the same calculations using C++.

Try It Out - Squares and Square Roots of Numbers

Program 6.3 calculates the square and square root of a number.

```
//   Program 6.3
//   Table of squares and square roots
#include <iostream.h>
#include <math.h>
#include <iomanip.h>
```

```
void main()
{
   cout << "\n\n\tTable of Squares and Square Roots\n\n"
        << "\t\tX²\t\tX\t\t√X\n";
   for (double i = 5.; i <= 100; i +=5)
      cout << setiosflags(ios::showpoint) << setprecision(3)
           << "\t  " << setw(8) << i * i << "\t  "<< setw(8)
           << i << "\t  "  << setw(8) << sqrt(i) << endl;
}
```

The variable **x** is declared in the **for** statement. If you run Program 6.3 you'll get the following table, which shows X^2 and $\sqrt{X}$ for values of X from 5 to 100, in increments of 5.

```
Table of Squares and Square Roots

     X2            X           √X
    25.000       5.000        2.236
   100.000      10.000        3.162
   225.000      15.000        3.873
   400.000      20.000        4.472
   625.000      25.000        5.000
   900.000      30.000        5.477
  1225.000      35.000        5.916
  1600.000      40.000        6.325
  2025.000      45.000        6.708
  2500.000      50.000        7.071
  3025.000      55.000        7.416
  3600.000      60.000        7.746
  4225.000      65.000        8.062
  4900.000      70.000        8.367
  5625.000      75.000        8.660
  6400.000      80.000        8.944
  7225.000      85.000        9.220
  8100.000      90.000        9.487
  9025.000      95.000        9.747
 10000.000     100.000       10.000
```

How It Works

If you want a table for a different range of values, all you have to do is change the initial values in the **for** loop.

```
cout << setiosflags(ios::showpoint) << setprecision(3)
     << "\t  " << setw(8) << i * i << "\t  "<< setw(8)
     << i << "\t  "  << setw(8) << sqrt(i) << endl;
```

You will probably have noticed the **setiosflag(ios::showpoint)**, **setprecision()**, and **setw()** that were used in the **cout** statement. What do they mean?

There are a group of functions that are used to decide how screen output will be formatted. You can use the associated flags without understanding how they work. Initially, you must include the header file **IOMANIP.H**.

```
setiosflags(ios::showpoint)
```

This expression ensures that the decimal point is always shown, even if the number has no fractional part. To set the flag, use **setiosflags** with the name of the flag, **showpoint**, as an argument. The flag name must be prefixed with the class name, **ios**, and the scope resolution operator (**::**). (Don't worry, we'll explain class name and the scope resolution operator later!)

```
setprecision()
```

This expression is used to set the number of digits to the right of the decimal point. The number of digits is specified as the argument.

```
setw()
```

The expression, **setw()**, is used to set the field width that the output is displayed in. The width is specified as the argument.

Press Any Key....

In Program 6.4 we use the **getch()** function from a standard library.

Try It Out - Getting Characters From the Keyboard

Let's see how this works in practice.

```
//   Program 6.4
//   Getting characters from the keyboard
#include <iostream.h>
#include <conio.h>

void main ()
{
  const int Esc = 27;

  cout << "\aPress any key to get its keycode. \n "
          "Press Esc to Quit.\n\n"
```

```
            "Key\tKeycode\n\n";
char Key;

do
{
    Key = getch();       // Wait for key pressed
    cout << Key;
    if ( ! Key )
        Key = getch();   // If 0, get scan code
    cout << '\t' << (int) Key << endl;
} while (Key != Esc);

cout << "\n\a Press any key to continue...";
if ( ! getch () )
    getch ();       // Wait for any key
}
```

How It Works

```
#include <conio.h>
```

To use **getch()** you need to include the **CONIO.H** header file. You will remember that you must write each preprocessor directive on a separate line.

```
Key = getch();    // Wait for key pressed
```

Although the function **getch()** has no arguments, it doesn't mean that you can get rid of the parentheses for the arguments. The function **getch()** isn't included in ANSI standard libraries. Nevertheless, this function is supported by many compilers for DOS (such as Borland C++). You may have problems compiling Program 6.4 under UNIX if the compiler's library doesn't contain the function **getch()**. In this case you will have to replace **getch()** in the source text with an equivalent function.

The function **getch()** waits for a character to be input from the keyboard, but operates in a different way from the **>>** operator. Firstly, it doesn't display the symbol being entered. That's why the character **Key** is output. Secondly, the **getch()** function terminates its operation immediately after you press any key (except the *Shift*, *Alt* and *Ctrl* keys and some other special keys).

Like the **>>** operator, the **getch()** function returns the ASCII code of the key pressed, though this only applies to ordinary keys that produce characters.

```
     if ( ! Key )
         Key = getch ();   // If 0, get scan code
```

For special keys - for example function keys, cursor control keys, and the combinations of *Ctrl* and *Alt* with other keys - the **getch()** function returns the value 0. For these keys, it's necessary to call the **getch()** function again to obtain the second byte which is generated when you press a special key. This byte contains a number known as the key's scan-code, which indicates which key you pressed. Therefore, for special keys, the key's scan code is output, and not the ASCII code.

Try running this program pressing different keys with or without *Shift*, *Alt* or *Ctrl*. To quit the loop, press *Esc*. Note that key codes for blank (32) and *Enter* (13) are also displayed, which you don't get with the **>>** operator. The *BkSp* and *Tab* keys also give the correct values of the ASCII code, but instead of a symbol being displayed, they control the cursor: the backspace erases the character **'\t'** output earlier, and the number 8 appears shifted to the left into the previous column; *Tab* shifts the number 9 to the right into the next column. The key combination *Ctrl-G*, enters the character **'\a'** and you'll hear a beep. To exit the loop you can press *Ctrl-[* as an alternative to *Esc*, as this enters the same code as the *Esc* key.

Program 6.4. could prove useful later on if you want to write your own programs that require you to analyze keyed input. It'll give you the values of the ASCII codes and scan codes of your computer keyboard, and will be particularly useful if there are any non-standard keys, or if the instruction manual with the codes in it has disappeared somewhere (this seems to be rather a common occurrence!).

```
   if ( ! getch () )
     getch ();       // Wait for any key
```

This program shows how to pause your program until a key is pressed. In Program 5.2 we did the same thing using the **>>** operator. However, this was more awkward as you had to press the *Enter* key as well.

The above statement illustrates an interesting feature of using a function: the value which it returns may be ignored. This is quite normal in C++, for example, a function may just output information, in which case there is no need to return a value.

How to Create Functions

The previous examples have shown you how to use the standard functions **sqrt()**, and **getch()**. You have seen how useful these functions are. You have also seen, in an earlier chapter, how to use some of the functions, in the **CTYPE.H** header file, to test character input. Once you have created your own function you can use it in your own programs, or give it to other programmers as a library on disk. You needn't hand over the source code, just provide a description of its interface. You need to divide programs into functions for the same reasons that this book is divided into chapters, sections and paragraphs. It makes it easier to comprehend, deal with and modify.

The Function main()

All the programs in this book so far have contained only one function - the function **main()**. Using Program 6.5 as an example, we'll try and explain why it's called this, and what distinguishes it from other functions.

Try It Out - Using the Function main()

Let's see this in action.

```
//   Program 6.5
//   main () starts first
#include <iostream.h>

void NotMain()
{
   cout << "Function doesn't work !!!!!!!!!! ";
}

void main()
{
   cout << "Function main () starts first.";
}
```

How It Works

There are two functions defined in this program: **main()** and **NotMain()**. They are very similar. You can assume that the syntax of this program is correct. Once you've compiled this program, you can be sure that it's correct and that there are no errors.

Try It Out!

From your knowledge of C++, and looking at Program 6.5, you might presume that program execution will be carried out from top to bottom, in other words, first the function **NotMain()** will be executed, then the function **main()**. However, it doesn't do this. If you run this program, you'll receive the message:

```
Function main () starts first.
```

output by the function **main()**. However, the function **NotMain()** is not called. Therefore, you will *not* see the expected message:

```
Function doesn't work !!!!!!!!!!
```

From this you can draw two conclusions. One, that the function **main()** is executed first; and two, that the function **NotMain()** for some reason doesn't work, in spite of the fact that its description isn't significantly different from function **main()**. As you are already aware, the reason for this is that the function **main()** has a special role in C++: program execution always begins automatically with the function **main()**. Any other function in a program must be called explicitly if it's to be executed.

There's one more detail in Program 6.5 that we need to explain which is the use of a return type **void** in the description of the function **main()**:

```
void main()
{
   ...
}
```

Returning the Wrong Type

The return type specifies the type of return that will be made. With regards to **main()**, any return would be made to the operating system. Therefore, you would normally have a return type of **void** unless you wanted to return a value to the operating system - possibly to be used as an **ERRORLEVEL** in a DOS batch file.

Other functions, either written by other people or created by you, will also have a return type. When you create a function, you should specify the type of return during the definition or declaration of all functions otherwise you may get an error. The type of return should match what the function will return. For example, if you tried to return a **float** and the compiler was expecting a **char** the compiler would treat this as an error.

If you don't specify the type of return for a function, the compiler will treat it as if it should return an integer argument.

```
void NotMain()
{
    ...
}
```

Even if the function doesn't return a value, you should still indicate **void** as the returned value type.

Call to a Function

Have a look at our next example, Program 6.6:

```
//   Program 6.6
//   Say 123

#include <iostream.h>

void Say_2(void)
{
    cout << 2;
}

void main(void)
{
    cout << 1;
    Say_2 ();
    cout << 3;
}
```

After the **#include** statement you will see that the function **Say_2()** is defined:

```
    void Say_2(void)
{
    cout << 2;
}
```

This function outputs the number 2 to the screen:

```
    cout << 1;
    Say_2 ();
    cout << 3;
```

In **main()** you will see four statements which are executed from top to bottom. The first statement in **main()** outputs 1 to the screen; then the statement **Say_2();** calls the function which outputs the number 2. Then control returns from the function **Say_2()** to the function **main()**, and the statement **cout << 3;** is executed. Finally, control returns to the operating system when the program terminates by passing the closing brace of **main()**. This process of how control is handed over from one statement to another is illustrated in the next figure.

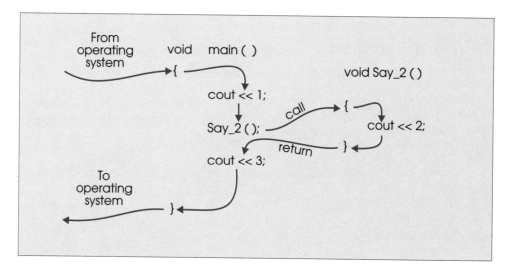

As you can see the call of the function in the statement:

```
Say_2();
```

is a jump that returns to the next statement after the function has been executed. So, you can see that the sequence of function execution is defined not by the order they are written in the program, but by the sequence of their calls.

Function Declaration

If the order in which the functions are described in a program doesn't play any role, then why can't we write the function **main()** earlier (or higher up) than the function **Say_2()**, as in the following example?

```
void main(void)
{
  cout << 1;
  Say_2 ();
  cout << 3;
}

void Say_2(void)
{
  cout << 2;
}
```

The trouble with this is that you'll receive a compiler error message.

The compiler needs to know how a function is declared before it is used. Therefore, we can avoid this error by using the statement:

```
void Say_2(void);          // Declaration
```

Try It Out - Function Declarations

Let's see how this works in the next program.

```
//   Program 6.7
//       Say 123 with declaration
#include <iostream.h>

void Say_2(void);          // Declaration

void main(void)
{
  cout << 1;
  Say_2 ();
  cout << 3;
}

void Say_2(void)           // Definition
{
  cout << 2;
}
```

Try It Out!

219

How It Works

```
void Say_2(void)          // Definition
```

This seems to be a repetition of the line following the include statements.

The first occurrence is the declaration, the second is the definition. The declaration of a function is also called a **function prototype**. A simplified illustration of how their syntax differs is given in the following figure.

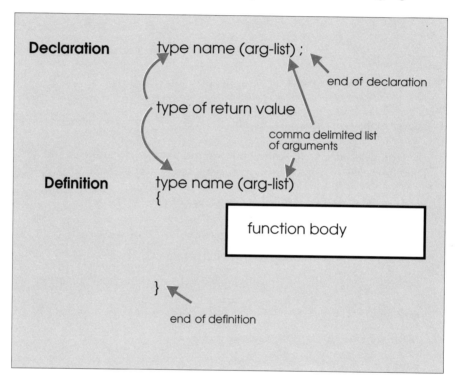

As you can see the definition of a function contains the body of the function which in turn includes the sequence of statement execution. You may be wondering what the purpose of the declaration is, and why we didn't need the declaration in Program 6.6, whereas it was needed in Program 6.7. This is simply one of the rules of the language. If a function is called from another then it must be defined or declared earlier in the program. You really need to know how a compiler operates to understand this more fully. It scans the program's text in the same way in which we would read it, in other words from left to right and top to bottom. When it encounters a new word like **Say_2**, for example, it must already have the information about what kind of an object it is, therefore the description of this object must be given before it's used.

The declaration of a function contains all the necessary information so that when a compiler meets a function call in the text it can form the required computer instructions and, equally importantly, check that it is being used correctly in the code. If there are no declarations, then the function definitions should be placed in a strict order, with function **main()** as the last.

Try It Out - Using Declarations

The next program demonstrates how function definitions can be located in an arbitrary sequence when declarations are used.

```
// Program 6.8
// Say 1234567 using declarations
#include <iostream.h>

// Declarations of functions in any order
void Say_23456(void);
void Say_345(void);
void Say_4(void);

// Definitions of functions in any order
void main(void)
{
   cout << 1;
   Say_23456();
   cout << 7;
}

void Say_23456(void)
{
   cout << 2;
   Say_345();
   cout << 6;
}

void Say_345(void)
{
   cout << 3;
   Say_4();
   cout << 5;
}

void Say_4(void)
{
   cout << 4;
}
```

How It Works

As you can see, you are free to place function declarations in any suitable order in C++, but it's better to group them together and place them at the beginning of a file, before the first function definition. This is described in the following figure.

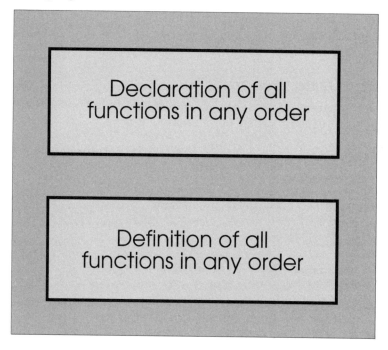

The function **main()** then usually follows, though this isn't obligatory, and then the rest of the function definitions in whatever order you prefer.

A function can also call itself in C++. This is called **recursion** but you must have a declaration for the function to do this.

The Hierarchy of Calls

If you want to show the interaction of a number of functions you can use a hierarchy scheme in your programs similar to that shown in the next figure.

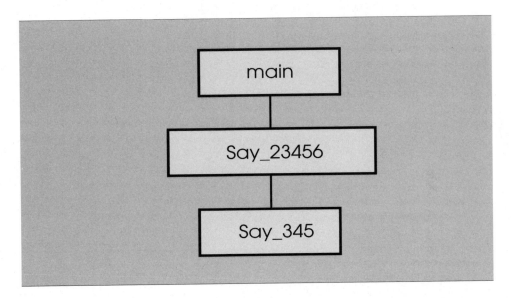

There are no arrows in this scheme as it shows the hierarchy of function calls not flow control. The line that connects the box main with the function **Say_23456()** means that the function **main()**, located higher up in the chart, calls the function **Say_23456()**. The latter in turn, calls the function **Say_345()**.

This chart can be compared to the hierarchical structure for an organization that shows who is in charge of who. In this analogy, the function **main()** is like the company president. However, function call charts differ considerably from the structures of organizations. For example, in the next program

(Program 6.9) the chart of function calls still looks like an organization chart (see the figure at the end of the program code), but you can't say this about Program 6.10 (again, see the figure at the end of the program code), although you could of course represent the function **Say_0()** as an "errand-boy". In this second figure you can see where the chart of function calls doesn't show the number and the sequence of function calls to **Say_0()** - it only shows which other functions call the function **Say_0()**.

Try It Out - Two Programs Showing Function Calls

Let's look at the program.

```
//   Program 6.9
//   Say 1234567 with 12 functions
#include <iostream.h>

void Say_1(void);
void Say_2(void);
void Say_3(void);
void Say_4(void);
void Say_5(void);
void Say_6(void);
void Say_7(void);
void Say_12(void);
void Say_34(void);
void Say_67(void);
void Say_345(void);

void main(void)
{
   Say_12();
   Say_345();
   Say_67();
}

void Say_12(void)
{
   Say_1 ();
   Say_2();
}

void Say_34(void)
{
   Say_3 ();
   Say_4();
}
```

```
void Say_67(void)
{
  Say_6 ();
  Say_7();
}

void Say_345(void)
{
  Say_34();
  Say_5();
}

void Say_1(void)
{
  cout << 1;
}

void Say_2(void)
{
cout << 2;
}

void Say_3(void)
{
  cout << 3;
}

void Say_4(void)
{
  cout << 4;
}

void Say_5(void)
{
  cout << 5;
}

void Say_6(void)
{
  cout << 6;
}

void Say_7(void)
{
  cout << 7;
}
```

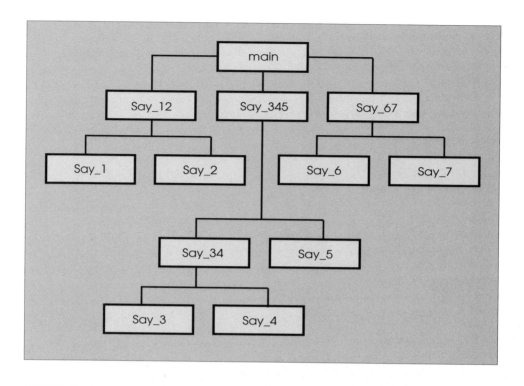

```
//   Program 6.10
//   Say 010203
#include <iostream.h>

void Say_0(void);
void Say_1(void);
void Say_2(void);
void Say_3(void);

void main(void)
{
  Say_1();
  Say_2();
  Say_3();
}

void Say_0(void)
{
  cout << 0;
}

void Say_1(void)
{
  Say_0();
```

```
   cout << 1;
}

void Say_2(void)
{
  Say_0();
  cout << 2;
}

void Say_3(void)
{
  Say_0();
  cout << 3;
}
```

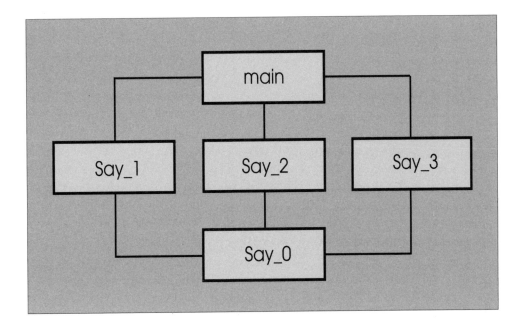

How It Works

Let's go through how these programs work.

Void Means Nothing

We must apologize for using the word **void** in a function's declaration and definition in Program 6.6 without explaining what it means. You've probably already guessed that **void** means nothing, for example, in the declaration in Program 6.6:

```
void Say_2(void)
{
   cout << 2;
}
```

the first **void** means that the function **Say_2()** doesn't return any value, and the second **void** means that the function doesn't have an argument.

The fact that the function doesn't have a return value means that it cannot be used in expressions or in an assignment operation. For example, it would be incorrect to write:

```
i = Say_2();  // Error
```

or:

```
if (Say_2()) ;  // Error
```

On the other hand you don't have to write the statement:

```
return;
```

in the body of such a function. The fact that the function doesn't have any arguments means that its call is written without an argument list, for example, the call of the function **Say_2()** is written:

```
Say_2();
```

The keyword **void** is a C++ type-specifier like **char**, **int** and so on.

Making A Header File

From the very first program we used the preprocessor directive:

```
#include <iostream.h>
```

The only thing you know about this is that it's necessary when using the **<<** and **>>** operators. Here **IOSTREAM.H** is the name of a header file (in other words, a text file, which means that you can look through it). It's provided with your compiler.

The preprocessor directive **#include** inserts the contents of a header file into the program at the location where it's specified. A header file can contain any text acceptable to a program in C++.

```
#include "myheader.h"
```

In the above statement the name of a header file is included in double quotes and not in brackets. If the name of a file is in double quotes then the compiler searches for this file first in the current directory, and afterwards (if it isn't detected) in a special directory, where system header files (for example, **IOSTREAM.H**) are located. If the name of a header file is in brackets then the compiler will only look in the system directory. Therefore, it's not incorrect to write:

```
#include "iostream.h"
```

although, you wouldn't usually do so.

Try It Out - Declaring Functions In a Header File

Normally, declarations of functions are placed into a header file. This is illustrated in Program 6.11.

```
//  Program 6.11
//  Say 1234567 with header
#include <iostream.h>
#include "P06_11.h"        // Contains declarations of functions

void main(void)             //main() does not have to return a value
{                           //and control will return to the operating
Say_12();                   //system after the call to Say_67() when the
Say_345();                  //program passes the final brace
Say_67();
}

void Say_12(void)
{
   Say_1 ();
   Say_2();
}

void Say_34(void)
{
   Say_3 ();
   Say_4();
}
```

```
void Say_67(void)
{
   Say_6 ();
   Say_7();
}

void Say_345(void)
{
   Say_34();
   Say_5();
}

void Say_1(void)
{
   cout << 1;
}

void Say_2(void)
{
   cout << 2;
}

void Say_3(void)
{
   cout << 3;
}

void Say_4(void)
{
   cout << 4;
}

void Say_5(void)
{
   cout << 5;
}

void Say_6(void)
{
   cout << 6;
}

void Say_7(void)
{
   cout << 7;
}
```

```
//  P06_11.H
//  Header file for program P06-11.CPP

// Function declarations

void Say_1(void);
void Say_2(void);
void Say_3(void);
void Say_4(void);
void Say_5(void);
void Say_6(void);
void Say_7(void);
void Say_12(void);
void Say_34(void);
void Say_67(void);
void Say_345(void);
```

If you compare Program 6.11 with Program 6.9 you will see that placing the declarations of functions in a header file gives you a more compact program.

The Return Value

The statement:

```
return expression;
```

hands over a returned value produced by **expression**.

Try It Out - Using the Return Value

Program 6.12 demonstrates the return of a function value. The output of this program is given in the comments.

```
//   Program 6.12
//   Returning int value 123
#include <iostream.h>

int GetInt(void);

void main(void)
{
  int  i;
                        //  Output
  GetInt();             //  0
  i = GetInt();         //  0
  cout << i;            //  123
```

Try It Out!

```
    cout << GetInt();  //  0123
    if ( GetInt() );   //  0
}

int GetInt(void)
{
    cout << endl << 0;
    return 123;
}
```

How It Works

The function **GetInt()** outputs the number 0 to the screen from a new line, and returns the value 123.

```
    GetInt();          //   0
```

This statement shows that the returned value can be ignored. The function at this time works by outputting 0 onto the screen.

```
    i = GetInt();          //   0
```

The above code shows how a returned value may be used in an assignment expression.

```
    cout << GetInt();          //    0123
```

This line outputs to the screen.

```
    if ( GetInt() );          //   0
```

This is a test expression.

A function can contain any number of **return** statements in different places, but good programming style requires only one **return** to be available and it should be the last statement in a function.

Arguments to Functions

Previously, when we used the **sqrt(x)** function we indicated the required value **x** and the function returned the square root of this value. Here **x** is an argument of the **sqrt(x)** function.

Try It Out - Using One Argument

If we modify Program 6.10, by adding a parameter to the function **Say()**, we'll get Program 6.13.

```
// Program 6.13
// Say to function what to do
#include <iostream.h>

void Say(int);

void main(void)
{
  Say(1);
  Say(2);
  Say(3);
}

void Say(int N)
{
  cout << 0 << N;
}
```

How It Works

Instead of four functions **Say_0()**, ... , **Say_3()**, each of which outputs a predetermined number, now only the function **Say()** is used. Any number which is output is an argument of this function. It can output any integer not only 0, 1, 2, 3.

```
   void Say(int);
```

Look at the declaration of the function. Here **int** means that a value of type **int** is an argument of the function.

```
   void Say(int N)
   {
     cout << 0 << N;
   }
```

The definition of this function shows the name of the argument **N** is indicated in parentheses, as well as the type of the argument. In the function body:

```
   cout << 0 << N;
```

Try It Out!

233

the name of the argument is used as a variable. It is already declared as **int** in the function argument declaration.

```
Say(1);
Say(2);
Say(3);
```

You can see how the function **Say()** is used to output the digits 1, 2, 3, as they are handed over to it in turn as arguments. It's clear that, in contrast to the source Program 6.10, Program 6.13 has been made much simpler by using a function argument.

Using Several Arguments

As you saw in the **sqrt()** function example, in C++ you can hand over a variable as a function argument.

Try It Out - Using Several Arguments

Program 6.14 shows how this is done.

```
//   Program 6.14
//   Several arguments
#include <iostream.h>

void Say1(int Number);
void Say2(int N1,int N2);
void Say3(int,int,int);

void main(void)
{
   Say2(1,2);
   Say3(3,4,5);
   Say2(6,7);
}

void Say1(int N)
{
   cout <<N;
}

void Say2(int N1,int N2)
{
   Say1(N1);
   Say1(N2);
}
```

```
void Say3(int N1,int N2,int N3)
{
  cout << N1 << N2 << N3;
}
```

How It Works

The program works the same way as Program 6.9, and outputs:

```
1234567
```

It demonstrates some peculiarities that you'll come across when using function arguments.

```
void Say1(int Number);
void Say2(int N1,int N2);
void Say3(int,int,int);
```

First of all note the difference in the declaration of the function **Say1()**, and the declaration of the function **Say()** in the Program 6.13 - **void Say(int);**

The name **Number** is found nowhere else in Program 6.14. The purpose of a function declaration (or prototype) is to show the compiler the number and type of the function's arguments, and the type of value it returns. Giving argument names is optional, but is encouraged to aid readability; these dummy argument names, if given, have no significance outside the function declaration.

As you will have noticed, **Say2()** has two arguments and **Say3()** has three arguments.

Using The Same Names in Different Functions

Consider the definitions of **Say2()** and **Say3()**. But when you look at these functions, you'll see that the same name **N1** is used in both of these functions. Earlier we told you that there couldn't be any variables with the same names in a program. This isn't completely true. The same names may be used in different argument lists, and refer to different objects as in our example. Later on in the chapter we'll look at using these names in greater detail.

Try It Out - Changing Arguments

In the examples we've looked at so far on the use of function arguments, these arguments didn't change in the function body. We'll now look at an example in which the value of an argument is changed.

```
//   Program 6.15
//   Changing arguments
#include <iostream.h>

void Change(int N);

void main(void)
{
  int i = 1;
  cout << i;
  Change (i);
  cout << i;
}

void Change(int N)
{
  N++;
  cout << N;
}
```

How It Works

As you can see, this program outputs:

121

We'll now look at how it's executed.

```
  int i = 1;
  cout << i;
```

Firstly, the value of the variable **i** which is equal to 1 is output to the screen.

```
  Change (i);
```

The function **Change()** is then called and this value of the variable **i** is passed on to function **Change()** as an argument.

```
void Change(int N)
{
  N++;
  cout << N;
}
```

In the **Change()** function, 1 is added to the resulting value and the result 2 is output.

```
cout << i;
```

Control then returns to **main()** where the value **i** is outputted. It turns out to be equal to 1 as before, in other words, equal to the source value which the variable **i** had before function **Change()** was called, but not equal to the new value 2, acquired by the variable **N**.

It seems that the function **Change()** didn't justify its name and change the value of the variable **i**. This depends on the method used to hand over the parameters, which is illustrated in the following figure.

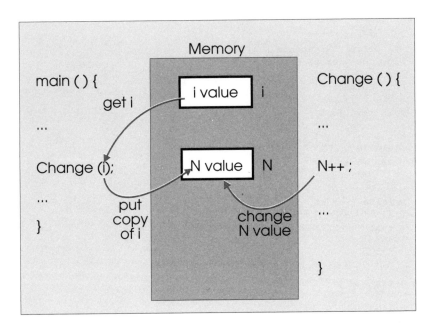

When the function:

```
Change (expression);
```

is called, the **expression** equal to the value of variable **i** is calculated and result is stored in a particular place. Then the value of this expression is copied to another place which is the location of argument **N** of the function **Change()**. All the subsequent changes of **N** result in the value of the copy changing, but not the original value in the variable **i**.

This way of handing over parameters is standard in C++, and applies to any types of arguments being handed over.

Default Arguments

This next program illustrates that you can indicate the default argument values when you define or declare a function.

Try It Out - Using Default Arguments

```
// Program 6.16
// Default arguments
#include <iostream.h>

void Say(int N1 = 1, int N2 = 2);

void main(void)
{              // Output
   Say ();     // 12
   Say (2);    // 22
   Say (3,4);  // 34
}

void Say(int N1, int N2)
{
   cout << N1 << N2 << ' ';
}
```

How It Works

Look at the function prototype:

```
void Say(int N1 = 1, int N2 = 2);
```

The default argument value **N1** is defined as 1, and the argument **N2**, 2.

If the default values are set, when a function is called, a fewer number of parameters can be indicated than are in its definition.

```
Say ();        // 12
```

When no argument is indicated, the default values will be taken. In the next line during a call one argument is indicated:

```
Say (2);       // 22
```

This value is assigned to the first argument and the second is taken by default as 2. Finally:

```
Say (3,4);     // 34
```

both arguments are indicated, and these are substituted for both default values.

Note that there is no method to indicate the value of the second argument explicitly, so that the first assumes the default value. In a declaration of a function you can't set a default value for the left argument until the defaults are set for all the arguments to the right. For example, the declaration:

```
void Say (int n1 = 1, int n2);    // Error
```

is wrong. You'll learn more about default arguments when we discuss the overloading of functions in the next chapter.

Data Communications

Function arguments are used as a data communication mechanism. In this section we'll introduce you to other methods of data communication between the functions, and also to such concepts as local and global data, and the scope of the identifiers.

Private Data

Imagine that in function **main()** the variable **x** is declared but another function **Use_x()** must also use this variable. Does this mean we can use the name **x** in the function **Use_x()** instead of organizing the communication of **x** "by post" via an argument? We will try to do this in Program 6.17 but as you'll see it's unsuccessful and we get an error message.

Try It Out - Using Private Data

Let's look at the program and analyze it.

```
//   Program 6.17
//   Scope demo 1. Program with error !!!
#include <iostream.h>

void Use_x(void);

void main(void)
{
  int x=0;  // Define x
  x++;      // Use
  Use_x ();  // Can't use x in other function
}

void Use_x(void)
{
  cout << x;  // Can't use x from other function
     // Error: x not defined in function Use_x
}
```

```
cout << x;  // Can't use x from other function
```

So why can you use the name **x** in the function **main()** but not in the function **Use_x()**?

How It Works

According to the rules of C++, any variable defined in a block (including a function) can only be used inside this block or, to be more precise, from the location of its definition down to the end of the block, in other words, to the closing brace **}**. This area is called the **scope** of an identifier, the part of a program text in which this identifier can be used. Therefore, the scope of the variable **x** is from where it's declared (the first statement in **main()**) to the closing brace of **main()**. It's as if the variable **x** is the private property of the function **main()**. In C++, such a variable is called a local variable.

In a similar manner, variables declared in the body of a function (not in **main()**) are local to this function and cannot be used in **main()** or any other function.

Try It Out - Using Local Data

This is shown in Program 6.18 where the variable **x** is declared in the function **Def_x()** and can't be used in **main()**.

```
//   Program 6.18
//   Scope demo 2. Program with error !!!
#include <iostream.h>

void Def_x(void);

void main(void)
{
   cout << x;   // Can't use x from other function
                // Error: x not defined in function main ()
}

void Def_x(void)
{
   int  x = 1;  // Define x
}
```

Islands In An Ocean

Functions with their local data are similar to islands in an ocean, inhabited by people who can't get from one island to another. However, in C++ you can communicate between function-islands using what is known as global data.

Try It Out - Using Global Variables

In Program 6.19, **x** is defined as a global variable. This variable is then used in **main()** and in the function **Use_x()**.

```
//   Program 6.19
//   Global variable
#include <iostream.h>

int x;        // Define global variable

void Use_x(void);
```

```
void main(void)
{
  cout << x;    // Use global x
  x = 1;        // Assign global x
  Use_x ();     // Use and change x in other function
  cout << x;    // Output changed value
}

void Use_x(void)
{
  cout << x;    // Use global x
  x++;          // Change global x
}
```

How It Works

We'll take a closer look at how this program works.

```
cout << x;  // Use global x
```

Execution begins with the value of the global variable **x**, which appears to be 0, being output to the screen. You already know that a variable has to be initialized before it's used, but where **x** is defined there is no initializing value, though there can be. However, all global data is initialized to 0 automatically by the compiler.

```
x = 1;    // Assign global x
```

The variable is assigned the value 1.

```
Use_x ();  // Use and change x in other function
```

The function **Use_x()** is then called:

```
void Use_x(void)
{
  cout << x;    // Use global x
  x++;          // Change global x
}
```

and in the function the current value of **x** equals 1 and is output to the screen. The next statement in the function increments **x** which becomes equal to 2 and control then returns to the next statement (after this function call) in **main()**:

```
cout << x;  // Output changed value
```

where the value of **x**, which is now 2, is output again. Therefore, the following sequence of digits is output to the screen:

```
012
```

The only difference between the definition of a global and local variable is the location. The definition of a global variable is placed outside any (in the ocean), whereas the definition of a local variable is located in the body of a function (on an island).

The scope of a global variable is the whole file of a program text (there are some limits but we won't mention them here).

Global or Local Data

This way of exchanging data between functions using a global variable is so simple that you're probably wondering why function arguments and return values are needed at all - surely it would be better to just use global data?

Unfortunately, we can't give you a simple answer to the question. Years of programming have shown that it's better to apply data communications through function arguments and that you should use global variables as seldom as possible. The fact is, you can control the process of data communications through arguments more easily, and so it's easier to detect errors in programs.

The Problem of Overpopulation

We're not talking about the population of the Earth here, but about data that resides in programs. You know that each object in C++ must have a name. Every time you define a new variable, label, function or other object you should give them a name. You should also make sure that the name reflects the nature of the object in some way. The more data there is in a program, the more difficult it is for you to assign them suitable names.

When we used just one function, the function **main()** in our examples, we had to use different names for the variables. However, you can use the same names in different functions which solves the problem of overloading the program with names.

Try It Out - Using Variable Names a Second Time

Program 6.20 shows variable names which are used a second time. Here local variables with the same name **x** are declared in two functions. Analyzing the program's output you'll see that these two variables refer to different objects. The program output is as follows:

```
Main 1
Say  ?
Say  -1
Main 2
Say  ?
Say  -1
Main 3
```

Here, the symbol '?' indicates random values which may vary during the function calls.

```cpp
// Program 6.20
// Using the same name
#include <iostream.h>

void Say(void);
void SaySay(void);

void main()
{
  float x;        // Local variable
  x = 1.;
  cout << "Main " << x << endl;
  Say ();
  x = 2.;
  cout << "Main " << x << endl;
  SaySay ();
  x = 3.;
  cout << "Main " << x << endl;
}

void Say(void)
{
  float x;        // Local automatic variable
  cout << "Say  " << x << endl;
  x = -1.;
  cout << "Say  " << x << endl;
}

void SaySay(void)
{
  Say ();
}
```

How It Works

```
x = 1.;
cout << "Main " << x << endl;
Say ();
```

In this program, the variable **x** in the function **main()** is initialized, and its value 1 is output to the screen. Then the function **Say()** is called.

```
void Say(void)
{
   float  x;      // Local automatic variable
   cout << "Say  " << x << endl;
   x = -1.;
   cout << "Say  " << x << endl;
}
```

We deliberately didn't initialize the variable **x** in the function **Say()**, to show you that the value 1 of the variable **x** from the function **main()** doesn't have any relation to the variable **x** from the function **Say()**. The output produced by the first **cout** statement is garbage. What is actually being output is the value that happened to be in the memory area allocated for the newly defined **x** in function **Say()**.

The variable **x** is then assigned the value -1 which is output to the screen. We did this to check whether this value would be retained during the .repeated call of the function **Say()**.

Variables are Born and Then Die

```
void SaySay(void)
{
   Say ();
}
```

Note that during the second call of the function **Say()** (which is carried out via the function **SaySay()**) the value -1, which was assigned to **x** during the first call, isn't output. Instead, garbage is output again.

So, the value of the variable **x** in the function **Say()** doesn't remain between the two calls. This is a common feature of what are known as automatic local variables. They are created during a function call (memory is allocated for them) and they are destroyed automatically (the allocated memory is freed) when the function terminates. The variable declarations that you've met so far have all been automatic.

Perhaps it seems that local variables are rather ineffective because of the time spent creating and destroying them each time a function is called. However, most processors have a special stack mechanism of memory organization to create and destroy local variables, which means it actually takes less than a dozen cycles of a processor operation.

Immortal Variables

Global variables are created when a program is initiated, and exist until the program exits. In this sense they are immortal. In C++ there is another type of variable which is immortal like a global variable, and is also like a local variable in that it is only visible within the limits of a function. To declare a variable of this type you need to write the keyword **static**, for example:

```
static float x;
```

as is shown in Program 6.21.

Try It Out - Static Storage Class

The following program demonstrates that the value of a variable of static storage class is retained between function calls.

```
//   Program 6.21
//   Static storage class
#include <iostream.h>

void Say(void);
void SaySay(void);

void main(void)
{
  float  x;        // Local variable

  x = 1.;
  cout << "Main " << x << endl;
  Say ();
  x = 2.;
  cout << "Main " << x << endl;
  SaySay ();
  x = 3.;
  cout << "Main " << x << endl;
}
```

```
void Say(void)
{
  static float x;      // Local static variable
  cout << "Say  " << x << endl;
  x += 1.0;
  cout << "Say  " << x << endl;
}

void SaySay(void)
{
  Say ();
}
```

How It Works

The above program differs from Program 6.20 by the inclusion of the word **static** in the function **Say()** and that instead of assigning the value of -1 to the variable **x** in **Say()**, the variable is incremented by **1.0**. It outputs the following:

```
Main 1
Say  0
Say  1
Main 2
Say  1
Say  2
Main 3
```

As you can see, during the first call, **Say()** outputs:

```
Say  0
Say  1
```

The first output 0 is an illustration of the fact that **static** variables, like global ones, are initialized with 0. The next output shows that the function has added 1.0 to this variable. During the subsequent calls, **Say()** outputs:

```
Say  1
Say  2
```

The first 1 is the **x** value which this variable retained after the first call. This shows that a **static** variable isn't destroyed during the breaks between the calls of a function in which it is declared.

A Local Name In a Block

The scope of a local name in C++ can be reduced to a block if the definition of a variable is written inside the block.

Try It Out - Scope for Local Variables

In Program 6.22 the variable **y** is declared inside a block, therefore its use outside the block is restricted.

```
//  Program 6.22
//  Block scope for local variable
#include <iostream.h>

void main(void)
{
  int x =1 ;        // Local in main
  cout << x;
  {
    int x = 2;      // Local in block
    int y = 3;      // Local in block
    cout << x << y;
  }
  cout << x;
}
```

How It Works

The variable **x** is declared twice: outside and inside a block. This is allowed, but remember that the variable **x** declared inside the block is a completely different variable from that outside. The output:

```
1231
```

shows that the value of the variable **x** defined outside the block and initialized with the value 1, remains the same after the block is exited. Note that there is another variable **x** with the value 2 inside the block.

Our introduction far from covers the whole variety of their relationships in C++, but it does lay the foundations for a key concept in C++, classes, which combines data and functions. In the next section we'll look at one more characteristic of an object - an address in a memory location.

Try It Out!

The Address of a Variable

During program execution, each object (for example, a variable or an array) is located in an area of memory. The location of an object in the memory is characterized by something called an address. In C++ there is an address (or referencing) operator, &, which allows you to obtain an object's address.

The value returned by this operator indicates the location of an object in memory. Since a program and its objects are located in the memory by the operating system, the addresses of the objects may be different during repeated executions of the program. Therefore, the value of an address alone is of no interest.

Try It Out - Addresses of Variables

Program 6.23 lets you see an address, because as they say, it's better to see something once than to hear it a hundred times.

```
//  Program 6.23
//  Addresses
#include <iostream.h>
#include <iomanip.h>

void main()
{
  int x;
  int A[3];

  cout << &x << endl << (unsigned long) &x << endl << endl;
  cout << (unsigned long) &A[0]  << endl << (unsigned long) &A[1]
       << endl << (unsigned long) &A[2]  << endl << endl;
  cout << (unsigned long) A << endl;
}
```

How It Works

In this program a variable **x** of type **int**, and an array **A** of three elements of type **int** are defined.

```
cout << &x << endl << (unsigned long) &x << endl << endl;
```

In the first **cout** statement the address of the variable **x**, is obtained by using the address of operator, **&x**, and is then output in hexadecimal form,

```
cout << (unsigned long) &A[0]  << endl << (unsigned long) &A[1]
      << endl << (unsigned long) &A[2]  << endl << endl;
```

and in the next line it is output in decimal form using a type cast (**long**). The same is done for the three elements of the array.

The program output on our computer is as follows:

```
0x29060ffe
688263166

688263160
688263162
688263164

688263160
```

Don't necessarily think that you will get the same output on your computer. You shouldn't attach literal meaning to the output value of an address. It isn't an ordinal number of a byte in the memory, it's only a way to represent an address.

However, look at the group of three numbers in the middle of the output. Reading from top to bottom they are the addresses of the elements of the array **A[0]**, **A[1]**, **A[2]**. Note that each of them differs from the preceding one by 2, which is how it should be. You know that the array elements of type **int** on our computer occupy 2 bytes each, therefore the address of the next element of an **int** array is always 2 greater than the preceding one.

The next figure shows the layout of the elements of the array **A** in the memory and its addresses.

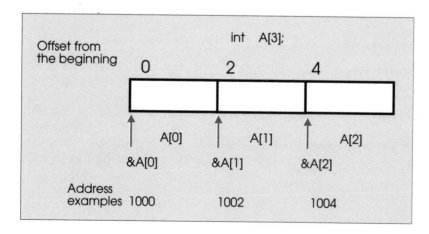

```
cout << (unsigned long) A << endl;
```

In this line of the code, you may be surprised by the fact that there is no **&** symbol before the name **A** of the array, and that the output value looks like an address and coincides exactly with the address of the element **A[0]**.The name of any array without brackets, references the address of the first element in the array.

There is something else worth noting in Program 6.23 which is that the operator **<<** applied to an **int** array, outputs an array address. You'll remember when we looked at Program 5.8 that for an array of type **char**, and only for this type, the action of the **<<** operator is different - it outputs a string of symbols until **'\0'** is encountered.

Obtaining a Value Through an Address

If you know the address of an object it isn't difficult to find out what is in the address. There is a special operator in C++, *****, called the dereference operator. Don't worry that it's the same as the multiplication operator - the compiler will determine from the context, which of these two operators it should use. If there is an address of an object to the right of the ***** operator, in other words:

```
* address
```

then the result of the operation is the value of the object which is at this address.

Try It Out - Using the Dereference Operator *

Program 6.24 demonstrates the use of this operator.

```
//   Program 6.24
//   De-reference operator *
#include <iostream.h>

void main(void)
{                            // Output
  int x = 0;
  cout << (*(&x));           // 0

  int A[3] = {1,2,3};
  cout << (*A)               // 1
       << (*(A+1))           // 2
       << (*(A+2))           // 3
       << (*A+1);            // 2
}
```

Try It Out!

251

How It Works

```
cout << (*(&x));      // 0
```

For example, **&x** designates the address of a variable of **int** type. Then:

```
* ( & x )
```

gives the value of the object of **int** type, which has this address, which in this case is equal to 0. **(*(&x))** is equivalent to writing **x**.

```
cout << (*A)        // 1
```

A is an address of an array of int type. ***A** gives the value of the **int** value that is located at this address, which is the value of the element **A[0]**.

Special Pointer Arithmetic

```
<< (*(A+1))     // 2
```

You may be wondering what:

```
*( A + 1 )
```

means. You don't need to be a great algebra expert to suppose that:

```
A + 1
```

means "add one to address **A**". However, this isn't the case. The statement **A + 1** in this case means "add 2 to address **A**"! This is an example of the special arithmetic for pointers, at which point we have to turn to C++ terminology, and look when the term **pointer** is used instead of the term **address**.

Two is added rather than one, because **A** is a pointer to an object of type **int**, the size of which is 2 bytes.

For an object with a size of N bytes the expression:

```
A + 1
```

means: "add the number N (the size of the object) to the address **A**".

```
<< (*(A+2))     // 3
```

By analogy, `A + 2` means: "add the length of 2 elements", in other words, 4.

To summarize:

`A + N`

simply means the address of the (N+1)-th element (the element with the index N). It should now be clear why the numbers 1, 2, and 3, are output: they are the values of the elements of the `A` array.

Therefore, the expressions, `A[2]` and `*(A + 2)` designate the same thing. You can decide which method suits you better. The following figure shows the relationship between the two.

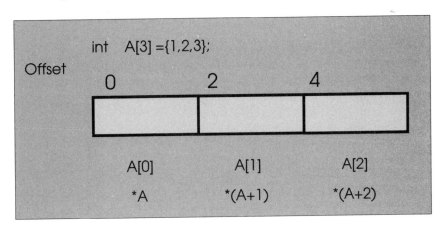

The parentheses in:

`* (A + 1)`

are needed because of the precedence of operations. `*` has a higher precedence than `+`. If you leave out the parentheses:

`* A + 1`

it means something completely different namely:

`(* A) + 1`

What this means is "add 1 to the value at address `A`". The result of this operation will be 2, not 1.

Changing Pointer Values

The pointer is an important variable type in C++. These objects contain the addresses of other objects. An object of pointer type may be defined for any other data type (as well as for pointer objects themselves).

Try It Out - Changing Pointer Values

Program 6.25 shows how an object pointer with the name **pInt** (pointer to integer) is defined.

```
// Program 6.25
// Variable of type pointer
#include <iostream.h>

void main(void)
{
  int *  pInt;                // Pointer to int
  int Int = 0;
  int A[3] = {1,2,3};

                             // Output
  pInt = & Int;
  cout << *pInt;             // 0

  pInt = A;
  cout << *pInt             // 1      *pInt is equivalent to A[0]
       << *(pInt + 1)       // 2      *(pInt + 1) is equivalent to A[1]
       << *(pInt + 2);      // 3      *(pInt + 2) is equivalent to A[2]

  *pInt = 4;
  cout << *A;               // 4
}
```

How It Works

Here the symbol * in the definition isn't the multiplication operator or a dereference operator! It just designates that **pInt** isn't an object of **int** type, but a variable-pointer to the object of **int** type. You can write * in any one of the four following places depending on which you find more convenient:

```
int*  pInt;
int  *pInt;
int *  pInt;
int*pInt;
```

Although we wouldn't exactly recommend the last example, you can still use it.

The variable **pInt** isn't initialized.

Since a pointer that is not initialized could be pointing to any location in the computers memory, trying to use it without initializing it could write values into a random memory location which could cause a serious error or cause the computer to crash.

Since non-initialized pointers present a serious threat to the health of programmers who look for errors in programs, it's initialized with the expression:

```
pInt = & Int;
```

The value assigned is equal to the address of the variable **Int**. in this case it's said that "**pInt** points to variable **Int**".

```
cout << *pInt;        // 0
```

a dereference operator is applied to **pInt** so that the value of the variable can be displayed. i.e. It accesses the value stored in the **Int** variable.

```
pInt = A;
```

In the next statement the value of **pInt** is changed. It now contains the address of the **A** array (in other words it points to the **A** array). The next **<<** operator outputs three array elements similar to those in the preceding program.

```
*pInt = 4;
```

means "assign value 4 to an object to which **pInt** points". However, **pInt** points to **A**, in other words, to the first array element. The next **cout** statement shows that the first array element has changed and is equal to 4.

Using a Pointer as a Function Argument

We'll now create a string copying function using a pointer. To do this we'll modify Program 5.10, to get Program 6.26.

Try It Out - Copying Strings Using Pointers

This program is the result of the modification.

```
//   Program 6.26
//   Copying strings
#include <iostream.h>

void StrCpy(char * To, char * From) ;

void main()
{
  char From [] = "I want to be copied.\n";
  char To [sizeof From] = "I want to get copy.\n";

  cout << From << To;
  StrCpy (To, From);
  cout << "To now contains: " << To;
}

void StrCpy(char * To, char * From)
{
  while ( (*To = *From) != '\0' )
  {
      To++;
      From++;
  }
}
```

How It Works

Here the function **main()** serves to test the function **StrCpy()**. Its arguments are pointers to objects of type **char**. The expression in the **while** loop,

```
*To = *From
```

copies the character, from the address the pointer **From** indicates, to the address to which the pointer **To** indicates.

After copying the '\0' that ends the string, the loop terminates. Both pointers are incremented by 1 in the body of the loop, and this provides the transition to the next element of each symbol array.

Designing a Program

We have almost reached the end of another chapter. Let's go through a final example of some of the topics we have covered.

The Problem

We are going to write a program that will perform certain operations on a string. The operations will be to calculate the length of a string, copy a string, reverse a string, and find the first occurrence of a character in the string.

The Analysis

The steps involved are:

1   Invite the user to input the string.

2   Perform the specified operations on the string.

3   Output the results of the operation.

The Solution

For 1 and 3 you could try the code:

```
cin >> string1;
```

but if you enter the string **This is a test** you will find that the contents of the string would be **This**. What happened to the rest of the string?

The problem is that the extraction operator, **>>**, considers a blank space to be a terminating character. It will read the first word and discard the rest of the string.

To get round this problem we use the following code:

```
cin.get(string1, MAX);
```

As we know what functions we will be using in the program we can set up a skeleton program.

```cpp
//  strings.cpp
//  a program to manipulate strings
#include <iostream.h>      //header file for Input/Output

void main()
{
const int MAX = 81;
int counter;
char string1[MAX], string2[MAX];

//function prototypes
int length(char str[]);
    //function to find length of string
void copy(char * source, char * dest);
    //function to copy string
void reverse(char * str);
    //function to reverse string
int LocateChar(char str[], char ch);
    //function to find first occurrence of a character

cout << "\n\n\tThis program manipulates strings.\n\n"
          << "\tEnter a string with a maximum of 80 characters\n\t";

cin.get(string1, MAX);
    //this function is used to input string
    //cin on its own would stop at first white space

cout << "\n\tYou entered: " << string1 << endl;

cout << "\tThe string is " << length(string1)
     << " characters long\n";

cout << "\tCopying string1 to string2 ... \n";

copy(string1, string2);

cout << "\tstring2 contains: " << string2 << endl;

int result = LocateChar(string1, 'a');
if(result == -1)
   cout << "\tThe character was not found in the string\n";
else
   cout << "\tThe first occurrence of the letter 'a' is element "
        << LocateChar(string1, 'a') << endl;

reverse(string1);
```

```
cout << "\tstring1 has been reversed and now reads ... \n\t"
        << string1;
}

int length(char str[])
{
}

void copy(char * source, char * dest)
{
}

void reverse(char * str)
{
}

int LocateChar(char str[], char ch)
{
}
```

2   We will write functions to perform the various operations.

Length
The following code will find the length of the string:

```
while(str[number] != '\0')
   number++;
```

The condition in the **while** loop looks for the null character which terminates the string. If the null character isn't found the counter is incremented.

Copy
How will you copy the contents of a string to another string? Unfortunately **string2 = string1;**   will not work.

You may well write some code like this:

```
while(*source != '\0')       //dereference operator used to look at value
stored
{                            //at memory address source is a pointer to a
string
  *dest = *source;           //character in source assigned to dest
  dest++;                    //move to next element in string
  source++                   //move to next element in string
}
*dest = '\0';                //insert null character at end of string
```

However, remember that 0 is taken as false and any other value as true. Therefore, ***source != '\0'** is akin with ***source** in the condition of the **while** loop.

Also, the incremental operator **++** can be used as a suffix. Therefore, a better version of the code would be:

```
while(*source)
   *dest++ = *source++;
*dest = '\0';
```

However, the **while** loop statement can be substituted into the condition. As the null character would be copied before the test to end the loop is made, we can omit the last statement in the function. This gives us

```
while(*dest++ = *source++);
```

Locate Character
In this case we will simply step through the string and check whether the character in the string is equal to the character we are looking for. If it is we will report the element number.

Reverse String
This is also a relatively simple operation. We assign the last character in the string we wish to reverse as the first character in our new string. We decrement the index of the original string and increment the index of the new string and assign the character in the original string to the new string. This continues until we reach the end of the string. We than have to add the null character to the new string.

```
while(count2 > -1)
   letter[count1++] = str[count2--];
letter[count1++] = '\0';
```

```
//   strings.cpp
//   a program to manipulate strings

#include <iostream.h>      //header file for Input/Output

void main()
{
  const int MAX = 81;
  int counter;
```

```
    char string1[MAX], string2[MAX];

    //function prototypes
    int length(char str[]);
        //function to find length of string
    void copy(char * source, char * dest);
        //function to copy string
    void reverse(char * str);
        //function to reverse string
    int LocateChar(char str[], char ch);
        //function to find first occurrence of a character

    cout << "\n\n\tThis program manipulates strings.\n\n"
            << "\tEnter a string with a maximum of 80 characters\n\t";

    cin.get(string1, MAX);
        //this function is used to input string
        //cin on its own would stop at first white space

    cout << "\n\tYou entered: " << string1 << endl;

    cout << "\tThe string is " << length(string1)
        << " characters long\n";

    cout << "\tCopying string1 to string2 ... \n";

    copy(string1, string2);

    cout << "\tstring2 contains: " << string2 << endl;

    int result = LocateChar(string1, 'a');
    if(result == -1)
        cout << "\tThe character was not found in the string\n";
    else
        cout << "\tThe first occurrence of the letter 'a' is element "
            << LocateChar(string1, 'a') << endl;

    reverse(string1);

    cout << "\tstring1 has been reversed and now reads ... \n\t"
            << string1;
}

int length(char str[])
{
    int number = 0;          //initialize variable to 0
while(str[number] != '\0')   //look for the null character
    number++;                //if not found increment count
return(number);              //return number of characters
}
```

```
void copy(char * source, char * dest)
{
   while(*dest++ = *source++);
}

void reverse(char * str)
{
   int count1 = 0, count2 = length(str) - 1;
const int SIZE = 81;
char letter[SIZE];            //temporary string

while(count2 > -1)
  letter[count1++] = str[count2--];
                              //assign last letter of str as first of
letter
letter[count1++] = '\0';      //insert null character
copy(letter, str);
                              //copy temporary string to our variable
}

int LocateChar(char str[], char ch)
{
   int number = 0;

while(str[number] != '\0')    //look for null character
{                             //if not found ...
  if(str[number] == ch)       //if character located
    return(number + 1);       //return its position
  else
    number++;

                              //if character not located increment counter
}
return(-1);                   //return -1 to signify character not found
}
```

You can now run the program. Typical output would be:

```
This program manipulates strings.

Enter a string with a maximum of 80 characters
Beginners Guide to C++

You entered: Beginners Guide to C++
The string is 22 characters long
Copying string1 to string2 ...
string2 contains: Beginners Guide to C++
The character was not found in the string
string1 has been reversed and now reads ...
++C ot ediuG srennigeB
```

Summary

We began this chapter looking at some standard functions, and now you can create the analog of a **strcpy()** standard function (the name of a standard function is written in lower-case). This is a significant step forward in your knowledge of C++. In the next chapter we'll continue looking at functions.

CHAPTER 7

Creating Programs Using Functions

In this chapter we'll describe how to use language features in C++ to construct programs made up of separate blocks, a bit like building a house brick by brick. To do this you'll have to acquire the skills and habits of a program architect. We'll show you how to divide programs into functions and how to design a program split into several files.

In this chapter you will:

- Divide a program into functions
- Learn about function overloading
- Split a program into several files
- Use header files to declare functions
- Write a program that analyzes a piece of text you type in

Dividing a Program Into Functions

We'll begin by taking a program consisting of a single function, **main()**, and breaking it up into several functions. If you compare the result with the original program you'll begin to realize why it's advisable to organize your programs in this way.

Try It Out - Using Functions

The following program is a good example. When compiled, the program allows two players to play tic-tac-toe (or noughts and crosses, if you prefer).

```
// Program 7.1
// tic-tac-toe

#include <iostream.h>
#include <conio.h>          //for clrscr();

int player, row, col, winner = 0;
char grid[3][3] = { {' ', ' ', ' '},  //game board 3x3 initialized
                    {' ', ' ', ' '},  //to spaces
                    {' ', ' ', ' '} };

void main()
{
  cout << "\n\n\tWelcome to the game of tic-tac-toe\n"
       << "\tThis is a game for two players and the computer will ask\n"
       << "\tEach player to input their row and column number.\n"
       << "\tThe computer shows whether the game has been won or drawn.\n";

  cout << "\n\n\tPress any key to continue .....";
  getch();                              //pause on screen - wait for key press

  for (int count = 0; count < 9 && winner == 0; count++)
  {
    clrscr();                           //clear screen

    cout << endl << endl             //display grid
         << "\t " << grid[0][0] << " | " << grid[0][1] << " | " << grid[0][2]
         << " \n" << "\t-----------\n"
         << "\t " << grid[1][0] << " | " << grid[1][1] << " | " << grid[1][2]
         << " \n" << "\t-----------\n"
         << "\t " << grid[2][0] << " | " << grid[2][1] << " | " << grid[2][2]
         << " \n" << endl << endl;

    player = (count % 2) + 1;           //determine player

    do
    {
```

Try It Out!

```cpp
  do                               //check row within limits
  {
    cout << "\n\nPlayer " << player << " please enter row number: ";
    cin >> row;
  }while(row < 0 || row > 3);

  row -= 1;                        //-1 from row, to use as array index

  do
  {
    cout << "Player " << player << " please enter column number: ";
    cin >> col;
  }while(col < 0 || col > 3);   //check col within limits

  col -= 1;                        //-1 from col, to use as array index

  if(grid[row][col] == 'X' || grid[row][col] == 'O') //see if position is
    cout << "\nThis space is occupied.  Try again."; //   occupied

}while(grid[row][col] == 'X' || grid[row][col] == 'O');
  //repeat loop if space occupied

grid[row][col] = (player == 1) ? 'X' : 'O';      //assign character to array
  for (int line = 0; line < 3; line++)          //check for win
  {
    if(grid[line][0] == 'X' &&  grid[line][1] == 'X' && grid[line][2] == 'X')
      winner = player;
    if(grid[line][0] == 'O' &&  grid[line][1] == 'O' && grid[line][2] == 'O')
      winner = player;
    if(grid[0][line] == 'X' &&  grid[1][line] == 'X' && grid[2][line] == 'X')
      winner = player;
    if(grid[0][line] == 'O' &&  grid[1][line] == 'O' && grid[2][line] == 'O')
      winner = player;
  }
  if(grid[0][0] == 'X' && grid[1][1] == 'X' && grid[2][2] == 'X')
    winner = player;
  if(grid[0][0] == 'O' && grid[1][1] == 'O' && grid[2][2] == 'O')
    winner = player;
  if(grid[0][2] == 'X' && grid[1][1] == 'X' && grid[2][0] == 'X')
    winner = player;
  if(grid[0][2] == 'O' && grid[1][1] == 'O' && grid[2][0] == 'O')
    winner = player;
}
clrscr();                                      //clear screen
cout << endl << endl                            //redisplay grid
    << "\t " << grid[0][0] << " | " << grid[0][1] << " | "
    << grid[0][2] << " \n"
    << "\t-----------\n"
    << "\t " << grid[1][0] << " | " << grid[1][1] << " | "
    << grid[1][2] << " \n"
    << "\t-----------\n"
```

```
        << "\t " << grid[2][0] << " | " << grid[2][1] << " | "
        << grid[2][2] << " \n" << endl << endl;

  if(winner == 0)                                 //make announcement
    cout << "\n\nThe game is a draw";
  else
    cout << "\n\nPlayer " << player << " is the winner\n\n";
}
```

How It Works

Tic-tac-toe is played on a square grid which has three rows and three columns. The two players take it in turns to enter either Xs or 0s into the grid. The player that manages to get their three symbols in a line wins.

You will almost certainly have played the game and will know what's needed.

Initially, we need a way to get the players to take turns and this is achieved by the use of a **for** loop. As there are only a maximum of nine moves, the loop variable is initialized to 0 and continues while the loop variable is less than 9. To decide whether player one or player two is to play we can check the loop. If it's an odd number, its player one's turn, if it's even, it's player two's. The modulus operator allows us to check this by showing the remainder when the counter is divided by two.

```
player = (count % 2) + 1;
```

We need to store the moves that each player makes. As the game is played on a square grid, an array seems an obvious choice.

```
char grid[3][3] = { {' ', ' ', ' '}, //game board 3x3 initialized
                    {' ', ' ', ' '}, //to spaces
                    {' ', ' ', ' '} };
```

A **char** array has been selected as this enables us to initialize it to contain spaces and we can subsequently store 0s or Xs. Don't let the syntax worry you. **grid** is a two-dimensional array which C++ treats as being a one-dimensional array where every element is itself an array. You can initialize a one-dimensional array with syntax like:

```
char array[3] = {'A', 'B', 'C'};
```

Therefore, to initialize a two-dimensional array we can use syntax like:

```
char array[3][2] ={ {'A', 'B', 'C'},
                    {'D', 'E', 'F'} }
```

As you can see, this is simply an array of arrays.

The grid is displayed with the following **cout** statement:

```
cout << endl << endl
    << "\t " << grid[0][0] << " | " << grid[0][1] << " | "
    << grid[0][2] << " \n"
    << "\t----------\n"
    << "\t " << grid[1][0] << " | " << grid[1][1] << " | "
    << grid[1][2] << " \n"
    << "\t----------\n"
    << "\t " << grid[2][0] << " | " << grid[2][1] << " | "
    << grid[2][2] << " \n" << endl << endl;
```

The program asks the players to specify the row number and the column number and these integers are used to access the desired element of the array. A check is made to see if the move can be made. It compares the requested move to what is stored in the array to check that the space isn't already occupied. You will see that a **do while** loop has been used to check that the correct entries are made. If a number outside the range is entered the loop repeats and the user is asked to enter details again.

Read through the source code to gain an understanding of what is happening.

Creating Functions

How do you decide what functions to create? First of all, you look for parts of the text in the program that are repeated. You will see that the code used to display the grid is repeated.

```
clrscr();
cout << endl << endl
    << "\t " << grid[0][0] << " | " << grid[0][1] << " | "
    << grid[0][2] << " \n"
    << "\t----------\n"
    << "\t " << grid[1][0] << " | " << grid[1][1] << " | "
    << grid[1][2] << " \n"
    << "\t----------\n"
    << "\t " << grid[2][0] << " | " << grid[2][1] << " | "
    << grid[2][2] << " \n"
    << endl << endl;
```

This pair of statements clear the screen and then display the grid. We can now make a function and will call it **showGameBoard()**. This function is shown below:

```
void showGameBoard()
{
  clrscr();

  cout << endl << endl
     << "\t " << grid[0][0] << " | " << grid[0][1] << " | "
     << grid[0][2] << " \n"
     << "\t----------\n"
     << "\t " << grid[1][0] << " | " << grid[1][1] << " | "
     << grid[1][2] << " \n"
     << "\t----------\n"
     << "\t " << grid[2][0] << " | " << grid[2][1] << " | "
     << grid[2][2] << " \n" << endl << endl;
}
```

As you can see, the function doesn't have any arguments and doesn't return a value.

Choosing function names is very important. If they reflect the action they perform then it makes the program text easier to understand. If, instead of the name **showGameBoard()**, we had called it **FunctionNo1** there would be little indication of the purpose of the function. Names should be unique and they shouldn't coincide with the names of functions in any standard library your program uses. Otherwise, you'll have problems making the executable file and the linker we'll report a fatal error. But you don't have to check the vast lists of standard functions each time you write your own - begin your function's name with any upper-case letter and you're guaranteed it won't duplicate any of the standard functions names which are all in lower-case. Users of Turbo C++ or Borland C++ can use the help facility to check that the name of the function doesn't correspond with a built in or library function.

Don't begin names with the underscore symbol (_). C++ often uses this style for its internal identifiers.

Try It Out - Making the Program Easier to Read

To make the program easier to read, it was decided to create the functions **checkForWin()** and **welcome()**. These are shown in the revised program listing.

```
// Program 7.2
// tic-tac-toe

#include <iostream.h>
#include <conio.h>          //for clrscr();

int player, row, col, winner = 0;
char grid[3][3] = { {' ', ' ', ' '}, //game board 3x3 initialized
                    {' ', ' ', ' '}, //to spaces
                    {' ', ' ', ' '} };

void welcome();
void showGameBoard();
void checkForWin();

void main()
{
  welcome();

  for (int count = 0; count < 9 && winner == 0; count++)
  {
    showGameBoard();                 //display grid
    player = (count % 2) + 1;        //select player 1 or 2

    do
    {
      do              //player enters row number - note error checks
      {
        cout << "\n\nPlayer " << player << " please enter row number: ";
        cin >> row;
      }while(row < 0 || row > 3);

      row -= 1;

      do              //player enters column number - note error checks
      {
        cout << "Player " << player << " please enter column number: ";
        cin >> col;
      }while(col < 0 || col > 3);

      col -= 1;

      if(grid[row][col] == 'X' || grid[row][col] == '0')  //check if space
        cout << "\nThis space is occupied.  Try again.";   //occupied
```

```
     }while(grid[row][col] == 'X' || grid[row][col] == 'O');

     grid[row][col] = (player == 1) ? 'X' : 'O';

     checkForWin();                      //check if player has won
  }                                      // loop continues until
                                         // nine moves or a win

  showGameBoard();                                 // After game completed
  if(winner == 0)                                  // show final board and
     cout << "\n\nThe game is a draw";                              //
announce win or lose
  else
     cout << "\n\nPlayer " << player << " is the winner\n\n";
}

void welcome()
{ /* Simple function to display welcome message and instructions */

  cout << "\n\n\tWelcome to the game of tic-tac-toe\n"
       << "\tThis is a game for two players and the computer will ask\n"
       << "\tEach player to input their row and column number.\n"
       << "\tThe computer shows whether the game has been won or drawn.\n";

     cout << "\n\n\tPress any key to continue .....";
     getch();
}

void showGameBoard()
{ /* This function clears screen and draws revised grid to screen */
  clrscr();

  cout << endl << endl
       << "\t " << grid[0][0] << " | " << grid[0][1] << " | "
       << grid[0][2] << " \n"
       << "\t-----------\n"
       << "\t " << grid[1][0] << " | " << grid[1][1] << " | "
       << grid[1][2] << " \n"
       << "\t-----------\n"
       << "\t " << grid[2][0] << " | " << grid[2][1] << " | "
       << grid[2][2] << " \n" << endl << endl;
}

void checkForWin()
{ /* This function checks for a win by comparing lines, rows, and
     diagonals for three of the same symbols */

  for (int line = 0; line < 3; line++)
  {
```

```
    if(grid[line][0] == 'X' &&  grid[line][1] == 'X' && grid[line][2] == 'X')
       winner = player;
    if(grid[line][0] == 'O' &&  grid[line][1] == 'O' && grid[line][2] == 'O')
       winner = player;
    if(grid[0][line] == 'X' &&  grid[1][line] == 'X' && grid[2][line] == 'X')
       winner = player;
    if(grid[0][line] == 'O' &&  grid[1][line] == 'O' && grid[2][line] == 'O')
       winner = player;
  }
  if(grid[0][0] == 'X' && grid[1][1] == 'X' && grid[2][2] == 'X')
    winner = player;
  if(grid[0][0] == 'O' && grid[1][1] == 'O' && grid[2][2] == 'O')
    winner = player;
  if(grid[0][2] == 'X' && grid[1][1] == 'X' && grid[2][0] == 'X')
    winner = player;
  if(grid[0][2] == 'O' && grid[1][1] == 'O' && grid[2][0] == 'O')
    winner = player;
}
```

Summing up

Now we've discussed the program and the functions, we'll consider the function **main()**   again. You can see that the program algorithm has become clearer due to the choice of function names and encapsulation of details inside the functions. The very fact that the program has become easier to read and understand now it is split into separate functions, makes the trouble worthwhile. But there is another important advantage which is that the code is now easier to modify.

Commenting Functions

An important element of a function is a comment that describes its purpose and algorithm. In the functions in this program there is an example (but not a model) of such a comment. A comment describes the action performed by the function and what it returns. If there were any arguments they should be described here too. We are using /* and */ as comment delimiters. These separators can enclose any number of lines of comments. Alternatively, you can use the normal C++ comment symbol //.

We should also mention that it is important to comment code within the body of the function to describe what it is doing.

Commercial programmers spend a fair bit of time documenting each and every function that they use in their programs.

Something like this is common:

```
/*
Purpose:  sums up column and produces standard deviation.

Input:   (float) Values        - a 2d array of float values
         (int)   Lastrow       - Highest row number
         (int)   Lastcol       - Highest column number

Returns:  The standard deviation (float)

Last Modified Record:
Date         Modifier   Reason
12/08/93     dhb           Fixed division by zero bud
13/08/93     dhb           Fixed calculation error introduced in previous bug fix
*/
```

Functions With the Same Names

From the previous chapter you know that C++ allows variables in one program to have the same names but designate different objects. Local variables defined in one block (as well as in a function body) must have different names, but those defined in different blocks or functions may have identical names. The scope of a local variable is the block in which it is defined.

Global variables defined outside a function body must all have different names. Function names are referred to as global names. They may be used anywhere in a file below their declaration or definition. You would think that function names must always be unique, but this isn't so.

Function Arguments and Function Overloading

C++ allows you to have functions with the same names in a file but only provided that all functions with identical names have different lists of arguments. This is quite a natural solution to the problem of resolving things named identically. If a dozen Smith families live in a town, then people begin to distinguish them by other additional features, for example, by where they live (near the river or the forest) or by their professions. The same applies to functions with identical names: in order to distinguish between them C++ uses additional features - **function arguments**. This practice is called **function overloading**.

Try It Out - Function Overloading

Function overloading is demonstrated in Program 7.3. Two functions with the same name **Say()** but with a different number of arguments are used.

```
//   Program 7.3
//   Two Say() overloaded functions
#include <iostream.h>

void  Say  (int N1);
void  Say  (int N1, int N2);

void main ()
{
  Say (1);
  Say (2,3);
}

void  Say (int N1)
{
  cout << N1;
}

void  Say (int N1, int N2)
{
  Say (N1);
  Say (N2);
}
```

Although in this example program the advantages of the replacement aren't so obvious, one thing is indisputable. Instead of two names there is only one. The advantages of function overloading become more evident in large programs and libraries containing hundreds of functions.

Try It Out - Function Overloading With Different Argument Types

The following example in Program 7.4 shows that even when the number of arguments is equal, the C++ compiler differentiates between the functions with the same names, if the argument types are different.

```
//   Program 7.4
//   One Say() says a lot
#include <iostream.h>

void  Say  (void) ;
void  Say  (char C) ;
void  Say  (int  I) ;
```

```
void  Say  (unsigned int U);
void  Say  (long L) ;
void  Say  (float F) ;
void  Say  (double D) ;
void  Say  (long double LD) ;
void  Say  (char * S) ;

void main ()
{  //  Testing Say() overloading functions

                      // Output
  Say ();        //   void
  Say ('0');     // 0 char
  Say (1);       // 1 int
  Say (2U);      // 2  unsigned int
  Say (3L);      // 3  long
  Say (4.F);     // 4  float
  Say (5.);      // 5  double
  Say (6.L);     // 6  long double
  Say ("7");     // 7  string
}

void  Say  (void)
{
  cout <<' '<< " void\n" ;
}

void  Say  (char C)
{
  cout << C << " char\n" ;
}

void  Say  (int  I)
{
  cout << I << " int\n" ;
}

void  Say  (unsigned int U)
{
cout << U << " unsigned int\n" ;
}

void  Say  (long L)
{
  cout << L << " long\n"    ;
}

void  Say  (float F)
{
  cout << F << " float\n" ;
}
```

```
void  Say  (double D)
{
  cout << D << " double\n"  ;
}

void  Say  (long double LD)
{
  cout << LD << " long double\n"  ;
}

void  Say  (char * S)
{
  cout << S << " string\n"  ;
}
```

How It Works

Let's go through the program and see how it works.

A Family of Functions

In the last program there are 9 functions with the same name. Each of them outputs the value of an argument using the operator <<, then outputs a test message to show which particular function is called. The output of this program is as follows:

```
    void
0 char
1 int
2 unsigned int
3 long ·
4 float
5 double
6 long double
7 string
```

Each of the overloaded functions is called in the function **main()**.

```
Say ();  //    void
```

In this line **Say()** is called without parameters. From the text displayed on the screen you can figure out that the function defined as:

```
void  Say  (void)
{
  cout <<' '<< " void\n"  ;
}
```

is called. To call each **Say()** we use a constant of the appropriate type.

Remember that constants with a decimal point (for example, 5.) are of type **double**.

Try writing a program with two functions that have the same names and sets of arguments (identical in number and type), but different types of returned values. You'll see that the compiler doesn't allow functions to differ only by the type of returned value.

A Program in Multiple Files

So far we've only dealt with programs each of which was in a single file. In this section we'll see how to write a program that is split into several files. And there are certain reasons why we might want to do this. One of them is that this allows several programmers to carry out a project as a team, each creating his own part of the program in a separate file (or files). Then all the files are compiled and linked to produce one complete program. This is the way large programs are written - huge commercial programs are developed by the collective efforts of groups of creative individuals.

Exit Into the Outer World

You can compare a program that resides in one file to a house. - the functions in the program are like rooms inside. A locked house is a closed world. We'll open the doors and make our way into the world outside!

Try It Out - Joining Files

We'll use two programs to do this - Programs 7.5a and 7.5b. We have added the letters a and b to emphasize the fact that they are actually one program split into two files, which you will need to enter as two separate files.

```
//   Program 7.5a
//   File 1. Joining files
#include <iostream.h>

void  External_function ();  // Declaration

void main ()
{
  cout << "File 1. Main calls External_function\n";

  External_function ();
}
```

```
// Program 7.5b
// File 2. Joining files
#include <iostream.h>

void External_function ()      // Definition
{
  cout << "File 2. External_function is speaking\n";
}
```

How It Works

We'll begin with Program 7.5a. It may surprise you that it contains only the declaration of `External_function()`, but not its definition. We've chosen this name to show that the definition is somewhere outside the file in which the function is used.

If you look at Program 7.5b, you'll see that the definition of `External_function()` is there, in other words in another file.

Compiling Two Files

How can we compile two functions and link them into one executable program? This depends upon the programming system you're using. For example, the BCC compiler from a Borland C++ package will compile and link the files `P07_05A.CPP` and `P07_05B.CPP` using the single command

```
BCC -P P07_05A.CPP P07_05B.CPP
```

The resulting executable program receives the name `P07_05A.EXE`, in other words, from the first file. In order to assign another name to the executable file, for example, `P07_05`, you have to add option `-e` (executable file name) to the command line:

```
BCC -P -eP07_05 P07_05   A.CPP P07_05B.CPP
```

To do the same under UNIX you have to run the compiler `CC` with the following command line:

```
CC P07_05A.CPP P07_05B.CPP
```

If you are using the Borland C++ integrated development environment (**IDE**), you should first create a project by selecting the Project option in the main menu, and list the files in it.

Then you press *F9*, and the executable program is compiled. Its name will be the same as the name of the project file.

Linking Files

The conversion of source code files into an executable program, which we called compilation for simplicity, is in fact done in two steps. The first one is compilation itself, and the second is called linking. We discussed this in Chapter 1 and it is described in the next figure.

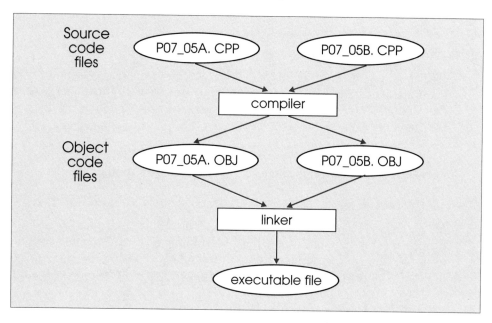

The first stage of the process is performed by the compiler. It creates an intermediate file, which is called an object file. In DOS, object files have the extension **.OBJ**. They are only needed to make an executable file and may be deleted afterwards.

For the second stage another program called a linker takes over and links object files together to create an executable file. Usually compilers call this program automatically, therefore there's no need to know its name and command line parameters. However, if you want to, you may tell the compiler to perform compilation only and not call the linker.

With the BCC compiler, for example, the option **-c** (compile) is used for this purpose. Using the command:

```
BCC -P -c P07_05A.CPP
```

the compiler will create the object file **P07_05A.OBJ** and stop at this point. Similarly, you may create the object file for the second part of the program with the command:

```
BCC -P -c P07_05B.CPP
```

Then, you can link these two object files using the command:

```
BCC -P P07_05A.OBJ P07_05B.OBJ
```

into the executable program **P07_05A.EXE**.

Separate compilation often saves you time. If you put corrections or modifications into one single source file, all you have to do is compile this one and link it with the other unmodified **.OBJ** files into the **.EXE**. There's no need to waste time compiling the whole bundle of source files over again.

Calling External Functions

Having compiled Programs 7.5a and 7.5b run the resulting program and you'll see the following two messages on the screen:

```
File 1. Main calls External_function
File 2. External_function is speaking
```

And now we'll see how it works. Its execution begins, as ever in C++, with the function **main()** in Program 7.5a, which contains the two executable lines:

```
cout << "File 1. Main calls External_function\n";
External_function ();
```

The first line outputs the message

```
File 1. Main calls External_function
```

and the second calls the **External_function()** that resides in Program 7.5b, in the second file. This function outputs the message:

```
File 2. External_function is speaking
```

After this control is returned to **main()** where the program terminates.

Imagine that initially you had the program in one file and it looked like this:

```cpp
#include <iostream.h>

void External_function () ;

void main ()
{
  cout << "File 1. Main calls External_function\n";
  External_function ();
}

void External_function ()
{
  cout << "File 2. External_function is speaking\n";
}
```

Then imagine it was divided into two parts and split into two files. As you can see, stepping out into the outside world is very easy in C++. All we needed to do was to move the definition of **External_function()** from one file into another, and not a single correction more.

Therefore, to conclude we can say that calling an external function, the definition of which is outside the current file, doesn't differ at all from calling a function located in the same file. As always, the declaration of an external function must precede the place where it's used.

Dividing a Program Into Files

It is also possible in C++ to divide programs into separate parts. Keeping different functions in different files is not only easy, but also practicable.

Try It Out - Dividing a Program Into Files

We'll divide the tic-tac-toe program into two parts so you can put them in two files. You can see the result in Program 7.6a and in Program 7.6b.

```cpp
// Program 7.6a
// tic-tac-toe

int player, row, col, winner = 0;
char grid[3][3] = { {' ', ' ', ' '}, //game board 3x3 initialized
                    {' ', ' ', ' '}, //to spaces
                    {' ', ' ', ' '} };

void welcome();
void showGameBoard(char g[3][3]);
```

```
void enter_move(char g[3][3], int p);
void checkForWin(char g[3][3], int& w, int p);
void display_result(int w, char g[3][3]);

 void main()
 {
  welcome();

   for (int count = 0; count < 9 && winner == 0; count++)
   {
     showGameBoard(grid);          //display grid
     player = (count % 2) + 1;     //select player 1 or 2

     enter_move(grid, player);
     checkForWin(grid, winner, player);   //check if player has won
   }                                      // loop continues until
                                          // nine moves or a win
   display_result(winner, grid);
 }



// Program 7.6b
// File 2 Functions for tic-tac-toe

#include <iostream.h>
#include <conio.h>          //for clrscr();

  void welcome()
  { /* Simple function to display welcome message and instructions */

  cout << "\n\n\tWelcome to the game of tic-tac-toe\n"
       << "\tThis is a game for two players and the computer will ask\n"
       << "\tEach player to input their row and column number.\n"
       << "\tThe computer shows whether the game has been won or drawn.\n";

     cout << "\n\n\tPress any key to continue ..... ";
     getch();
  }

  void showGameBoard(char g[3][3])
  { /* This function clears screen and draws revised grid to screen */
    clrscr();

    cout << endl << endl
         << "\t " << g[0][0] << " | " << g[0][1] << " | "
         << g[0][2] << " \n"
         << "\t-----------\n"
         << "\t " << g[1][0] << " | " << g[1][1] << " | "
         << g[1][2] << " \n"
         << "\t-----------\n"
         << "\t " << g[2][0] << " | " << g[2][1] << " | "
         << g[2][2] << " \n" << endl << endl;
```

```
}

void enter_move(char g[3][3], int p)
{
   int row;
   int col;

   do
   {
    do                    //player enters row number - note error checks
    {
      cout << "\n\nPlayer " << p << " please enter row number: ";
      cin >> row;
    }while(row < 0 || row > 3);

    row -= 1;

    do                    // player enters column number - note error checks
    {
      cout << "Player " << p << " please enter column number: ";
      cin >> col;
    }while(col < 0 || col > 3);

    col -= 1;

    if(g[row][col] == 'X' || g[row][col] == 'O')         //check if space
      cout << "\nThis space is occupied.  Try again.";   //occupied

   }while(g[row][col] == 'X' || g[row][col] == 'O');

   g[row][col] = (p == 1) ? 'X' : 'O';
}

void checkForWin(char g[3][3], int &w, int p)
{ /* This function checks for a win by comparing lines, rows, and
   diagonals for three of the same symbols - note this function as been
   modified slightly.  There is no need to check if both players have won
   after each move.  We now only check if the current player has won    */

   if (p == 1)
   {
   for (int line = 0; line < 3; line++)
   {
     if(g[line][0] == 'X' &&  g[line][1] == 'X' && g[line][2] == 'X')
       w = p;
     if(g[0][line] == 'X' &&  g[1][line] == 'X' && g[2][line] == 'X')
       w = p;
   }
   if(g[0][0] == 'X' && g[1][1] == 'X' && g[2][2] == 'X')
     w = p;
   if(g[0][2] == 'X' && g[1][1] == 'X' && g[2][0] == 'X')
     w = p;
   }
   else
```

```
  {
    for (int line = 0; line < 3; line++)
    {
      if(g[line][0] == 'O' &&  g[line][1] == 'O' && g[line][2] == 'O')
        w = p;
      if(g[0][line] == 'O' &&  g[1][line] == 'O' && g[2][line] == 'O')
        w = p;
    }
    if(g[0][0] == 'O' && g[1][1] == 'O' && g[2][2] == 'O')
      w = p;
    if(g[0][2] == 'O' && g[1][1] == 'O' && g[2][0] == 'O')
      w = p;
  }
}

void display_result(int w, char g[3][3])
{
  showGameBoard(g);                           // After game completed
  if(w == 0)                                  // show final board and
    cout << "\n\nThe game is a draw";         // announce win or lose
  else
    cout << "\n\nPlayer " << w << " is the winner\n\n";
}
```

Program 7.6a contains the function **main()**, and all the other functions are contained in the second file, Program 7.6b. The declarations of all the functions are left in the first file. We don't need the declarations in the second file. This file is like a function storehouse from which **main()** takes functions when necessary.

We have extracted another two functions out of **main()**. These are called **enter_move()** and **display_result()**. At last **main()** has acquired a compact form which demonstrates the principal elements of the algorithm:

       welcome   (displays welcome message and usage)

In the **for** loop, which continues for 9 moves or until there is a winner:

       showGameBoard   (shows state of play after last move)

       select player

       enter_move   (enter move and store in array)

       checkForWin   (checks to see if a winner)

       display_result   (displays final grid and announces whether the game was a win or a draw)

There's one more thing to note. There aren't any preprocessor directives, I/O operators, or functions from a standard library in Program 7.6a. They are only required in Program 7.6b.

We have had to make a few changes to the existing functions.

`welcome()`	No changes were made
`showGameBoard()`	So that this function has access to the array, we have to pass the array to the function as an argument.
`enter_move()`	Again we have had to pass the array as an argument together with `player`.
`checkForWin()`	This function is discussed below.

```
void checkForWin(char g[3][3], int &w, int p)
```

You will notice that the argument list contains `int &w`. This is known as passing an argument to a function by reference; it enables the value of the argument to be changed by the function, and is explained in Chapter 9.

We have also altered this function because there is no need to check if both players have won after each move. We now only check if the current player has won.

By dividing the program into two parts in different files we gain the following general advantages:

- Two different programmers could work on the program independently.

- If you make corrections in one part, you don't have to recompile the other, so you save time.

- You can use the second part (b) without any changes when writing other programs that use the same functions.

Try It Out - A Function Here, a Function There

The next program, composed of three files (Program 7.7a, Program 7.7b, and Program 7.7c) shows that you are completely free to place functions in as many files as you want and call them from any file you need.

```
//   Program 7.7a
//   File 1. Program in three files
#include <iostream.h>

void  FunctionInFile2();  // Declaration
void  FunctionInFile3();  // Declaration

void main ()
{
  cout << 1;
  FunctionInFile2();
}

void  FunctionInFile1()
{
  FunctionInFile3();
}
```

```
//   Program 7.7b
//   File 2. Program in three files
#include <iostream.h>

void  FunctionInFile1();  // Declaration

void  FunctionInFile2()
{
  cout << 2;
  FunctionInFile1();
}
```

```
//   Program 7.7c
//   File 3. Program in three files
#include <iostream.h>

void  FunctionInFile1();  // Declaration
void  FunctionInFile2();  // Declaration
void  FunctionInFile3();  // Declaration

void  FunctionInFile3()
{
  cout << 3;
}
```

Try It Out!

287

To compile the whole program you have to mention all the partial files in the compiler command line (or in a project file), for example, in this case:

```
BCC -P P07_07A.CPP P07_07B.CPP P07_07C.CPP
```

The resulting program outputs:

```
123
```

How It Works

Now we'll see how this output is produced.

```
void main ()
{
  cout << 1;
  FunctionInFile2();
}
```

First the function **main()** in the first file (Program 7.7a) outputs "1" onto the screen and calls **FunctionInFile2()**, which is in the second file.

```
void  FunctionInFile2()
{
  cout << 2;
  FunctionInFile1();
}
```

This function in Program 7.7b outputs "2" and calls **FunctionInFile1()**, located in the first file, which in turn calls the **FunctionInFile3()** from the third file. This function outputs the last digit, "3". After this, control is passed back through the chain of functions (like a bubble coming up through the water) and the program terminates.

The Problem with Function Declarations

Now we'll consider the function declarations in each part of the program. In Program 7.7a the functions **FunctionInFile2()** and **FunctionInFile3()** are called, which is why the declarations of these two functions are placed here. In Program 7.7b only **FunctionInFile1()** is called and so only the declaration of this function is present.

You may be thinking that there aren't any calls to external functions in Program 7.7c, so what are those three declarations doing there. You are right, they aren't needed. We put them there only to show that they don't hinder the compiler - it simply ignores them. It's also just to give you an idea about where to declare functions in large programs.

While a program consists of just a few lines it's not at all difficult to see what functions it calls, and write the appropriate declarations. But what if the program files contain hundreds of lines and call dozens of functions?

Fortunately C++ provides a simple solution to this problem. This was demonstrated in Program 7.7c where you can write the declarations of all functions from all the files in every file. The compiler will ignore declarations of functions that aren't used in the current file. But this solution also has a negative side. Each file will begin with the same list of declarations. If you need to include a new function or change the name or arguments of a function then you have to make changes in all the files. Not only is this approach time-wasting, it's fraught with errors.

Using Header Files to Declare Functions

The aim of the following program is to show how the preprocessor directive **#include** is used to solve the problem of interactive function declarations. This program (see Program 7.8a, Program 7.8b, and Program 7.8c) is nearly identical to the previous one. We've changed the function names: **F1()** instead of **FunctionInFile1()** and so on. This was a minor change just to make the names shorter. The major one is that instead of the function declarations we now see the directive

```
#include "P07-08.h"
```

This directive to the preprocessor means "insert the contents of the file "**P07-08.H** here". The extension **.H** stands for header, because headers with functions declarations are always included at the beginning of program files.

Try It Out - Using Header Files to Declare Functions

Our header contains the following:

```
//  P07-08.h
//  Header file with all function declarations
#include <iostream.h>

void F1();
void F2();
void F3();
```

When you key in this program, be sure to name this file correctly, otherwise the include operation will fail.

Try It Out!

How It Works

As you can see, file **P07-08.H** contains the standard directive

```
#include <iostream.h>
```

and the "omitted" declarations of all three functions used in Programs
7.8abc, which, by the way, produces the same output as our previous one:

123

```
//  Program 7.8a
//  File 1. Program in three files with header
#include "P07-08.h"

void main()
{
  cout << 1; F2();
}

void  F1()
{
  F3 ();
}
```

```
//  Program 7.8b
//  File 2. Program in three files with header
#include "P07_08.h"

void  F2()
{
  cout << 2;
  F1();
}
```

```
//  Program 7.8c
//  File 3. Program in three files with header
#include "P07_08.h"

void  F3()
{
  cout << 3;
}
```

Try modifying Program 7.8abc to trace calls to the functions and the return
of control. For example, for **F1()**:

```
void F1()
{
  cout << "Entry file 1";
  F3();
  cout << "Exit  file 1";
}
```

and so on with the other functions.

In the Public View

The way a function can be called from other files constituting a program is both simple and convenient. Each function is always at hand or in the public view, so to speak. In this sense a function is something like a global variable (see Program 6.19) - your program can access it, and all modifications in its body can be done within the limits of a single file.

In C++, external linkage allows functions to be visible from other files. But it has a negative aspect, too. No two function definitions can be the same within one program or its files, apart from overloaded functions.

Try It Out - Errors Produced By Duplicate Function Definitions

In Program 7.9, consisting of two parts (Program 7.9a and Program 7.9b) there is an error. The function **Any_function()** is defined in program 7.9a, and again in Program 7.9b, but with a different body.

The linker can't decide which of the two functions should be called in Program 7.9a. Therefore, an error occurs when the program is compiled and the **.EXE** file is not created.

```
//  Program 7.9a
//  File 1. Error: duplicate definition of Any_function
#include <iostream.h>

void  Any_function();      // Declaration
void  Any_function()       // Definition
{
  cout << 1;
}

void main()
{
  Any_function();
}
```

```
// Program 7.9b
// File 2. Error: dublicate definition of Any_function
#include <iostream.h>

void  Any_function();      // Declaration
void  Any_function()       // Definition
{
   cout << 2;
}
```

Static Functions

External linkage of functions requires strict matching of function specifications (names, number and types of arguments) when people work together on a program. But you may want to write some functions that are purely local to your program file. It would be very inconvenient if you had to keep their names unique because of possible confusion with programs with the same name in another file. Luckily, there's no need to do this since C++ can make a function invisible to other files. You just have to declare a function as **static** (you already know this keyword):

```
static type function-name (arg-list);
```

Try It Out - Using Static Functions

The following two files (Programs 7.10a and 7.10b) contain an example of using **static** functions.

```
// Program 7.10a
// File 1. Static function
#include <iostream.h>

static  void  StaticFunction();
extern  void  ExternFunction();

extern  int  main()
{
   cout << "File 1. Main function  calls ExternFunction\n";

   ExternFunction();

   cout << "File 1. Main function  calls StaticFunction\n";

   StaticFunction();

   return 0;
}
```

```
static void StaticFunction()
{
  cout << "File 1. StaticFunction is speaking\n";
}
```

```
//  Program 7.10b
//  File 2. Static function with the same name
#include <iostream.h>

static void StaticFunction();
extern void ExternFunction();

extern void ExternFunction()
{
  cout << "File 2. ExternFunction is speaking\n";

  cout << "File 2. ExternFunction calls StaticFunction\n";

  StaticFunction();
}

static void StaticFunction()
{
  cout << "File 2. StaticFunction is speaking\n";
}
```

The output of this program speaks for itself:

```
File 1. Main function  calls ExternFunction
File 2. ExternFunction is speaking
File 2. ExternFunction calls StaticFunction
File 2. StaticFunction is speaking
File 1. Main function  calls StaticFunction
File 1. StaticFunction is speaking
```

How It Works

Both files have a function, **StaticFunction()**, with the same declaration:

```
static void StaticFunction();
```

And yet, unlike the previous program (7.9abc), this one can be compiled and executed.

```
static void StaticFunction()
{
  cout << "File 2. StaticFunction is speaking\n";
}
```

The keyword **static** makes **StaticFunction()** in Program 7.10b invisible from the outside, for example to Program 7.10a.

```
StaticFunction();
```

In Program 7.10a the compiler doesn't hesitate over which of the two **StaticFunction()** to call here. In this context it "sees" only the **StaticFunction()** which is defined in the lines:

```
static void StaticFunction()
{
  cout << "File 1. StaticFunction is speaking\n";
}
```

in the file.

```
StaticFunction();
```

The same applies to the call to **StaticFunction()** in Program 7.10b. Here the **StaticFunction()** defined in the lines:

```
static void StaticFunction()
{
  cout << "File 2. StaticFunction is speaking\n";
}
```

of the second file is invoked.

So declaring a function as **static** makes it visible only within the limits of the file where it's defined. It can be said that these functions are **encapsulated** into your file. This gives you more freedom to name internal functions the way you like. They are only used in your files, in your personal part of the project. You don't have to worry about what your partners will say - they won't even know that these functions exist, as they can only use those functions that you leave visible to other files.

External Specifier

```
extern void ExternFunction();
```

In this line of Program 7.10a there is a keyword **extern**, which you don't know yet, and which is applied to the declaration of **ExternalFunction()**.

You can also see it in the definition of **main()**:

```
extern  int  main()
{
```

and in the definition of **ExternalFunction()** in Program 7.10b:

```
extern  void  ExternFunction()
{
```

This keyword didn't appear before in a similar context in Program 7.5a, so what's the difference? Well, there's no actual difference. The word **extern** may be discarded from the declaration of a function and nothing will change: the function will be linked as external anyway, in other words if the linkage type is not specified explicitly as **extern** or **static**, then **extern** is assumed by default. This is the reason why **extern** is usually omitted in function declarations.

Try removing the keyword **static** from the declaration and the definition of one or both **StaticFunction()**, and you'll see that the compilation will be aborted by an error.

You can experiment and see what happens if you remove the word **static** from only the declaration or from only the definition of a function. The result may depend upon the compiler type, but in any case the declaration must match the definition.

Try It Out - Testing the Static Specifier

You can see in Programs 7.11a and 7.11b which follow, that the specifier **static** really does make functions **SF1()** and **SF2()** "invisible". Correct the error by discarding the word **static** and the functions will become visible.

```
//  Program 7.11a
//  File 1. Error: undefined name SF2
#include <iostream.h>

static  void  SF1();    // Defined here
static  void  SF2();    // Defined elsewhere
void  EF();     // Defined elsewhere

void main()
{
  SF1();
  EF();
  SF2();      // Error: undefined symbol SF2
}
```

Try It Out!

```
static void SF1()
{
  cout << 1;
}



// Program 7.11b
// File 2. Error: undefined name SF1
#include <iostream.h>

static void SF1();  // Defined elsewhere
static void SF2();  // Defined here
void EF();       // Defined here

static void SF2()
{
  cout << 2;
}


void EF()
{
  SF2();
  cout << 3;
  SF1();      // Error: undefined symbol SF1
}
```

Using External Data

Just like functions, data can be made visible from outside the file using the specifier **extern**.

Try It Out - Using External Data

In Program 7.12a a global array of characters, **ExternalData[]**, is defined and initialized with a literal string:

```
extern char ExternalData [] = "array is defined in file 2\n";
```

This is the definition of the array. A memory block equal to the size of the string plus 1 byte is allocated for it. Note that Program 7.12b doesn't contain any functions.

In Program 7.12a there's the declaration

```
extern char ExternalData [];
```

It isn't initialized, which indicates that it's a declaration but not a definition. Its size isn't indicated either.

The output of the program

```
ExternalData array is defined in file 2
```

shows that the function **main()** in the first file has access to the data located in the second file.

```
//   Program 7.12a
//   File 1. External data
#include <iostream.h>

extern  char  ExternalData [];

void main()
{
  cout << "ExternalData " << ExternalData;
}
```

```
//   Program 7.12b
//   File 2. External data

extern  char  ExternalData [] = "array is defined in file 2\n";
```

In our discussion on global variables we mentioned that using them is not considered good programming style. The same applies to external data to an even greater extent. The correct way is to exchange data between functions through their arguments, though it may seem less convenient. Nevertheless, external data is sometimes useful so we'll discuss briefly some aspects of its usage.

Declaring and Defining External Data

To use external functions you must declare them. The same applies to external data. You know the difference between the definition of a function and its declaration: the definition contains the function body in braces, for example:

```
    void FunctionDefinition ()
  {
    ...
  }
```

A function declaration doesn't have a body, for example:

```
    void FunctionDeclaration ();
```

Try It Out - Declaring and Defining External Data

We can explain this better by looking at some examples.

```
//    Program 7.13a
//    File 1. External data declarations and definitions
#include <iostream.h>

extern    int  V2;
extern    const  int  C2;

void  ExternalFunction ();

int  V1 = 1;
extern const int  C1 = 1;

void main()
{                               // Output
  cout << C1 << C2 << endl;      // 12
  cout << V1 << V2 << endl;      // 12

  V1 = 3; V2 = 4;
  ExternalFunction();
  cout << V1 << V2 << endl;       // 56
}
```

```
//    Program 7.13b
//    File 2. External data declarations and definitions
#include <iostream.h>

extern    int  V1;
extern    const  int  C1;

void  ExternalFunction();

int  V2 = 2;
extern const  int  C2 = 2;

void  ExternalFunction()
{                               // Output
  cout << C1 << C2 << endl;      // 12
  cout << V1 << V2 << endl;       // 34

  V1 = 5; V2 = 6;
}
```

We'll now take a look at the data definitions. In Program 7.13a, a variable **v1** and a constant **c1** are defined. They are assigned the value 1. In the same way **v2** and **c2** initialized with the value 2 are defined in Program 7.13b.

The program outputs the following:

```
12
12
12
34
56
```

This shows that external constants and variables may be freely used in each file regardless of where they are defined. For example, variables **v1** and **v2** are assigned values 3 and 4 in the first file:

```
V1 = 3; V2 = 4;
```

then **ExternalFunction()** located in the second file is called and outputs these modified values of **v1** and **v2**:

```
cout << V1 << V2 << endl;       // 34
```

Similarly, in Program 7.13b **v1** and **v2** assume values 5 and 6:

```
V1 = 5; V2 = 6;
```

which are then output in Program 7.13a:

```
cout << V1 << V2 << endl;       // 56
```

Hiding Data in a File

When you need global data to be inaccessible from another file, for example, to avoid conflicts between variables with the same names, you can use the keyword **static**.

The rules of default for external and **static** data are not so simple as those for functions. That's why it's always better to write these specifiers explicitly in declarations or definitions of data.

Designing a Program

It is now time to look at the end of chapter program for this chapter to see how we can put what we have learnt into practice.

The Problem

The problem we have to solve is to write a program that can analyze text entered via the keyboard. The program will count the number of letters in each word and the number of words in each sentence. Some simple statistics can then be calculated.

The Analysis

The steps involved are:

1   Invite the user to enter the text.

2   Count the number of letters in each word and the words in each sentence.

3   Calculate the statistics.

4   Display the results to the screen.

The Solution

1   Unfortunately, we can't use **cin** to input the string as this will skip the embedded white space. We will input the string a character at a time to enable us to increment the appropriate counters depending on what has been entered by the user. We can use the following code

```
cin.get(character);
```

2   We next count the number of letters in each word and the number of words in each sentence.

While the terminating character has not been entered, we can check to see if the character is a letter and if a letter has been entered we will increment the counter.

```
  while(character != '*')
  {
    if(isalpha(character))
      letters++;
    else
    {
      if(letters > 20)
        letters = 20;
      length[letters]++;
      letters = 0;
    }
```

We use the function **isalpha()** to check whether a letter has been entered. If a letter hasn't been input then we increment the appropriate element of the array.

If the previous character was a letter and the current character is not a letter, then we know that we have reached the end of a word and can increment the counter.

```
if((isalpha(previous_character)) && (!isalpha(character)))
  words++;
```

If the current character is a full stop, an exclamation mark, a question mark, or the terminating character we know we have come to the end of a sentence and can increment the appropriate element in the array.

```
if(character == '.' || character == '!' || character == '?'
       || character == '*')
  {
    if(words > 20)
      words = 20;
    no_of_words[words]++;
    words = 0;
    sentences++;
  }
```

3   We can now perform the calculations, and then:

4   display the results on the screen.

```
// textanal.cpp
// a program to analyze the number of letters in words
// and words in sentences

#include <iostream.h>    //header file for I/O
#include <conio.h>       //header file for getch()
#include <ctype.h>       //header file for isalpha()
```

```
void main()
{
  void analyze(void);
  char answer = 'N';

    clrscr();           //clear the screen

    cout << "\n\t\t ANALYZING TEXT ENTERED VIA THE KEYBOARD \n"
         << "\t\t ************************************** \n\n"
         << "\n\tThis program analyzes text entered via the keyboard"
         << "\n\tand reports on the number of letters in words and the"
         << "\n\tnumber of words in a sentence.\n\n";

    do            //this loop repeats, and allows the user to analyze more
    {             //   text, until the user does not enter Y or y
      analyze();  //calls analyze function

                  //ask user if they want another go
      cout << "\n\tDo you want to analyze some more text? (Y/N) ";
      cin >> answer;              //users response

    } while(answer == 'Y' || answer == 'y');//repeat loop if Y or y entered
}

void analyze()                     //function to analyse text
{
//function prototype - this function displays the results
void results(int l[], int n[], int s);

char character = ' ';             //character being analyzed
char previous_character = ' '; //previous character analyzed
int letters = 0, i;
int words = 0, sentences = 0;
int length[21];
int no_of_words[21];

    for(i = 0; i <= 20; i++)    //initialize arrays
    {
      length[i] = 0;
      no_of_words[i] = 0;
    }

    cout << "\n\tPlease enter your text which should be terminated"
         << "\n\tby leaving a space and then typing *.\n\n";

  cin.get(character);            //get first character

  while(character != '*')        //repeat loop until * entered
    {
      if(isalpha(character))     //is character a letter
        letters++;               //  if so increase count
      else                       //  if not
```

```
    {
        if(letters > 20)        //   if letters greater than 20
          letters = 20; //  assign letters value 20 (for display and array)
        length[letters]++; // increment element corresponding to length
        letters = 0;        //   re-initialize variable
    }

    //if previous character a letter and currenet one isn't ...
    if((isalpha(previous_character)) && (!isalpha(character)))
        words++;               // ... increment word

    if(character == '.' || character == '!' || character == '?'
                   || character == '*')
    {//if character terminates a sentence, i.e. . ! ? or *
        if(words > 20)        //if words greater than 20
          words = 20;         // assign words value 20 (for display and array)
        no_of_words[words]++; //  ++ element corresponding to no of words
        words = 0;            //  re-initialize variable
        sentences++;          //  increment count of sentences
    }
    previous_character = character;
    cin.get(character);          //get new character
                                 //loop will repeat unless * entered
  }

    clrscr();                          //clear screen

    results(length, no_of_words, sentences);   //display results
}


void results(int length[], int no_of_words[], int sentences)
{
  int i;
  float total = 0.0, total1 = 0.0, mean = 0.0;

    cout << "Number of Characters" << "\t"
         << "Number of Words \n";

    for(i = 1; i <=20; i++)
      cout << i << "\t\t\t\t" << length[i] << endl;

    cout << "\n\t Press any key to continue ... ";
    getch();     //wait until a key is pressed

    clrscr();

    cout << "Number of words in sentence"
         << "\t Number of occurrences \n";

    for(i = 1; i <= 20; i++)
      cout << i << "\t\t\t\t\t" << no_of_words[i] << endl;

    cout << "\n\t Press any key to continue ... ";
```

```
    getch();    //waits until a key is pressed

    clrscr();

    cout << "The total number of sentences processed was : "
        << sentences << endl;

  for(i = 1; i <= 20; i++)
    {
      total  += length[i];
      total1 += (i * length[i]);
    }

  mean = total1 / total;

    cout << "\n\nThe average word size is " << mean << " letters."
        << "\n\nThe total number of words is " << total << "."
        << "\n\n\tPress any key to continue ... ";
    getch();
}
```

We can now try the program.

```
        ANALYZING TEXT ENTERED VIA THE KEYBOARD
        ****************************************


    This program analyzes text entered via the keyboard
    and reports on the number of letters in words and the
    number of words in a sentence.


    Please enter your text which should be terminated
    by leaving a space and then typing *.

  This book is called The Beginners Guide to C++.
The author of the book is Oleg Yaroshenko.
The book is published by Wrox Press.  Wrox
Press publish several books that will be of use
to people interested in computer programming.

  This program demonstrates the use of user-defined
functions in computer programming. *



Number of Characters Number of Words
1                    1
2                    12
3                    7
4                    11
5                    4
6                    3
```

7	4
8	2
9	3
10	2
11	2
12	1
13	0
14	0
15	0
16	0
17	0
18	0
19	0
20	0

    Press any key to continue ...

Number of words in sentence	Number of occurrences
1	0
2	0
3	0
4	0
5	0
6	0
7	1
8	1
9	1
10	0
11	0
12	1
13	0
14	0
15	0
16	1
17	0
18	0
19	0
20	0

    Press any key to continue ...

The total number of sentences processed was : 5

The average word size is 4.865385 letters.

The total number of words is 52.

    Press any key to continue ...
Do you want to analyze some more text? (Y/N) N

Summary

In this chapter we discussed the means and methods to write programs that consist of many functions and files. These methods are inherent to all the C++ languages and programming systems. You will have to use and master these methods to write any software of significant complexity.

CHAPTER 8

Using Disks

Up until now, we have only used data located in the random access memory (RAM) for all the programs. This data only exists while the program is being executed and disappears when the program finishes.

In this chapter you'll learn how to work with data stored on a disk in the form of a file. This data is kept when the program has been executed as well as after the computer has been switched off. You'll also familiarize yourself with data streams and ANSI C++ standard library functions used to operate with files.

In this chapter you will:

> Look at data streams

> Read from and write to disk files

> Look at text files and binary files

> Learn how to use file pointers

> Write a program that prints your files

Data Streams

We'll begin with the idea of the "data stream" in C++. This concept is directly related to files on disk. A stream is an abstract term referring to any flow of data from a source to a destination. In fact, you have already used streams in your first program: the terms **cout** and **cin** are the names of two standard streams of C++: the Console **OUT**put stream and the Console **IN**put stream. As you can see, a stream in C++ is an object type, and **cin** and **cout** are objects of the type stream.

For a **cout** stream, program objects (such as variables or constants) are the sources of data, and the console, in other words, the computer screen, is the destination. For a **cin** stream, a console (in this case, the computer keyboard) is the source of data, and program objects (variables) are the destination. Of course, the real source of data in this case is the program user entering data from the keyboard.

Try It Out - Using Stream I/O

In the next program, characters from the input stream **cin** are sent into the output stream **cout**. As the saying goes, in one ear and out the other...

```
//   Program 8.1
//   Stream I/O. In one ear... Quit with $
#include <iostream.h>

void main ()
{
  cerr << "\nConsole Input/Output demo\n\n"
          "Input text then press Enter "
          "to send it to input stream\n"
          "You'll get an echo string from the output stream\n"
          "You may press Enter and try again\n"
          "Enter a dollar sign $ to quit the program\n";

  char  Char = '!';
  while (Char != '$')
  {
     cin  >> Char;          // In one ear
     cout << Char;          // Out the other
  }
}
```

The output from the program looks like this:

```
Console Input/Output demo

Input text then press Enter to send it to the input stream
You'll get an echo string from the output stream
You may press Enter and try again
Enter a dollar sign $ to quit the program
123
123
$
```

How It Works

Having initialized it you'll receive a message on screen. After this you can input characters from the keyboard and they will be displayed on the screen. As you already know, it's the operator "get from" or extractor (>>) that operates here. It extracts the next character from an input stream (the keyboard) and displays it on screen. The operator >> finishes its operation when *Enter* is pressed. For example, input the string:

```
123
```

and press *Enter*. On the screen you'll see:

```
123
123_
```

and the cursor will be where the underscore character is here.

```
cerr << "\nConsole Input/Output demo\n\n"
        "Input text then press Enter "
        "to send it to input stream\n"
        "You'll get an echo string from the output stream\n"
        "You may press Enter and try again\n"
        "Enter a dollar sign $ to quit the program\n";
```

This uses another standard stream, called **cerr**, which stands for Console **ERR**or stream. This is another object, identical to a **cout** stream, but with another name.

How Does the >> Operator Work?

The previous result looks very strange. After all, why are the input characters "123" displayed twice? From the lines:

```
while (Char != '$')
{
    cin >> Char;          // In one ear
    cout << Char;         // Out the other
}
```

you might expect a different result. If the statement:

```
cin >> Char;
```

only inputs a character, and:

```
cout << Char;
```

displays it, then the string "123" should appear only once! However, this is not some great riddle. This is simply the way the operator >> is implemented. Until the *Enter* key is pressed, the operator >> continues to input and display characters. This is where the first screen copy of the string "123" comes from. However, the variable **Char** can store only one character, so where does the operator "get from" input them to? As it happens the operator >> inputs characters, displays them and then temporarily stores them in a separate memory area called a buffer. This buffer is an integral part of a **cin** object.

```
cin >> Char;      // In one ear
```

Only after you press *Enter* does the above statement terminate its operation. Meanwhile, the cursor is moved to the beginning of the next line on the screen, and the first character from the buffer is extracted into the variable **Char**.

```
cout << Char;     // Out the other
```

Now the "put to" operator (insertion), <<, starts operating. It outputs the value **Char** (the first character input into the buffer) at the beginning of the next line and then finishes its operation. The loop is then repeated, and the statement:

```
cin >> Char;
```

only extracts the next character from the buffer (without displaying it), storing it in **Char** and terminating its operation. The **<<** operator then outputs again, and so on. Only when all characters from the buffer are extracted and the end of the buffer is reached, will the operator **>>** wait for input from the keyboard again.

You can check on the availability of the **cin** buffer and even find out its size, if you keep keying characters without pressing *Enter*. Sooner or later, depending on the implementation, the input will cease. This signifies that the buffer is full.

How to Get Out of a Stream

To get out of this vortex of two streams, just as in life, you need money, or, more precisely in this case, its sign. Input the dollar sign, $, and press *Enter*. The condition:

```
Char != '$'
```

will interrupt the loop and the program will end.

Blank Spaces are Ignored

You will see another feature of the operator **>>** when executing Program 8.1 if you input blank spaces between the characters. For example:

```
123     456  $
```

In this case the output of the program will be:

```
123     456  $
123456$
```

As you can see, there are blank spaces in the upper string, but none in the lower one. This is the because of the operator **>>** (not the operator **<<**). The extraction operator ignores blanks, tabs, newline characters and other non-displayable characters when extracting them from the stream.

Redirecting Console Input

It is possible to redirect console input in DOS and UNIX. For our program, assuming our source file is **P08_01.CPP**, we can do this as follows:

```
P08_01 < P08_01.CPP
```

The symbol < (redirection) means that the program will get its input data, not from the keyboard, but from the file **P08_01.CPP**. This is the source code for the program if you have named the source file appropriately. In other words, standard console input is redirected to the file. Input this command and you'll see on screen (with the prompt, of course):

```
//Program8.1//StreamI/O.Inoneear...Quitwith$
```

This is just a part of the source code file **P08_01.CPP** from where it begins, to the **$** sign. It's clear that all the blank spaces have disappeared (including the newline), which is why the code isn't as easy to recognize.

The second thing worth mentioning is the absence of line repetition on the screen. If the standard input is redirected from a file then the operator **>>** doesn't display the characters as it does with keyboard input, it just extracts them.

Extracting Whitespace Characters

The following program shows how to control the operation of the operator **>>**, making it extract whitespace characters in the same way as it extracts all the ordinary characters.

Try It Out - Extracting Whitespace Characters

This is done using the code:

```
cin.unsetf (ios::skipws);  // Not to skip whitespace
```

This calls the function **cin.unsetf()** (unset flag), which, as you may have guessed from the name itself, resets the flag designated **ios::skipws**. If this flag is not reset, then the operator **>>** omits whitespace characters.

```
//   Program 8.2
//   Extracting whitespace. Using input redirection <
#include <iostream.h>

void main()
{
  cerr << "\nConsole Input redirection\n\n"
          "Usage with redirection:\n\n"
          "  P08-02 < P08-02.CPP\n\n"
          "Use for redirection ONLY file P08-02.CPP !!!\a\n\n"
          "Usage without redirection:\n"
```

```
            "   Input text then press Enter\n"
            "   You'll get an echo string\n"
            "   You may try again\n"
            "   Enter a dollar sign to quit the program\n";

   char  Char = '!';
   cin.unsetf (ios::skipws);     // Not to skip whitespace
   while (Char != 36)            // 36 - ASCII code for dollar sign
   {
     cin  >> Char;               // Get from stream
     cout << Char;               // Put to   stream
   }
 }                               // ! Don't delete this line ! EOF$
```

How It Works

You see unusual characters in the name of the function (a period) and in the name of the flag (two colon characters). Accept this for the present as it is. We will discuss this later.

By executing the program, you'll find out that blank spaces are no longer ignored and the result of inputting the string "123 456" is:

```
123 456
123 456
_
```

The underscore here, as before, shows where the cursor is, and also indicates that the newline character (one of the whitespace characters) is not ignored by the operator >> either.

Where is the End of File?

Assuming your source file is **P08_02.CPP**, when you redirect the input using the command:

```
P08_02 < P08_02.CPP
```

the contents of the file **P08_02.CPP** is displayed on the screen.

```
 }                              // ! Don't delete this line ! EOF$
```

You can see that we put a **$** sign at the end of the program, since it represents a loop termination flag.

```
     while (Char != 36)       // 36 - ASCII code for dollar sign
```

In the **while** loop condition instead of the **$** sign, we put its ASCII code, 36. If we hadn't, the program would be output only up to this point.

```
     while (Char != 36)       // 36 - ASCII code for dollar sign
     {
       cin  >> Char;          // Get from stream
       cout << Char;          // Put to   stream
     }
```

If the **$** sign is discarded from the program, then the loop will be repeated endlessly. It can be interrupted by pressing *Ctrl-C*, but this is really a rescue facility in case of emergency.

The problem lies in the fact that a stream of characters has an end. When it reaches the end of the file, the operator **>>** stops extracting characters and placing them in the variable **Char**. However, it doesn't automatically transfer control out of the program loop. The loop is continued, and the operator **<<** continues to output the same character from **Char**.

Reading Text Files

To find out where the end of the file is, you have to call a special function, **cin.eof()**.

Try It Out - Reading Text Files

Look at the following program.

```
//   Program 8.3
//   Reading text file. Using eof () and ^Z
#include <iostream.h>

void main()
{
  cerr << "\nText file typing:\n\n"
          "To type any text file:\n\n"
          "  P08_03 < any_text_file\n\n"
          "Don't type executable file\n\n"
          "Without redirection use ^Z to stop console input:\n"
          "  Input text then press Enter\n"
          "  You'll get an echo string\n"
          "  You may try again\n"
          "  Enter ^Z (Ctrl/Z) to exit\n\n";
```

```
char  Char = '!';
cin.unsetf (ios::skipws);      // Not to skip whitespace
while (1)
{
   cin  >> Char;               // Get from stream
   if (cin.eof())
      break;                   // Exit on End Of File
   cout << Char;               // Put to    stream
}
}                              // End of file is here ->
```

How It Works

```
if (cin.eof())
   break;
```

The function **cin.eof()** normally returns 0, but doesn't return 0 if the end of the file is reached. Using this function allows you to interrupt the loop and exit the program when the end of the file is detected.

Now you have a working program which allows you to display on screen the information contained in files at the command:

```
P08_03 < name_of_a_file
```

In DOS and UNIX, you can use the **MORE** command to present the output of a long file one full screen at a time. For example:

```
P08_03 < P08_03.CPP | MORE
```

End of File Control Character

In the last program we solved the problem of how to get out of a loop with the help of the end-of-file. Now we are faced with a new problem - how to quit the loop when input is from the keyboard, but not from the file. You can solve this problem by inputting a special control character with the code 26. To do this, press *Ctrl* and *Z* at the same time. This is usually written as *Ctrl-Z*, or *^Z* (this last notation is what is displayed on screen). Start the program and input:

```
123
```

then press *Ctrl-Z* and *Enter*. You'll get

```
123^Z
123
```

and the program will be terminated. You will find that ^Z serves as an end-of-input indicator wherever it is encountered, even within a file. So use this program only for text files which contain no control characters, except for `'\t'`, `'\n'`, `'\r'`, `'\f'` (the last character, "form feed", is to control the printer - it feeds a sheet of paper).

A C++ program is an example of a text file. The same program in executable form is an example of a binary file. Bear in mind that text documents written on many word processors are in fact recorded not as text files but as binary files. Program 8.3 won't display binary files.

Creating Text Files

Now you are ready to create or copy a text file.

Try It Out - Creating Text Files

This next program does this. It is similar to Program 8.3 with additions for processing of output and input errors. Enter the source text with the file name **P08_04.CPP**.

```
// Program 8.4
// Writing text files
#include <iostream.h>

void main ()
{
  cerr << "\nText file creating and copying:\n\n"
         " Be careful !!!\a\n"
         " Existing file will be erased\n\n"
       "To create file:\n\n"
         " P08_04 > file_name\n\n"
         " Input text strings ending with Enter\n"
         " Enter ^Z (Ctrl/Z) to exit\n\n"
       "To copy any text file:\n\n"
         " P08_04 < any_text_file > new_file_name\n";

  char  Char = '!';
  cin.unsetf (ios::skipws);        // Not to skip whitespace
  while (1)
  {
    cin >> Char;                   // Get from stream
    if (cin.eof ())
        break;                     // Exit on End Of File
    if (cin.bad ())
    {
```

```
            cerr << "Input error\n";
            break;                    // Exit on error
    }
    cout << Char;                     // Put to stream
    if (cout.bad())
    {
        cerr << "Output error\n";
        break;                        // Exit on error
    }
}
}
```

When executed, the program outputs the message:

```
Text file creating and copying:

 Be careful !!!
 Existing file will be erased

To create file:

 P08_04 > file_name

 Input text strings ending with Enter
 Enter ^Z (Ctrl/Z) to exit

To copy any text file:

 P08_04 < any_text_file > new_file_name
```

How It Works

This program gives a warning about the danger of destroying the current file, if in the command:

```
 P08_04 > file_name
```

file_name refers to an existing file. Using this command, you can create a text file with the name you require by entering the required lines of text, and terminating them by pressing *Enter*. You can use the *BkSp* key to discard any characters entered erroneously in a line up until you press *Enter*.

Getting Out of Sticky Situations

When data is input from or output to a disk, you can get error situations independent of the program. For example, when creating a file on disk, you may find that the disk has filled up. As you saw in the above program:

```
if (cout.bad())
{
        cerr << "Output error\n";
        break;
}
```

Here the function **cout.bad()** is called, and returns a non-zero value if an error has been detected, and 0 otherwise.

```
if (cin.bad())
{
    cerr << "Input error\n";
    break;        // Exit on error
}
```

A similar function **cin.bad()** is used to test the **cin** stream.

Copying Text Files

You can copy text files using Program 8.4, redirecting both console input and output streams. For example, the command:

```
P08_04  <  FILE_1.TXT  >  FILE_2.TXT
```

copies **FILE_1.TXT** to the file called **FILE_2.TXT**. However, you must remember that the existing **FILE_2.TXT** file will be erased without warning.

Processing Text Files

Now that you know how to perform input and output operations for text files, you can apply this knowledge to write a program that performs text processing.

Try It Out - Processing Text Files

The next program is designed to process C++ source code files. It counts the total number of characters in a file, and also separately counts the number of strings, whitespace characters, and the approximate number of statements and comments.

```
// Program 8.5
// Processing text files: counting characters
#include <iostream.h>

//   Global data
// Numbers of chars in stream
long BlankTabs,   // Blank + Tab
  NewLines,       // NewLine
  Semicolons,     // ;
  Slashes,        // /
  Others;         // All other chars

//   Function declarations
void  SayAboutUsage (void);
void  Count     (char Char);
int   Err_or_EOF (void);
void  SayAboutChars (void);

void main ()
{
  char  Char = '!';

  SayAboutUsage ();

  cin.unsetf (ios::skipws);    // Not to skip whitespace
  while (1)
  {
      cin >> Char;             // Get from stream
      if (Err_or_EOF ())
          break;               // Exit on error or EOF
      Count (Char);            // Count chars
  }
  SayAboutChars ();
}

void SayAboutUsage(void)
{
  cerr << "\nCounting characters:\n\n"
          "File input:\n\n"
          "  P08_05 < any_text_file\n\n"
          "Console input:\n"
          "  Input text strings ending with Enter\n"
          "  Enter ^Z (Ctrl/Z) to exit\n";
}

int Err_or_EOF(void)
{//this function returns non-zero if an error is detected
 //or if the end-of-file is detected.

  int status = 0;
```

```
    if( cin.eof() )
      status = -1;
    else
        if ( cin.bad() )
      {
            cerr << "Input error\n";
            status = -2;
        }
    return status;
}

void Count(char Char)
{
  switch (Char)
  {
      case ' ' :
      case '\t':
        BlankTabs++;
        break;
      case '\n':
        NewLines++;
        break;
      case ';' :
        Semicolons++;
        break;
      case '/' :
        Slashes++;
        break;
      default  :
        Others++;
  }
}

void SayAboutChars(void)
{
  long Whitespaces = 2 * NewLines + BlankTabs;
  /* Every pair of chars
     Carriage Return and Line Feed
     is translated by >> into one
  */
  long Comments = Slashes/2;  // Not too precise
  long Total = Whitespaces + Semicolons + Slashes + Others;

  cout << "\nFile has:\n\n" << " Total characters " << Total
       << endl << "  Lines            " << NewLines << endl
       << "  Whitespaces      " << Whitespaces << endl
       << "  Statements       " << Semicolons  << endl
       << "  Comments         " << Comments  << endl;
}
// EOF
```

How It Works

Look at the text of the function **main()**, which contains the main loop for processing characters. The function **SayAboutUsage()** outputs a message about program usage. The testing of an input stream state is performed in a separate function **Err_or_EOF()**, which returns non-zero if there is an error or an end-of-file detected, and 0 otherwise.

The function **Count()** counts characters. The current character is transferred to it as an argument. Lastly, after exiting the loop, the function **SayAboutChars()** outputs the results of processing to the screen.

```
long  BlankTabs,   // Blank + Tab
   NewLines,       // NewLine
   Semicolons,     // ;
   Slashes,        // /
   Others;         // All other chars
```

The global variables defined in the above lines are used to transfer information. The function **Count()** computes the values of these variables and the function **SayAboutChars()** uses them.

```
void Count(char Char)
{
  switch (Char)
  {
    case ' ' :
    case '\t':
      BlankTabs++;
      break;
    case '\n':
      NewLines++;
      break;
    case ';' :
      Semicolons++;
      break;
    case '/' :
      Slashes++;
      break;
    default  :
      Others++;
  }
}
```

Notice how the function **Count()** operates. It receives the current character as the argument **Char**, and, depending upon the value of this variable, adds 1 to the appropriate counter. It is handy in these conditions to use a **switch** statement, rather than a series of **if** statements. Here, character constants serve as constant expressions in **case** labels. Note that the two labels:

```
case ' ' :
case '\t':
```

apply to one statement:

```
BlankTabs++;
```

Now look at how the results of counts are displayed in the function **SayAboutChars()**.

```
void SayAboutChars(void)
{
  long Whitespaces = 2 * NewLines + BlankTabs;
    /* Every pair of chars
      Carriage Return and Line Feed
      is translated by >> into one
  */
  long Comments = Slashes/2;  // Not too precise
  long Total = Whitespaces + Semicolons + Slashes + Others;

  cout << "\nFile has:\n\n" << " Total characters " << Total
       << endl << "  Lines          " << NewLines << endl
       << "  Whitespaces    " << Whitespaces << endl
       << "  Statements     " << Semicolons  << endl
       << "  Comments       " << Comments  << endl;
}
```

While counting the number of blank spaces, there is a new fact taken into account. This concerns the operator **>>**, which transforms each pair of characters **'\r'**, **'\n'** into one carriage return character **'\n'**, which is why the number of **NewLines** is multiplied by two. We've included only four characters in the concept of "whitespace":

```
' '   '\t'   '\n'   '\r'
```

The aim here isn't to make exact accounts of the number of statements and comments. We have limited ourselves to making approximate calculations. So the count of the number of comments as the number of slashes divided by 2:

```
long Comments = Slashes/2;   // Not too precise
```

is approximate. The fact that **'/'** is met also as the division sign, in string literals, and in the comments themselves is discounted. In the same way the number of semi-colons approximately matches the number of statements.

Check how this program is executed based on its source code:

```
P08_05 < P08_05.CPP
```

You'll get:

```
Counting characters:

File input:

  P08_05 < any_text_file

Console input:
  Input text strings ending with Enter
  Enter ^Z (Ctrl/Z) to exit

File has:

  Total characters 2222
  Lines            108
  Whitespaces      583
  Statements       35
  Comments         25
```

Counting Words

In previous sections of this chapter we considered the methods of character input/output using the **cin** and **cout** streams. In the ANSI standard library of functions there are several functions for stream processing which are kept for compatibility with previous language versions.

Try It Out - Counting Words

The next program uses two functions, **getchar()** and **printf()**, to count characters, blank spaces, words, sentences, and lines in a text file. Program 8.6 is derived from Program 8.5. Have a look at the changes that have been made.

```
//   Program 8.6  P08_06.CPP
//   Counting words with old I/O stream functions
#include <stdio.h>

//   Global data
                     // Numbers of:
long  BlankTabs,     // Blank + Tab
  NewLines,          // NewLine
  Fullstops,         // End of sentence
  Others,            // All other chars
  Words;             // whitespace delimitered words
```

```
//  Function declarations
void  SayAboutUsage  (void);
void  Count       (char Char);
void  SayAboutChars  (void);

void main()
{
  int IChar = 0;

  SayAboutUsage();
  while (1)
  {
     IChar = getchar ();          // Get from stream
     if (IChar == EOF)
       break;                     // Exit on EOF
     Count ((char)IChar);        // Count chars
  }

  SayAboutChars();
}

void SayAboutUsage(void)
{
  printf ("\nCounting characters, words and sentences:\n\n"
          "File input:\n\n"
          "  P08-06 < any_text_file\n\n"
          "Console input:\n"
          "  Input text strings ending with Enter\n"
          "  Enter ^Z (Ctrl/Z) to exit\n" );
}

void Count(char Char)
{  /*  Count chars and words
    Flag InWord has value No if Char is whitespace
      Yes - otherwise
    Static variable WasInWord remember
      previous InWord value     */

  const  int No       = 0;
  const  int Yes      = 1;
  static int WasInWord = No;       // Where was
         int InWord    = Yes;      // Where now

  switch (Char)
  {
     case ' ' :
     case '\t':
       BlankTabs++;
       InWord=No;
       break;
```

```
        case '\n':
          NewLines++;
          InWord=No;
          break;
        case '.' :
          Fullstops++;
          break;
        default  :
          Others++;
  }

  if (InWord && !WasInWord)
    Words++;
  WasInWord = InWord;          // Save for next entry
}

void SayAboutChars(void)
{
  long Whitespaces = 2 * NewLines + BlankTabs;
  /* Every pair of chars
     Carriage Return and Line Feed
     is translated by getchar () into one char
  */
  long Total = Whitespaces + Fullstops + Others;

  printf ("\nFile has:\n\n");
  printf ("  Total characters %ld\n", Total);
  printf ("  Whitespaces      %ld\n", Whitespaces);
  printf ("  Words            %ld\n", Words);
  printf ("  Sentences        %ld\n", Fullstops);
  printf ("  Lines            %ld\n", NewLines);
}
// EOF
```

How It Works

```
#include <stdio.h>
```

Firstly, the **#include** directive has been changed. While using the standard input/output functions you need to include the file **STDIO.H**.

```
int IChar = 0;
```

Instead of **Char** in the function **main()**, the variable **IChar** of type **int** is used, as required by the function **getchar()**, which returns the character input from a stream as an integer.

The check on the end of the file condition has been changed. The function **getchar()**, on detecting the end of the file, returns a value (-1) that doesn't coincide with any of the 256 characters. This value has a symbolic designation **EOF** (it is defined in the file **STDIO.H**). That's why the control for reaching the end of the file has the form:

```
if (IChar == EOF)
   break;
```

The function **getchar()** inputs the characters from a stream in the same way as the operator **>>**.

```
  void Count(char Char)
{  /*  Count chars and words
    Flag InWord has value No if Char is whitespace
      Yes - otherwise
    Static variable WasInWord remember
      previous InWord value    */

  const  int No       = 0;
  const  int Yes      = 1;
  static int WasInWord = No;     // Where was
         int InWord    = Yes;    // Where now

  switch (Char)
  {
      case ' ' :
      case '\t':
        BlankTabs++;
        InWord=No;
        break;
      case '\n':
        NewLines++;
        InWord=No;
        break;
      case '.' :
        Fullstops++;
        break;
      default  :
        Others++;
  }
  if (InWord && !WasInWord)
    Words++;
  WasInWord = InWord;            // Save for next entry
}
```

Now have a look at how the words in the function **Count()** are counted. Here, a word is bounded on both sides by any one of three characters:

blank space, tab or carriage return. To count the words, two variables are used:

```
static int WasInWord = No;
       int InWord    = Yes;
```

As the variable **WasInWord** is static, it's initialized once at the start of the program (by the value No), and its previous value is stored at repeated calls of the function **Count()**. This variable is a flag and it assumes one of two meanings: **Yes** or **No**. **No** means that the previous character was a blank space, it was outside a word. **Yes** means that the previous character was a part of a word.

```
    case '\t':
       BlankTabs++;
       InWord=No;
       break;
    case '\n':
       NewLines++;
       InWord=No;
       break;
```

The variable **InWord** is automatic. It is initialized by the value **Yes** at each entry into the function **Count()**. If the current character **Char** is a blank space, then **InWord** is set to **No** in **case '\t'** or **case '\n'**, otherwise it remains **Yes**, as initialized.

```
    if (InWord && !WasInWord)
       Words++;
```

The word counter is incremented by 1 during "entry" into a word, in other words if the current character is a part of a word, but the previous one was outside it.

```
    WasInWord = InWord;        // Save for next entry
```

The current value of the **InWord** variable is kept in the **static** variable **WasInWord** to use when processing the next character.

The output functions, **SayAboutUsage()** and **SayAboutChars()**, use the function **printf()**, which is the C programming language's output function. This function formats and prints its arguments on the standard output device. The format of this function is:

```
    printf(format, argument1, argument2, argument3, .... )
```

The format string contains ordinary characters to be output and **conversion specifiers** which cause the arguments to be converted in a specified manner before they are displayed. Here **%ld** is the conversion specifier for the format of a **long int** (not **long double**).

```
printf ("  Sentences        %ld\n", Fullstops);
```

To count the number of sentences, the above code fragment (taken from **SayAboutChars()**) counts the number of full stops (an approximate count).

File Streams

Up to this point in the chapter you have dealt with three standard streams:

cin - console input stream

cout- console output stream

cerr- console error stream

These three streams are predefined. They are accessible (open for use), if the program contains the directive:

```
#include <iostream.h>
```

All necessary declarations and definitions of these objects are made in the header file **IOSTREAM.H**.

However, a programmer can create other streams connecting them with files on a diskette. The number of streams being created isn't limited by the C++ language, but by the operating system. The maximum number of streams opened may be 20 or more depending on the parameters of the operating system configuration.

A stream is a general name given to the flow of data and are normally associated with I/O operations. Streams are your first encounter with object-oriented programming. The I/O operations are arranged in a complex hierarchy of classes. However, you don't have to understand this hierarchy to use the operations successfully.

You have already seen input statements like **cin >> ch;** or **cin >> number;** and output statements like **cout << "Welcome to this book";** or **cout << number;**.

Streams allow a standard notation to be used with different data types allowing the compiler to work out the necessary details.

Try It Out - Opening a Text File for Reading

Look at the following example:

```
//   Program 8.7
//   Opening text file for reading
#include <stdlib.h>      //hesder file needed for exit()
#include <fstream.h>     //header file needed for file I/O
                         //this header file includes IOSTREAM.H
                         //so there is no need to #include it

void main()
{
  const int MAX = 80;
  char buffer[MAX];

  ifstream input("a:\\file1.cpp");

  if(!input)
  {
    cout << "\n\n\tCouldn't Open File\n";
    exit(-1);                          //function to terminate the program
  }
  while(input)
  {
    input.getline(buffer, MAX);
    cout << buffer << endl;
  }
}
```

How It Works

This example opens a disk file, reads the text, and displays the text on the screen.

```
#include <stdlib.h>
#include <fstream.h>
```

The header file **STDLIB.H** is needed so that the **exit()** function can be used. The header file **FSTREAM.H** is needed for file handling. As **FSTREAM.H** includes **IOSTREAM.H** there is no need for us to **#include IOSTREAM.H** in our program.

The ifstream File Object

```
ifstream input("a:\\file1.cpp");
```

An object called **input** has been defined to be a member of the **ifstream** class. In the same statement, input is initialized to the file name **A:\FILE1.CPP**. This initialization opens the file and sets aside resources for the file. You will notice that the file name in the code has two slashes, ****. This is because the file name is a string and **** is a special character.

Testing for Errors

```
if(!input)
{
  cout << "\n\n\tCouldn't Open File\n";
  exit(-1);
}
```

Errors can occur during stream operations. The program may try to open a file that isn't in the directory or may read past the end of the file. There are several ways to test for errors, but in this program we have used the **if** statement.

An **ifstream** object has a value that can be tested. If an error occurs the object has a zero value otherwise the value is non-zero.

In this case, if an error occurs a message will be displayed and the program will terminate as the **exit()** function will be called. The **exit()** function is a standard ANSI function. To use this function you must include the header file **STDLIB.H**. We would point out that it is standard practice to use a negative number as an argument to **exit()** to denote that something has gone wrong. Similarly:

```
while(input)
{
  input.getline(buffer, MAX);
  cout << buffer << endl;
}
```

while(input) checks that no errors have occurred and if this is true the statements in the loop are executed.

There are other tests that can be carried out to check for errors:

```
if (input.good())
```

tests if no errors have occurred.

```
if(input.bad())
```

tests if errors have occurred.

```
if(input.eof())
```

tests if the end-of-file marker has been found.

Try It Out - Opening a Text File For Writing

Let's look at another example.

```
//   Program 8.8
//   Opening text file for writing
#include <stdlib.h>
#include <fstream.h>

void main()
{
  ofstream output("a:\\text.out");
  if(!output)
  {
    cout << "\n\n\tCouldn't Open File\n";
    exit(-1);
  }
  output << "This program demonstrates outputting to a text file\n";
  output << "You should notice how we can use the << operator to output\n"
         << "in the same way as when we use cout.\n\n";
}
```

How It Works

This program outputs some text to a file. The file that is produced is a **text file** which is a sequence of ASCII characters divided into lines. Each line is terminated with the newline character.

Try It Out!

Run the program and then check to see that the file has been generated. The file will be on drive **a:** and you will need to have a disk in that drive (unless you alter the program). A directory listing will show whether **TEXT.OUT** has been created. Open the file with any standard editor and you will see what has been written to the file. This is shown below:

```
This program demonstrates outputting to a text file
You should notice how we can use the << operator to output
in the same way as when we use cout.
```

The program uses the same header files as in the previous example.

The ofstream File Object

```
ofstream output("a:\\text.out");
```

This is a similar statement to the one you saw in Program 8.7. In this case an object called **output** has been defined to be a member of the **ofstream** class and output has been initialized to the file name **A:\TEXT.OUT**. A full path name can be used but this isn't necessary if the file is to be placed in the current directory.

```
if(!output)
{
  cout << "\n\n\tCouldn't Open File\n";
  exit(-1);
}
```

As in the previous example, an **if** statement is used to check for errors. As with the **ifstream** object a **while** loop or the other test functions - **output.bad()**, **output.good()**, **output.eof()** - can be used.

```
output << "This program demonstrates outputting to a text file\n";
output << "You should notice how we can use the << operator to output\n"
       << "in the same way as when we use cout.\n\n";
```

The strings are then output to the file using the **ofstream** file object, **output**, together with the **<<** operator.

Closing the File

When the program terminates the object **output** goes out of scope. This causes the text file to close. Therefore, it isn't necessary to close the file in the program, although it would be prudent to do so as this ensures all reading/writing is complete. To specifically close the file we would use the following code:

```
output.close();
```

Try It Out - Appending to a Text File

Another way of writing to a file is demonstrated by Program 8.9. In this program, the file is opened with the flag (or mode bit) **ios::app** which means "append text", in other words text will be added to the end of the current file (if there wasn't a file then it is created).

```
//   Program 8.9
//   Appending to text file
#include <stdlib.h>
#include <fstream.h>

void main()
{
  ofstream output("a:\\text2.out", ios::app);
  if(!output)
  {
    cout << "\n\n\tCouldn't Open File\n";
    exit(-1);
  }
  output << "\nThis program demonstrates appending text to a file\n";
  output << "Each time the program is run more lines of text are\n"
         << "added to the file.\n\n";
}
```

How It Works

Each time it's run, this program adds more lines to the file **TEXT2.OUT**. The file contains the following text after the program has been executed twice:

```
This program demonstrates appending text to a file
Each time the program is run more lines of text are
added to the file.


This program demonstrates appending text to a file
Each time the program is run more lines of text are
added to the file.
```

Try It Out!

333

There are a number of mode bits as shown in the following table.

Mode Bit	Result
ios::in	Open for reading
ios::out	Open for writing
ios::app	Start reading or writing at end of file (APPend)
ios::ate	Erase file before reading or writing (truncATE)
ios::nocreate	Error when opening if file does not already exist
ios::noreplace	Error when opening for output if file already exists, unless ios::ate or ios::app is also specified
ios::binary	Open file in binary (not text) mode

Binary Files

Data is written to a binary file exactly as it appears in memory. No examination or processing of the data is performed and all characters are written to the file, as is. Obviously you can't use any of the standard text mode stream input/output functions.

To use a file in binary mode open the file using the mode bit **ios::binary**.

Try It Out - Writing a Binary File

Writing a binary file isn't that different to writing a text file: the difference being that character conversion isn't performed. This next program shows how all 256 characters are written into the file **BINARY1.OUT**.

```
// Program 8.10
// writing to a binary file
#include <stdlib.h>
#include <fstream.h>

void main()
{
  ofstream output("a:\\binary1.out", ios::binary );
  if(!output)
  {
    cout << "\n\n\tCouldn't Open File\n";
    exit(-1);
  }
  char text1[80] = "\n\tThe Beginners Guide to C++\n";
  char text2[80] = "\tby Oleg Yarosh";
  char text3[80] = "\n\n\tPublished by Wrox Press Ltd, 1994\n";
```

```
    output.write((char *) &text1, sizeof(text1));
    output.write((char *) &text2, sizeof(text2));

    for (int i = 0; i < sizeof(text3); i++)
      output.put(text3[i]);
    for (i = 0; i < 256; i++)
      output.put((char) i);
    output.close();
}
```

How It Works

```
    output.write((char *) &text1, sizeof(text1));
    output.write((char *) &text2, sizeof(text2));
```

The first two strings were output to the file using the function **write()**.
This function will write to either a text file or a binary file. As you can see,
the function takes two arguments. The first argument is the address of the
variable to be written using the address of operator, **&**. The second
argument is the size of the variable in bytes. The **sizeof** keyword is used
to ascertain this. However, the address of the variable has to be cast to be a
pointer to a **char**. This is achieved by **(char *)**.

```
    for (int i = 0; i < sizeof(text3); i++)
      output.put(text3[i]);
```

The third string is output using a **for** loop to step through the array and
output each character in turn.

```
    for (i = 0; i < 256; i++)
      output.put((char) i);
```

Another **for** loop is used to output the 256 characters.

If you open the binary file you will see how the strings and characters have
been stored. You may have a problem displaying or printing the first 31
non-printing characters. To illustrate the process of reading from a binary
file, the above program was modified so that the first 31 non-printing
characters weren't output to the file. The **for** loop was altered as shown
below:

```
    for (i = 32; i < 256; i++)
      output.put((char) i);
```

Try It Out - Reading From a Binary File

The next program demonstrates reading from a binary file.

```
//   Program 8.11
//   reading from a binary file
#include <stdlib.h>
#include <fstream.h>

void main()
{
  ifstream input("a:\\binary2.out", ios::binary );
  if(!input)
  {
    cout << "\n\n\tCouldn't Open File\n";
    exit(-1);
  }

  char text1[80], text2[80], text3[80];

  input.read((char *) &text1, sizeof(text1));
  input.read((char *) &text2, sizeof(text2));
  for (int i = 0; i < sizeof(text3); i++)
    input.get(text3[i]);

  cout << text1 << text2 << text3;

  char ch;
  for (i = 32; i < 256; i++)
  {
    if (i % 40 == 0)
      cout << endl;
    input.get(ch);
    cout << ch;
  }
  input.close();
}
```

How It Works

As you can see from Program 8.11, there is no problem in reading a binary file. As you would expect, the **ofstream** object is declared and initialized to the filename. The file is opened in binary mode.

```
    input.read((char *) &text1, sizeof(text1));
    input.read((char *) &text2, sizeof(text2));
```

We use the **read()** function to read the first two text strings. The **read()** function takes the same arguments as the **write()** function. Again the address of the variable must be cast to be a pointer to **char**.

```
for (int i = 0; i < sizeof(text3); i++)
  input.get(text3[i]);
```

A **for** loop is used to read the third text string.

```
for (i = 32; i < 256; i++)
{
  if (i % 40 == 0)
    cout << endl;
  input.get(ch);
  cout << ch;
}
```

and a **for** loop is used to read the characters.

```
if (i % 40 == 0)
  cout << endl;
```

To make the characters easier to read we decided to limit the size of the lines to 40 characters. This is achieved by calculating the modulus of the loop counter. If the modulus (remainder) is equal to 0, then a new line is started. This actually means that the first line only has 9 characters on it.

Try It Out - Copying Binary Files

Program 8.12 enables you to copy any files (binary and text). It extends Program 8.4 which only copies text files.

```
//  Program 8.12
//  copying a file
#include <stdlib.h>
#include <fstream.h>

void main()
{
  ifstream input1("a:\\binary2.out", ios::app | ios::binary );
  ifstream input2("a:\\file8.cpp", ios::app);
  ofstream output1("a:\\binary2.cpy", ios::binary);
  ofstream output2("a:\\file8.cpy");

  if(!input1)
    cout << "\n\n\tCouldn't Open Input1\n";
  if(!input2)
    cout << "\n\n\tCouldn't Open Input2\n";
  if(!output1)
  {
    cout << "\n\n\tCouldn't Open Output1\n";
    exit(-1);
  }
}
```

Try It Out!

```
    if(!output2)
    {
      cout << "\n\n\tCouldn't Open Output2\n";
      exit(-1);
    }

    while(!input1.eof())
    {
      char ch;
      input1.get(ch);
      output1 << ch;
    }
    input1.close();
    output1.close();
    while(!input2.eof())
    {
      char buffer[120];
      input2.getline(buffer, 120);
      output2 << buffer << endl;
    }
    input2.close();
    output2.close();
}
```

How It Works

This program also demonstrates that it's possible to have several files open at once.

```
ifstream input1("a:\\binary2.out", ios::app | ios::binary );
ifstream input2("a:\\file8.cpp", ios::app);
ofstream output1("a:\\binary2.cpy", ios::binary);
ofstream output2("a:\\file8.cpy");
```

Four files are opened: two binary files - one for reading (the one to copy) and one for writing, and two text files - one for reading and one for writing.

The files are then checked for errors.

```
    while(!input1.eof())
    {
      char ch;
      input1.get(ch);
      output1 << ch;
    }
```

The binary file is copied by using a **while** loop which is checking for the end-of-file marker in the file that's being copied. Whilst the end-of-file marker is not found, a character is read from the file being copied and output to the file being written to. When the copy is completed the two files are closed.

```
    while(!input2.eof())
    {
      char buffer[120];
      input2.getline(buffer, 120);
      output2 << buffer << endl;
    }
```

The text file is also copied using a **while** loop. This time the **getline()** function is used to read a complete line. The function reads a character at a time until the `'\n'` is found. The function puts the string into the character array, **buffer**. This string is then output to the copy file. The files are then closed.

Try It Out - Opening Several Files

The last program showed how to open and process more than one input file. The next program, Program 8.13, also looks at this. In this program two files are defined which contain the three best results in the speed descent for men from the 1994 Winter Olympic Games in Lillehammer.

```
//   Program 8.13
//   using more than one file
#include <stdlib.h>        //header file for exit()
#include <fstream.h>       //header file for file I/O
#include <iomanip.h>       //header file for I/O manipulators

void main()
{
  ifstream input1("a:\\p08_13.nam");
  ifstream input2("a:\\p08_13.res");
  if(!input1)
  {
    cout << "\n\n\tCouldn't Open Input1\n";
    exit(-1);
  }
  if(!input2)
  {
    cout << "\n\n\tCouldn't Open Input2\n";
    exit(-1);
  }
  cout << "\t13-Feb-1994 Lillehammer\n"
          "\tAlpina Skiing Downhill Men\n\n";

  while(!input1.eof() || !input2.eof())
  {
    char name[80], res[80];
    input1.getline(name, 80);
    input2.getline(res, 80);
```

Try It Out!

```
        cout << setw(30) << name << "\t\t" << setw(15) << res << endl;
    }
    input1.close();
    input2.close();
}
```

How It Works

You need to create two files to be used by this program. The file
P08_13.NAM contains the names and countries of each sportsman:

> Tommy Moe (USA)
> Andre Amot (NOR)
> Edvard Podivinski (CAN)

The file **P08_13.RES** contains the results and places of the sportsmen (in the
same order as the first file):

```
1.45.75  1
1.45.79  2
1.45.87  3
```

You could imagine that the first file was filled before the competitions, and
the second was filled separately after the competitions. The task is to output
the table of results. Program 8.13 outputs:

```
13-Feb-1994 Lillehammer
Alpina Skiing Downhill Men

          Tommy Moe  (USA)        1.45.75  1
        Andre Aamot  (NOR)        1.45.79  2
  Edvard Podivinski  (CAN)        1.45.87  3
```

Notice how it does it.

```
    ifstream input1("a:\\p08_13.nam");
    ifstream input2("a:\\p08_13.res");
```

Firstly, two files are opened for reading. It is indicated in the comments
which functions each of three header files contains. The function **exit()**
provides an emergency program termination and exit from any point in the
program directly to the operating system.

```
    input1.getline(name, 80);
    input2.getline(res, 80);
```

The function **getline()** is used to read a line from each file and store it in
a character array. By the term "line from each file" you should understand a

sequence of characters that is terminated by the character pair '\r' and '\n'. Names are read from one file pointed to by **input1** and the results - from another, pointed to by **input2**.

```
cout << setw(30) << name << "\t\t" << setw(15) << res << endl;
```

The **cout** statement is used to display the results on the screen. The expression **setw()** is used to set the field width. You can imagine that each value displayed by **cout** is contained in a box which has a certain width. The default width is just big enough to hold the value. The **setw()** manipulator allows you to alter this width.

The File Pointer

How does the program know where it is in the file? You will have noticed that in some of the preceding examples the characters or strings were read from the stream from the beginning, one character at a time. To indicate the character to be extracted with the next read operation, a file pointer is connected with each file stream. A file pointer is an offset of the number of characters from the beginning of the file.

For example, if after opening a file you read three characters (three bytes) from the file, the value of the file pointer is 3, and it points to the fourth byte in the stream. This is shown in the next figure. As you can see the file pointer value is similar to an array index.

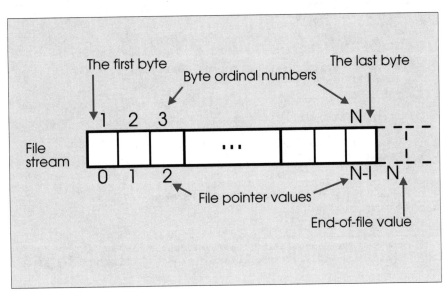

Don't confuse the idea of a file pointer with the type "pointer to data".

Each file object has two integer values associated with it. These are called:

- ▶ The get pointer
- ▶ The put pointer

These values signify the location from the start of the file where reading or writing will occur. As you have seen, the default actions allow a file to be read from the start continuing to the end. When writing to a file, the default action deletes any existing contents and starts from the beginning unless the file is opened with the **ios::app** mode bit when the contents won't be deleted and writing will start from the end.

There will be times when you want to control where reading or writing occurs. The **seekg()** and the **tellg()** functions allow you to set and ascertain the value of the get pointer, and the **seekp()** and the **tellp()** functions perform the same operations for the put pointer.

Try It Out - Getting the File Pointer Value

Look at the following example:

```
//  Program 8.14
//  getting file pointer value
#include <stdlib.h>
#include <fstream.h>
#include <iomanip.h>

void main()
{
  ofstream output("a:\\p08_14.dat", ios::binary);
  long FP;
  char ch;

  if(!output)
  {
    cout << "\n\n\tCouldn't Open file\n";
    exit(-1);
  }

  char line[] = "ABCDEFGHIJKLMNOPQRSTUVWXYZ";
  output << line;
  output.close();

  cout << "Reading binary file file8.dat...\n\n";
  cout << setw(25) << "Operation  " << "        File Pointer after it\n\n";
```

```
    ifstream input("a:\\p08_14.dat", ios::binary);
    FP = input.tellg();

    cout << setw(25) << "File Open " << " " << setw(15) << FP << endl;

    input.get(ch);
    FP = input.tellg();
    cout << setw(25) << "Get first character " << ch << setw(15)
        << FP << endl;

    input.get(ch);
    FP = input.tellg();
    cout << setw(25) << "Get second character " << ch << setw(15)
        << FP << endl;

    input.get(ch);
    FP = input.tellg();
    cout << setw(25) << "Get third character " << ch << setw(15)
        << FP << endl;
    input.close();
}
```

How It Works

The program first creates a file

```
    ofstream output("a:\\p08_14.dat", ios::binary);
...
    char line[] = "ABCDEFGHIJKLMNOPQRSTUVWXYZ";
    output << line;
    output.close();
```

that contains the 26 letters of the alphabet in upper case letters. This file is then closed.

```
    ifstream input("a:\\p08_14.dat", ios::binary);
```

and is opened to be read.

```
    FP = input.tellg();
```

Further on, the program displays the current value of the file pointer which is obtained by the function **tellg()** after opening the file:

```
    input.get(ch);
    FP = input.tellg();
    cout << setw(25) << "Get first character " << ch << setw(15)
        << FP << endl;
```

```
    input.get(ch);
    FP = input.tellg();
    cout << setw(25) << "Get second character " << ch << setw(15)
        << FP << endl;

    input.get(ch);
    FP = input.tellg();
    cout << setw(25) << "Get third character " << ch << setw(15)
        << FP << endl;
```

and after each of the next three operations reading one character. The program outputs:

```
Reading binary file p08_14.dat...

                Operation         File Pointer after it

                File Open              0
    Get first character A              1
    Get second character B             2
    Get third character C              3
```

As you can see, after the file is opened, the file pointer value is 0. Its value is then incremented by 1 after each character is read.

Try It Out - Moving a File Pointer

Much of the data that is stored in files needs to be processed sequentially. However, it's often necessary to read or write data in a file, not sequentially, but in a random order, as the computer processor does when addressing RAM (random access memory). Program 8.15 shows how random access is provided with the help of the **fseekg()** and **fseekp()** functions.

```
//   Program 8.15
//   moving the file pointer from A to Z
#include <stdlib.h>
#include <fstream.h>
#include <iomanip.h>

void main()
{
    ofstream output("a:\\p08_15.dat", ios::binary);
    long FP;
    char ch;
```

```
if(!output)
{
  cout << "\n\n\tCouldn't Open file\n";
  exit(-1);
}

char line[] = "ABCDEFGHIJKLMNOPQRSTUVWXYZ";
output << line;
output.close();
cout << "Moving file pointer in p08-17.dat...\n\n";

ifstream input("a:\\p08_15.dat", ios::binary);
input.seekg(0, ios::beg);
FP = input.tellg();
input >> ch;

cout << "First byte " << ch << " " << (int) ch
     << " at file pointer " << FP << endl;

input.seekg(-1, ios::end);
FP = input.tellg();
input.read((char *) &ch, sizeof(ch));

cout << "Last byte " << ch << " " << (int) ch
     << " at file pointer " << FP << endl;

input.seekg(0, ios::cur);
FP = input.tellg();
input.get(ch);

cout << "EOF byte " << ch << " " << (int) ch
     << " at file pointer " << FP << endl;
input.close();
}
```

How It Works

This program uses the **seekg()** and the **tellg()** functions.

The **seekg()** function can be used in two ways. The first is where a single argument represents a position in the file - for example, **input.seekg(20)**. The start of the file is byte 0 and in this case the file pointer would move to byte 20. The second is using **seekg()** with two arguments. The first argument represents an offset from a specific location in the file, and the second stipulates the location from where the offset is measured, for example **input.seekg(0, ios::beg)**. There are only three possibilities for the second argument, `ios::beg` is the beginning of the file, `ios::cur` is the current pointer position, and `ios::end` is the end of the file. For example, the statement:

```
seekg(-5, ios::end);
```

will set the get pointer to 5 bytes before the end of the file.

This file pointer movement is demonstrated by Program 8.15. As in the previous example, a file is created containing the 26 letters of the alphabet.

```
input.seekg(0, ios::beg);
FP = input.tellg();
input >> ch;
```

The file pointer is then moved to three different positions. In each position the character is read and displayed. The program outputs:

```
Moving file pointer in p08_15.dat...

First byte A 65 at file pointer 0
Last byte Z 90 at file pointer 25
EOF byte    -1 at file pointer 26
```

Look at how the function `seekg()` is used. It is initially invoked to move to the beginning of file with zero values for the offset and `ios::beg` as the location arguments. The value of the file pointer returned by the function `tellg()` is equal to 0. In the next line the character from the beginning of the file is read. This is the character 'A'. It is output together with its ASCII (numeric) value of 65.

```
input.seekg(-1, ios::end);
```

Further on, the `seekg()` function serves to move the file pointer to one byte before the end-of-file position. Note that `tellg()` gives the value of the file pointer as 25. In our file there are 26 characters; its length is 26. The file pointer value of the last position, corresponding to the 'Z' character, is 25. So the next call:

```
input.seekg(0, ios::cur);
```

moves not to the last byte of the file, but beyond the last byte. You can see that the value of the character obtained from the end-of-file position is equal to -1 in our case (this may depend on implementation).

Try It Out - Using Random Access to a File

Program 8.16 shows how to randomly access a file.

```
//  Program 8.16
//  Random read/write demo
#include <stdlib.h>        //for exit() and rand()
#include <fstream.h>       //for fileI/O
#include <ctype.h>         //for islower(), toupper(), etc
#include <iomanip.h>       //for I/O manipulators
#include <string.h>        //for strcpy()

long N = 1000;             // Number of reads/writes
int ReverseCaseFlag = 0;   // Not change letter case

void filename ( char * );
void Indicator(void);
void Print(long Count []);

void main()
{
  long FileLen;            // File length
  long Count [256]={0};    // Array for counting chars
  char FName[128];         // Place for file name

  cout << "\nCounting statistical distribution of characters in file\n\n";

  filename(FName);         // Get file name and open

  fstream discfile;

  discfile.open(FName, ios::app | ios::in | ios::out | ios::binary);
  // Note the vertical bars indicate that the mode bits are being
  // OR'd together so that several flags can be used simultaneously

  discfile.seekg(0, ios::end);     // Set file to its end
  FileLen = discfile.tellg();      // Get file length

  for (long i=0; i<N; i++)         //Repeat file access N times
  {
    unsigned char C;               // Current char
    long Pos;                      // Current position

    Pos = rand() % FileLen;        // Random Pos from 0 to FileLen
    discfile.seekg(Pos);           // Move file pointer
    discfile.get(C);               // Read 1 byte
    if(discfile.bad())
      exit (-1);                   // Exit on error

    if (ReverseCaseFlag)
    { // Reverse case of letter only for p08-16.tst file
```

```
      if (islower(C))
        C=toupper(C);
      else
        C=tolower(C);

      discfile.seekp(Pos);        // Return to previous position
      discfile.put(C);            // Write 1 byte
      if(discfile.bad())
        exit (1);                 // Exit on error
    }
    Count[tolower(C)]++;          // Increment for current char
    Indicator ();                 // Progress indicator
  }
  Print (Count);                  // Output results
}

void filename(char * name)
{/* Get file name from console
   and open file in binary mode for read and write

   If file not exists then file "p08_16.tst" is used
   (if it is not exists, it is created)
   When file "p08_16.tst" is used,
   the ReverseCaseFlag is set to 1
   and case of letters will be reversed  */

   cout << "Enter file name (if not exist - p08-18.tst will be used): ";
   cin  >> name;

   ifstream input(name, ios::in | ios::binary );
   if (!input)
   { // Test file name
     char TestName[128]="a:\\p08_16.tst";

     ReverseCaseFlag = 1;   // Letter case will be changed

     cout << "File " << name << " not found\n";

     ofstream output(TestName, ios::in | ios::out | ios::binary | ios::app);
     if (output)
     { // Create and open test file
       char Line [] = "ABCDEFGHIJKLMNOPQRSTUVWXYZ";
       if (! output)                //test file line
         exit (-1);

       cout << "Creating file " << TestName << endl;
       output << Line;
       output.close();
     }
     cout << "Test file " << TestName << " is used\n";
```

```
      strcpy(name, TestName);
    }
    cout << "Enter number of seeks (1-100000): ";
    cin >> N;
    if (N < 1L || N > 100000L)
    {
      N = 1000;
      cout << "Value is out of range, 1000 is used\n";
    }
    input.close();
}

void Indicator(void)
{/* Output Progress_Indicator character
   for every Progress_Count bytes read  */

     static int Count=0;
     char Progress_Indicator = '.';
     int  Progress_Count = 100;

   if ( !(++Count % Progress_Count) )
     cout << Progress_Indicator;
}

void Print(long Count [])
{
   long Sum = 0;
   int  i = 0;
   unsigned char C = 0;

   for (Sum=0,i=0; i < 256; i++)
     Sum += Count [i];
   cout << "\nTotal characters:\t" << Sum << endl;

   for (Sum = 0, C = 'a'; C <= 'z';  C++)
     Sum += Count [C];
   cout << "Alpha characters aA to zZ:\t " << Sum << endl << endl;

   cout << setw(8) << "Char" << setw(8) << "Q-ty" << setw(8) << "%"
        << setw(8) << "Char" << setw(8) << "Q-ty" << setw(8) << "%"
        << endl << endl;

   for (C = 'a'; C <= 'z'; C++)
   {
     cout << setw(8) << C << setw(8) << Count[C] << setw(8)
          << (100. * Count[C]) / Sum;
     if((C - 'a') % 2)
       cout << endl;        // Next line
   }
}
```

How It Works

The program uses the random number generator function **rand()**, declared in **STDLIB.H**, to count the statistical distribution of characters in a file. The general algorithm is as follows. After running the program, the user must enter the name of the file to be tested, and the number of seek operations, which is stored in the variable **N**. The length of the file is then determined, and a byte from a random position in the file is read in the loop which is iterated **N** times. This position is defined with the help of the function **rand()** within the limits from 0 to **FileLen** (the length of the file).

In the loop, the appearances of every alphabetic character aA - zZ are counted. After the loop has been terminated, a table is displayed with information on how many times each character was read, and the percentage of the total number of characters that the character represents.

For example, if you create the test file **P08_16.TST** containing the 26 letters:

ABCDEFGHIJKLMNOPQRSTUVWXYZ

typical output from the program will be:

```
Counting statistical distribution of characters in file

Enter file name (if not exist - p08_16.tst will be used): a:\anyfile.tst
File a:\anyfile.tst not found
Creating file a:\p08_16.tst
Test file a:\p08_16.tst is used
Enter number of seeks (1-100000): 1000
..........
Total characters: 1000
Alpha characters aA to zZ:  1000
```

Char	Q-ty	%	Char	Q-ty	%
a	57	5.7	b	51	5.1
c	31	3.1	d	47	4.7
e	46	4.6	f	57	5.7
g	38	3.8	h	33	3.3
i	31	3.1	j	41	4.1
k	41	4.1	l	33	3.3
m	42	4.2	n	60	6
o	25	2.5	p	20	2
q	31	3.1	r	49	4.9
s	32	3.2	t	56	5.6
u	30	3	v	16	1.6
w	38	3.8	x	26	2.6
y	30	3	z	39	3.9

These results may differ on your computer as the random numbers generated may be different.

You can test the random number generator and program with different data stored in the file to be tested, and different numbers of accesses, **N**. For example, you can deal with files containing:

▶ Only one character which may be duplicated.

▶ A pair of characters (AB or ABBBB or AAAAABBBBB and so on) * More characters (ABC or ABBCCCC or ABCDE and so on).

▶ A real text file (use big N).

Use different values of **N** from 10 to 10000 in each case.

Testing Input Data

Let us now consider the separate parts of Program 8.14. Its execution starts from the function **filename()**. It executes the basic data input, checking and choosing default values. It sets the values of the three global variables.

```
cout << "Enter file name (if not exist - p08_16.tst will be used): ";
cin  >> name;
ifstream input(name, ios::in | ios::binary );
```

First, the function **filename()** gets the name of a file from the standard input stream (keyboard), and tries to open that file.

The vertical bars between the flags cause the bits representing the flags to be logically 'ORed' together, so several flags can be used simultaneously.

```
if (!input)
{ // Test file name
  char TestName[128]="a:\\p08_16.tst";

  ReverseCaseFlag = 1;  // Letter case will be changed

  cout << "File " << name << " not found\n";

  ofstream output(TestName, ios::in | ios::out | ios::binary | ios::app);

  if (output)
  { // Create and open test file
    char Line [] = "ABCDEFGHIJKLMNOPQRSTUVWXYZ";
    if (! output)              //test file line
      exit (-1);
```

```
      cout << "Creating file " << TestName << endl;
      output << Line;
      output.close();
   }
   cout << "Test file " << TestName << " is used\n";
   strcpy(name, TestName);
}
```

If the file isn't found, it tries to use the test file `P08_16.TST`. If that isn't found either, then it's created with the contents:
ABCDEFGHIJKLMNOPQRSTUVWXYZ

When the test file is used, the global flag `ReverseCaseFlag` is set to 1.

```
   cout << "Enter number of seeks (1-100000): ";
   cin  >> N;
```

The number of searches `N` (number of random accesses) is also entered in this function.

```
   if (N < 1L || N > 100000L)
   {
     N = 1000;
     cout << "Value is out of range, 1000 is used\n";
   }
```

Its value is checked and if it is outside the admissible range a default value of 1000 is set. As you can see, the data being entered is carefully controlled by using default values and actions when invalid values are being input.

After `filename()` has returned control to `main()`:

```
   fstream discfile;
   discfile.open(FName, ios::app | ios::in | ios::out | ios::binary);
```

we encounter a new statement. In the previous examples the file objects were either for input or output. However, there will be times when you will want a file that can be read from or written to. An istream object is only for input and an ostream object is only for output. Therefore, an `fstream` file object is created as this can be used for both. However, the file is not opened or specified. To open the file we use the function `open()`.

Using Random Numbers

```
Pos = rand() % FileLen;   // Random Pos from 0 to FileLen
```

Almost all game programs apply a random number generator to create a variable pattern of game characteristics. In our program the standard function **rand()** is used. It returns a random integer in the range 0 to **RAND_MAX** (this macro constant is defined in **STDLIB.H** and may be up to 65535). Using **rand()**, a random value for the file pointer **Pos** is calculated. If **FileLen** is less than **RAND_MAX**, then the random **Pos** value will lie in the range from 0 to **FileLen - 1**, which are legitimate values of the file pointer.

```
discfile.seekg(0, ios::end);    // Set file to its end
FileLen = discfile.tellg();     // Get file length
```

The file length is calculated. First, **seekg()** sets the file pointer to the end-of-file, then **tellg()** returns the value of the file pointer which is equal to the file length in bytes.

```
discfile.seekg(Pos);    // Move file pointer
discfile.get(C);        // Read 1 byte
```

Using a random **Pos** value, **seekg()** sets the file pointer to a new position and a character is read. The numerical value of the character (**unsigned char** from 0 to 255) is used as the index of the **Count[]** array. This array is defined to store the number of hits of each character. For example, **Count[0]** contains the number which show how many times the byte with the value 0 appears in a random sample, and **Count['a']** reveals how many times the character 'a' or 'A' was encountered.

```
Count[tolower(C)]++;    // Increment for current char
Indicator ();           // Progress indicator
```

The function **tolower()** is used to convert an alphabetic character from upper to lower-case in order not to count upper and lower-case letters separately.

The function **Indicator()** outputs a period indicator after each 100 accesses to the file.

Random Write

```
discfile.seekp(Pos);    // Return to previous position
discfile.put(C);        // Write 1 byte
```

A special case of processing takes place if the global variable **ReverseCaseFlag** is not 0: random write operations are performed. **ReverseCaseFlag** is set to 1 by the function **filename()**, only if the file **P08-18.TST** is used. This is done so as not to destroy the contents of an arbitrary file.

```
if (islower(C))
    C=toupper(C);
else
    C=tolower(C);
```

When **ReverseCaseFlag** is not 0 the case of the character read is reversed (the lower-case character becomes upper-case and vice versa). This is done with the **toupper()** and **tolower()** functions. After being changed, the character is written to its previous position. This allows you to see which positions were chosen by examining the file **P08_16.TST** when the program has finished its execution. (You can experiment with this by choosing small values of **N**).

Designing a Program

We have now reached the end of this chapter and can see how to put what we have learnt into practice in a useful way.

The Problem

This chapter's problem will produce a simple program that demonstrates a very useful facility. We are going to write a program that can open an existing file and send the contents of the file to the printer.

The Analysis

The steps involved are:

1 Invite the user to enter the name of the file to print.

2 Open the file and check that there are no errors.

3 Open the printer file.

4 Send the contents of the file to the printer.

The Solution

The compiler has to know what device the program will use. DOS defines a number of special filenames for hardware devices and the following program makes use of PRN which sends output to the default parallel printer.

1   We need to ask the user to enter the name of the file to print. The `cin.get()` function, which we have met before, is used.

2   The program opens the file and checks that there are no errors.

```
ifstream infile(filename);
if(!infile)
{
    cerr << "\nUnable to access file.  Program terminating.\n";
    exit(-1);
}
```

An object called `infile` has been defined to be a member of the `ifstream` class. In the same statement, `infile` is initialized to the name of the file stored in the string filename. The initialization opens the disk file and sets aside the necessary resources for the file.

As no value is returned, you don't know whether you have been successful.

Errors can occur during stream operations. The program may try to open a file that isn't in the directory or read past the end of the file. These, and other conditions, cause errors and must be detected. There are several ways to detect errors and we are using the **while** loop. The **ifstream** object has a value that can be tested. If an error has occurred the object will return a zero value.

3   In a similar way, an object called `printer` has been defined to be a member of the **ofstream** class. In the same statement, `printer` is initialized to the name of **PRN** which relates to the first parallel printer.

```
ofstream printer("PRN");
```

355

4   The contents of the file are read a line at a time and sent to the printer.

```
  infile.getline(buffer, LENGTH);
  printer << buffer << endl;


//  printer.cpp
//  this program opens an existing disc file and
//  outputs it to the printer
#include <fstream.h>        //header file needed for file input/output
#include <stdlib.h>         //header file needed for exit()

void main()
{
  const int MAX    = 20;
  const int LENGTH = 80;

  char filename[MAX];
  char buffer[LENGTH];

  cout << "\n\tThis program opens an existing disc file and "
       << "\n\toutputs the file to the printer.\n\n"
       << "Enter filename to print: ";

  cin.get(filename, MAX);

  //open file
  ifstream infile(filename);        //create file object

  if(!infile)
  {
    cerr << "\nUnable to access file.  Program terminating.\n";
    exit(-1);
  }

  ofstream printer("PRN");          //create file object

  while(infile)
  {
    //get a line
    infile.getline(buffer, LENGTH);
    //print the line
    printer << buffer << endl;
  }
}
```

You can now try the program.

Summary

In this chapter you have learned how to use disks: how to input data from a disk, and output it to a disk. Now that you know more about sequential and random access to disk files, you can write programs that store the results of data processing on disk and retrieve from it. In addition you are able to output to the printer. We can now go on to Chapter 9 and look at data types.

Making Up Your Own
Data Types

You can now declare and define variables that can hold a variety of data types, including integers, floating point numbers, and characters. You are able to work with arrays of these types and use pointers to memory locations containing this data. However, there are many occasions when you will want greater flexibility.

In C++, there is virtually an infinite number of derived types that you can construct from the fundamental types. In this chapter you'll learn how to create your own data types by grouping the existing types into what are called structures. The greater part of the chapter will be devoted to the rules of structure creation and how to use them. In the next chapter you'll see how the addition of functions into structures leads to the idea of object oriented programming (OOP) - the central feature of C++.

In this chapter you will:

▶ Create and use structured data types

▶ Use pointers to structures and create arrays of structures

▶ Look at array and pointer arithmetic

▶ Examine unions

▶ Write a program that will store information about your books or CDs

Creating and Using Structure Data Types

In this section you'll learn how to group interrelated data into new data types called structures. We can combine any number of data types into a structure which can then be used to define variables of this new type. This is easier to explain with specific examples, so let's revisit our old friends, the mountains.

Joining Data About Mountains

In Chapter 4 we considered data about the heights of 7 mountain summits and then combined this into one array of the type **int**. In Chapter 5 we then joined the names of 7 mountains into an array of strings. How can we join together different data about the mountains?

Try It Out - Joining Data

Program 9.1 shows how to join different data on mountains together into a single structure. In this program, two data items are defined to describe a mountain:

```
char   MountainName[21] = "Everest ";
int   MountainHeight;
```

The first is the name of the mountain as a character array. The second is the mountain height. Its type is **int**.

```
//       Program 9.1
//       Joining data into a structure
#include <iostream.h>

//       Definition of 2 data items: of array and int type
char     MountainName[21] = "El'brus   ";
int      MountainHeight = 5642;

//       Definition of 1 object: structure Mountain
struct
{
  char     Name[21];
  int      Height;
}  Mountain = {"Everest ",8848};

void main()
{
  cout << MountainName << MountainHeight  << endl;
  cout << Mountain.Name << Mountain.Height << endl;
}
```

How It Works

```
struct
{
```

Here the keyword **struct** indicates the kind of object we are defining,

```
{
   char     Name[21];
   int      Height;
}
```

This is followed by declarations of its elements (called "members") between the braces. Each member has a name. Here two members are defined: **Name** and **Height**. The declarations of members are written in the same manner as the declarations of ordinary variables.

Structure Initialization

```
} Mountain = {"Everest ",8848};
```

The initialization of the structure is defined immediately following the name of a structure variable, as you can see here. The structure is initialized as a whole, with the initial values for each of the members being written in the same manner as that used for an array. In other words the values of the members are listed, separated by commas, in the order they are defined in the structure, and are enclosed between braces. If the number of values in the list is less than the number of members in the structure, then the remaining members are initialized with zeroes, for example in the next declaration the **Height** member will be initialized to 0:

```
struct {...} Mountain = {"Everest "};
```

Naming Members

```
cout << Mountain.Name << Mountain.Height << endl;
```

To reference a particular structure member, you use a name constructed from the name of the structure object and the name of its member, as you can see. The period (or full stop) separating the structure variable name, **Mountain**, and the member name **Name** or **Height**, is called a member selection operator. Blanks are not permitted before or after the period in such compound names, so all of the following are illegal:

```
Mountain     .Height = 8848;
Mountain.     Height = 8848;
Mountain   .  Height = 8848;
```

361

Such compound names referencing a structure member can be used anywhere where you can use ordinary variable names.

The definition of a structure type object is illustrated in the following figure. The types **type1**, **type2** and so on and the member names may be any legal C++ identifiers.

```
struct

{

        type1        MemberName1;

        type2        MemberName2;
         .
         .
         .
        typeN        MemberNameN;


}      Struct Name = { value1, value2, ... valueN } ;
```

Try It Out - Structure Type Declaration

Having combined two data items into one structure in Program 9.1, we haven't obtained any obvious advantages for the present. We will do better when we define a new data type in the next program.

```
//      Program 9.2
//      Structure type declaration
#include <iostream.h>

// Declaration of type mountain and definition of type mountain object
struct mountain
{
  char Name[21];
  int  Height;
}  TheBiggestMountain = {"Everest ",8848};

void SayAbout(mountain M) ;

void main()
{
```

```
   mountain K1;                    // Definition of the type mountain object
   K1 = TheBiggestMountain;        // Assigning structures
   SayAbout(K1);
}

void  SayAbout(mountain M)
{
   cout << M.Name << M.Height;
}
```

How It Works

```
struct   mountain
{
```

You can see the word **mountain** in the structure definition. This is the name of the new data type **mountain**. Now we can say that the object **Mountain** has the type **mountain**. The syntax of the structure type declaration is shown in the next figure.

```
Type declaration :

    struct
    {
            type1          MemberName1;
            type2          MemberName2;

                 .
                 .
                 .

            typeN          MemberNameN;
    };
Object definition :
            Struct Type    Object Name ;
```

You can declare a type without any object definition:

```
struct  mountain
{
  char    Name [21];
  int     Height;
};
```

This is simply the declaration of a new data type, **mountain**. This declaration doesn't create any new objects. No memory whatever is allocated here. Having declared a new type in such a way, you can define variables (objects) of this type in a similar way to variables of type **int** or **char**:

```
mountain TheBiggestMountain = {"Everest ",8848};
mountain K1;
```

The first example is initialized explicitly. The second isn't initialized.

```
void SayAbout(mountain M)
{
  cout << M.Name << M.Height;
}
```

Look how the argument **M** of type **mountain** is used in the function definition. In order to access the members of this structure a member selector operator is used.

```
SayAbout(K1);
```

During the function call, one argument of the type **mountain** is passed to the function.

Assigning Structures

To assign a value from one structure object to another, you can use the assignment operator to copy data from one structure to the other, member-by-member. For example, the assignment:

```
K1 = TheBiggestMountain;
```

means that the value of the member **TheBiggestMountain.Name** (the string "Everest") is copied into **K1.Name**, and the value of member **TheBiggestMountain.Height** is assigned to the member **K1.Height**.

You can compare the use of structures in C++ with the use of ideas in a general language. In a language it's convenient to have the abstract idea "mountain", behind which there is a set of characteristics (a name, height and so on). If there wasn't some idea like this then instead of being able to use just one word "mountain", you would have to use a long phrase like "high piece of dry land with a certain height above sea-level called XYZ".

Returning a Structure Type from a Function

As you saw in Program 9.2 a structure can be passed as a function argument. You can also return a structure from a function.

Try It Out - A Function Returning a Structure

This is demonstrated in the next program where the function **Get()** is defined which returns a value of the type **mountain**.

```
//      Program 9.3
//      Function returning a structure
#include <iostream.h>

struct  mountain            // Type mountain
{
  char    Name[21];
  int     Height;
};

mountain Get();             //  Function returning a structure

void main()
{
  mountain M;               // Object
  M = Get();                // Assigning returned structure
  cout << M.Name << M.Height;
}

mountain Get()              //  Function returning a structure
{
  mountain  Mountain = {"Everest ",8848};
  return    Mountain;
}
```

How It Works

```
return    Mountain;
```

The return of the value of type **mountain** is provided by the above statement.

```
M = Get();                        // Assigning returned structure
```

This returned structure is then assigned to the variable **M** of the type **mountain**. You should note that if a structure occupies a lot of memory, then passing the structure as a function argument or as a return value will be inefficient, as the copying of the structure from one function to another takes memory space and time.

Pointer to a Mountain

An effective way of passing structure arguments to functions and returning structure values is provided with the help of pointers to structures.

Try It Out - Pointers to Structures

This next program shows the use of pointers for accessing structure elements. Here we define two variables of the type **mountain**. The member **Height** isn't initialized in either of these objects. Its value is set to 0. Therefore, the function call **Say(1,E)** outputs:

```
1 Everest 0
```

You can see that we use header file **MOUNTAIN.H** which contains the type **mountain** declaration. The contents of this file is defined following the program. This will be used in other programs in this chapter.

```
//         Program 9.4
//         Pointer to structure
#include "mountain.h"      // Type mountain
#include <string.h>        // for strcpy()
#include <iostream.h>

void main()
{  //        Objects of type mountain
   mountain E={"Everest "};       // 0 height
   mountain M={"? "};             // Any mountain

   //       Pointers to mountain
   mountain *pE = &E;             // pE points to Everest
   mountain *pM;                  // Not initialized
```

```
   Say (1,E);                      // 1 Everest 0
   Say (2, *pE);                   // 2 Everest 0

   pM = pE;                        // pM points to Everest
   pM -> Height = 8848;            // Indirect member selector ->
   Say(3,E);                       // 3 Everest 8848

   Say(4,M);                       // 4 ? 0
   pM = &M;                        // pM now points to M
   (*pM).Height = 8848;            // Same as pM->Height=8848;
   Say(5,M);                       // 5 ? 8848

   *pM = *pE;                      // Copy structure E to M
   Say(6,M);                       // 6 Everest 8848

   strcpy(pM -> Name, "The biggest mountain");
   Say(7,M);                       // 7 The biggest mountain 8848
}
void    Say(int N, mountain M);
[
   cout   << N << '' << M.Name << M.Height << endl;
]
```

```
// File "mountain.h"

struct  mountain           // Type mountain
{
   char Name[21];
   int  Height;
};
```

How It Works

The first argument of the function **Say()** is the sequence number of the call of the function. This will allow you to connect the lines of code with the output on the screen.

```
   mountain *pE = &E;       // pE points to Everest
   mountain *pM;            // Not initialized
```

Two pointers **pE** and **pM** are defined. These are pointers to objects of the type **mountain**, or, more briefly, pointers to **mountain**. We use the letter 'p' (from a pointer) first in the names of pointers.

Pointer **pE** is initialized by the address of the structure **E**. To access the structure pointed to by **pE**, we use the dereference operator (*), which means that ***pE** is the same as **E**. Therefore, the call to **Say(2,*pE)** outputs onto the screen the values of the members of **E**:

```
2 Everest 0
```

In the program the value of the pointer **pE** remains unchanged.

```
pM = pE;                // pM points to Everest
pM -> Height = 8848;    // Indirect member selector ->
```

The value of the pointer **pM** becomes the same as **pE**. In the next line the operator **->** is used which is new to you. It's called the **indirect member selector** because it accesses the member of a structure through a pointer. There mustn't be any blanks between the symbols that form this operator. The statement in the second line here means that value 8848 is assigned to the member **Height** in the structure **E** which **pM** points to. Instead of the indirect member selector **->**, you could use the direct member selector (.). For example, the statement:

```
(* pM).Height = 8848;
```

is equivalent to the second line above. You can use either of these two forms. The form with **->** is clearer and is usually preferred. The next figure shows the correspondence between the various ways of accessing data through pointers.

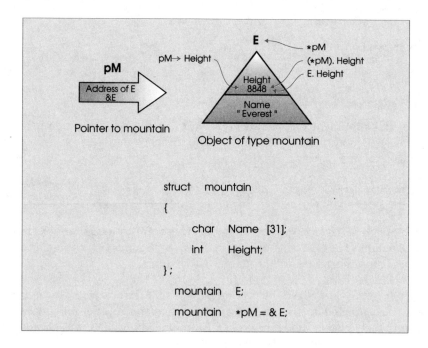

```
pM = &M;                           // pM now points to M
(*pM).Height = 8848;               // Same as pM->Height=8848;
Say(5,M);                          // 5 ? 8848
```

In the statement, the value of **pM** is changed to point to **M**. Then the value of the member **Height** is set for the object **M**, to be the same as that of **E**. That's why the next **Say(5,M)** outputs

```
5 ? 8848
```

```
*pM = *pE;                         // Copy structure E to M
```

This statement copies the contents of the structure **E** into the structure **M** which is equivalent to saying **M = E**. Now **Say(6,M)** outputs:

```
6 Everest 8848
```

```
strcpy(pM -> Name, "The biggest mountain");
Say(7,M);                    // 7 The biggest mountain 8848
```

In order to change the name, we used the function **strcpy()** in the line which copies the string "The biggest mountain " into the character array **Name** of **M**. As a result **Say(7,M)** gives:

```
7 The biggest mountain 8848
```

Size of a Mountain

Now with the help of the operator **sizeof** we can obtain the size of the **mountain** structure meaning the amount of memory in bytes occupied by an object of type **mountain**, not it's height above sea level. As we have mentioned before, the values given by the operator **sizeof** can differ on different computers. It also depends on the compiler parameters.

Try It Out - Using sizeof

Let's see how this works in practice.

```
//        Program 9.5
//        Size of a mountain
#include <iostream.h>
#include "mountain.h"                              // Type mountain

void main()
{
  mountain M;
                                                   // Output
  cout << sizeof M.Name  << '+'                    // 21+2=23?
       << sizeof M.Height << '='
       << sizeof (mountain)  << '\?' << endl;
  cout << sizeof (char *)                          // ?
       << sizeof (int *)                           // as above
       << sizeof (mountain *);                     // as above
}
```

The output of the program on our computer is as follows:

```
21+2=23?
222
```

How It Works

As you can see, 11+2 gives 14. This is not because our computer doesn't like the number 13. It appears that the compiler can add empty bytes into the structures (this is called an alignment) to increase the speed of operation. Variables of the basic data types are typically placed in addresses that are multiples of their length.

> You should rely only on the value of a structure size given by the operator `sizeof`, and not on the sum of sizes forming the structure of members.

```
  cout << sizeof (char *)                     // ?
       << sizeof (int *)                      // as above
       << sizeof (mountain *)                 // as above
```

These lines output the sizes of three different pointers. These output three identical numbers. In our case it was 2. This is the number of bytes occupied by a pointer. This shows that our pointers are of the same length, regardless of what they point to. (Here we have simplified the situation to some extent.)

Nested Structures

When talking about mountains, we mustn't forget the people who conquered them. Let's add data about the first conqueror of the mountain and the date of the first ascent to the information we already have. We can do this in the following way:

```
struct mountain
{
   char    MountainName[21];
   int     Height;
   char    Name[21];
   int     Day;
   char    Month[11];
   int     Year;
};
```

We had to substitute **MountainName** for the name of the mountain so as not to confuse it with the name of the person who first climbed it, **Name**. The names of all the members in one structure must be different.

Imagine now that we want to hold information about a person's name and date of birth. This information can be collected in the form of a structure:

```
struct person
{
   char Name[21];
   int  Day;
   char Month[11];
   int  Year;
};
```

Comparing two structures you see that our latest structure type **person** contains a subset of the members of the structure type **mountain**. C++ allows us to use structures as structure members, so we can write:

```
struct mountain
{
   char MountainName[21];
   int  Height;
   person Climber;
};
```

Here **Climber** is the name of a structure member of the type **person**.

Try It Out - Using Nested Structures

The use of nested structures is demonstrated in Program 9.6.

```
//      Program 9.6
//      A Climber and a Mountain. Nested structures
#include <iostream.h>

//      Structure definitions
struct  date                            // Type date
{
  int  Day;
  char Month[11];
  int  Year;
};

struct  person                          // Type person
{
  char Name[21];
  date Date;                            // Nested structure
};

struct  mountain                        // Type mountain
{
  char    Name[21];
  int     Height;
  person Climber;                       // Nested structure
};

void SayAbout(date);

void main()
{
  mountain M = {                        // M
              "Everest ",               // M.Name
              8848,                     // M.Height
              {                         // M.Climber
              "Edmund Hillary",         // M.Climber.Name
                {                       // M.Climber.Date
                 29,                    // M.Climber.Date.Day
                "May",                  // M.Climber.Date.Month
                 1919                   // M.Climber.Date.Year
                }
              }
            };
  cout << "One of the first people to reach the summit of " << M.Name
       << '(' << M.Height << ")\nwas " << M.Climber.Name << " in ";

  M.Climber.Date.Year = 1953;
  SayAbout(M.Climber.Date);
}
```

```
void  SayAbout(date D)
{
   cout << D.Day << "th of " << D.Month << ", " << D.Year;
}
```

The program outputs the information:

```
One of the first people to reach the summit of Everest (8848)
was Edmund Hillary on 29th of May, 1953
```

How It Works

Three types of structures are defined in this program: **date**, **person**, and **mountain**. The structure **Climber** of type **person** is a member of structure **mountain**, and the structure **Date** of type **date** in its turn is a member of the structure **person**.

Note that the structures **mountain** and **person** contain members with similar names. This is another important advantage of using structures. The names of structure members may coincide with the names of the members of other structures or with the names of normal variables.

```
SayAbout(M.Climber.Date);
```

The structure of the type **date**, which is a member of the structure **person**, is used as an argument of the function **SayAbout()**. Here, the compound name **M.Climber.Date** designates the structure **Date**, that is a member of the structure **Climber**, that in turn is a member of the structure **M**.

```
M.Climber.Date.Year = 1953;
```

The above statement shows how a member of a nested structure is referenced. For access to the member **Year** of a structure **Date**, that is a member of a structure **Climber**, from a structure **M**, the direct member selector operator is used three times.

As you see in Program 9.6, the initialization of a nested structure is executed with the help of nested pairs of braces. The comments indicate the compound names of the structure members being initialized.

An Array of Mountain Structures

Having dealt with the highest summit in the world you are now faced with arrays of mountains. In C++ an array can be declared for any data type.

Try It Out - Arrays of Structures

The declaration of an array of mountains is shown in Program 9.7:

```
//        Program 9.7
//        Array of mountain structures
#include "mountain.h"          // Type mountain
#include <iomanip.h>           // as IOMANIP.H includes IOSTREAM.H there is
                               // no need to include IOSTREAM.H here
void SayAbout(mountain M);

void main()
{
  mountain AM[] =              // Array of structures of type mountain
                  {            // Initializer list for 7 structures
             {"Kosciusko", 2228}, // Initializer sublist for a structure
             {"Vinson Massif", 5140},
             {"El'brus", 5642},
             {"Kilimanjaro",5895},
             {"McKinley", 6193},
             {"Aconcagua", 6960},
             {"Everest", 8848}    // <- No comma at the end of the list
                  };

  int N = sizeof AM / sizeof AM[0];        // Number of array elements
  for (int i=0; i<N; i++)
    SayAbout( AM[i] );
}


void  SayAbout(mountain M)
{// Display members Name and Height
 // of a structure M of type mountain
   cout << setw (20) << M.Name << setw (6) << M.Height << endl;
}
```

The output list has the form:

```
    Kosciusko  2228
Vinson Massif  5140
      El'brus  5642
   Kilimanjaro  5895
      McKinley  6193
     Aconcagua  6960
       Everest  8848
```

How It Works

The name of the array is **AM** (Array of Mountains). Its elements are structures of the type **mountain**. The number of array elements isn't indicated explicitly. It's computed by the compiler from the initializer list, and is equal to 7. Each array element is initialized with the help of a nested list, each element having its own set of initial values between braces.

```
int N = sizeof AM / sizeof AM[0];          // Number of array elements
for (int i=0; i<N; i++)
   SayAbout( AM[i] );
```

You can calculate the number of array elements (if it isn't explicitly given) as we have seen previously, by dividing the size of the array by the size of a single element, as we have done. Then we use the number of elements, **N**, for controlling the loop to output a list of mountains to the screen.

Each element of the array **AM** is transferred (copied) into the function **SayAbout()** which outputs the members of that element as a single line on the screen.

Moving an Array of Mountains

Often, arrays are defined in one function but need to be used in others. We can do this by moving an array from one function to another.

Try It Out - Moving Arrays

Let's modify the function **SayAbout()** so that it can receive the whole array **AM** as an argument, and output the whole list of mountains. This is done in Program 9.8 in the function **Say()**.

```
//       Program 9.8
//       Moving array of mountain structures
#include "mountain.h"                       // Type mountain
#include <iomanip.h>

void Say(mountain am[], int N);

void main()
{
mountain AM[] =
    { {"Kosciusko", 2228}, {"Vinson Massif", 5140}, {"El'brus",5642},
      {"Kilimanjaro",5895}, {"McKinley", 6193}, {"Aconcagua",  6960},
      {"Everest",    8848} };
```

```
    int N = sizeof AM / sizeof AM [0];          // Number of array elements
    Say(AM,N);                                  // Display list of mountains
}

void Say(mountain am[], int N)
{// Display N elements of array am of type mountain
  for (int i=0; i<N; i++)
    cout << setw (20) << am[i].Name << setw (6) << am[i].Height << endl;
}
```

How It Works

```
void Say(mountain am[], int N)
{
```

The first argument of **Say()** is declared as an array of mountains, and the second argument as an integer count of the number of elements. The **for** loop used to output the array elements has been transferred into the body of the function **Say()**.

```
cout << setw (20) << am[i].Name << setw (6) << am[i].Height << endl;
```

In the output statement in the loop, **am[i].Name** designates the member **Name** in the **(i+1)**-th element of array. This program outputs the same list on the screen as the Program 9.7.

```
Say(AM,N);                                  // Display list of mountains
```

When the function **Say(AM,N)** is called, the structure array **AM** is passed to it as an argument. Is it reasonable to transfer a structure array into the function? We have already said that to pass a structure as an argument of a function would result in copying the whole structure. This way processor time and memory would both be wasted. You would think that the transfer of an array of structures must be even more wasteful and inefficient. However, it's not like this. In fact, when the function **Say()** is called, the **AM** structure array isn't copied. Only the address of the first array element is transferred.

As we saw in Chapter 6, an array name by itself specifies the address of the first array element, so in our case **AM** is the same as **&AM[0]**. Therefore, the argument **am** of the function **Say()** isn't an array but only a constant of the type pointer to a mountain.

You could try in Program 9.8 to declare a pointer

```
mountain * pM = M;
```

after the definition of the array `AM`, and try to pass it to `Say(pM,N)`. Such an attempt to pass a variable and not a constant into the function `Say()`, will be perceived by the compiler as an error. It's easy to correct this error by changing the declaration of the function `Say()` to:

```
void Say(mountain *pM, int N);
```

The Size of an Array

Now that it's clear that the parameter `am` in the function `Say()` in Program 9.8 isn't an array, but is only a pointer you may wonder why the second argument `N` - the number of array elements being output - is needed in the function `Say()`.

You could conceivably put a statement in the function `Say()` to perform the same calculations we have in `main()` for `N`, but applied to the array `am`:

```
N = sizeof am / sizeof am[0];
```

If you try this you won't get the result you want. On our computer, we get the result:

```
sizeof am / sizeof am[0] = 2 / 23 = 0
```

so we completely fail to calculate the number of elements in the `am` array. It appears to be equal to 0. The reason is that the argument declared as:

```
mountain am[]
```

is considered by the compiler to be a pointer and, accordingly, `sizeof(am)` gives the size of the pointer, and not the size of the array, `sizeof(AM)`. Therefore, it's necessary to pass the number of elements `N` as the second argument.

Array and Pointer Arithmetic

There is a close connection between pointers and arrays in C++. Let's see what this means in practice.

Try It Out - Arrays and Pointers

In this next program the array **A** of **mountain** type structures is defined. The names of the mountains are numbered in such a way that the number coincides with the element index in the array. In the program there are a variety of expressions using both the array name **A** (the constant pointer to the beginning of the array), and the variable **P** which is of type pointer to **mountain**.

```
//        Program 9.9
//        Pointers and arrays
#include "mountain.h"                                    // Type mountain
#include <iostream.h>

void main()
{ // Array of montains
   mountain A[] =
   { {"0 Everest", 8848}, {"1 Aconcagua", 6960}, {"2 McKinley", 6193},
     {"3 Kilimanjaro",5895}, {"4 El'brus", 5642}, {"5 Vinson Massif", 5140},
     {"6 Kosciusko", 2228} };

   cout << "\nTesting pointer arithmetic\n"
                                                // Output
       << ( A->Name) << endl                    // 0 Everest
       << ( (&A[0])->Name) << endl << ( (*A).Name) << endl
       << ( A[0].Name) << endl
       << ( (A + 2)->Name) << endl              // 2 McKinley
       << ( (&A[2])->Name) << endl << ((*(A + 2)).Name) << endl
       << ( A[2].Name) << endl << ( A[3].Name) << endl  // 3 Kilimanjaro
       << ( 4[A].Name) << endl                  // 4 El'brus      <-- 3
       << endl;

   mountain *P = A + 2;                          // P points to "2 McKinley"
   cout << ( (P - 2)->Name) << endl             // 0 Everest
       << ( (&P[-2])-> Name) << endl << ((*(P - 2)).Name)
       << endl << ( P[-2].Name) << endl
       << (P->Name) << endl                     // 2 McKinley
       << ( (&P[0])->Name) << endl << ( (*P).Name) << endl
       << (   P [0] .  Name)  << endl;

   cout << ((++P)->Name) << endl;               // 3 Kilimanjaro
   cout << ((++P)->Name) << endl;               // 4 El'brus
}
```

How It Works

Let's take a look at some of the expressions typical for pointer arithmetic in C++. You already know that the name of an array is the address of the beginning of the array. That's why the expression:

```
A->Name
```

means the name of the mountain for the first array element. In the next line the expression `&A[0]`, owing to the priority of the operation `[]`, means the expression `&(A[0])`, in other words, the address of the first element, which is the same as A.

```
<< ( (*A).Name) << endl
```

Here `*A` means "the value at the address A", so it designates the first array element, and `(*A).Name` specifies the value of the member `Name` of this element. Parentheses are obligatory as the operation (.) takes precedence over (*). Further, in the next line `A[0]` designates the first array element. You can see that in C++ the expressions `*(A+i)` and `A[i]` are equivalent.

Any expression of the form `x[y]` in C++ is interpreted as `*(x + y)`. Since the sum doesn't change during the exchange of the places of `x` and `y`, the expression means the same as `y[x]`.

We would recommend that you never code like this! We have included this code simply to give you a better understanding of array and pointer arithmetic.

```
<< ( 4[A].Name) << endl                 // 4 El'brus      <-- 3
```

You may be convinced of this in view of the line that contains `4[A]`. The form `A[4]` is clearer and usually preferred, though the forms are the same for the compiler.

```
mountain *P = A + 2;                     // P points to "2 McKinley"
```

In this statement, the variable `P` of the type "pointer to mountain" is initialized by the value `A+2`, so according to the rules of pointer arithmetic, `P` points to the element with index 2 which is the third element.

```
cout << ( (P - 2)->Name) << endl              // 0 Everest
    << ( (&P[-2])->Name) << endl << ((*(P - 2)).Name)
    << endl << ( P[-2].Name) << endl
```

Here you can see that pointers can also be decremented. Is this case the count of array elements is towards the beginning of the array.

```
cout << ((++P)->Name) << endl;               // 3 Kilimanjaro
cout << ((++P)->Name) << endl;               // 4 El'brus
```

The operation ++ is used, which means "go to the next array element" in pointer arithmetic. Since the operation is prefixed, P is first increased and then P->Name is calculated. Notice that here we had to repeat cout otherwise the operation ++ results in side effects, as we have seen before.

This program is illustrated in the following figure. Here we show the correlation between different ways of referencing elements.

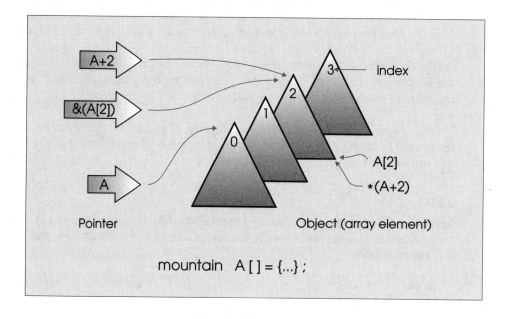

mountain A [ ] = {...} ;

Try It Out - Using a Pointer as a Structure Member

C++ allows you to combine various kinds of data into structures, including pointers. In Program 9.10 two types of data are declared: **MOUNTAIN** and **mountain**.

```
//        Program 9.10
//        Using pointers as structure members
#include <iostream.h>
#include <iomanip.h>

struct  MOUNTAIN                            // Big MOUNTAIN
{
  char Name[21];                            // Array of chars
  int Height;
};

struct  mountain                            // Little mountain
{
  char *Name;                               // Pointer to char
  int Height;
};

void Say(MOUNTAIN *,int);
void Say(mountain *,int);

void main()
{
  MOUNTAIN M[]={ {"Everest", 8848},{"McKinley",6193} };
  mountain m[]={ {"Kilimanjaro",5895},{"El'brus", 5642} };

  cout << "\nBig MOUNTAIN:\t\t" << sizeof M << ' '
       << sizeof (MOUNTAIN) << endl << endl;

  Say(M, sizeof M / sizeof M [0]);

  cout << "\nLittle mountain:\t" << sizeof m << ' '
       << sizeof (mountain) << endl << endl;

  Say(m, sizeof m / sizeof m [0]);
}

void Say(MOUNTAIN *pM,int N)
{
  for (int i=0; i<N; i++, pM++)
    cout  << setw (20) << pM->Name << setw (6) << pM->Height << endl;
}

void Say(mountain *pM,int N)
{
  for (int i=0; i<N; i++, pM++)
    cout  << setw (20) << pM->Name << setw (6) << pM->Height << endl;
}
```

How It Works

We have used the **MOUNTAIN** type in previous programs. Unlike the type **mountain**, it contains a pointer to a character rather than an array of characters. If you run this program you will obtain the output:

```
Big MOUNTAIN:      46 23

Everest       8848
McKinley      6193

Little mountain:    8 4

Kilimanjaro      5895
El'brus         5642
```

This shows that the size of the structure **Mountain** (23 on our computer) is far larger than the size of the structure of the type **mountain** (4). Therefore, it's reasonable to apply pointers as structure members instead of arrays, since you can significantly reduce the size of a structure. However, you must initialize the pointer or no space will be allocated.

```
MOUNTAIN M[]={ {"Everest", 8848},{"McKinley",6193} };

mountain m[]={ {"Kilimanjaro",5895},{"El'brus", 5642} };
```

Note that in these lines the initialization of arrays of both types look similar.

Sharing Memory - Unions

In addition to structures there is another way of combining data in C++. Syntactically it looks the same as a structure, but instead of the keyword **struct** you use the keyword **union**. In the next program a union object with the name **UNION1** is defined. As you will see, its definition is identical to the definition of the structure with the name **STRUCT1**. The aim of the program is to demonstrate the difference in the sizes of the objects **STRUCT1** and **UNION1**. Execute the program and you will get:

```
sizeof People      5000
sizeof Mountains  10000
sizeof STRUCT1    15000
sizeof UNION1     10000
```

The first number is the size of the array **People** consisting of 500 elements of 10 bytes each. The second is the size of the array **Mountains** which has 1000 elements of 10 bytes each. The third is the size of the structure **STRUCT1** that includes both arrays identical to the previous ones. Therefore, the size of the structure **STRUCT1** is equal to the sum of the previous two sizes: 15000. But what about **UNION1**? Is it a mistake?

Try It Out - Unions

To answer the above question, let's see all this in action.

```
//        Program 9.11
//        Union of person and mountain
#include <iostream.h>

struct person                               // Type person
{
  char Name[10];
};

struct mountain                             // Type mountain
{
  char Name[10];
};

person People[500];                         // Array of type person
mountain Mountains[1000];                   // Array of type mountain

struct
{
  person People[500];
  mountain Mountains[1000];
} STRUCT1;                                  // Structure STRUCT1 (one object)

union
{
  person People[500];
  mountain Mountains[1000];
} UNION1;                                   // Union UNION1 (one object)

void main()
{                                                       // Output
cout << "sizeof People\t\t"  <<  sizeof People    << endl  // 5000
     << "sizeof Mountains\t" << sizeof Mountains << endl   // 10000
     << "sizeof STRUCT1\t\t" << sizeof STRUCT1   << endl   // 15000
     << "sizeof UNION1\t\t"  << sizeof UNION1    << endl;  // 10000
}
```

Try It Out!

How It Works

Look at the output from the program. The last result 10000 for the size of the **union UNION1** is correct, though it may surprise you. You might think it should be 15000, but not 10000. The difference is that all members declared in the **union** are located in memory, not one after another as in a structure, but each beginning at the same place.

In a structure, each member (data element) has its own unique memory address. However, the members in a union share the same memory area. In a union, only one member is stored at any one time. Therefore, the size of the union is equal to the size of the largest member (in our case **Mountains**, 1000*10 bytes), and all the other members share the same memory. This is the principal distinction between a **union** and a structure and is shown in the following figure.

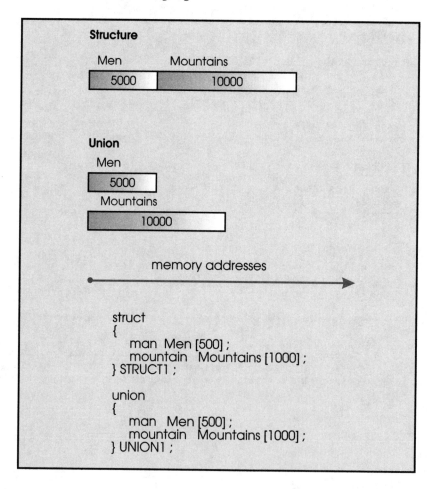

Unions may be used to save memory in situations when data isn't needed all at the same time in a program. Imagine that the program at first inputs data about 500 people, sorts them and outputs the result. Then it inputs data about 1000 mountains, also sorts them and outputs the result. In this case a union of two arrays can be used quite safely, and is the best from a memory saving point of view.

Perhaps we should mention that unions are not used very often and almost never by novice programmers.

Try It Out - Using Unions

If the data from the arrays **People** and **Mountain** are used jointly, then this solution won't do. Program 9.12 illustrates this. Here the union contains structures rather than arrays. There is also a tag **UNION2** in the declaration of the union which is the name of a new data type.

```
//      Program 9.12
//      Using union of person and mountain
#include <iostream.h>

struct person                                 // Structure type person
{
   char Name[10];
};

struct mountain                               // Structure type mountain
{
   char Name[10];
};

union UNION2                                   // Union type UNION2
{
   person Climber;
   mountain Mountain;
};

void main()
{
   person H = {"Hillary"};
   mountain E = {"Everest"};
   UNION2 U;

   U.Climber = H;
   cout << "Climber:\t\t" << U.Climber.Name << endl;

   U.Mountain = E;
   cout << "Mountain:\t" << U.Mountain.Name << endl;

   cout << "Climber:\t\t" << U.Climber.Name << "!\?" << endl;
}
```

Try It Out!

385

How It Works

```
person H = {"Hillary"};
mountain E = {"Everest"};
UNION2 U;
```

In Program 9.12 three objects are defined in the above lines. You can see that access to a member of a union is obtained in the same way as to a member of a structure.

```
U.Climber = H;
```

The member **Climber** (structure) of union **U** is initialized by the value of the structure **H**. The next statement outputs onto the screen:

```
Climber:          Hillary
```

Similarly, the statements:

```
UNION1.Mountain = E;
cout << "Mountain:\t" << U.Mountain.Name << endl;
```

produce the output:

```
Mountain:        Everest
```

The output produced by the next line just confirms the last figure. It shows that both members (**People** and **Mountain**) occupy a common memory area, so the change of the value of **Mountain** results in a loss of the value of **Climber**. As a consequence you need to keep track of which member was written last when using unions.

Reference Types

In this section we will consider another kind of C++ type - reference types. They are closely related to pointers. The major use of references in C++ is for passing arguments to functions and for returning values.

Up to now you have learnt two ways of passing an argument to a function:

▶ Passing an object

▶ Passing a pointer to an object

C++ also includes a third way of passing an argument:

> Passing a reference to an object

Let's take a look at each of these ways in turn.

Passing an Object

When an object is passed to a function, a copy is made of the object and this copy is passed to the function. All subsequent changes to the transferred copy of an object are not reflected in the original. You saw this in Program 6.15.

Passing a Pointer

If an object is a large structure then passing the object to a function is very inefficient. In such a case, a more efficient solution is to pass a pointer to the object. While passing a pointer to a function, a copy is also made and is passed to the function. But a pointer is small and the cost of copying it is minimal.

A function uses a pointer copy passed to it in order to access the object to which this pointer points and all changes made will be reflected in the original object.

Try It Out - Passing a Pointer

This is illustrated in the next program. To make it easy to follow, the object was taken to be a simple variable of **int** type, but the principle of using a pointer here is the same as for any kind of object including structures.

```
//      Program 9.13
//      Pass 'pointer to object' to change object
#include <iostream.h>

int X = 1;                              // Object

void ChangeP(int * x);
void Say(int x);

void main()
{                                       // Output
  Say(X);                               //  1
  ChangeP( &X );                                // Pass &X to change X
  Say(X);                               //  2
}
```

Try It Out!

```
                              // Pass 'pointer to object' as function argument
void     ChangeP(int * x)
{// Argument x is of type 'pointer to int'
  // When calling ChangeP(&X) x points to X

   *x = 2;                              // Same as X = 2
}
                                       // Pass object as function argument
void Say(int x)
{
   cout << x << endl;
}
```

How It Works

In this program a global variable **x** is defined and initialized with the value 1. Therefore, the first call of the function **Say()**:

```
   Say(X);                         //  1
```

results in an output of 1 to the screen.

```
   ChangeP( &X );                  // Pass &X to change X
```

Then the function **ChangeP()** is invoked, with a pointer **&X** - an address of the variable **x** - as the argument. The address is copied into the parameter **x** of the function and **x** then points to **X**. Then, with the help of the dereference operator (*):

```
   *x = 2;                         // Same as X = 2
```

the value of the object **x** is changed.

Passing a Reference

Now let's see how the next program executes the same, with the use of a reference to an object **x**. The program is very similar to the previous one. Comparing them line by line you will find four main differences. They are given in the following table.

Program	9.13	9.14
Function	ChangeP()	ChangeR()
Call	ChangeP(&X)	ChangeR(X)
Argument	int * x	int & x
Body	* x = 2;	x = 2;

Try It Out - Passing a Reference

You see that in Program 9.14, when calling the function **ChangeR()** the name of the object **x** is used as the argument, not its address **&X**, as in Program 9.13. This tends to look more natural and is easier to read.

```
//       Program 9.14
//       Pass 'reference to object' to change an object
#include <iostream.h>

int X = 1;                           // Object

void ChangeR(int & x);
void Say(int x);

void main()
{                        // Output
   Say(X);               // 1
   ChangeR ( X );                    // Pass X to change it !!!
   Say(X);               // 2
}

void ChangeR(int & x)    // Pass 'reference to object' as function argument
{ //       Argument x is of type 'reference to int'
   //       When calling ChangeR (X) x refers to X

   x = 2;                            // Same as X = 2
}

void Say(int x)                      // Pass object as function argument
{
   cout << x << endl;
}
```

How It Works

Note that we only used the letters **R** and **P** in the function names to distinguish these functions in the two examples. Letter **P** suggests that a pointer is used, and letter **R** that a reference is applied.

The definition of the parameter to the function **ChangeR()** indicates that it is a 'reference to **int**'. As a result, in the body of the function **ChangeR()**, the name of the argument **x** is used without a dereference operator. A reference acts rather like an alias for the original value as no dereferencing is necessary.

How a Reference is Transferred

The most unusual thing about the operation of the function **ChangeR()** is the fact that a change of the local argument **x** results in a change of the global object **X**, which is shown in the program output:

```
1
2
```

The reason is that calling a function with a reference argument transfers a pointer. What's more, we don't have to dereference the argument in the body of the function. That's why we can say that passing a reference to a function is more effective than passing the object itself.

In the next table three ways of passing argument are compared.

Pass	Object	Pointer	Reference
Call	**f (&X)**	**f (X)**	**f (X)**
Argument	**int x**	**int * x**	**int & x**
Passing	Object	Pointer explicitly	Pointer implicitly
Access to X from **f()** body	none	***x**	**x**

Try It Out - Using Reference as Aliases

Reference types are also used for the creation of object synonyms, or aliases. Program 9.15 gives some examples of these.

```cpp
//      Program 9.15
//      Reference types
#include <iostream.h>

void main()
{
  int X = 0;
  int & rX = X;                      // Reference declaration
                                     // Name rX is alias for X
                                     // rX must be initialized
                            // Output
  rX = 1;                            // Same as X=1
  cout << X << rX   << endl;  // 11
```

Try It Out!

```
    X++;
    cout << X << rX   << endl;      // 22

    int * prX = &rX;                              // &rX is the same as &X;

    (*prX)++;                                     // Same as rX++, same as X++
    cout << X << *prX << endl;      // 33

    int & rrX = rX;                               // One more alias for X

    rrX++;                                        // Same as X++
    cout << X << rrX   << endl;      // 44

    const int & crX = X;                          // One more alias for X

    X++;
    cout << X << crX << endl;       // 55
}
```

How It Works

```
    int & rX = X;                                 // Reference declaration
```

This line of the example declares the name **rX** to be a synonym for the
name **X**. After such a declaration, any operation on **rX** has precisely the
same effect as an operation on **X** itself. For example, in the line:

```
    rX = 1;                                       // Same as X=1
```

the value 1 is assigned to the variable **X** , the statement being the
equivalent of:

```
    X = 1;
```

The next statement:

```
    cout << X << rX   << endl;           // 11
```

outputs the value of **X** twice since again **rX** means the same as **X**. The name
rX serves only for the purpose of referencing the object **X**. In a very real
sense it isn't an object, but the name **rX** has the type: 'reference to **int**', so
using **rX** in the program implicitly means using a pointer to the object **X**.

Initialization of a Reference

You should note that a reference to a given type **T** must be initialized by an object of the type **T**. Therefore, if a variable **Var** of type **T** is declared:

```
T Var;
```

then the declaration of a reference to **Var** should have the form:

```
T &RefVar = Var;
```

Once declared, the reference **RefVar** can't be changed to refer to another object. Note that the equals sign in the initialization of a reference is treated very differently to an assignment. Therefore, the assignment:

```
rX = 1;                                    // Same as X=1
```

operates on the object referred to (**x**). But the initialization sign (**=**) in the statement:

```
int & rX = X;                              // Reference declaration
```

indicates the name of an object (**x**), the synonym of which is **rX**.

You could try discarding the initialization expression in the declaration of **rX** obtaining:

```
int & rX;
```

The compiler will output an error message.

You can also confirm that blanks in a declaration of a reference don't matter, by trying the following forms of writing the declaration:

```
int&  rX  = X;
int     &rX = X;
int & rX  = X;
int&rX    = X;
```

What Does a Pointer to a Reference Point to?

```
int *  prX = &rX;                                    // &rX is the same as &X;
```

Let's consider what the definition in the last program means. Here a pointer **prX** of the type 'pointer to **int**' is declared and is initialized by the address, **&rX**.

Here **&rX** means ' the address of **x**', and not 'the address of a reference'. It's a general rule that any operation with a reference gives the same effect as an operation with the object to which it references. Therefore, **&(rX)** means the same as **&X** and the pointer **prX** points to **x**.

```
(*prX)++;                                            // Same as rX++, same as X++
```

This means that the above statement increments **x** by 1.

What Does a Reference to a Reference Refer to?

In the last program there is one more interesting definition:

```
int & rrX = rX;
```

Here a reference **rrX** is declared and initialized by the name **rX**. You can obtain the same effect by substituting **x** for **rX**. That is, **rrX** is another alias for **x** along with **rX**. So incrementing **rrX** :

```
rrX++;                                               // Same as X++
```

increments **x** by 1.

Reference to a Constant

In order to prevent the accidental modification of an object, you often use a declaration of a reference of the form:

```
const int & crX = X;
```

This means that the reference **crX** mustn't be changed. Any attempt to use the name **crX** to change **x**, such as:

```
crX++;   // Error
```

will be flagged by the compiler as an error. A 'reference to **const**' type argument can be used as an effective alternative to calling by value, to protect values being passed from modification.

Try It Out - Returning a Reference

In Program 9.16, we shall look at a function that returns a reference.

```
//        Program 9.16
//        Pass a REFERENCE and return it
#include <iostream.h>

void Use(int & x);
int & UseRet(int & x);
void  Say(const int & x);

void main()
{
  int X  = 1;              // Output

  Say(X);                  // 1
  Say(UseRet(X));          // 2
  Use (X);
  Say(X);                  // 3
}

void Use(int & x)          // Pass reference to use it
{
  ++x;
}

int & UseRet(int & x)      // Pass reference and return it
{
  return ++x;
}

void Say(const int & x)  // Pass 'reference to const'
{
  cout << x;
}
```

The program outputs:

3

How It Works

```
void Use(int & x)
{
  ++x;
}
```

Here a function **Use()** is defined, which accepts an argument **x** of the type "reference to **int**" and increments the object referred to by **x**. The function doesn't return a value.

```
int & UseRet(int & x)
{
  return ++x;
}
```

The second function **UseRet()** differs from the previous one only in that it returns a value. It returns the reference which was passed to it.

```
Say(UseRet (X));          // 2
```

Here you can see how this function is used. The returned value is used as an argument of the function **Say()**. To achieve the same result with the function **Use()** that doesn't return a reference, requires the two statements:

```
Use (X);
Say(X);                   // 3
```

Try discarding the four **&** signs in Program 9.17. The functions will then accept and return the objects themselves, but not references. Can you work out why the program output will be 121?

The Advantages of Using References

In order that you can evaluate the advantages of using references, we have prepared two more programs which do the same as Program 9.16, but with different methods. In Program 9.17, arguments are transferred, and a result is returned using the 'pass by value' method. Program 9.18 uses pointers. It's easy to see that Program 9.16, which uses references, is by far the most readable.

Try It Out - Passing By Value

Let's look at the first example.

```
//        Program 9.17
//        Pass VALUE and return it
#include <iostream.h>

int UseRet(int x);
void Say(const int x);

void main()
{
  int X  = 1;
                            // Output
  Say(X);                   // 1
  X=UseRet(X);
  Say(X);                   // 2
  X=UseRet(X);
  Say(X);                   // 3
}

int UseRet(int x)           // Pass value and return it
{
  return ++x;
}

void  Say(const int x)      // Pass const value
{
  cout << x << endl;
}
```

Try It Out   Passing Using Pointers

Now let's look at the second example.

```
//        Program 9.18
//        Pass POINTER and return it
#include <iostream.h>

void Use(int * x);
int * UseRet(int * x);
void Say(const int * x);

void main()
{
  int X  = 1;
                            // Output
  Say(&X);                  // 1
  Say (UseRet(&X));         // 2
  Use(&X);
```

```
    Say(&X);                  // 3
}

void Use(int * x)            // Pass pointer to use it
{
   ++(*x);
}

int * UseRet(int * x)        // Pass pointer and return it
{
   ++(*x);
   return x;
}

void Say(const int * x)      // Pass 'pointer to const'
{
   cout << *x << endl;
}
```

Designing a Program

You have now reached the end of this chapter and we can see how we can make use of what we have learnt in a complete program.

The Problem

The problem we have to solve is to write a program that can store details of books entered via the keyboard in a binary disk file. It's a simple matter to alter this program so that it stores names and addresses, details of your CD collection, or something similar.

The Analysis

The steps involved are:

1 Display a menu inviting the user to enter a choice.

2 Perform the appropriate operations on the file - add record, read a single record, or read all records - and display the results on screen.

3 After the operations have been performed the program returns to the menu screen waiting for the user to make another choice.

The Solution

1   The program starts off by displaying a menu and inviting the user to select the operation to be performed. There will also be a message that says how many records are in the file.

The user will press a number between 1 and 4. This value will be returned to **main()** to be used with the switching variable. For example:

```
number = menu();
```

We need to open the file. The file is in binary form and in this function we need to read from it.

```
library.open("a:\\books.dat", ios::in | ios::binary);
```

We will check to see that there are no errors.

```
if(!library)
   cout << "\nCould not open file\n";
```

We now want to calculate the number of records in the file so that we can display the appropriate message.

```
library.seekg(0, ios::end);
endOfFile = library.tellg();
NoOfRecords = endOfFile / sizeof(book);
```

We are using the **seekg()** and the **tellg()** functions. The **seekg()** function can be used in two ways. It can be used with a single argument that represents a position in the file - the start of the file is byte 0. Alternatively, the function can be used with two arguments as shown in the above code fragment. As we discussed in the last chapter, the first argument represents an offset from a specific location and the second stipulates the location from which this offset is to be measured. There are three possibilities for the second argument:

beg   the beginning of the file
cur   the current position
end   the end of the file.

In the code fragment above, the file pointer is moved to the end of the file. The **tellg()** function returns the file pointer's position in bytes. In this case the function returns the length of the file in bytes. The number of records can then be calculated by dividing the length of the file in bytes by the size of an individual record.

After the function has obtained the information that is needed, the file is closed. This is because the user may want to exit from the program.

2   As you can see from the program, a **switch** statement is used to call the appropriate functions.

add()

If you look at this function you will see that it uses another function, **enter_data()**.

```
void enter_data(data& x)
{
  cout << "\nEnter title: ";
  gets(x.title);
  cout << "Enter author: ";
  gets(x.author);
  cout << "Enter publisher: ";
  gets(x.publisher);
  cout << "Enter date of publication: ";
  cin >> x.date;
  cout << "Enter ISBN number: ";
  gets(x.isbn);
  cout << "Enter price: ";
  cin >> x.price;
}
```

This function uses **gets()** to store the string in the appropriate structure variable. The function **gets()** is an ANSI standard function and you need to include the header file **STDIO.H** to use it. When you run the program you will see that white spaces in the string don't cause any problems.

In addition you will notice the argument to **add()** indicates that the variables will be passed by reference. This means that the **add()** function works with the actual structure variable and not a copy.

The **add()** function opens the file so that records can be added at the end. We will also check for errors.

```
library.open("a:\\books.dat", ios::app | ios::out | ios::binary);
if(!library)
   cout << "\nCould not open file\n";
```

A call to the **enter_data()** function prompts the user to enter the data. The record can then be written to the file.

```
library.write((char *) &book, sizeof(book) );
```

The data is written to the file using the **write()** function. This take two arguments. The first is the address of the variable to be written using the address of operator, **&book**, and the second is the size of the variable in bytes. The **sizeof** keyword is used. You will also see that the address of the variable must be cast to type 'pointer to **char**'.

```
read_rec()
```

This function will read a single record from the file. This function makes use of the **display_data()** function.

The **read_rec()** function opens the file and checks for errors. The user is asked to specify the record number and the program then moves the file pointer to the appropriate record.

```
position = (record - 1) * sizeof(book);
library.seekg(position);
```

Can you see how this works? The position is calculated by multiplying the record number by the size of a record. However, before this calculation is done, we have to subtract one from the record number. This is because the first record is at the start of the file, 0 bytes into the file. If a record is 130 bytes long then record two starts 130 bytes into the file, record three starts 260 bytes into the file, etc. The **seekg()** function is then used to position the file pointer at the appropriate position.

The record is then read and the information is displayed on the screen.

```
library.read((char *) &book, sizeof(book) );
display_data(book);
```

To read the data we use the **read()** function. This takes the same arguments as the **write()** function. The **display_data()** function outputs the information on the screen.

There is a function called **getch()** which we are using to halt the program until a key is pressed. To use this function in other programs you will have to include the header file **CONIO.H**.

The file is then closed.

read()

The **read()** function is used to display all the records on the screen. This is very similar to the **read_rec()** function except that we read all the records and don't have to calculate the position of individual records.

```
while(library)
{
  library.read((char *) &book, sizeof(book) );
  if(!library.eof())
    display_data(book);
}
```

A **while** loop is used to read all the records until the end-of-file marker is found.

3   As a **do while** loop is used in **main()** the program returns to the menu screen after each operation.

```
// book.cpp
// a program to store details of books to a disc file

#include <fstream.h>        //header file for file i/o
#include <stdio.h>          //header file for gets()
#include <conio.h>          //header file for clrscr(), getch()
#include <dos.h>            //header file for sleep()

struct data
{
char title[50];
char author[30];
char publisher[30];
int date;
char isbn[15];
float price;
};
```

```
data book;
int number, record, position;
fstream library;

void main()
{
  void enter_data(data&);
  void display_data(data&);
  int menu();
  void add();
  void read_rec();
  void read();

  do
  {
    number = menu();
    switch(number)
    {
      case 1:
        add();
        break;
      case 2:
        read_rec();
        break;
      case 3:
        read();
        break;
      case 4:
        clrscr();
        cout << "The program is now ending.";
        break;
      default:
        clrscr();
        cout << "You should enter a number between 1 and 4.  Try again.";
        sleep(6);
    }
  }while(number != 4);
}

int menu()
{
  int select, endOfFile, NoOfRecords;

  clrscr();
  cout << endl << "This program manipulates a file containing details of
books\n\n";

  library.open("a:\\books.dat",  ios::in | ios::binary);
  //check for errors
  if(!library)
    cout << "\nCould not open file\n";
```

```
    library.seekg(0, ios::end);
    endOfFile = library.tellg();
    NoOfRecords = endOfFile / sizeof(book);

    cout << "At the present time there are " << NoOfRecords
         << " records in the file.\n";
    cout << "\n\t\tDo you wish to\n"
         << "\t1\tAdd a Record\n" << "\t2\tRead a Record\n"
         << "\t3\tRead all Records\n" << "\t4\tExit from the Program\n"
         << "\nEnter number: ";
    cin >> select;

    library.close();
    return(select);
}

void enter_data(data& x)
{
    cout << "\nEnter title: ";
    gets(x.title);
    cout << "Enter author: ";
    gets(x.author);
    cout << "Enter publisher: ";
    gets(x.publisher);
    cout << "Enter date of publication: ";
    cin >> x.date;
    cout << "Enter ISBN number: ";
    gets(x.isbn);
    cout << "Enter price: ";
    cin >> x.price;
}

void display_data(data& x)
{
    cout << endl << x.title << " written by " << x.author << endl
         << "published by " << x.publisher << " in " << x.date << endl
         << "price £" << x.price << endl << "ISBN number " << x.isbn
         << endl;
}

void add()
{
    library.open("a:\\books.dat", ios::app | ios::out | ios::binary);

    //check for errors
    if(!library)
        cout << "\nCould not open file\n";

    clrscr();
    enter_data(book);
    library.write((char *) &book, sizeof(book) );
```

```
  cout << endl << endl << "Press a key to continue ...";
  library.close();
  getch();
}

void read_rec()
{
  library.open("a:\\books.dat", ios::in | ios::binary);

  //check for errors
  if(!library)
    cout << "\nCould not open file\n";

  clrscr();
  cout << "Which record do you wish to read? ";
  cin >> record;
  cout << endl << endl;
  position = (record - 1) * sizeof(book);
  library.seekg(position);
  library.read((char *) &book, sizeof(book) );
  display_data(book);
  cout << endl << endl << "Press a key to continue ...";
  library.close();
  getch();
}

void read()
{
  library.open("a:\\books.dat", ios::in | ios::binary);

  //check for errors
  if(!library)
    cout << "\nCould not open file\n";

  clrscr();
  library.seekg(0, ios::beg);
  while(library)
  {
    library.read((char *) &book, sizeof(book) );
    if(!library.eof())
      display_data(book);
  }
  cout << endl << endl << "Press a key to continue ...";
  library.close();
  getch();
}
```

We can now try the program.

```
This program manipulates a file containing details of books

At the present time there are 3 records in the file.

   Do you wish to
1  Add a Record
2  Read a Record
3  Read all Records
4  Exit from the Program

Enter number: 3

Instant C++ Programming written by Ian Wilks
published by Wrox Press in 1994
price £18.49
ISBN number 1-874416-29-X

The Beginners Guide to C++ written by Oleg Yaroshenko
published by Wrox Press in 1994
price £22.99
ISBN number 1-874416-26-5

The Revolutionary Guide to Visual C++ written by Ben Ezzell
published by Wrox Press in 1994
price £37.49
ISBN number 1-874416-22-2


Press a key to continue ...


This program manipulates a file containing details of books

At the present time there are 3 records in the file.

   Do you wish to
1  Add a Record
2  Read a Record
3  Read all Records
4  Exit from the Program

Enter number: 4
The program is now ending.
```

Summary

In the C++ language there are two kinds of types: fundamental types and derived types. The fundamental types are: **char**, **short**, **int**, **long int**, **float**, **double**, and **long double**. We have looked at all these types except **short** which is a variety of **int**. The specifiers **unsigned** and **signed** are used to construct varieties of the integer types **char**, **short**, **int**, and **long int**.

Derived types may be constructed from the fundamental types in the following main ways:

- As constants which are values of a given type
- As arrays of objects of a given type
- As pointers to objects of a given type
- As references to objects of a given type
- As structures which are a group of objects of various types
- As unions which are a special kind of structures
- As functions which take arguments of a given type and return objects of a given type

One more user-defined type is a **class**. It is a data type that combines data and functions together. The concept **class** is one of the most important in C++. This is what we will introduce in the next chapter.

CHAPTER 10

Combining Data And
Code Into Classes

This chapter is an introduction to one of the principal concepts of C++ which differentiates it from C - the concept of **classes**. For this reason, C++ was originally given the name "C with Classes". By using classes in C++ you aren't restricted to programming using functions that execute operations on data that is essentially separate from the functions. Instead you will be able to use object-oriented programming (OOP), in which data and functions become closely coupled parts of an object of the type class.

First we'll look again at the concept of a structure. You will see how to combine data and functions into a single structure, how to control the structure, how to initialize and destroy objects using constructors and destructors, and how to control access to structure members using access modifiers. In C++ structure and class are almost identical concepts!

In this chapter you will:

⟫ Use structures that contain functions as well as data

⟫ See how constructors and destructors are utilized

⟫ Examine the differences between private and public members

⟫ Realize that classes and structures are almost identical

⟫ Write a program that can be used to store names and addresses

Structures Containing Functions

Until now we've dealt with two places where we can put data relative to functions as you can see in the following figure.

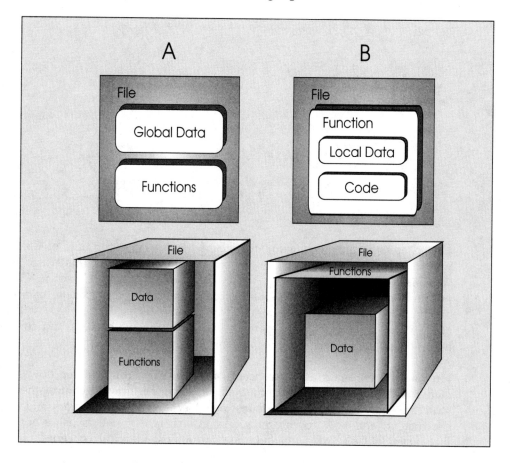

In A, the data definitions are located outside the function definitions, and so the data is called global data. In B, the data definitions are located inside the function definition and so the data is local. Most programs contain both types of data.

Defining a Function Inside a Structure

There is another way that data and functions can be positioned relative to one another. This is illustrated in the next figure.

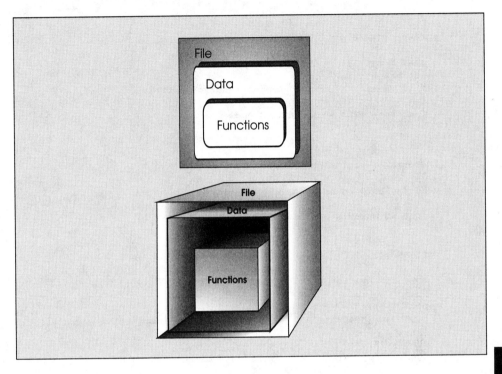

Here, the function definitions are located inside the data definitions.

Try It Out - Defining a Function Inside a Structure

Program 10.1 shows that in C++ it's possible for function definitions to be located inside a data structure. You can see that the definition of the function **Say()** is located inside the declaration of the type **mountain**. A function that is located inside the declaration of a structure is called a member function.

```
//        Program 10.1
//        Structure with function

#include <iostream.h>

//        Structure declaration

struct  mountain
{
  char Name[21];     // Data member declarations
  int Height;
  void Say()               // Member function definition
  {
    cout << Name << Height << endl;
  }
};

// Normal function definition

void SayAbout(mountain M)
{
  cout<<M.Name<<M.Height<<endl;
}

void main()
{
  mountain Everest = {"Everest ",8848};

  cout <<"1. ";
  SayAbout (Everest);        // Using a normal function

  cout <<"2. ";
  Everest.Say ();            // Using a member function
}
```

The program output:

```
1. Everest 8848
2. Everest 8848
```

shows that both functions operate identically.

How It Works

For the purposes of comparison, we will look at the definitions of the member function **Say()** and the normal function **SayAbout()**. The function **SayAbout()** is defined, as usual, outside the data declaration. While the syntax of the definitions are the same, there is an important distinction. For the function **SayAbout()** to obtain access to the structure data members

Name and **Height**, the structure, or a pointer to the structure, must be passed to it as an argument. In contrast to this, a member function has direct access to all data members of the structure just by using the appropriate member name, and doesn't need an argument. Therefore, the ways in which the two functions are called are different.

```
SayAbout (Everest);       // Using a normal function

cout <<"2. ";
Everest.Say ();           // Using a member function
```

In the call to the member function, the selector operator (.) is used in the same way as for a data member of a structure object.

When the function **SayAbout()** is called, an argument in the form of a structure is passed to it. Note that a structure containing a member function is passed as an argument in the same way as a structure without a member function.

Try changing the name of the member function **SayAbout()** to **Say()**. You need to change the program in two places: in the definition, and the call of the function. The program should compile and run without error in spite of the coincidental names of the two functions. This is because the member function has structure scope, and so its name is invisible outside the structure, whereas the normal function has file scope.

Try It Out - Identical Declarations of Two Functions

You may think that this is because the interfaces of the functions are different: one has arguments, and the other doesn't, but this isn't the case. In Program 10.2 the interfaces of both **Say()** functions are identical. The compiler can see the difference between the call to the member function and the call to the normal function.

```
//        Program 10.2
//        Identical declaration of 2 functions Say()

#include <iostream.h>

struct  mountain
{
  char  Name[21];      // Data member declarations
  int   Height;
  void  Say()          // Member function definition
  {
```

Try It Out!

```
        cout << Name << Height << endl;
    }
};

// Normal  function definition

void Say()
{
   cout << "Name " << "Height" << endl;
}

void main()
{
   mountain  Everest = {"Everest ",8848};

   cout <<  "1. ";
   Say();                   // Call common function

   cout <<  "2. ";
   Everest.Say ();          // Call Everest member function
}
```

A Member Function Outside the Structure

In Program 10.1 we used a short member function which we put in one line. The size of a member function is arbitrary, but it wouldn't be a good idea to include the definition of a large function in the declaration of a structure. For this reason, C++ allows you to place a member function definition outside the structure declaration.

Try It Out - Defining Member Functions Outside the Structure

This is illustrated in Program 10.3. If you compare it with Program 10.1, you can see that in the structure declaration, only the declaration of the member function say() has remained inside the structure. Its definition is outside the structure declaration. It can actually be anywhere in the file, not necessarily immediately after the structure declaration.

```
//        Program 10.3
//        Member function definition outside the structure

#include <iostream.h>

struct  mountain
{
   char Name[21];      // Data member declarations
   int  Height;
```

```
   void Say();          // Member function declaration
};

// Member function definition
void  mountain::Say()
{
   cout << Name << Height << endl;
}

void main()
{
   mountain Everest = {"Everest ",8848};

   Everest.Say ();      // Using member function
}
```

How It Works

The definition of a member function located outside the structure declaration
is notable only for the fact that the name of the member function is
qualified by the structure type (**mountain**), using the scope resolution
operator (**::**). This allows the computer to distinguish a member function
from a normal function, and to differentiate member functions with similar
names from different structures. For example, if two structures **s1** and **s2**
have a member function **f()** with the same name:

```
struct s1
{
  void f ();
  // ...
}

struct s2
{
  void f ();
  // ...
}
```

then the definitions of the member functions will have the form:

```
void s1::f()
{
  //...
}
```

or

```
void s2::f() { //... }
```

Here '//...' means any sequence of C++ statements.

Outside the structure declaration, the definition of a member function is still considered to be within the scope of its structure, and can use the names of the members of its structure directly by name.

Using Separate Files

Look at the next example which shows that structures can be used over several files as we saw in Chapter 7.

```
//  P010_04.H
//  Header for P10_04a.cpp and P10-04b.cpp

struct  mountain        // Structure declaration
{
   char  Name[21];      // Data member declarations
   int   Height;
   void  Say();         // Member function declaration
};
// EOF
```

```
//       Program 10.4a
//       Creating library with member function Say ()

#include <iostream.h>
#include "P10_04.h"

//       Member function definition
void  mountain::Say() {cout << Name << Height << endl;}
// EOF
```

```
//       Program 10.4b
//       Using library with member function Say ()

#include "P10_04.h"

void main()
{
   mountain Everest = {"Everest ",8848};

   Everest.Say();       // Call member function from library
}
```

There is nothing in these program files that we haven't encountered before.

Constructing Mountains

Each time a structure is defined in a program, storage is allocated for it. Other actions, initialization for example, can be executed. Some actions can be performed during compilation, others during program execution.

The constructor Function

C++ makes it possible for you to influence the process of creating a structure object with the help of a special member function called a **constructor**. The constructor has a number of features that differentiate it from other member functions, for example:

> The name of a constructor is the same as the name of the structure.

> A constructor doesn't return a value and a **return** statement doesn't have to appear in its body.

> A constructor, if present, is called implicitly when a structure object is defined.

Try It Out - Using a Constructor

Program 10.5 gives an example of a constructor. This constructor has two arguments: **N** - a mountain name, and **H** - its height. The values of the arguments are copied into the corresponding members of the structure being constructed.

```
//      Program 10.5
//      Constructor

#include <iostream.h>
#include <string.h>

struct  mountain
{
  char Name[21];
  int  Height;

  void Say()
  {
    cout << Name << Height << endl;
  }
```

```
// Constructor definition
  mountain(char* N,int H)
  {
    strcpy(Name,N);
    Height=H;
  }
};

void main()
{
// Constructor is invoked explicitly
  mountain  NM = mountain("!mountain ",0);

// Constructor is invoked implicitly
  mountain  Everest ("Everest ",8848);

// An initializer list isn't allowed
// if a constructor is defined in a structure
// mountain       Err = {"Err ",-1};
// Error !


                      // Output
  NM.Say();           // !mountain 0
  Everest.Say();      // Everest 8848
}
```

How It Works

```
mountain  NM = mountain("!mountain ",0);
```

When the structure **NM** is defined, the constructor is called explicitly just like an ordinary function. It appears to the right of the equals sign as if its value being returned had the type **mountain**, although this isn't the case.

When the structure **Everest** is defined:

```
mountain Everest ("Everest ",8848);
```

the constructor is called implicitly and its name isn't mentioned. Look at the syntax. The argument values of a constructor are listed after the name of the object being created, in parentheses not in braces. This makes it look like a function call of a function called **Everest**. In fact, the constructor **mountain** is called to create the object **Everest**.

In Program 10.5 one of the comments tells us that if a constructor is declared in a structure then you can't use the usual initializer list between braces. This means that the initialization of an object is entrusted entirely to your constructor.

If no constructor is declared for a structure, then the compiler generates a default constructor. This default constructor is called automatically when you define a structure object, and the initial values for members are taken from the initializer list between braces.

A Constructor With a Default Argument

If a constructor has many arguments and for many objects the same values of the arguments are repeated, then you can use a constructor with default arguments. The arguments of member functions are assigned default values in the same way as ordinary functions. We saw how to do this in Chapter 6. Remember that if any argument has a default value, then all arguments located to its right must also have default values.

Try It Out - A Constructor With a Default Argument

In Program 10.6 the constructor is declared with two arguments. The second argument assumes the value 0 by default. This means that when the constructor is called implicitly, the second argument (**height**) assumes the default value 0. Note that argument names in a function declaration (but not in a definition) can be omitted. Therefore, it's quite acceptable to write the declaration of a constructor as follows:

```
mountain (char*,int=0);
```

```
//       Program 10.6
//       Constructor with default argument

#include <iostream.h>
#include <string.h>

struct  mountain
{
  char Name[21];
  int  Height;
  void Say() {cout << Name << Height << endl;}

// Constructor declaration with default argument
  mountain(char* name,int height=0);
};

void main()
{
// Constructor with both arguments
  mountain M ("McKinley ", 6193);
// Constructor with default (height) argument
  mountain E ("Everest ");
```

Try It Out!

```
// Pointer to mountain, points to E
   mountain *  pM = &E;

// Access to members through a pointer
                        // Output
  pM->Say();            // Everest 0
  pM->Height = 8848;
  pM->Say();            // Everest 8848
  pM = &M;
  pM->Say();            // McKinley 6193
}


//        Constructor definition
mountain::mountain (char* name,int height)
{
  strcpy(Name,name);
  Height = height;
}
```

How It Works

Let's go over the main parts of the program.

Constructors Outside of Structures

```
mountain::mountain (char* name,int height)
{
  strcpy(Name,name);
  Height = height;
}
```

In the above program, the constructor definition is outside the structure declaration. Here the prefix **mountain::** is like any member function defined outside a structure declaration. You should note that the constructor name must be the same as the structure name. Hence, **mountain::mountain**. The constructor doesn't have a returned value. You can see that the default value for **height** isn't indicated in the definition of the constructor. Repeating it would cause the compiler to flag an error, as you are only allowed to initialize arguments once.

If you delete the default **height=0**, and write the declaration as:

```
mountain (char* name,int height);
```

and you then place the initial value in the definition:

```
mountain::mountain (char* name,int height=0)
{
  strcpy(Name,name);
  Height = height;
}
```

the compiler will tell you that you have an error in the line:

```
mountain E ("Everest ");
```

as the declaration above this line states that the constructor has not one but two arguments. It follows that it's sensible to indicate all the required defaults for arguments in the declaration (or **prototype**) of a constructor.

Using a Pointer to Call a Member Function

```
mountain *      pM = &E;
```

A pointer to **mountain pM** is defined, which is initialized by an address of an object **E**. The pointer may be used to call a member function as well as to obtain access to a data member using the indirect member selector **->**. Since **pM** points to **E**, then:

```
pM->Say();      // Everest 0
```

outputs information about the object **E**. When **pM** points to **M**:

```
pM->Say();     // McKinley 6193
```

the call **pM->Say ()** outputs information about the object **M**.

Overloaded Constructors

A constructor in which both arguments have default values:

```
mountain (char* = "Everest ",int = 0);
```

allows you to give default values for both arguments as in the declaration:

```
mountain E;
```

or for just the last argument:

```
mountain M ("McKinley ");
```

But there is no way you can specify a value for the second argument and allow the default for the second to apply. For example, the definition

```
mountain E (8848);
```

would be an error.

Try It Out - Using Overloaded Constructors

Program 10.7 shows you how to get around this difficulty by using overloaded constructors which differ by their number and types of arguments. We saw overloaded functions in Chapter 7. In this example four constructors are declared, one for each possible combination of the two arguments.

```
//       Program 10.7
//       4 overloaded constructors

#include <iostream.h>
#include <string.h>

struct mountain
{
  char Name[21];
  int Height;
// init () is called from constructors
  void init(char* N,int H)
  {
    strcpy (Name,N);
    Height = H;
  }

// 4 constructors
  mountain();        // Default (without arguments)
  mountain(int);
  mountain(char*);
  mountain(char*,int);
};

void main()
{
                          // Output
  mountain M0;            // Using default constructor
```

```
    mountain M1(0);        // Using int-constructor
    mountain M2("");       // Using char-constructor
    mountain M3("",0);     // Using char-int-constructor
}

//   Definition of default constructor
mountain::mountain()
{
    init("",0);
    cout << "Using default constructor\n";
}

//   Definition of constructor with one int argument
mountain::mountain(int H)
{
    init("",H);
    cout << "Using int-constructor\n";
}

//   Definition of constructor with one char argument
mountain::mountain(char* N)
{
    init(N,0);
    cout << "Using char-constructor\n";
}

// Definition of constructor with both types of argument
mountain::mountain(char* N,int H)
{
    init(N,H);
    cout << "Using char-int-constructor\n";
}
```

How It Works

A constructor without arguments is called a "default" constructor. It is called this if the definition of an object doesn't have initializing values, such as in the line:

```
mountain M0;            // Using default constructor
```

We have added output messages to the constructor definitions so that you can follow which constructor is called at each initialization.

Note that the member function **init()** is used by each of the constructors because they each require the actions performed by this function.

Try It Out - Using Overloaded Constructors Again

Program 10.8 demonstrates the use of both argument default values and constructor overloading.

```
//        Program 10.8
//        2 overloaded constructors

#include <iostream.h>
#include <string.h>

struct  mountain
{
  char Name[21];
  int  Height;
  void init(char* N,int H) {strcpy (Name,N);Height = H;}
  mountain(int);
  mountain(char* ="M0",int=0);
};

void main()
{
                        // Output
  mountain M0;          // Using char-int-constructor...
  mountain M1(1);       // Using int-constructor...
  mountain M2("M2");    // Using char-int-constructor...
  mountain M3("M3",3);  // Using char-int-constructor...
}

//        Definition of constructor with one argument
mountain::mountain(int H)
{
  init("M1",H);
  cout << "Using int-constructor\t\twith Name=\""
       << Name << "\", Height=" << Height << endl;
}

//        Definition of constructor with two arguments
mountain::mountain(char* N,int H)
{
  init(N,H);
  cout << "Using char-int-constructor\twith Name=\""
       << Name << "\", Height=" << Height << endl;
}
```

The program outputs the following:

```
Using char-int-constructor with Name="M0", Height=0
Using int-constructor       with Name="M1", Height=1
Using char-int-constructor with Name="M2", Height=0
Using char-int-constructor with Name="M3", Height=3
```

As you can see, a constructor with one argument is called in only one of the cases.

How It Works

It would be an error to use a default for the first constructor in its declaration.

```
mountain (int=0);
```

If you were to do this, when analyzing the statement in the line:

```
mountain MO;          // Using char-int-constructor...
```

the compiler would be unable to determine whether to call the first constructor using its default argument, or the second constructor with both arguments as defaults.

A Constructor Can Do All the Work

Just from looking at the first program in which a constructor was used (Program 10.5) you can see that constructors are able to use the data members of their structure, can call member functions of their structure, and also call ordinary functions.

Try It Out - Using Constructors to Do All The Work

In Program 10.7 constructors began to speak, using the console output stream **cout** to output to the screen. At the same time it became obvious that in this program the constructor operates at data definition time, before the first executable statement in the function **main()**.

Everything indicates that constructors can not only initialize an object but also perform complicated data processing. Program 10.9 shows how an implicit call of a constructor in the object definition, executes a sequence of actions in the constructor body. Note, that the function **main()** doesn't contain any executable statements. It contains just one definition. This type of program is typical in C++.

Try It Out!

```
//        Program 10.9
//        A constructor can do all work

#include <iostream.h>

//        Type declaration

struct  s
{
  s();     // Struct has only one member - constructor };
};

void main()
{
//        Local object definition

  s  S;        // Constructor s () is implicitly invoked here
}

//        Constructor definition
s::s()
{
//        May define any necessary data and call any required functions
  cout << "Hello, Programmer!\n"
         "A constructor can do all the necessary work for you.\n";

  cout << "\nSize of structure without data members is "
       << sizeof (s) << endl;
}
```

Note that the structure declaration doesn't contain data members. This is quite legal in C++. The size of this type of structure appears in the program output:

```
Hello, Programmer!
A constructor can do all the necessary work for you.

Size of structure without data members is 1
```

Try It Out - Using a Constructor For Global Data

This next program seems even more radical as the function **main()** is executed after a call to the constructor, as you can see from the program output:

```
Constructing global object BEFORE main ()
Executing main ()
```

This is because global data will be created before program execution starts and destroyed after it exits. The constructor **s()** is called when the global variable **s** is declared.

```
//        Program 10.10
//        A constructor for global data works BEFORE main ()

#include <iostream.h>

void main()
{
    cout <<  "Executing main()\n";
}

//        Type declaration

struct  s
{
    s();     // Constructor declaration
};

//        Global object definition

s  S;          // Constructor s() is invoked BEFORE main ()

//        Constructor definition
s::s()
{
    cout << "Constructing global object BEFORE main()\n";
}
```

A Destructor

In Program 10.11 you will meet one more special member function: a **destructor**. It's designed to perform the actions just before an object (structure) is destroyed. Its name is that of the structure proceeded by a tilde character (~) as you can see in its declaration.

Blank spaces are allowed between the character (~) and the structure name. A destructor can't accept parameters nor can it have a return type (even **void**). If a destructor isn't explicitly defined (as in all the previous programs using structures) the compiler generates one.

As we have already seen, a constructor is called to initialize the members of a newly created variable. A destructor does any necessary tidying up when the variable goes out of scope. For example, if the constructor in the program switched the screen to graphics mode, the destructor would reset the screen to text mode.

Try It Out - Using a Destructor

Let's see how all this works in practice.

```
//        Program 10.11
//        Destructor

#include <iostream.h>

//        Type declaration
struct  s
{
  ~s();    // Destructor declaration
};

// Destructor definition
s :: ~s()
{
  cout << "Destroying local structure\n";
}

void any_function()
{
  cout << "Starting any_function()\n";
  s S;        // Local automatic structure
  cout << "Ending   any_function()\n";
//        Destructor ~s() is called just AFTER exit
}

void main()
{
  cout << "Starting main()\n";
  any_function();
  cout << "Continue main()\n";
}
```

If you execute Program 10.11 you get the following output:

```
Starting main()
Starting any_function()
Ending   any_function()
Destroying local structure
Continue main()
```

How It Works

A destructor is called implicitly when a variable is outside of its declared scope. For example, for automatic variables (non-static local variables) declared inside a function, a destructor is called just after exiting from the function.

```
cout << "Starting main()\n";
any_function();
```

The first line is output by the function **main()**. Then it calls
any_function(), where an automatic variable which is a structure **s** of the
type **s** is declared:

```
s  S;        // Local automatic structure
```

The message output by the destructor:

```
Destroying local structure
```

is displayed on the screen between the messages about terminating
any_function(), and returning to **main()**, so proving that the destructor is
called after exiting from **any_function()**.

Try It Out - Destructor For Global Data

With global variables, a destructor is called automatically after program
termination, which is after the function **main()** is exited. This is
demonstrated by Program 10.12 which outputs:

```
Executing main ()
Destroying global object AFTER main ()
```

The first line is output by the function **main()**. At this point **main()** is
terminated, and the destructor operates and outputs the second line.

```
//        Program 10.12
//        Destructor for global data works AFTER main ()

#include <iostream.h>

struct  s
{
  ~s();      // Destructor declaration
};

// Destructor definition
s::~s()
{
  cout << "Destroying global object AFTER main ()\n";
}
```

Try It Out!

```
//        Global object definition
s   S;        // Destructor ~s() is called AFTER main ()

void main()
{
   cout <<   "Executing main ()\n";
}
```

In a destructor you can declare data and call functions from it, so when you need to, you can program various actions to terminate a program in the destructor of a global variable.

In Program 10.11 try declaring the local variable **s** as **static** with:

```
static s S;
```

Check that the **static** variable is destroyed after **main()**, and not after exiting from **any_function()**.

Try It Out - Illegal Use of a Pointer

Program 10.13 demonstrates the illegal use of a pointer to an object which has been destroyed. It also shows when a constructor call takes place for a local variable.

```
//        Program 10.13
//        Illegal usage of a pointer to an object which has been destroyed

#include <iostream.h>

//        Type declaration
struct   s
{
   int m;        // Data member
    s();          // Constructor
    ~s();         // Destructor
};

//        Constructor and destructor definitions
s :: s()
{
   cout << "Constructing local structure S\n";
    m=1;
}

s ::~s()
{
```

```
   cout << "Destroying local structure S\n";
}

s * any_function()
{
  cout << "Starting any_function ()\n";

  s  S;               // Automatic structure
  s *  pS = &S;       // pS points to S

  cout << "Displaying value of local structure member pS->m: " << pS->m
       << endl;
  cout << "Returning pointer pS from any_function()\n";

  return pS;
  //       Destructor ~s() is called just AFTER exit
}

void main()
{
  s *  pS;

  cout << "Starting main()\n";
  cout << "Calling any_function ()\n";

  pS = any_function();

  cout << "Returning to main()\n";

/*       Now pS points to an automatic variable in any_function (),
         the structure S whose value is destroyed by the destructor
         It is illegal to use a pointer to such objects
*/
  cout << "Displaying value of destroyed structure member pS->m: "
       << pS->m << endl;

  cout << "Ending main ()\n";
}
```

The program outputs the following:

```
Starting main ()
Calling any_function ()
Starting any_function ()
Constructing local structure S
Displaying value of local structure member pS->m: 1
Returning pointer pS from any_function ()
Destroying local structure S
Returning to main ()
Displaying value of destroyed structure member pS->m: 1298
Ending main ()
```

How It Works

```
pS = any_function();
```

After outputting two lines to the screen, **main()** calls **any_function()**.

```
s  S;                    // Automatic structure
```

In **any_function()**, an automatic variable **s** is defined. This causes a constructor to be called which outputs a message and initializes the data member **m** of the structure **s** with the value 1.

Then the pointer **pS** is defined in **any_function()**. It is initialized by the address of structure **s** in the line:

```
s *  pS = &S;            // pS points to S
```

This pointer is then used to output the value of the member **m** (equal to 1). Then the value of the pointer is returned to the calling function **main()**, where it's retained in another local variable with the same name.

But just after the exit from **any_function()**, a destructor of the object **s** is executed. This is signaled by the seventh line of output. In this way, the object to which the pointer **pS** in **main()** still points, is destroyed and its contents are lost. Therefore, the output of the value of the member **m** using the value of the pointer **pS** is random (not necessarily the one presented here), and not the expected value 1. This confirms that the previous object **s** has been destroyed, and some other data is located at its address.

Structures With Private Members

You can climb most mountains for free. A structure of the form:

```
struct mountain
{
  // ...
  int Height;
  // ...
};
```

is like a real mountain. Access to it is open. Figuratively speaking, anyone can cope with this summit. If this type of structure is defined as global, then in order to access a member **Height** of object **M**, defined as:

```
mountain M;
```

from any function, all you need to do is indicate the name of the structure and the name of the member and connect them with a dot:

```
M.Height;
```

Free access to structure members in C++ is called 'public access'. Be careful not to mix up the idea of access to a name, with the idea of name scope. In the next code fragment:

```
struct mountain
{
  // ...
  int Height;
  // ...
};
mountain M;

Height = 0;            // Error
M.Height = 8848;       // Ok
```

the member **Height** is easy to access, but the name **Height** taken alone without the prefix **M** is in the scope of the structure mountain, and can't be used outside the structure without a member scope specifier. You can, for example, use a variable with the name **Height**:

```
mountain M;
int      Height = 0; // Ok
M.Height = 8848;     // Ok
```

without conflicting with the name of the structure member. Public access to structure members is illustrated in the following figure.

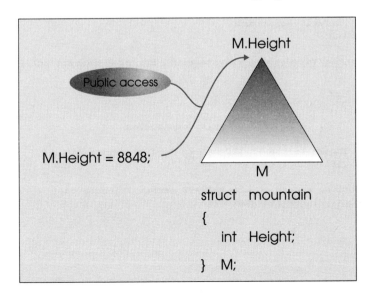

A Private Club

You can make structure members inaccessible to non-member functions. The keyword **private** followed by a colon serves this purpose. This is called an **access specifier**.

Try It Out - Using struct with A Private Member

In Program 10.14 an access specifier is used in order to inhibit access to a member of the structure of the type **club**. All members declared in the structure below the access specifier **private** are private members, for example the member **PrivateMember** in the structure object **Club** can't be accessed externally.

```
//         Program 10.14
//         Struct with private member

#include <iostream.h>
#include <string.h>

struct club
{
                    // Public members (by default)
  club();           // Constructor
  void PublicFunction()
  {
    cout << PrivateMember;
  }

private:                 // Access specifier
                         // Private member
  char PrivateMember[81];
};

//      Default constructor
club::club()
{
  strcpy(PrivateMember,"Private club. For club members only!");
}

void main()
{
  club Club;     // Call default constructor

// Ok! Access to the PUBLIC member PublicFunction()
  Club.PublicFunction ();

// Error! No access to the PRIVATE member PrivateMember
// cout << Club.PrivateMember;
}
```

You can make certain that a private member is inaccessible outside the structure if you discard the comment:

```
// cout << Club.PrivateMember;
```

and compile the program. The compiler will output an error to the effect that **PrivateMember** is not accessible.

All members declared in the structure above the access specifier **private** are public members by default. If an access specifier is absent, then all the structure members are public. For example, in the structure **club**, a constructor and the function **PublicMember()** are public members. The function **PublicMember()** is easy to access outside the structure and its call in the line:

```
Club.PublicFunction ();
```

outputs the message:

```
Private club. For club members only!
```

The following figure illustrates the separation of structure members into **public** and **private** groupings.

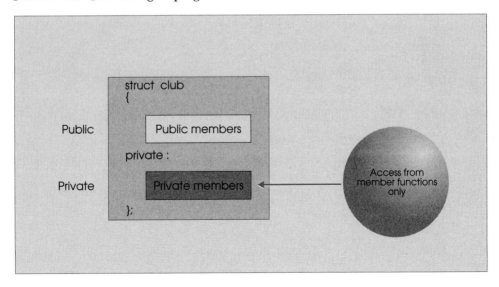

Private members (data and structure) are inaccessible to the functions that don't belong to the structure. They are accessible only for member functions of this structure. For example, the member function `PublicMember()` as well as the constructor have access to the private member `PrivateMember`.

Members that are declared to be `public` or are `public` by default (as in the case of a structure) can be used or called by any function. The calling function does not need to be a member function. Members that are declared to be `private` or are `private` by default can only be used or called by member functions of the same structure or friends. We will explain friends in the next chapter.

Introducing a Class Type

This whole chapter has been leading you towards something called class. Now you are only one step from it and this one step is made in the next program.

Try It Out - Using a Class

Here the only thing that has changed is the description of the type `club`. In Program 10.14 we had a structure type `club`.

```
//        Program 10.15
//        Class is a struct with members private by default

#include <iostream.h>
#include <string.h>

//        Type club (class)

class club
{
// Private member (by default)
  char PrivateMember[81];

public:                    // Access specifier
                           // Public members
  club();                  // Constructor
  void PublicFunction()
  {
    cout << PrivateMember;
  }
};
```

```
//      Default constructor
club::club()
{
  strcpy(PrivateMember,"Private club. For club members only!");
}

void main()
{
  club C;        // Call default constructor

// Ok! Access to the PUBLIC member PublicFunction ()
  C.PublicFunction();

// Error! No access to the PRIVATE member PrivateMember
// cout << C.PrivateMember;
}
```

How It Works

```
class   club
{
// Private member (by default)
  char PrivateMember[81];

public:                      // Access specifier
                             // Public members
  club();                    // Constructor
  void PublicFunction()
  {
    cout << PrivateMember;
  }
};
```

Here in Program 10.15 we have a **class** type **club**. As you can see, the difference is in the keyword **class** instead of **struct**. In the declaration of the class you find one more access specifier:

```
public:
```

It's there because class members are **private** by default, unlike structure members which are **public** by default. Aside from the keyword, the default member access is the only difference between **class** and **struct**, which is why we say that there is only this last step to classes. Everything you know about the structure data type applies equally to the data type class. The two descriptions are identical:

```
struct <name>
{
   // Any members
};
```

and

```
class  <name>
{
  public:
   // Any members
};
```

If we were to use an explicit access specifier at the beginning of both a structure and a class description, then the descriptions of the structure and class can be distinguished only by the name of the type (**struct** or **class**), as is illustrated in the following figure.

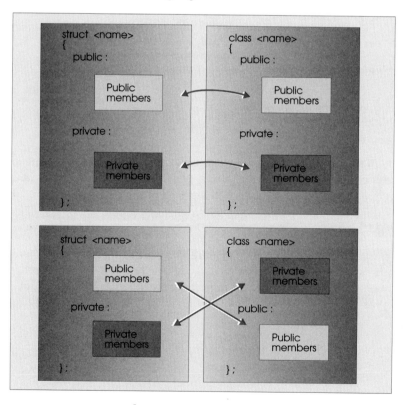

You may well ask why there are two different names, struct and class, used for practically the same thing in C++. There is a purely historical reason for this. In C there is the concept of structure, but there is no concept of class. C++ appeared as an extension of C in which one of the main changes was the introduction of the class concept (hence the name "C with Classes"). The class concept extended the concept of structure by introducing member functions side by side with data members. In today's C++ the keyword **struct** has been kept so that it's compatible with the old C language, but at the same time the structure concept was expanded to mean the same thing as the class concept (with the exception of the access specifier by default).

Object-oriented programming encourages the concept of **information-hiding**. C++ enables the implementation of user-defined types, and data, to be hidden from a user of the type. The user accesses the data via an interface. This is achieved by separating member data and functions into **private** and **public** sections. C++ uses the **class** for this. A **class** is the same as a **struct**, except that all its members are **private** (hidden) unless they are explicitly declared **public**.

Designing a Program

Now we have reached the end of this chapter, it's once again time to look at how we can use all the things we have learnt here in a useful program.

The Problem

The problem we are now going to solve is very similar to the one at the end of the previous chapter. We will write a program that stores names and addresses to a disk file. We are going to make use of the code from the last chapter, but rework it to use classes.

The Analysis

As in the previous chapter, the steps involved are:

1   Display a menu inviting the user to enter a choice.

2   Perform the appropriate operations on the file - add a record, read a single record, or read all records - and display the results on screen.

3   After the operations have been performed the program returns to the menu screen waiting for the user to make another choice.

The Solution

1   Initially we have to define our structure.

```
struct data
{
  char firstnames[30];
  char surname[30];
  char address1[20];
  char address2[20];
  char address3[20];
  char postcode[10];
};
```

However, as we have seen in this chapter, the functions that operate on the data can be incorporated into the structure as member functions.

```
struct data
{
  char firstnames[30];
  char surname[30];
  char address1[20];
  char address2[20];
  char address3[20];
  char postcode[10];

  int menu();
  void add();
  void read_rec();
  void read();

private:
  void enter_data();
  void display_data();
};
```

As the functions **enter_data()** and **display_data()** are only called by member functions of the structure they can be placed in the **private** section of the structure.

As you saw in the previous chapter, the program will start off by displaying the menu and inviting the user to select the operation to be performed. There will also be a message that says how many records are in the file. The user will press a number between 1 and 4. This value will be returned to **main()** to be used with the switching variable. For example:

```
number = menu();
```

```
int data::menu()
{
  int record, position, select, endOfFile, NoOfRecords;
  fstream address_book;

  clrscr();                                    //clear the user
screen

  cout << endl
       << "This program manipulates a file containing names and
addresses\n\n";

  address_book.open("a:\\addr.dat", ios::in);  //open the disc file
  //check for errors
  if(!address_book)
    cout << "\nCould not open file\n";

  address_book.seekg(0, ios::end);    //calculate number of records in file
  endOfFile = address_book.tellg();   //with this group of three statements
  NoOfRecords = endOfFile / sizeof(data);

  cout << "At the present time there are " << NoOfRecords
       << " records in the file.\n";

  cout << "\n\t\tDo you wish to\n"
       << "\t1\tAdd a Record\n" << "\t2\tRead a Record\n"
       << "\t3\tRead all Records\n" << "\t4\tExit from the Program\n"
       << "\nEnter number: ";
  cin >> select;

  address_book.close();                        //close disc file

  return(select);                              //return value for use in switch
}
```

As the function wasn't defined in the structure declaration it is qualified by the use of the structure type and the scope resolution operator (::).

```
int data::menu()
```

2   As you can see from the program, a **switch** statement is used to call the appropriate functions. The functions are called by specifying the structure variable and using the dot operator:

```
address.add();
```

Look at the function declaration:

```
void data::add()
{
  int record, position;
  fstream address_book;

  address_book.open("a:\\addr.dat", ios::app | ios::out ); //open disc file

  //check for errors
  if(!address_book)
    cout << "\nCould not open file\n";

  clrscr();                                          //clear screen
  enter_data();                              //call function to enter data
  address_book.write((char *) this, sizeof(data) );
  //write information to file
  cout << endl << endl << "Press a key to continue ...";
  address_book.close();                              //close disc file
  getch();                          //wait on screen until key pressed
}
```

Again, the function is very similar to the code used in the last chapter. The main difference being the statement:

```
address_book.write((char *) this, sizeof(data) );
```

You will notice the use of the keyword **this**. The keyword **this** refers to a pointer which can only be used in member functions. It always points to the particular object whose member function is being called. This will be clarified in the next chapter.

The other functions are declared in a similar way.

3   As a **do while** loop is used in **main()** the program returns to the menu screen after each operation.

```
//    addr.cpp
//    a program to store names and addresses to a file

#include <fstream.h>          //header file for file i/o
#include <stdio.h>            //header file for gets()
#include <conio.h>            //header file for clrscr(), getch()
#include <dos.h>              //header file for sleep()

struct data                   //declare structure
{                             //These members are public by default
  char firstnames[30];
  char surname[30];
  char address1[20];
  char address2[20];
  char address3[20];
  char postcode[10];

  int menu();                 //function prototypes
  void add();
  void read_rec();
  void read();

private:                      //these members are private
  void enter_data();
  void display_data();
};

int data::menu()         //function to display menu and return users choice
{
  int record, position, select, endOfFile, NoOfRecords;
  fstream address_book;

  clrscr();                   //clear user screen

  cout << endl
  << "This program manipulates a file containing names and addresses\n\n";

  address_book.open("a:\\addr.dat", ios::in );       //open disc file

  //check for errors
  if(!address_book)
    cout << "\nCould not open file\n";

  address_book.seekg(0, ios::end);    //calculate number of records in file
  endOfFile = address_book.tellg();     //   with these three statements
  NoOfRecords = endOfFile / sizeof(data);

  cout << "At the present time there are " << NoOfRecords
       << " records in the file.\n";
```

441

```
    cout << "\n\t\tDo you wish to\n"                          //display menu
        << "\t1\tAdd a Record\n" << "\t2\tRead a Record\n"
        << "\t3\tRead all Records\n" << "\t4\tExit from the Program\n"
        << "\nEnter number: ";
    cin >> select;                                            //user enters choice

    address_book.close();                                //close disc file

    return(select);                      //return users choice for use with switch
}

void data::add()                               //function to add record to disc file
{
   int record, position;
   fstream address_book;

   address_book.open("a:\\addr.dat", ios::app | ios::out );   //open file

   //check for errors
   if(!address_book)
      cout << "\nCould not open file\n";

   clrscr();                                               //clear screen
   enter_data();                                           //call enter
data function
   address_book.write((char *) this, sizeof(data) ); //write record to file
   cout << endl << endl << "Press a key to continue ...";
   address_book.close();                                   //close file
   getch();                              //wait on screen until a key is pressed
}

void data::read_rec()                          //function to read record
{
   int record, position;
   fstream address_book;

   address_book.open("a:\\addr.dat",  ios::in );              //open file

   //check for errors
   if(!address_book)
      cout << "\nCould not open file\n";

   clrscr();                                               //clear screen
   cout << "Which record do you wish to read? ";
   cin >> record;                                  //user enters record number
   cout << endl << endl;
   position = (record - 1) * sizeof(data);//calculate correct position in file
   address_book.seekg(position);                   //move to correct record
   address_book.read((char *) this, sizeof(data) );       //read record
   display_data();                                //call display data function
   cout << endl << endl << "Press a key to continue ...";
```

```
  address_book.close();                                   //close file
  getch();                               //wait on screen until a key is pressed
}

void data::read()                                  //function to read all records
{
  int record, position;
  fstream address_book;

  address_book.open("a:\\addr.dat",  ios::in );             //open file

  //check for errors
  if(!address_book)
    cout << "\nCould not open file\n";

  clrscr();                                               //clear user screen
  address_book.seekg(0, ios::beg);                    //go to beginning of file
  while(address_book)                                 //while not at end of file
  {                                                   //  or some other error
    address_book.read((char *) this, sizeof(data) );         //read record
    if(!address_book.eof())  //to prevent last record being output twice
      display_data();                                         //display data
  }
  cout << endl << endl << "Press a key to continue ...";
  address_book.close();                                       //close file
  getch();                               //wait on screen until a key is pressed
}

void data::enter_data()                                //function to enter data
{
  cout << "\nEnter first names: ";
  gets(firstnames);
  cout << "Enter surname: ";
  gets(surname);
  cout << "Enter first line of address: ";
  gets(address1);
  cout << "Enter second line of address: ";
  gets(address2);
  cout << "Enter third line of address: ";
  gets(address3);
  cout << "Enter postcode: ";
  gets(postcode);
}

void data::display_data()                              //function to display data
{
  cout << endl << firstnames << " " << surname << endl
       << address1 << endl << address2 << endl << address3
       << endl << postcode << endl << endl;
}
```

```
void main()
{
  data address;
  int number;

  do
  {
    number = address.menu();    //call menu function and use returned value
                                //in switch statement
    switch(number)
    {
      case 1:
        address.add();
        break;

      case 2:
        address.read_rec();
        break;

      case 3:
        address.read();
        break;

      case 4:
        clrscr();
        cout << "The program is now ending.";
        break;

      default:
        clrscr();
        cout << "You should enter a number between 1 and 4. Try again.";
        sleep(6);
    }
  }while(number != 4);
}
```

We can now try the program.

```
This program manipulates a file containing names and addresses

At the present time there are 3 records in the file.

   Do you wish to
1  Add a Record
2  Read a Record
3  Read all Records
4  Exit from the Program

Enter number: 2
Which record do you wish to read? 1
```

```
Oleg Yaroshenko
c\o Wrox Press Ltd
1334 Warwick Road
Birmingham
B27 6PR


Press a key to continue ...
This program manipulates a file containing names and addresses

At the present time there are 3 records in the file.

   Do you wish to
1  Add a Record
2  Read a Record
3  Read all Records
4  Exit from the Program

Enter number: 2
Which record do you wish to read? 2


Wrox Press Ltd
1334 Warwick Road
Birmingham
United Kingdom
B27 6PR


Press a key to continue ...
This program manipulates a file containing names and addresses

At the present time there are 3 records in the file.

   Do you wish to
1  Add a Record
2  Read a Record
3  Read all Records
4  Exit from the Program

Enter number:3

Oleg Yaroshenko
c\o Wrox Press Ltd
1334 Warwick Road
Birmingham
B27 6PR
```

```
Wrox Press Ltd
1334 Warwick Road
Birmingham
United Kingdom
B27 6PR


Wrox Press Inc
2710 W. Touhy
Chicago
Illinois
60645



Press a key to continue ...
This program manipulates a file containing names and addresses

At the present time there are 3 records in the file.

  Do you wish to
1  Add a Record
2  Read a Record
3  Read all Records
4  Exit from the Program

Enter number: 4
The program is now ending.
```

We have already seen that the syntax of a structure is the same as the
syntax of a class. The only difference is that class members are **private** by
default and structure members are **public** by default. Now we need to alter
the program so that a class is used instead of a structure.

There are only two alterations to make:

1   The keyword **struct** must be changed to **class**; and as the members
of a **class** are private by default we must include a **public** section.

```
//    addr2.cpp
//    a program to store names and addresses to a file

#include <fstream.h>       //header file for file i/o
#include <stdio.h>         //header file for gets()
#include <conio.h>         //header file for clrscr(), getch()
#include <dos.h>           //header file for sleep()
```

```
class data                        //class declaration
{
public:                           //these members are public
  char firstnames[30];
  char surname[30];
  char address1[20];
  char address2[20];
  char address3[20];
  char postcode[10];

  int menu();
  void add();
  void read_rec();
  void read();

private:                          //these members are private
  void enter_data();
  void display_data();
};

int data::menu()
{
  int record, position, select, endOfFile, NoOfRecords;
  fstream address_book;

  clrscr();

  cout << endl << "This program manipulates a file containing names and
addresses\n\n";

  address_book.open("a:\\addr.dat",  ios::in );
  //check for errors
  if(!address_book)
    cout << "\nCould not open file\n";

  address_book.seekg(0, ios::end);
  endOfFile = address_book.tellg();
  NoOfRecords = endOfFile / sizeof(data);

  cout << "At the present time there are " << NoOfRecords
       << " records in the file.\n";

  cout << "\n\t\tDo you wish to\n"
       << "\t1\tAdd a Record\n" << "\t2\tRead a Record\n"
       << "\t3\tRead all Records\n" << "\t4\tExit from the Program\n"
       << "\nEnter number: ";
  cin >> select;

  address_book.close();

  return(select);
}
```

```
void data::add()
{
  int record, position;
  fstream address_book;

  address_book.open("a:\\addr.dat", ios::app | ios::out );

  //check for errors
  if(!address_book)
    cout << "\nCould not open file\n";

  clrscr();
  enter_data();
  address_book.write((char *) this, sizeof(data) );
  cout << endl << endl << "Press a key to continue ...";
  address_book.close();
  getch();
}

void data::read_rec()
{
  int record, position;
  fstream address_book;

  address_book.open("a:\\addr.dat",  ios::in );

  //check for errors
  if(!address_book)
    cout << "\nCould not open file\n";

  clrscr();
  cout << "Which record do you wish to read? ";
  cin >> record;
  cout << endl << endl;
  position = (record - 1) * sizeof(data);
  address_book.seekg(position);
  address_book.read((char *) this, sizeof(data) );
  display_data();
  cout << endl << endl << "Press a key to continue ...";
  address_book.close();
  getch();
}

void data::read()
{
  int record, position;
  fstream address_book;

  address_book.open("a:\\addr.dat",  ios::in );

  //check for errors
```

```
    if(!address_book)
      cout << "\nCould not open file\n";

    clrscr();
    address_book.seekg(0, ios::beg);
    while(address_book)
    {
      address_book.read((char *) this, sizeof(data) );
      if(!address_book.eof())  //to prevent last record being output twice
        display_data();
    }
    cout << endl << endl << "Press a key to continue ...";
    address_book.close();
    getch();
}

void data::enter_data()
{
  cout << "\nEnter first names: ";
  gets(firstnames);
  cout << "Enter surname: ";
  gets(surname);
  cout << "Enter first line of address: ";
  gets(address1);
  cout << "Enter second line of address: ";
  gets(address2);
  cout << "Enter third line of address: ";
  gets(address3);
  cout << "Enter postcode: ";
  gets(postcode);
}

void data::display_data()
{
  cout << endl << firstnames << " " << surname << endl
       << address1 << endl << address2 << endl << address3
       << endl << postcode << endl << endl;
}

void main()
{
  data address;
  int number;

  do
  {
    number = address.menu();

    switch(number)
    {
      case 1:
```

```
          address.add();
          break;

       case 2:
          address.read_rec();
          break;

       case 3:
          address.read();
          break;

       case 4:
          clrscr();
          cout << "The program is now ending.";
          break;

       default:
          clrscr();
          cout << "You should enter a number between 1 and 4. Try again.";
          sleep(6);
     }
   }while(number != 4);
 }
```

Summary

In this chapter you have got to know the basic concept of C++ - class.
Objects of the type class and structure in C++ may combine data and
functions, which is the first step on the way to object-oriented
programming. A member function of a class has access to all data of that
class, while access by other functions to data and functions of the class,
may be limited or closed completely. Hiding information inside classes is
called encapsulation. In the next chapter we will discuss this and various
other features of classes.

CHAPTER 11

Operating With Class Objects

In the preceding chapter you were introduced to the basic C++ concept of class. Figuratively speaking, we completed the first training ascent to one of the summits of the mountain range called class. Now it's time to explore it in more detail.

In this chapter we'll concentrate on the characteristics of an isolated class not connected with other classes. We'll discuss friend functions, static data members, static functions, and operator overloading. You'll also become familiar with information hiding or **encapsulation**, which is based on the idea of limiting access to class data and functions. This chapter is closely linked with the next chapter, so our end of chapter program for this topic comes at the end of Chapter 12.

In this chapter you will:

- Examine class properties
- Use the **this** pointer
- Understand friends of classes
- Look at static class members

An Overview of Class Properties

In this section we'll summarize the class properties you already know. By now you are fairly familiar with structures, and classes in C++ are very similar to structures. The only difference between a structure and a class is that class members are **private** by default, while structure members are **public**, and of course a class is defined using the keyword **class**.

A Class is a Type

Consider a class specified in the following way:

```
class myclass             // Type (class) name
{
public:                   // Access specifier
  int    mydata;          // Data member
  void   myfunction();    // Member function
};
```

A class specification is usually referred to as a class declaration. A class with the name **myclass** introduces a new type **myclass**. The terms *type myclass* and *class myclass* are synonyms.

A class object of type **myclass** can be declared and defined according to exactly the same rules as an object of a fundamental type, such as **char**, or **int**. For example:

```
myclass Class1;
```

is the definition of an object of type **myclass** with the name **Class1**, and:

```
myclass * pClass1;
```

is the definition of an object of the type pointer to an object of type **myclass**. Usually instead of the long phrase "a pointer to an object of type **myclass**", we will call it "a pointer to **myclass**".

This table gives some definition examples of objects of various types.

Definition	Meaning
`myclass Class1;`	`Class1` is an object of `myclass`
`const myclass cClass1;`	`cClass1` is a constant class object of type `myclass`
`myclass * pClass1;`	`pClass1` is an object of the type 'pointer to `myclass`'
`myclass & rClass1 = Class1;`	`rClass1` is an object of the type 'reference to `myclass`'
`myclass aClass1[2];`	`aClass1` is an array of 2 elements of type `myclass`
`myclass1 funct(myclass2);`	`funct` is a function that returns an object of class, `myclass1` and accepts an argument of class `myclass2`

Class Declarations

The simplified format of a class declaration statement is as follows:

```
class    <class-name>
{
  <member-list>
};
```

class-name is defined by the programmer. The rules and limitations for class names are the same as for ordinary variables. A name must be unique within its scope, so for instance, if a class declaration is global, then the class name mustn't coincide with the names of other global variables, constants, or types. It mustn't coincide with C++ keywords either.

The Member List

The member list in a class declaration is a sequence of data declarations (of any type including other classes and enumerations), function declarations (without the function bodies), and function definitions (with the bodies). These functions are called member functions, or sometimes **methods**. (We have used the term enumerations - this will be defined shortly.)

A class is a data type that combines both data and functions. Objects of two different classes are objects of different types, even if their member lists are identical For example:

```
class c1
{
   int m;
};

class c2
{
   int m;
};
```

The objects **C1** and **C2** of the two classes above, declared as:

```
c1 C1;
c2 C2;
```

are considered incompatible, and so the following assignment:

```
C2 = C1;   // Illegal
```

is incorrect.

You can use the name of a class in its member list to declare a pointer to the same class, for example:

```
class c
{
   c *  pC;      // Ok: pointer to c
   // ...
};
```

But you can't include a declaration of an object of the same class being declared in the member list:

```
class c
{
  c C;        // Error
  // ...
};
```

If you define a new type and put it in a member list, then this type must be declared somewhere in the program preceding the member list in which it appears. If a class declaration contains a function declaration, the definition of this function can be located anywhere in the source file, or even in another source file or library.

Access Specifiers

The member list can also contain the access specifiers **public:** or **private:**, which define access to a member from outside the class. All class members are private by default, in other words inaccessible from outside the class. Any member function has access to all class members (to data members as well as member functions), regardless of where it's defined - inside or outside the class declaration.

Ordinary functions that aren't members of the class only have access to public class members. This is done using the direct (.) or indirect (->) member selection operators. For example, if a class **c** and a pointer **pC** are declared as follows:

```
class c
{
public:
  int   m;
  void  mf ();
};

c   C;
c * pC = &C;
```

then we can access the data member **m** in either of the following ways:

```
C.m   = 1;
pC->m = 1;
```

and we can access a member function like this:

```
C.mf();
pC->mf();
```

Access specifiers can be listed arbitrarily, for example:

```
class c
{
  // Private members
public:
  // Public members
private:
  // Private members
public:
  // Public members
  // ...
};
```

but in our opinion it's better to put all the private members first, followed by all the public members:

```
class c
{
  // All private members
public:
  // All public members
};
```

The Scope of Class Member Names

The scope of all class member names is limited to the class. This means you can use the same member names in different classes, or use them outside classes for other objects. For example, the following declarations of **m** and **f()** are correct:

```
class c1        // Type c1
{
  int  m;
  void f();
};

class c2        // Type c2
{
  int  m;
  void f();
};

int  m;
void f();
```

Three separate functions **f()** are defined, as well as three separate objects **m**.

Enumeration types, enumeration constants, and **typedef** synonyms defined inside a class are also local to that class, so you can declare the following:

```
class c
{
  enum  e{e1,e2};
  typedef  int i;
};

enum  e{e1,e2};
typedef int I;
```

An enumerated type is another method to name integer constants. Don't worry if this isn't completely clear at this stage, as it's explained further later in the chapter.

As you have seen, structures, unions and classes allow programmers to create their own data types. In the *original* C language, structures and unions couldn't define a type and the keywords **struct** or **union** had to be repeated every time a programmer declared a variable of these types. The **typedef** keyword allows programmers to create a new name for an existing data type.

The general form of the **typedef** statement is:

```
typedef  type  newname;
```

where **type** is any regular data type and **newname** is the new name for this type. The defined new name is in addition to the existing type name.

Predefined Operations For Class Objects

As well as the access operation, there are other operations defined for classes. You can copy one object to another (if, of course, they are of the same type):

```
c  C1, C2;
C1 = C2;      // Ok.
```

and take the address **&C1**. A class object can also be passed to or returned by a function. However, it's more efficient to use a pointer or a reference to a class for this purpose.

Try It Out - Studying the Mountain Class

With the help of Program 11.1, we'll take a look at some new features of classes. In this program, the structure **mountain**, which you already know, has had a number of member functions added, and is now declared as the class **mountain**.

```
//        Program 11.1
//        Studying the mountain class

#include <iostream.h>
#include <string.h>

//Class (type) declaration
class mountain                              // class mountain
{
// Private data members:
  char N[21];                               // The mountain name
  int  Height;                              // Height of the mountain

// Private member functions:
  char * GetName();                         // Get name
  int GetHeight();                          // Get height

// Public member functions:
public:
  mountain();                               // Constructor
  void Say(int N);                          // Tell about the mountain

  // The next two functions are overloaded
  void Set(char* n);                        // Set name
  void Set(int h);                          // Set height

  void Copy(mountain M);                    // Copy to this mountain
  mountain Get();                           // Get this mountain
  mountain & GetR();                        // Get reference to this mountain
  mountain * GetP();                        // Get pointer to this mountain

// Friend function:
  friend int cmpM (mountain, mountain);     // Compare 2 mountains
};                      // End of class declaration

//Member function definitions
//constructor
mountain::mountain()
{   //note - no return type specified as this would be an error
  *N = 0;
  Height = 0;
}
```

```
//this function, and the others, can be written in this form
/*
  mountain::mountain() {*N=0; Height=0;}
*/

char *    mountain::GetName() {return N;}              // Get name
int       mountain::GetHeight() {return Height;}       // Get height
void      mountain::Set(char* n) {strcpy(N,n);}        // Set name
void      mountain::Set(int h) {Height=h;}             // Set height
void      mountain::Copy(mountain M) {*this=M;}        // Copy to this
mountain
mountain mountain::Get() {return *this;}          // Get this mountain
mountain & mountain::GetR() {return *this;}       // Get reference to this
mountain * mountain::GetP() {return this;}        // Get pointer to this

void main ()
{
  mountain E,M2,M3,M4,M5;        // Create (plain) mountains
                                 //    initialized to zero
  E.Say (0);                     // 0.0

  E.Set ("Everest ");            // Set name
  E.Set (8848);                  // Set height
  E.Say (1);                     // 1. Everest 8848

  M2=E;                          // Member by member assignment
  M2.Say (2);
  M3.Copy(E);                    // Copy E to M3
  M3.Say (3);

  // E.Get() returns *this, i.e. E
  M4=E.Get();                    // The same as M4=E
  M4.Say(4);
  M4.Get().Say (4);              // The same as M4.Say (4)


  // E.GetR() returns
  //   reference to this (E)
  M5.GetR() = E.GetR();          // The same as M5=E
  M5.Say(5);
  M5.GetR().Say (5);             // The same as M5.Say(5)


  mountain *  pM;                // Pointer to mountain

  // E.GetP() returns this (&E)
  pM = E.GetP ();                // The same as pM=&E;

  // pM points to E (&E)->Say(6);
  pM->Say (6);                   // The same as (&E)->Say(6)
  E.GetP ()->Say (6);            // The same as (&E)->Say(6)
```

```
   if (cmpM (M2,E) == 0 && cmpM (M3,E) == 0 &&
       cmpM (M4,E) == 0 && cmpM (M5,E) == 0)
     cout << "They are all the same!\n";
}

void mountain::Say (int N)
{//      Say about a mountain
   cout << N << ". " << GetName () << Height << endl;
}

int cmpM (mountain M1,mountain M2)
{
/*      Compare the heights of 2 mountains
        friend function of the class mountain

        Returns
        -1 if M1 <  M2
         0 if M1 == M2
        +1 if M1 >  M2
*/

// Access to mountain class private data member
   if(M1.Height < M2.Height)
     return -1;

// Access to mountain class private member function
   if (M1.GetHeight() > M2.GetHeight())
     return +1;

   return 0;
}
```

How It Works

```
class mountain                // class mountain
{
// Private data members:
   char N[21];                // The mountain name
   int  Height;               // Height of the mountain

// Private member functions:
   char * GetName();          // Get name
   int GetHeight();           // Get height
```

In the class **mountain** there are two private data members and two private member functions. These private members can only be accessed by functions that are in the list of class members. We can now take a look at each of the functions.

The private function **GetName()** returns the value of the private member **N** (the address of the character array). The private function **GetHeight()** returns the value of the private member **Height**. These two functions demonstrate how a private function accesses private members.

```
// Public member functions:
public:
   mountain();              // Constructor
   void Say(int N);         // Tell about the mountain

   //The next two functions are overloaded
   void Set(char* n);       // Set name
   void Set(int h);         // Set height

   void Copy(mountain M);   // Copy to this mountain
   mountain Get();          // Get this mountain
   mountain & GetR();       // Get reference to this mountain
   mountain * GetP();       // Get pointer to this mountain
```

The function **Say()** outputs the values of the data members **N** (the mountain name) and **Height** to the screen. The argument **N** (an integer) is used to number the output lines so that you can trace the lines of the program text. Note that the name of the argument **N** overrides the name of the data member **N** and the latter becomes hidden in the function.

The function **GetName()** helps us to extract the name of the mountain. You could avoid the need for **GetName()** by changing the name of the argument for the function **Say()**, as follows:

```
void mountain::Say(int n)
{
   cout << n << ". " << N << Height << endl;
}
```

Or you could use the scope resolution operator **::** which reveals hidden members:

```
void mountain::Say(int N)
{
   cout << N << ". " << mountain::N << Height << endl;
}
```

Here the class name **mountain** is used as a prefix to select the **N** that is a class member.

```
mountain::mountain()
{    //note - no return type specified as this would be an error
  *N = 0;
   Height = 0;
}
```

The default constructor **mountain()** initializes the objects created with zeroes.

Therefore, the statement, **E.Say(0);** outputs:

```
0. 0
```

```
void Set(char* n);      // Set name
void Set(int h);        // Set height
```

The two member functions **Set()** are overloaded, since they have identical names but different types of arguments. They assign the values to the private members **N** or **Height** depending on the type of the argument. These functions are public, which means they are accessible from any function, including **main()**, where they are used to initialize the object **E**. Here we have to use the prefix **E.**, otherwise the statement:

```
Set();
```

would mean a call to a normal global function, not to a member function of class **mountain**.

Note that the two functions **GetName()** and **GetHeight()** can't be overloaded, as they have similar (empty) argument lists. The fact that they return different types is not enough to permit overloading.

```
M2=E;                    // Member by member assignment
```

We used the assignment operation to initialize the second object, **M2**. This is actually member-by-member copying. For example, this is equivalent to the following two statements:

```
strcpy (M2.N, E.N);
M2.Height = E.Height;
```

The this Keyword

```
void        mountain::Copy(mountain M) {*this=M;} // Copy to this mountain
```

In the function `Copy()`, you will notice a C++ keyword that you haven't met yet, **this**.

The keyword **this** refers to a pointer. It can only be used in member functions, where it always points to the particular object whose member function is now being called. It is an invisible parameter passed to every member function.

```
M3.Copy(E);                    // Copy E to M3
```

For instance, during the call to the function `Copy()`, the pointer **this** will point to the object **M3** (in other words, have the value **&M3**), and therefore ***this** will mean the object **M3** itself. This means that the statement:

```
*this = M;
```

will at that moment mean:

```
M3 = M;
```

As the result, the argument **M** (which contains the object **E**) will be copied into the object **M3**. So the statement, **M3.Copy(E);** actually does the same thing as:

```
M3 = E;
```

It copies the contents of **E** into the object **M3**.

If we didn't use the pointer **this**, the function `Copy()` would have to be defined with two arguments:

```
void mountain::Copy (mountain M1, mountain M2) {M1 = M2;}
```

and we would have to call it in the following way:

```
M3.Copy(M3, E);
```

It is obvious that using the pointer **this** simplifies the interface and makes the program text clearer.

```
mountain   mountain::Get() {return *this;}     // Get this mountain
```

The function **Get()** demonstrates using a class object as the returned value of a function. It returns **this** - the object for which the function is called. For example:

```
M4=E.Get();              // The same as M4=E
```

Get() is called for the object **E**, so it returns the value **E** which is then copied into **M4**. Of course, we've used this function instead of:

```
M4 = E;
```

only for demonstration purposes. Now you will be able to understand the statement:

```
M4.Get().Say (4);              // The same as M4.Say (4)
```

It means that the function **Say()** is to be called for the object returned by **M4.Get()** - for object **M4**.

```
mountain & mountain::GetR() {return *this;}    // Get reference to this
```

The function **GetR()** returns the reference to ***this**. Therefore, it can be located in the left part of an assignment statement, as in:

```
M5.GetR () = E.GetR ();
```

which gives us the same as:

```
M5 = E;
```

which is the preferred method of coding.

```
mountain * mountain::GetP() {return this;}              // Get pointer this
```

The next function, **GetP()** returns the pointer **this** itself, in other words the address of the object for which the function **GetP()** is called. Therefore, the expression **E.GetP()** returns **&E**, so the statement:

```
E.GetP()->Say (6);
```

means the same thing as **(&E)->Say(6)** or **E.Say(6)**.

You should note that it's more efficient to pass and return a reference, or a pointer to a class object, to a function, than to operate with the object itself (by value). The difference in performance is especially noticeable with large class objects.

Friends of Mountains

In class **mountain** a special function **cmpM()** is declared as:

```
friend  int cmpM (mountain, mountain);
```

It compares the heights of two mountains. It's distinguished from the other functions by the specifier **friend**. This is another new C++ keyword. Its role is very simple. It allows a non-member function to gain access to all members of the class, including **private** members. In all other respects it's an ordinary function. It's called without using an object name or member access operator (**.**). The definition of **cmpM()** is as follows:

```
int cmpM (mountain M1,mountain M2)
{
  if(M1.Height < M2.Height)
    return -1;

  if (M1.GetHeight() > M2.GetHeight())
    return +1;

  return 0;
}
```

Note that to access the members of an object of the class **mountain** here, we have to use the members' names together with the object name, as in **M1.Height** for example.

You can use the statement:

```
cout << M1.Height;
```

which is not a friend of class **mountain**, in the function **main()** and you'll see that the compiler generates an error.

Friend functions are important as they can increase the efficiency of your objects. As friends can access all class members they can be used to provide an interface to your objects and may replace several member functions designed to give a user interface. In Chapter 12 you will see how friend functions are used to define overloaded operators.

Data Access Control

One of the key concepts of object-oriented programming is **encapsulation** (hiding information). In this section we'll look at how this works in C++.

Data members of a class object hold information, and member functions process it. Each class member has one of three possible access categories or attributes: **private, public,** or **protected**. Private members (data as well as functions) are inaccessible to ordinary functions (we say that they are hidden inside the class). This is illustrated in the following figure, which shows to which data and functions there is access.

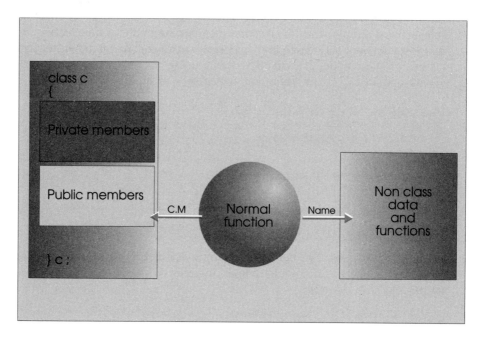

The information in the shaded sections of class **c** is inaccessible. This applies to data and functions equally. **Name** written near an arrow means that data or a function is accessed by name, and **c.M** means Class.Member, which means that as well as the member name, we have to indicate the class object name.

The Access Rights of Member Functions

Member functions have full access to all members of their class (see the following figure), either via the member name alone (in the figure this is shown by M) or the pointer **this**.

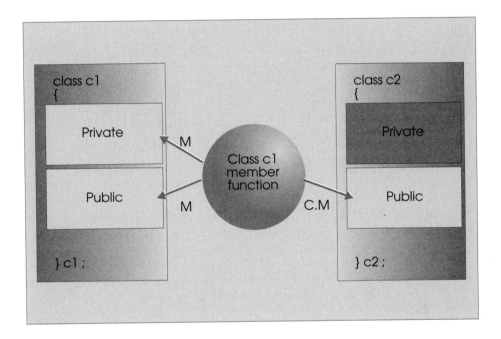

Access to an object of another class is possible if the class object name is specified (this is marked in the figure by C.M), but is restricted to public members only (data as well as functions).

Classes are often designed so that class data members (all or the majority of them) are declared as **private** and hidden from ordinary functions, while class member functions (all or the majority of them) are declared as **public** and are accessible from ordinary functions. In this case, ordinary functions can access data in a class object only by using the public member functions, as shown in the following figure.

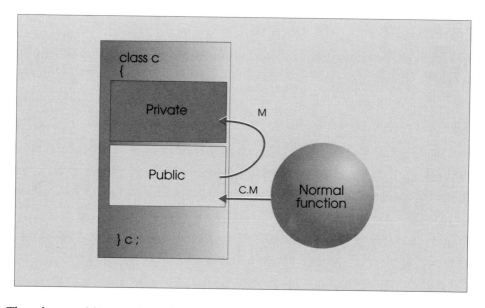

Therefore, public member functions can act as an interface between data hidden in the class object, and the world outside the object. Public member functions define an object's behavior and how it's accessed from outside.

In some instances, public member functions can't provide all the capability you need in manipulating members of a class. Friend functions that aren't class members, which we demonstrated in Program 11.1, can provide added capability.

Before we continue to examine friend functions, we ought to mention protected members (they are not illustrated in the figures or the example). If a member is protected, its access is the same as it is for private. In addition, the member can be used by member functions, as well as friends of classes derived from the declared class.

The Access Rights of friend Functions

In all respects a **friend** function is an ordinary function, with one exception: it has full access to all members of the class in which it is declared as a **friend** (in other words, with the keyword **friend**). As shown in the following figure, a **friend** function of the class **c1** has full access to all members of **c1**. However, it only has access to public members of another class **c2**, in which it isn't declared as a **friend**.

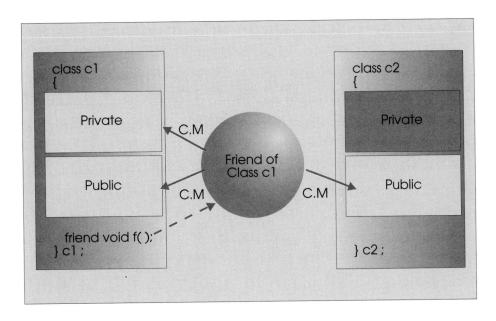

Mutual Friends

A function can be declared as a **friend** of two or more classes. As a result this function has full access to all the information in the objects of these classes (see the next figure).

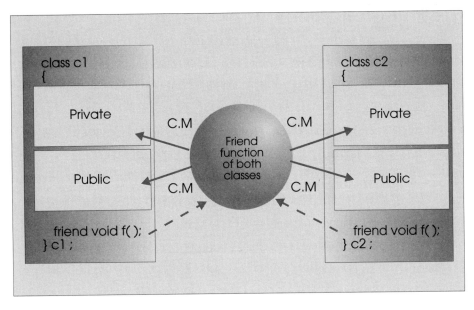

Try It Out - Using a Function That is a friend of Two Classes

Program 11.2 demonstrates the use of a function that is a **friend** of two classes, **mountain** and **continent**. Each class contains **private** information. The friend function **Say()**, that has access to the **private** members of both classes, displays the name of the mountain and the continent where it is found.

```
//        Program 11.2
//        Function - friend of two classes

#include <iostream.h>
#include <string.h>

class continent;                       // Incomplete declaration

class mountain                         // Class mountain
{
  // Friend function of class mountain
  friend void Say (mountain&, continent&);

  char N[21];                          // Name of the mountain
public:
  mountain(char *);                    // Constructor
};

class continent                        // Class continent
{
  // Friend function of class continent
  friend void Say (mountain&, continent&);

  char N[21];                          // Name of the continent
public:
  continent(char *);                   // Constructor
  void Say(mountain&, continent&);     // Member function
};

//        Constructors definitions

  mountain::mountain(char * N) {strcpy (mountain::N,N);}
  continent::continent(char * N) {strcpy (continent::N,N);}

//        -------------------------------------------------------

void Say(mountain& M, continent& C)
{
/*  Say about a mountain and a continent
```

```
      This global function, which is a friend function of classes mountain
      and continent, can access all members of both classes
*/

  cout << M.N << C.N << endl;

// Error: Field N cannot be used without an object
// cout << mountain::N << continent::N << endl;
}

//       -------------------------------------------------------

void continent::Say(mountain& M,continent& C)
{
/*  Say about a mountain and a continent

    continent class member function can call any global function, including
a friend.
    To avoid name ambiguity we must use the scope resolution operator (::)
*/

  ::Say (M,C);     // Call Say() defined in global scope

/*  Say (M,C); would cause an error: call member continent::Say(),
    i.e. itself, which would result in the endless loop.
*/
}

void main ()
{
  mountain E = "Everest ";      // Using constructor with one argument
  continent C = "Asia ";        // for type conversion

  Say (E,C);                    // Call the friend function
  C.Say (E,C);                  // Call the member function
}
```

How It Works

Let's go through the program to see how it works.

The Declaration of a Mutual Friend Function

```
friend void Say (mountain&, continent&);
```

Both classes **mountain** and **continent** contain the same declaration which declares the function **Say()** as a friend of both classes. When we declare a friend of both classes one problem arises. To obtain access to the members of both classes, we have to include the names of the objects (or references, or pointers) of both classes in the argument list. Here, we used the references **mountain&continent&**.

```
class continent;              // Incomplete declaration
```

However, C++ requires that a declaration or a definition precedes the use of any name. Therefore, in **Say(mountain&, continent&)** in the declaration of the class **mountain**, we can't use the type **continent** until it has been declared. To escape the vicious circle we use the incomplete class declaration which simply declares that a class with the name **continent** will be declared later. This indication is sufficient for the compiler to interpret the declaration of the friend function **Say()** in the class **mountain**. This is called a forward reference or a forward declaration. In the class **continent**, a similar incomplete declaration is unnecessary (though possible), as by the time class **mountain** is used in the declaration of class **continent**, the name mountain is already known.

Try removing the incomplete declaration:

```
class continent;              // Incomplete declaration
```

and you'll see that the compiler gives you an error message about the use of the undefined name **continent**.

The main purpose of friend functions is to provide concurrent access to members of several classes. Some programmers prefer to use a friend function instead of a member function, even if it's defined for just one class. They consider that the traditional calling syntax of friend functions:

```
SayAbout(E);        // Friend functions
Y = Change(X);      //    calling syntax
```

is more convenient than the syntax of member functions:

```
E.SayAbout();       // Member functions
Y = X.Change();     //    calling interface
```

Which method will you use? Friend functions can be very useful especially if you want a function that will operate on more than one class but could lead to a spaghetti-code situation if too many are used. Therefore, we would recommend that you only use friend functions occasionally.

Friends are Ordinary Functions

The friend function **Say()** has full access to all members of both classes in Program 11.2. But in all other respects (scope, definition, access rules, or calling) it's a normal function. Although the **friend** declaration is at the beginning of the class declaration, which is private by default, the function **Say()** is accessible from the ordinary function **main()**. Access attributes have no effect on the declarations of friend functions. Friend functions are outside of the class scope, and so they are accessed by using just their name, and can't use the pointer **this**.

Using the Scope Resolution Operator

In the last program there are two examples showing how the scope resolution operator (**::**) is used.

```
mountain::mountain (char * N) {strcpy (mountain::N,N);}
continent::continent (char * N) {strcpy (continent::N,N);}
```

In the definitions of both constructors, the two names **N** refer to different data: the name of a function argument and the name of a data member **N** (the name of a mountain and a continent). The first name, which is declared later, hides the second one, but doesn't make it inaccessible. We can access the hidden name of a class member using the class name and the scope resolution operator, therefore:

```
mountain::N
```

means "the member **N** of the class **mountain**". If, for example, we were more sensible, and called the argument **Name**:

```
mountain::mountain(char * Name) {strcpy (N,Name);}
```

then we wouldn't need to use the operator **::**, as there are no duplicate names.

We would point out that the last program used the same name N as the name of data members in both classes. This is not something we would recommend as it would make your programs hard to modify and debug. Think up unique and suitable names.

```
class continent                    // Class continent
{
  // Friend function of class continent
  friend void Say(mountain&, continent&);

  char N[21];                      // Name of the continent
public:
  continent(char *);               // Constructor
  void Say(mountain&, continent&); // Member function
};
```

Another example refers to functions. In the class **continent** two functions with the name **Say** and the same arguments are declared: a friend function and a member function. Their names don't conflict as the member function has class scope, while the friend function is outside of the class scope. However, if you look at the definition of the member function **Say()**,

```
void continent::Say(mountain& M,continent& C)
{
/*  Say about a mountain and a continent

    continent class member function can call any global function, including
    a friend. To avoid name ambiguity we must use the
    scope resolution operator (::)
*/

  ::Say (M,C);     // Call Say() defined in global scope

/*  Say (M,C); would cause an error: call member continent::Say(),
    i.e. itself, which would result in the endless loop.
*/
}
```

you will see that it differs from the definition of the **friend** function **Say()**.

```
void Say(mountain& M, continent& C)
{
/*  Say about a mountain and a continent

    This global function, which is a friend function of classes mountain
    and continent, can access all members of both classes
*/

  cout << M.N << C.N << endl;

// Error: Field N cannot be used without an object
// cout << mountain::N << continent::N << endl;
}
```

First of all, note the presence of the scope resolution operator in the member function. The member function **continent::Say()** calls the global friend function:

```
::Say (M,C);
```

This syntax always indicates a reference to a globally defined name, be it a function or data. If we leave out the operator **::** then the statement:

```
Say (M,C);
```

will cause the function to repeatedly call itself, in other words, we end up with an endless loop (don't try it!).

A Constructor with One Argument

```
mountain E = "Everest ";      // Using constructor with one argument
```

The last program, Program 11.2 shows another way to initialize a class object, using the assignment operator.

This is possible only when a constructor (or more than one overloaded constructor) with just one argument is declared for a class. The constructor:

```
mountain::mountain (char *);
```

is called during the object definition, and the value of the expression to the right of the assignment operator is passed to it as an argument. As a result, the program outputs the following:

```
Everest Asia
Everest Asia
```

The first line is output by the friend function and the second by the member function (which does this via the friend function, too).

A Friend Member Function

A member function of one class can be declared as a friend in another class. In this case it has access to all members of both classes (see the following figure).

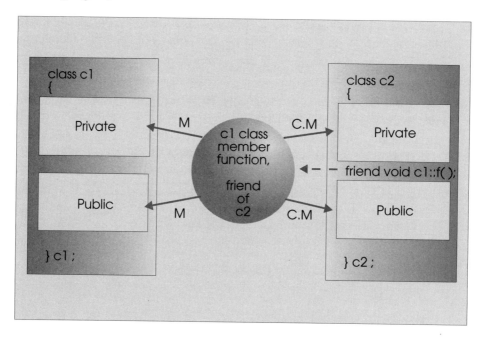

Try It Out - Using a Friend Member Function

The next program illustrates using friends of another class.

```
//      Program 11.3
//      Member function - a friend of another class

#include <iostream.h>
#include <string.h>

class continent;

class mountain
{
  char N[21];
```

```
public:
  mountain (char *);
  void Say(continent&);       // Member function (continent class friend)
};

class continent
{  // Friend function of this class
  friend void mountain::Say(continent&);
  char N[21];

public:
  continent (char *);
};

//       Constructors definitions

  mountain::mountain(char * N) {strcpy (mountain::N,N);}
  continent::continent(char * N) {strcpy (continent::N,N);}

//       ----------------------------------------------------

void mountain::Say(continent& C)
{
/*  Say about a mountain and a continent

    mountain class member function, which is a friend of the class
    continent, can access all continent class members
*/

  cout << N << C.N << endl;
}

//       ----------------------------------------------------

void main()
{

  mountain E = "Everest ";
  continent C = "Asia ";

  E.Say (C);                  // Call class mountain member function,
                              // which is a friend of the class continent

}
```

How It Works

Let's look at the program.

```
void mountain::Say(continent& C)
{
/*  Say about a mountain and a continent
```

```
    mountain class member function, which is a friend of the class
    continent, can access all continent class members
*/

  cout << N << C.N << endl;
}
```

In this program, the function `Say()` is defined. If you compare it with the ordinary function `Say()` we had in Program 11.2, you'll see that the member function `mountain::Say()` doesn't need the argument `M`, as it has direct access to the member by name.

Try It Out - A Strange Friendship Between Classes

If you want to declare all the functions of one class as friends of another, then instead of repeating the `friend` declaration for each function, you can declare the whole class as a friend of the other. Look at Program 11.4.

```
//         Program 11.4
//         Strange friendship of two classes

#include <iostream.h>
#include <string.h>

// Classes
class mountain
{ // The class continent is a friend of the class mountain
  friend class continent;

  char N [21];
public:
  mountain (char *);
  void Say(continent&);
};

class continent
{
  //friend class mountain;
  // Class mountain isn't a friend of class continent !!!
  char N[21];
public:
  continent (char *);
  void Say(mountain&);
};

//      Constructors definitions
  mountain::mountain (char * N) {strcpy (mountain::N,N);}
  continent::continent (char * N) {strcpy (continent::N,N);}

//      ---------------------------------------------------------
```

```
void continent::Say(mountain& M)
{
/*      Say about a mountain and a continent

   continent class member function, which is a friend of class mountain,
   can access all mountain class members
*/
   cout << M.N << N << endl;
}

//        ----------------------------------------------------------

void mountain::Say(continent& C)
{  //  Say about a mountain

   cout << N
   //    << C.N       // Error: "continent::N" isn't accessible
                      // Class mountain isn't a friend of the class continent,
                      // so the class mountain member function mountain::Say()
                      // can't access the class continent member continent::N

        << endl;
}

//        ----------------------------------------------------------

void main ()
{
   mountain E = "Everest ";
   continent C = "Asia ";

   E.Say (C);
   C.Say (E);
}
```

How It Works

```
class mountain
{  // The class continent is a friend of the class mountain
   friend class continent;
```

Note how it's done in this program. The class **continent** is declared as a **friend** of the class **mountain**. Therefore, all the functions of the class **continent** are friend functions of class **mountain**, in other words they have access to the class **mountain** members (see the following figure).

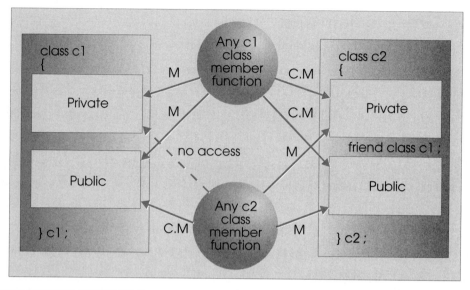

```
class continent
{
  //friend class mountain;
```

Note that a similar declaration in class `continent` is commented out of the program. Without this declaration, the class `mountain` won't be a friend of the class `continent`, regardless of the fact that `continent` is a friend of `mountain`.

```
void continent::Say(mountain& M)
{
/*      Say about a mountain and a continent

  continent class member function, which is a friend of class mountain,
  can access all mountain class members
*/
  cout << M.N << N << endl;
}

//      -----------------------------------------------------------

void mountain::Say(continent& C)
{ //  Say about a mountain

  cout << N
```

```
//    << C.N        // Error: "continent::N" isn't accessible
                    // Class mountain isn't a friend of the class continent,
                    // so the class mountain member function mountain::Say()
                    // can't access the class continent member continent::N
      << endl;
}
```

Compare the functions `Say()` of both classes. Since the class `continent` is a friend of the class `mountain`, then `continent::Say()` has access to `M.N`. However, `mountain::Say()` doesn't have access to `C.N` (as indicated by the comment), since the class `continent` isn't a friend of `mountain`. Therefore `mountain::Say()` doesn't use the argument `c` and only prints the name of the mountain. The output of Program 11.4 therefore looks as follows:

```
Everest
Everest Asia
```

If you uncomment the following two lines in Program 11.4:

```
// friend class mountain;
```

```
// << C.N
```

the classes `mountain` and `continent` will become mutual friends and the program will output:

```
Everest Asia
Everest Asia
```

Static Members of a Class

Class members (both data and functions) may be declared using the keyword `static`, for example:

```
class c
{
  static int sm;
  static void smf();
};
```

The features of static members differ greatly from the features of ordinary (non-static) members. They also differ from the features of ordinary data and functions which aren't class members and are defined using the keyword **static** (for examples of static variables see Program 6.21, and for examples of static functions see Programs 7.10a and 7.10b).

Static Data Members

We'll start by examining the features of static data members. The keyword **static** in this context means that there is one (and only one) copy of the data item, which is common to all instances (objects) of the class.

Look at Program 11.5, three classes (**emptyClass**, **nonStaticClass**, and **staticClass**) are declared. Five objects (**E**, **N1**, **N2**, **S1**, and **S2**) are also defined.

Try It Out - Classes With Static Data Members

Let's look at the program.

```
//        Program 11.5
//        A class with a static data member

#include <iostream.h>

class emptyClass     {                           } E;       // Empty
class nonStaticClass {        char m[1000];} N1,N2;  // Non static
class staticClass    {static char m[1000];} S1,S2;  // Static

void main ()
{
                                                 // Output:
   cout << sizeof (emptyClass)   << endl         // 1
        << sizeof (E)  << endl                   // 1
        << sizeof (nonStaticClass)  << endl      // 1000
        << sizeof (N1) << endl                   // 1000
        << sizeof (N2) << endl                   // 1000
        << sizeof (staticClass)   << endl        // 1
        << sizeof (S1) << endl                   // 1
        << sizeof (S2) << endl;                  // 1
}
```

How It Works

```
class emptyClass     {                       } E;        // Empty
```

The class **emptyClass** doesn't have any members.

```
class nonStaticClass {        char m[1000];} N1,N2;   // Non static
class staticClass     {static char m[1000];} S1,S2;   // Static
```

The class **nonStaticClass** contains an ordinary, non-static member: an array of 1000 characters. An array with the same name is declared in class **staticClass** as **static**. The program outputs the sizes of the classes and the objects in each class.

The empty class, **emptyClass,** and the object **E** of this class have the size of 2 on our computer. The size of class **nonStaticClass** and both of its objects (**N1** and **N2**) is equal to 1000, in other words, the size of the data member. The thing of interest here is that the size of class **staticClass** and the size of its objects (**S1** and **S2**) are the same as an empty class. This means that no memory is allocated for a static data member in a class, which in turn means that there is a principal difference between static and non static members.

When each new object is defined, a separate copy of each non static member is created and the necessary amount of memory is allocated (see the following figure).

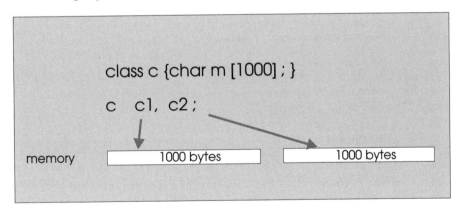

Try It Out - Static Data Member Definition

For a static member the situation is completely different. It isn't created when an object is defined and no memory is allocated for it. The definition of a static member is required somewhere else, as shown in Program 11.6. To simplify the example, a member **s** of type **char** is used instead of an array, and **struct** is used instead of class (to eliminate the **public** access specifier).

```
//       Program 11.6
//       Static data member definition is required somewhere

#include <iostream.h>

// Declarations

struct nonStaticStruct {        char C;}; // Non static
struct staticStruct     {static char C;}; // Static

// Static member definition (global)

char staticStruct::C =  'C'; // Static member C of staticStruct is defined

// Class objects definitions (global)

nonStaticStruct N1 = {'A'};              // N1.C is defined
nonStaticStruct N2 = {'B'};              // N2.C is defined
staticStruct S1;                         // No member S1.C is defined    <--
staticStruct S2;                         // No member S2.C is defined    <--

//       -------------------------------------------------------

void main()
{                                        // Output
  cout << N1.C << endl                   // A
       << N2.C << endl                   // B
       << staticStruct::C << endl        // C
       << S1.C << endl                   // C
       << S2.C << endl;                  // C
}
```

How It Works

```
char staticStruct::C =  'C';             // Static member C of staticStruct is
defined
```

The **static** member **C** of the structure **staticStruct** is defined in a separate statement, which looks like the definition of an ordinary variable with the special compound name **staticStruct::C**. This name includes the name of the type, which is **staticStruct**, and the scope resolution operator (**::**). Note that the static member **staticStruct::C** is defined before the definition of any object of type **staticStruct**. This is indicative of the fact that a static member is a separate object which exists independently of the objects of the class of which it's a member.

Try commenting out the two definitions of objects **S1** and **S2** in Program 11.6, and the two lines where these objects are used. You will see that the program operates exactly as before, and that the static object **staticStruct::C** still exists, even without **S1** and **S2**.

There is a single copy of a static member which is associated with a whole class, illustrated in the following figure.

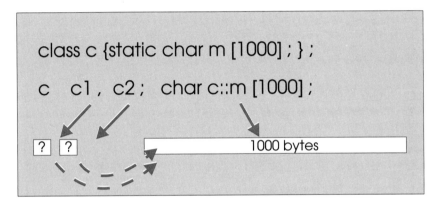

This means that **staticStruct::C**, **S1.C**, and **S2.C** refer to the same object and any one of these objects can change the value of **c** which will be available to other instances of the class. Of the three styles, **staticStruct::C** is preferable, as it implicitly indicates that the static member isn't associated with the objects of the class **staticStruct**. We can say that one static member is shared by all the objects of the class. This is evident in the program output which appears in the comment to the **cout** statement, where **S1.C** and **S2.C** contain the value **'C'**, with which the static member **staticStruct::C** has been initialized. Note that **S1** and **S2** were not initialized at all. Moreover, we can't initialize them using a list as we did for the objects **N1** and **N2**. It would be incorrect to write, for example:

```
staticStruct  S1 = {'C'};  // Error
```

The cause of the error is clear: you know that in the object **S1** no memory is allocated for the static member, so there is no place to which the value of the initializing expression can be copied.

Static Member Functions

Static member functions differ from non-static ones in the way that they access class members.

Try It Out - Static Member Functions

This is demonstrated in the following program.

```
//        Program 11.7
//        A static member function

#include <iostream.h>

class example
{
          int   m;
    static int   sm;

public:
    example();                              // Constructor
    void Inc();                             // Increment m and sm
    static void Say(example&,example&);     // Say about m and sm (static)
};

//   Static member definition

int example::sm = 0;

//   Member functions

example::example() {m=0;}
void example::Inc() {m++; sm++;}

//        ----------------------------------------------------------

void example::Say(example& ex1, example& ex2)
{
    cout << " ex1.m = " << ex1.m
         << " ex2.m = " << ex2.m
         <<   " sm = "  << sm << endl;

// Error: 'm' can't be used in a static member function
// cout << m;
}

//        ----------------------------------------------------------

void main()
{
    example ex1,ex2;                // Use example::example(); initialize m with 0

    example::Say (ex1,ex2);         // Call static member function
    ex1.Inc ();                     // Call nonstatic member function
```

```
   example::Say (ex1,ex2);
   ex2.Inc ();
   example::Say (ex1,ex2);
}
```

How It Works

```
class example
{
        int  m;
  static int   sm;

public:
  example();                             // Constructor
  void Inc();                            // Increment m and sm
  static void Say(example&,example&);    // Say about m and sm (static)
};
```

Here, class **example** contains a static member function **Say()** along with a static data member **sm**. The syntax of a static member function definition is the same as that of a non static one. The only difference is that a static function has only direct access (by name) to static members of its class (both data and functions, **public** and **private**), and unlike non-static member functions, it doesn't have the pointer **this** and can't access non static members by name.

Using Static Objects

What can we use a static function for? As you will remember, a static data member is a single data item shared by all instances of the class. You could write a program that used a static data member to keep a record of the number of objects of a class there were. For example:

```
class data
{
private:
    static int numberOfObjects;
    //other statements

public:
    data()
    {
        numberOfObjects++;
    }

    ~data()
    {
        numberOfObjects--;
    }
    //other statements
};
```

The static data member is incremented by the constructor and decremented by the destructor. To access the data member to see how many objects there are we can create a function. How do we access the function? What happens if there are no objects? Obviously, the number of objects will be zero but we have no object to use a member function with! To create an object to access the function seems wrong. In fact, wouldn't it be better if we could call the function with the name of the class, for example,

```
data::reportNumber();
```

This won't work unless the member function is declared **static**.

Nevertheless, a static member function has access all the class members via compound names like **ex.M**, where **ex** is the name of the object (or, as in our case, the name of the reference), which is passed to the function as an argument. The following figure shows how static member functions and normal functions access static and non-static members.

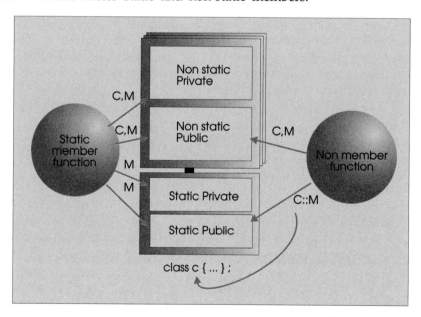

You can see that to access the static member **M** from a normal function, the class name prefix is required, so you must use the expression **example::M**.

For example, the statement:

```
example::Say (ex1,ex2);
```

is used to call the static member function **Say()** from the normal function `main()`. However, you can't use `sm` in a similar way , for example:

```
example::sm = 1;
```

as `sm` is a private member inaccessible from `main()`.

```
void example::Inc() {m++; sm++;}
```

Now we'll see how the static member `sm` is used in the program to count the calls to the member function `Inc()`, which adds 1 to `m` and `sm`. When it's called for object `ex1` (`ex1.Inc()`), it adds 1 to `ex1.m`, and when it's called for object `ex2` (`ex2.Inc()`), it adds 1 to `ex2.m`. But the value of the static member `sm` is incremented by 1 with every call, as you can see from the output of the program:

```
ex1.m = 0 ex2.m = 0 sm = 0
ex1.m = 1 ex2.m = 0 sm = 1
ex1.m = 1 ex2.m = 1 sm = 2
```

Using Static Members

You can use static members to eliminate the need for global names, by hiding global data and functions in classes. In the next figure, access to global names is compared with access to public static members of a class. The names of the static members are invisible from outside the class. To gain access to them we need to specify the class name as a prefix.

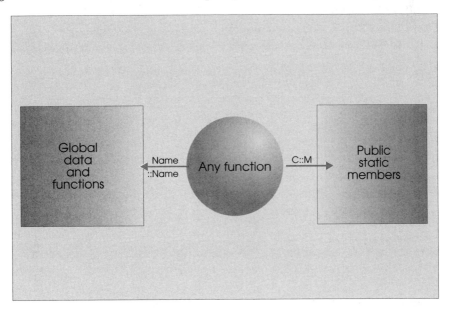

Try It Out - Using Static Members

We can see this in action in the next program.

```cpp
//        Program 11.8
//        Globals with the same names

#include <iostream.h>

class example1
{
public:
  static int  GlobalObject;
  static void Say ();
};

class example2
{
public:
  static int  GlobalObject;
  static void Say ();
};

//  Global data definitions

int example1::GlobalObject;        // example1 class static member
int example2::GlobalObject;        // example1 class static member
int GlobalObject;                  // global variable

//  Static member functions definitions

void example1::Say() {cout<<"Class example1 "<< GlobalObject <<endl;}
void example2::Say() {cout<<"Class example2 "<< GlobalObject <<endl;}

//  Global function definition

void Say() {cout<<"Global    "<< GlobalObject<<endl;}

//  ---------------------------------------------------------

void main ()
{
  example1::GlobalObject = 1;
  example2::GlobalObject = 2;
  GlobalObject = 3;

                    // Output
  example1::Say (); // 1
  example2::Say (); // 2
  Say ();           // 3
}
```

How It Works

The same names can be used for members in different classes at the same time. They don't conflict with each other as they are local within the limits of a class.

```
int example1::GlobalObject;    // example1 class static member
int example2::GlobalObject;    // example1 class static member
int GlobalObject;
```

Program 11.8 shows how the name **GlobalObject** is used for three different objects. The first name is defined is defined in class **example1**, the second in class **example2**, and the third is a global variable.

```
//  Static member functions definitions

void example1::Say() {cout<<"Class example1 "<< GlobalObject <<endl;}
void example2::Say() {cout<<"Class example2 "<< GlobalObject <<endl;}

//  Global function definition

void Say() {cout<<"Global    "<< GlobalObject<<endl;}
```

In the same way, three identical names **Say()** refer to three different functions. The program's output:

```
Class example1 1
Class example2 2
Global    3
```

shows that each function uses the name of its own **GlobalObject**, which is defined in the same scope as the function itself.

Using Enumerations Locally in a Class

Another example of hiding information is given in Program 11.9.

This program looks at enumerated types. An enumerated type is another method to name integer constants. For example:

```
enum {ZERO, ONE, TWO};
```

This defines three integer constants, or enumerators, and assigns values to them. By default, enumerated types are assigned values starting at 0.

Therefore, our example is equivalent to writing:

```
const ZERO = 0;
const ONE = 1;
const TWO = 2;
```

Try It Out - An Enumeration Local in a Class

As Program 11.9 shows, an enumerated type can be named. The name becomes a distinct type and can be used to create variables. For example:

```
YesNo response;
response = ONE;
int j = ONE;        //puts the value 1 into j
```

However:

```
response = j;           //error
response = YesNo(j); //correct. However, can only have value of 0 or 1 or 2
```

```
//        Program 11.9
//        An enumeration local in a class

#include <iostream.h>

class example
{
public:
  enum YesNo {No=0,Yes=1};        // Local type YesNo
};

enum YesNo {No=2,Yes=3};          // Global type YesNo

//      -------------------------------------------------------

void main ()
{                                      // Output
  cout << example::No   << endl    // 0
       << example::Yes  << endl    // 1
       <<     No  << endl    // 2
       <<    Yes  << endl    // 3
       << ios::skipws;       // 1
}
```

How It Works

```
class example
{
public:
  enum YesNo {No=0,Yes=1};       // Local type YesNo
};
```

Here in the class **example** an enumeration type **YesNo** is defined, which includes two constants **No** and **Yes** that have values 0 and 1 respectively.

```
enum YesNo {No=2,Yes=3};          // Global type YesNo
```

At the same time, a global type with the same name and the same enumeration constant names is defined, but with different constant values.

```
    cout << example::No    << endl      // 0
         << example::Yes  << endl      // 1
         <<     No   << endl            // 2
         <<    Yes  << endl            // 3
         << ios::skipws;               // 1
```

The rules for enumeration constants local to a class, are the same as for static members. This can be seen from the above statement which outputs the values of the enumeration constants. In the last line you can see an expression that was used in Program 8.2. **ios** is the name of a class which is declared in the file **IOSTREAM.H**, which is included in the program by the **#include** directive. But what does the name **skipws** mean? If you look through the file **IOSTREAM.H** you'll find the declaration of the class **ios**, and inside this declaration there is the declaration of an enumeration type, and finally inside this is **skipws** as the name of one of the enumeration constants. This example shows how you can use a class to hide the names of enumeration types and constants.

Summary

In this chapter we have covered a lot of new ground. We have looked at class properties and the **this** keyword. We have discussed data access control and friends and looked at static and non-static members of classes.

The topic is quite hard so you may want to read the chapter through again before launching into the next one. We haven't included an end of chapter program here because this chapter runs very nicely into the next. By the end of Chapter 12 you will see how what you have learnt can be used in a useful program.

More About Class Objects

This chapter carries straight on from the last, but we are covering a lot of ground so let's quickly recap what we know. We started looking at classes in Chapter 10 where we saw how similar they are to structures.

Chapter 11 started with an overview of class properties and we looked at access specifiers. We saw how useful the **this** keyword is because it always points to the object whose member function is being called. We examined friends of classes and how a **friend** can access all members of a class - including the private members.

In addition we have looked at encapsulation. This embodies the hiding of information (both data and code): local variables are hidden in functions, private members are hidden in classes. As a result, external direct access to data and functions by name is prevented.

This chapter you will:

- Learn how to add operator functions to objects
- Understand overloaded operators
- Design a calculator (a bit more complicated than the last one) using some of what we have covered in the last two chapters

Adding Operator Functions for Class Objects

In this section we'll discuss a special kind of function in C++, which allows you to define the effect of operators on class objects. These functions are called operator functions. We'll take the example of the addition operator (+) for a simple class that consists of just one data member **N** of type `int`:

```
class number
{
  int n;
// member functions
};
```

The problem here is that the operator + cannot be applied to objects of the class **number**, so we can't simply write **X + Y**, where **X** and **Y** are objects of the class number. We are sure you can see that the intuitive way to add numbers would be to write **X + Y** and we will develop a mechanism for doing this.

How then can we add numbers?

Using the Add() Member Function

The straightforward solution is to use a member function which performs addition. In the next example a member function **Add()** is used to add together two objects of the class **number**. For example:

```
Z = X.Add(Y);
```

Try It Out - Using the Add() Member Function

Let's look at the example.

```
//        Program 12.1
//          Adding number objects

#include <iostream.h>

class number
{
public:
  int n;
  number() {n = 1;}
  number Add(number);
};
```

```
number number::Add (number N)
{
/*      member function Add()
        Adds two objects of type number
        and places result into a temporary object
        Returns temporary object
*/

  number T;                    // Temporary object
  T.n = n + N.n;
  return  T;
}

void main ()
{
  number  X,Y,Z;               // Initialized to 1 by constructor

  Z = X.Add (Y);               // Z=X+Y
  cout << Z.n;                 // 2

  Z = Z.Add(X.Add (Y));        // Z=Z+X+Y
  cout << Z.n;                 // 4

  // Z = X + Y;                // Error: operator + cannot be applied
                               //   to 'number' + 'number'
}
```

How It Works

In this program, we use the member function **Add()** to add objects of the class **number**.

```
  number  X,Y,Z;

  Z = X.Add (Y);               // Z=X+Y
```

To add two numbers, **X** and **Y** we call the **Add()** function.

```
number number::Add (number N)
{
/*      member function Add()
        Adds two objects of type number
        and places result into a temporary object
        Returns temporary object
*/

  number T;                    // Temporary object
  T.n = n + N.n;
  return  T;
}
```

The expression:

```
T.n = n + N.n;
```

in the body of the function **Add()** means the same as:

```
T.n = X.n + Y.n;
```

```
Z = X.Add (Y);            // Z=X+Y
```

The result of the addition is stored in the temporary number **T**. Then a copy of the value of **T** is returned from the function **Add()**, and the result of the addition is assigned to another object of the class **number**.

```
class number
{
public:
  int n;
  number() {n = 1;}
  number Add(number);
};
```

Note that the default constructor of the class initializes the member **n** of the objects being created with the value 1. Therefore **X.n + Y.n** results in 2, as we can see from the output of the program:

```
24
```

Although this method solves the problem of adding objects of the class **number**, it is too cumbersome and unnatural to be completely satisfactory. Instead of the usual simple statement:

```
Z = Z + X + Y;
```

we have to write a more complicated and unusual expression:

```
Z = Z.Add(X.Add (Y));
```

Try uncommenting the line:

```
// Z = X + Y;
```

and then try to compile the program. You'll see that the compiler will not allow you to apply the operator **+** to objects of the class **number**.

When adding integers, such as in the statements:

```
int x,y;z;
z = x + y;   // Ok
```

the compiler "knows" what the operator + means and what operations (machine instructions) are required to perform addition. The same applies to all the other predefined types. However, with objects of user-defined types (for example, of type **number**) the compiler doesn't know in what sense we'd like to apply the operation of addition, in other words what operations are needed to produce the result.

Addition Using the Operator+() Member Function

C++ has a way of 'telling' the compiler which procedure should be executed when the operator + is applied to objects of a derived type. It does this using an **operator** function and this overloads the operator.

Try It Out - Using the +() Member Function

In Program 12.2 you'll notice a member function with the unusual name **operator+**. This is the operator function. It is declared in the class **number**.

```
//      Program 12.2
//      Adding numbers with the operator+() member function

#include <iostream.h>

class number
{
public:
  int n;
  number() {n=1;}
  number operator+ (number);
};

number number::operator+ (number N)
{
/*      operator+() member function

        Adds two objects of the type number
        and places the result into the temporary object
        Returns the temporary object
*/
  cout << "\noperator+() function is working ";
  number T;               // Temporary object
  T.n = n + N.n;
  return  T;
}
```

Try It Out!

```
void main()
{
  number  X,Y,Z;

  Z = X.operator+(Y);       // Explicit call to operator+()
  cout << Z.n;              // 2

  Z = X + Y;                // Implicit call to operator+()
  cout << Z.n;              // 2

  Z = Z + X + Y;            // Chain of calls
  cout << Z.n;              // 4

  // Z = X + 1;             // Error: operator + cannot be applied
                            //  to 'number' + 'int'
}
```

How It Works

In this program, you see the C++ keyword **operator** in the name of the function. The sign that follows it is part of the function name. The sign specifies the C++ operator to which this operator function refers. The word **operator** and the operation sign can be separated by spaces.

```
number number::operator+ (number N)
{
/*        operator+() member function

        Adds two objects of the type number
        and places the result into the temporary object
        Returns the temporary object
*/
  cout << "\noperator+() function is working ";
  number T;                 // Temporary object
  T.n = n + N.n;
  return  T;
}
```

The function **operator+()** works in the same way as the function **Add()** in the previous example. The only difference is that a test message has been added.

```
    Z = X.operator+(Y);       // Explicit call to operator+()
```

The explicit call to the **operator+()** function to add **X** and **Y** is also similar to that of **Add()**.

```
z = X + Y;                    // Implicit call to operator+()
```

However, the main advantage of the operator function facility is that it can be called implicitly (without its name). This is demonstrated by the output from the program:

```
operator+() function is working 2
operator+() function is working 2
operator+() function is working
operator+() function is working 4
```

The function **operator+()** is implicitly called for each operator **+**, where both operands are objects of the class **number**. For example, whenever the compiler encounters an expression such as **X + Y**, it calls the operator function in the following way:

```
X.operator+(Y)
```

And, similarly:

```
Y + X
```

actually stands for:

```
Y.operator+(X)
```

Overloaded Operators

If different functions have the same name but different arguments, they are called overloaded functions. In the same way, operators that execute different operations depending upon the type and/or number of operands are called overloaded operators. Most C++ operators can be overloaded. Some of them are overloaded already. For example, the operator **+** in the expression **i + 1** means "add 1 to **i**", if **i** is an integer variable. Whereas, the expression **p + 1** where **p** is a pointer to a structure, means "add the structure size to the address contained in **p**" but not "add 1 to **p**". Since we have included a member function **operator+()** in the class **number**, we have created one more overloaded operator **+**, which the compiler will use for adding objects of class number.

Try It Out!

Try It Out - Adding a Number Object and an Integer

```
// Z = X + 1;              // Error: operator + cannot be applied
                           // to 'number' + 'int'
```

The function **operator+()** introduced in Program 12.2 can add objects of the class **number**, but can't add an object of type **number** and an integer.

However, we now know how we can do this. We have to include an additional **operator+()** function in the class **number**, with an argument of type **int**. This is done in Program 12.3.

```
//        Program 12.3
//        Adding a number and an integer

#include <iostream.h>

class number
{
public:
  int n;
  number() {n = 1;}
  number operator+ (number);
  number operator+ (int);
};

number number::operator+ (number N)
{
  number  T;
  cout << "\nAdding two numbers ";
  T.n = n + N.n;
  return T;
}

number number::operator+ (int N)
{
  number  T;
  cout << "\nAdding number to integer ";
  T.n = n + N;
  return T;
}

void main()
{
  number  X,Y,Z;

  Z = X + Y;                // Call operator+ (number)
  cout << Z.n;
```

```
Z = X + 1;                    // Call operator+ (int)
cout << Z.n;

// Z = 1 + X;                 // Error: operator + cannot be applied
                             //    to 'int' + 'number'
}
```

How It Works

This program has an additional **operator+()** function in the class **number**, with an argument of type **int**.

```
Z = X + 1;                    // Call operator+ (int)
```

It is invoked as shown, which is effectively:

```
Z = X.operator+(1);
```

This is demonstrated by the second line of the program output:

```
Adding two numbers 2
Adding number to integer 2
```

You may be wondering whether it will it be invoked for:

```
Z = 1 + X;
```

where the integer is in the left side of the addition expression. The answer to this is no, it won't, so how can we solve this problem?

The Non-member Operator Function

We can't solve this new problem with the help of a member function, we need a non-member function. The following program illustrates why.

Try It Out - Adding With a Non-member Function

Program 12.4 shows how to define a non-member **operator+()** function.

```
//        Program 12.4
//        Adding with a non-member function

#include <iostream.h>

class number
{
```

Try It Out!

```
public:
  int n;
  number() {n = 1;}
};

number operator+ (number N1,number N2)
{
  number  T;

  cout << "\nAdding two numbers ";
  T.n = N1.n + N2.n;
  return  T;
}

number operator+ (int N1,number N2)
{
  number  T;

  cout << "\nAdding integer to number ";
  T.n = N1 + N2.n;
  return  T;
}

void main()
{
  number  X,Y,Z;

  Z = operator+(X,Y);     // Explicit call to
  cout << Z.n;            //   operator+ (number,number)

  Z = X + Y;              // Implicit call to
  cout << Z.n;            //   operator+ (number,number)

  Z = operator+(1,X);     // Explicit call to
  cout << Z.n;            //   operator+ (int,number)

  Z = 1 + X;              // Implicit call to
  cout << Z.n;            //   operator+ (int,number)
}
```

How It Works

Two operands are required by the binary **+** operator. Therefore both non-member **operator+()** functions have two arguments each: the first argument is for the left operand, the second is for the right.

```
    Z = operator+(X,Y);     // Explicit call to
                            //   operator+ (number,number)
```

This statement calls a non-member **operator+()** function explicitly to add **x** **+ y**, and the statement:

```
    Z = operator+(1,X);        // Explicit call to
                               //    operator+ (int,number)
```

produces the sum **1 + X**.

```
    Z = X + Y;                 // Implicit call to
                               //    operator+ (number,number)
```

An implicit call here doesn't differ at all from an implicit call to a member function.

```
    Z = 1 + X;                 // Implicit call to
                               //    operator+ (int,number)
```

The compiler takes care to choose the appropriate **operator+()** function. It searches for the one whose left and right argument types match the left and right operands of the operator **+**.

When we considered function overloading, we saw the compiler needs the name together with the number and types of arguments to be able to identify a function. In order to use operators with user-defined types we can overload most of the existing C++ operator set. You have to overload the operator for it to work with your data types. Consider the division operator, **/** , which performs integer arithmetic if its two operands are both integers. It will perform floating-point arithmetic if at least one of the operands is a **float**.

Friend Operator Functions

In the previous programs our class **number** had only public members. We did this so as not to over-complicate the programs. However, in real life, some class members will be declared as **private**. These are usually data members. How would we need to modify our operator functions in this case?

We shall use the friend keyword. Without this, we wouldn't be able to use an overloaded operator with an integer variable as the first parameter. This is because we cannot call an integer member function with syntax like:

```
    int.operator+ (object)
```

Try It Out - Adding With a Friend Function

If we declare the data member **n** private, Program 12.4 will compile with
errors, as the member **n** will have become inaccessible from the
operator+() functions and **main()**. In Program 12.5 we have tried to get
around this problem.

```
//      Program 12.5
//      Adding with a friend function

#include <iostream.h>

class number
{
  int n;        // Private member
public:
        number() {n = 1;}
  friend number& operator+ (number&,number&);
        void Say ();
};

number T;       // Temporary object (global)

number& operator+ (number& N1,number& N2)
{
/*      operator+() a friend function of the class number

    Adds two objects of type number
    and stores the result in a temporary object (global).
    Returns the reference to the temporary object.
*/

  T.n = N1.n + N2.n;
  return  T;
}

void number::Say ()
{
  cout << ' ' << n << ' ';
}

void main ()
{
  number  X,Y,Z = X + Y;
                    //output
  X.Say();          // 1
  cout << '+';      // +
  Y.Say();          // 1
  cout << '=';      // =
  Z.Say();          // 2

  // cout << Z;     // Error: operator << cannot be applied
                    // to operand of type 'number'
}
```

How It Works

```
class number
{
  int n;        // Private member
public:
        number() {n = 1;}
   friend number& operator+ (number&,number&);
        void Say ();
};
```

Here a **friend** specification is applied to the **operator+()** function, which opens up access for this function to all members of the class **number**. To display the results we have to use the member function **Say()**, which we didn't need before. These are all changes we needed to make to use the operator **+** for adding objects of the class **number**. The interface of the **operator+()** function is changed to demonstrate the use of references when passing arguments and returning a value.

```
  number T;        // Temporary object (global)
```

Note that at the same time, we had to declare the temporary object **T** as global, since we can't return a reference to a local object because a local object is destroyed on exiting the function.

```
                   //output
   X.Say();        // 1
   cout << '+';    // +
   Y.Say();        // 1
   cout << '=';    // =
   Z.Say();        // 2
```

The output of Program 12.5:

```
1 + 1 = 2
```

is produced by the above statements.

```
   // cout << Z;     // Error: operator << cannot be applied
                     // to operand of type 'number'
```

However, we can't use the operator **<<** with objects of the class **number** as is stated in the comment to the program.

Displaying the Objects of a Class

To add objects of the class **number** we defined the **operator+()** function. Similarly, to make the following a valid statement:

```
cout << Z;
```

we have to define an appropriate operator function with the name **operator<<**. Its second (or right) argument must have the type **number**. The first argument, however, must be of the type **ostream&**.

What is the Type ostream?

The type **ostream** is declared in the file **IOSTREAM.H**. It is a class, with a lot of members. Among them are several overloaded operator member functions of the format:

```
ostream& operator<< (<type>);
```

where **type** can assume different values (**int**, **long**, **double**, etc.). These overloaded functions are used for outputting data of various types via the **<<** operator.

Try It Out - Using the Function operator<<()

In Program 12.6 the **operator<<()** function is used to output an object of the class **number**.

```
//  Program 12.6
//  Displaying numbers

#include <iostream.h>

class number
{
  int n;        // Private member
public:
        number() {n = 1;}
  friend number&  operator+  (number&,number&);
  friend ostream& operator<< (ostream&,number&);
};

number T;         // Temporary object (global)

number& operator+ (number& N1,number& N2)
{
/*     operator+() friend function of class number
```

```
    Adds two objects of type number
    and stores the result into a global temporary
    object. Returns the reference to the temporary
    object.
*/

  T.n = N1.n + N2.n;
  return  T;
}

ostream& operator<< (ostream& Cout,number& N)
{
/*      operator<<() friend function of class number
        and public member function of class ostream

  Inserts N.n into stream Cout (global)
  Returns reference to Cout
*/

  Cout << ' ' << N.n << ' ';
  return Cout;
}

void main()
{
  number  X,Y,Z = X + Y;

  cout << X << '+' << Y << '=' << Z;        // 1 + 1 = 2
}
```

How It Works

The function **operator<<()** is defined in the program.

```
ostream& operator<< (ostream& Cout,number& N)
{
/*      operator<<() friend function of class number
        and public member function of class ostream

  Inserts N.n into stream Cout (global)
  Returns reference to Cout
*/

  Cout << ' ' << N.n << ' ';
  return Cout;
}
```

Its first argument **Cout** has the type "reference to the class **ostream**", and the second has the type "reference to the class **number**". It can be compared to the function **operator+()** whose arguments were also references.

Using arguments of the type 'reference to a class' instead of type 'class' is characteristic of C++, as it's more effective. It wasn't completely by chance that the name **Cout** was chosen for the first argument. In actual fact, **cout**, which you met in the very first program, is a globally defined object of a class connected with the class **ostream**. A reference to this object is passed to the function and then is returned from it so that we can build the **<<** operators into a chain, for example:

```
X << Y << Z
```

```
cout << X << '+' << Y << '=' << Z;        // 1 + 1 = 2
```

Using the overloaded **<<** operator we can program the output of Program 12.6 in just the one statement instead of the five statements in Program 12.5.

Designing a Program

We have reached the end of this chapter, which really led on from the last. Now we can see how to implement what we have covered in the last two chapters in a real program.

The Problem

This chapter's problem is to produce a simple calculator that performs addition, subtraction, multiplication, division, calculates percentages, and can find the square root of a number.

The Analysis

The steps involved are:

1   Decide on the class specification. What operations will be member functions? What operations will be friend functions?

2   Define the functions.

3   Decide on the interface. How will the functions be called? Will the user have to execute the program each time they want to perform a calculation? How do we check that the user asks for a specified operation?

The Solution

1   The last few example programs have used a class **number** and this seems a suitable place to start. The only data member we need is a real number (a number that has a fractional part). We could have a **float**, **double**, or a **long double**. To help achieve a reasonable range of values and a suitable degree of accuracy, let's use a **double**.

We will use **friend** operator functions for the addition, subtraction, multiplication, division, and percentage calculations. The square root function will be written as a member function. A function to output the value to the screen is also needed. The **say()** function was used. We also need a way of assigning values to the object. The simplest way is to overload the **=** operator.

Additionally, a non-member function, **enter_data()** is used to obtain the user's numerical input and assign these values to our objects.

```
class number
{
public:
  number()                          //constructor - initialize object to zero
  {
    val = 0.0;
  }

  number(double n)                  //constructor - assign a double to object
  {
    val = n;
  };

  //functions
  void sqrt(void)                   //square root function
  {                                 //calls standard sqrt() function in maths.h
    if(val <= 0)
    {
      cout << "The square root of a negative number is not"
           << " a suitable calculation.";
    }
    else
    {
      number z;
      z.val = ::sqrt(val);
      z.say();
    }
  }
```

```
    void say(void)                  //display val
    {
      cout << val << endl;
    }

    void operator= (double d)       //overloaded assignment operator
    {                               //we can now use X = y; where X is an
      val = d;                      //object of the class number
    }

private:
    double val;                     //double used for size of numbers and precision

    friend void operator+ (number& X, number& Y);
    friend void operator- (number& X, number& Y);
    friend void operator* (number& X, number& Y);
    friend void operator/ (number& X, number& Y);
    friend void operator% (number& X, number& Y);
};
```

2   The functions can now be defined.

sqrt()

This function uses the function **sqrt()** from the header file **MATH.H**. To resolve the conflict in names between our class member function and the global function, the scope resolution operator, **::** , is used.

```
    void sqrt(void)
    {
      if(val <= 0)
      {
        cout << "The square root of a negative number is not"
             << " a suitable calculation.";
      }
      else
      {
        number Z;
        Z.val = ::sqrt(val);     //math.h header file needed
        Z.say();
      }
    }
```

To keep this program simple, let's not handle negative numbers as this will require the use of complex numbers.

```
    number Z;
    Z.val = ::sqrt(val);      //math.h header file needed
    Z.say();
```

A temporary **number** object is created and the data member of this object is used to store the answer. The answer is output using the **say()** function.

operator=

This member function simply assigns the **double** on the right hand side of the = operator to the private member data, **val**, on the left hand side of the operator. For example, **X = number1;** assigns the value stored in the memory location accessed by the variable name **number1** to **X.val**.

```
  void operator= (double d)       //overloaded assignment operator
  {                               //we can now use X = y; where X is an
    val = d;                      //object of the class number
  }
```

operator+

We can use a **friend** overloaded operator to perform the addition.

```
  void operator+ (number& X, number& Y)
  {
    number Z;
    Z.val = X.val + Y.val;
    Z.say();
  }
```

A temporary **number** object is created and the data member of this object is used to store the answer. The addition is performed using the binary **+** operator to add the two numbers together.

The subtraction function and the multiplication function can be performed in a similar way by overloading the - operator and the * operator.

operator/

This function has to ensure that the program will not crash if the user attempts to divide by zero.

```cpp
void operator/ (number& X, number& Y)
{
  number Z;
  if(Y.val == 0.0)
    cout << "\tAttempt to Divide by 0";
  else
  {
    Z.val = X.val / Y.val;
    Z.say();
  }
}
```

The value of the divisor is checked to see that it is not equal to 0.0. If it is, the function displays a warning message and terminates. Otherwise the calculation is performed in a similar manner to the other overloaded operator functions.

operator%

This function also performs some checks.

```cpp
void operator% (number& X, number& Y)
{
  number Z;
  if(X.val == 0.0)
    Z.say();
  else
    if(Y.val == 0.0)
      Z.say();
    else
    {
      Z.val = X.val * Y.val / 100.00;
      Z.say();
    }
}
```

enter_data()

This function asks the user to enter a number. Provided the user hasn't asked for a square root to be obtained, the user is asked to input a second number. These values are then assigned to our objects using the overloaded = operator. The function then displays the calculation that was requested on the screen.

```
void enter_data(char ch)
{
 double number1 = 0.0, number2 = 0.0;

  cout << "\n\tEnter number: ";
  cin >> number1;

  if(ch != 'r' && ch != 'R')
  {
    cout << "\tEnter number: ";
    cin >> number2;
  }

  X = number1, Y = number2;

  if(ch != 'r' && ch != 'R')
  {
    cout << "\n\n\t" << number1 << " " << ch
      << " " << number2 << " = ";
  }
  else
    cout << "\n\n\t√" << number1 << " = ";

}
```

3   The interface can now be considered.

The program should continue to run until it is terminated by the user. Therefore, the **main()** function will have a **do while** loop.

A menu is to be displayed on the screen and the user is asked to enter a choice. This could be coded in the following manner.

```
    do
    {
      cout << "\n\tSimple Calculator" << "\n\n\tOptions"
          << "\n\t+\tAddition" << "\n\t-\tSubtraction"
          << "\n\t*\tMultiplication" << "\n\t/\tDivision"
          << "\n\t%\tPercentage" << "\n\tR\tSquare Root"
          << "\n\tF\tFinish" << "\n\n\tEnter Option: ";

      cin >> choice;
    }while (choice != '+' && choice != '-' && choice != '*'
      && choice != '/' && choice != '%' && choice != 'R'
      && choice != 'r' && choice != 'F' && choice != 'f');
```

Tests are made in the **while** condition to see if the user has entered one of the expected responses. If an incorrect response has been made, the menu will be redisplayed. The user's input can then be used in a **switch** statement.

However, the statement in the **while** condition is rather complicated and it would probably be wise to put the **switch** statement in with this code which should simplify things!

The following code will, therefore, be used:

```
do
{
    cout << "\n\tSimple Calculator" << "\n\n\tOptions"
        << "\n\t+\tAddition" << "\n\t-\tSubtraction"
    << "\n\t*\tMultiplication" << "\n\t/\tDivision"
    << "\n\t%\tPercentage" << "\n\tR\tSquare Root"
    << "\n\tF\tFinish" << "\n\n\tEnter Option: ";

    cin >> choice;

    switch(choice)
    {
        case '+':
            enter_data(choice);
            X + Y;
            break;
        case '-':
            enter_data(choice);
            X - Y;
            break;
        case '*':
            enter_data(choice);
            X * Y;
            break;
        case '/':
            enter_data(choice);
            X / Y;
            break;
        case '%':
            enter_data(choice);
            X % Y;
            break;
        case 'R':
        case 'r':
            enter_data(choice);
            X.sqrt();
            break;
        case 'F':
    case 'f':
            select = 'N';
            break;
```

```
        default:
            cout << "\n\tYou have made an invalid choice\n";
            select = 'N';
    }
}while (select == 'Y');
```

Provided the user has not asked to finish the program, the user is asked if they want to make another calculation.

```
if (choice != 'f' && choice != 'F')
{
    cout << "\n\n\tDo you want another go? (Y/N): ";
    cin >> choice;
}
```

The program listing is as follows:

```
//  calc1.cpp
//  using class number to implement a simple calculator

#include <iostream.h>              //header file for I/O
#include <math.h>                  //header file for library sqrt()

class number                       //class number
{
public:                            //public members
  number()                         //constructor initializes data to 0.0
  {
    val = 0.0;
  }

  number(double n)                 //constructor that assigns a double to
object
  {
    val = n;
  };

  //functions
  void sqrt(void)                  //member sqrt()
  {
    if(val <= 0)                   //if val is less than 0, output message
    {
      cout << "The square root of a negative number is not"
      << " a suitable calculation.";
    }
    else                           //pass val to library function and store
    {                              //answer in our Z.
      number Z;
      Z.val = ::sqrt(val);
      Z.say();                     //display answer
    }
  }
}
```

```
   void say(void)                    //display data on screen
   {
     cout << val << endl;
   }

   void operator= (double d)         //overloaded assignment operator
   {
     val = d;
   }

private:                             //private members
   double val;                       //double used for size of numbers
            //   and precision

   friend void operator+ (number& X, number& Y);
   friend void operator- (number& X, number& Y);
   friend void operator* (number& X, number& Y);
   friend void operator/ (number& X, number& Y);
   friend void operator% (number& X, number& Y);
};

//overloaded operators

void operator+ (number& X, number& Y)
{
   number Z;
   Z.val = X.val + Y.val;
   Z.say();
}

void operator- (number& X, number& Y)
{
   number Z;
   Z.val = X.val - Y.val;
   Z.say();
}

void operator* (number& X, number& Y)
{
   number Z;
   Z.val = X.val * Y.val;
   Z.say();
}

void operator/ (number& X, number& Y)
{
   number Z;
   if(Y.val == 0.0)
   cout << "\tAttempt to Divide by 0";
   else
   {
```

```
   Z.val = X.val / Y.val;
   Z.say();
   }
}

void operator% (number& X, number& Y)
{
  number Z;
  if(X.val == 0.0)
  Z.say();
  else
  if(Y.val == 0.0)
    Z.say();
  else
  {
    Z.val = X.val * Y.val / 100.00;
    Z.say();
  }
}

//objects
number X, Y, Z;

void main()
{
  char choice, select = 'Y';

  //function prototype
  void enter_data(char ch);

  do                                //do until user has no more calculations
  {                                 //   to do
    do                              //do display menu and call functions
until
    {                               //   user wishes to Finish
      cout << "\n\tSimple Calculator" << "\n\n\tOptions"
           << "\n\t+\tAddition" << "\n\t-\tSubtraction"
      << "\n\t*\tMultiplication" << "\n\t/\tDivision"
      << "\n\t%\tPercentage" << "\n\tR\tSquare Root"
      << "\n\tF\tFinish" << "\n\n\tEnter Option: ";

      cin >> choice;                //obtain users choice

      switch(choice)                //select options via switch
      {
    case '+':                       //addition
      enter_data(choice);
      X + Y;
      break;
    case '-':                       //subtraction
      enter_data(choice);
```

```
     X - Y;
     break;
   case '*':                    //multiplication
     enter_data(choice);
     X * Y;
     break;
   case '/':                    //division
     enter_data(choice);
     X / Y;
     break;
   case '%':                    //percentage
     enter_data(choice);
     X % Y;
     break;
   case 'R':                    //square root - if R entered
   case 'r':                    //square root - ir r entered
     enter_data(choice);
     X.sqrt();
     break;
   case 'F':                    //finish - if F entered
   case 'f':                    //finish - if f entered
     select = 'N';
     break;
   default:                     //default - in case invalid choice made
     cout << "\n\tYou have made an invalid choice\n";
     select = 'N';
     }
   }while (select == 'Y'); //loop continues until select is changed to N

   if (choice != 'f' && choice != 'F')     //if not Finish, ask question
   {
      cout << "\n\n\tDo you want another go? (Y/N): ";
      cin >> choice;
   }

 } while(choice != 'n' && choice != 'N' && choice != 'f' && choice != 'F');
}

//non-member function declaration

void enter_data(char ch)
{
  double number1 = 0.0, number2 = 0.0;

  cout << "\n\tEnter number: ";
  cin >> number1;

  if(ch != 'r' && ch != 'R')
  {
    cout << "\tEnter number: ";
    cin >> number2;
```

```
   }

X = number1, Y = number2;

if(ch != 'r' && ch != 'R')
{
  cout << "\n\n\t" << number1 << " " << ch
     << " " << number2 << " = ";
}
else
  cout << "\n\n\tû" << number1 << " = ";
}
```

Sample output:

```
Simple Calculator

Options
+ Addition
- Subtraction
* Multiplication
/ Division
% Percentage
R Square Root
F Finish

Enter Option: +

Enter number: 5.5
Enter number: 7.75

5.5 + 7.75 = 13.25


Do you want another go? (Y/N): y

Simple Calculator

Options
+ Addition
- Subtraction
* Multiplication
/ Division
% Percentage
R Square Root
F Finish
```

```
Enter Option: /

Enter number: 582
Enter number: 10

582 / 10 = 58.2


Do you want another go? (Y/N): Y

Simple Calculator

Options
+ Addition
- Subtraction
* Multiplication
/ Division
% Percentage
R Square Root
F Finish

Enter Option: /

Enter number: 582
Enter number: 0

582 / 0 =  Attempt to Divide by 0

Do you want another go? (Y/N): Y


Simple Calculator

Options
+ Addition
- Subtraction
* Multiplication
/ Division
% Percentage
R Square Root
F Finish

Enter Option: r

Enter number: 81

√81 = 9
```

```
Do you want another go? (Y/N): Y

Simple Calculator

Options
+ Addition
- Subtraction
* Multiplication
/ Division
% Percentage
R Square Root
F Finish

Enter Option: R

Enter number: -9

√-9 = The square root of a negative number is not a suitable calculation.

Do you want another go? (Y/N): n
```

Summary

This chapter continued on from where we finished in Chapter 11 and has concentrated on operator functions. These are a very useful part of the C++ language as they allow us to redefine the normal operators so that they can be used with our objects. The result is that objects that we have defined can be used in as natural a manner as the pre-defined types. Therefore, our objects seem to be part of the language rather than something we have created.

CHAPTER 13

Basics of Object-Oriented Programming

Object-oriented programming was developed as a result of limitations in earlier approaches to programming. The basic idea was to combine data and the functions that operate on that data into a single unit, called an object. The intention of object-oriented programming is to model the real world in a program.

When you approach a problem you should no longer be thinking about how to divide it into functions. Instead you will be considering what objects to use. Thinking about objects should result in a close match between objects in your program and objects in the real world.

There are three ideas that are the basis of object-oriented programming: Encapsulation, Inheritance and Polymorphism

You already know about encapsulation. The other two are still foreign ground. In this chapter we will look at these in depth and by the end of the chapter you will be confident in the basics of object-oriented programming.

In this chapter you will:

- Understand about OOP
- Learn about inheritance and multiple inheritance
- Learn about polymorphism
- Write a program that will sum and average data

The Three Summits of Object-Oriented Programming

Let's go through each of the three ideas of OOP in turn.

Encapsulation

We have already covered this subject, but we will go over it again as it leads nicely on to the other two The concept of encapsulation embodies the hiding of information (both data and code): local variables are hidden in functions, private members are hidden in classes. As a result, external direct access to data and functions by name can be prevented. Therefore, the programmer has greater freedom in the choice of object names, and the probability of programming errors is reduced at the expense of stricter control of data access by the compiler.

Inheritance

This concept is similar to one idea being derived from other, more general, ideas. For example, a C++ programmer is a person that writes C++ programs. Here the idea of a C++ programmer is derived from two other ideas: a person and C++. Another example might be that of a mountain-skier. We understand that this is a person who skis down mountains.

Derived concepts (a mountain-skier, a programmer) in their turn can be basic definitions for other derived concepts, forming a hierarchical system similar to that shown in the following figure.

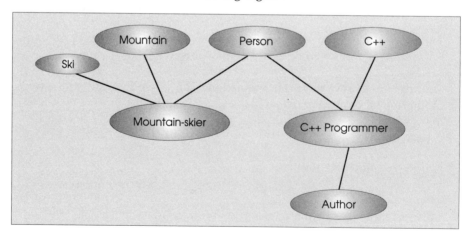

Classes in C++ can have the same sort of relationship, with a hierarchical structure and inheritance of the features from the basic classes to the derived classes. These relations are called inheritance.

Polymorphism

This conception of C++ can be expressed by the following comparison. The inscription "Do it!" on a signboard or pointer is executed by a programmer and a mountain-skier in different ways, depending on what sort of object is indicated by the pointer. If it points in the direction of a mountain then "Do it!" may mean: "Ascend the mountain and ski down it!" and if it points in the direction of a computer then "Do it!" may mean: "Write a program". Here it is important that it is not the pointer that defines what is to be done, but the object to which the pointer points.

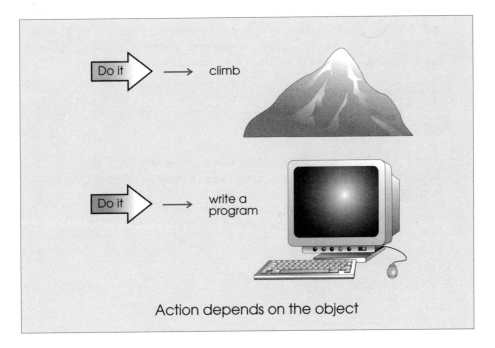

Action depends on the object

An Introduction to Inheritance

Seeing that comparisons are no more than shadows of objects, and remembering the saying: "It is better once to see, than a hundred times to hear" let us pass from just words to action.

Using Nested Classes

You know that a mountain contains rocks, ice, snow. In C++ the same idea may be expressed by a structure, for example:

```
struct mountains
{
  rock  R[];
  ice   I[];
  snow  S[];
};
```

You may wonder how in C++ you can express the idea of relations of another kind, for example, that a mountain is a site on a map? Here the idea of "mountain" is being derived from a more general concept of "site" or "location". All material objects, including mountains, have the property of being located at a place. This suggests that the idea of "location" is a basic one, and the idea "mountain" should be derived from it. In C++, a relationship between two ideas, illustrated in the next figure, is expressed by the following declaration of the class **mountain**:

```
class mountain : location
{
  ...
};
```

Here a **location** is a basic class, and a **mountain** is a derived class. The colon (:) after the type name **mountain**, means "is derived from".

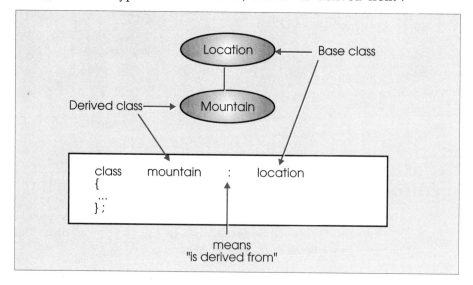

The idea of location is simple enough. For a mountain it includes a longitude and a latitude, and for a satellite in space it includes three coordinates of a location in a space and three more coordinates that depict rotations.

In order not to complicate the example program with unnecessary details we shall take a simplified example of a coordinate, **x**, which could, for example, represent the x-coordinate of a character position on a computer screen.

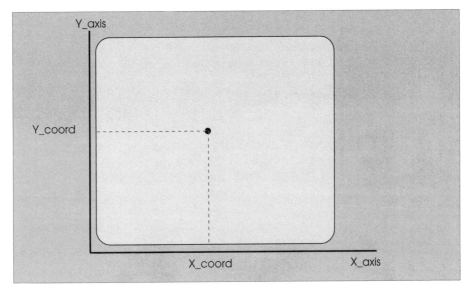

Try It Out - Using a Nested Class

Let's first look how, in Program 13.1, we can declare the type **x_coord** as consisting of one member which is of the type **coordinate**:

```
//      Program 13.1
//      Nested class (struct)

#include <iostream.h>

struct  coordinate {int N;};    // Coordinate (general type)
struct  x_coord {coordinate C;}; // x coordinate (special type)

void main ()
{
  x_coord  X;         // Definition

  X.C.N = 1;          // Access to member in nested class
  cout << X.C.N;
}
```

How It Works

Here, and in several of the following programs, we use structures instead of classes. This is done only for the simplicity of the examples. Everything we say applies equally well to classes. Therefore we shall use the term class to mean both classes and structures.

The declaration of **x_coord** used in Program 13.1 formally is quite acceptable, but the appearance of a coordinate value in the form:

    X.C.N

looks very cumbersome. Moreover the sense of the declaration "**x_coord** consists of coordinate" doesn't seem quite right.

Base and Derived Classes

In Program 13.2 the relations between the two ideas - coordinate (in general) and x-coordinate in particular - are expressed in another way.

Try It Out - Using Base and Derived Classes

Let's look at the example.

```
//   Program 13.2
//   Derived class x

#include <iostream.h>

struct coordinate {int N;};      // Base class
struct  x_coord : coordinate {};  // x_coord derived from coordinate

void main ()
{
  x_coord X;

  X.N = 1;            // Member N is inherited from base class
  cout << X.N;        // Access to N as it was declared in x_coord
}
```

How It Works

```
struct x_coord : coordinate {};   // x_coord derived from coordinate
```

This declaration means that the particular idea of x-coordinate is derived from a more general (base) idea of a coordinate in general. Here **coordinate** is a base class, and **x_coord** is a derived class.

Superficially this declaration looks as if **x_coord** doesn't contain members. But this isn't correct. In reality, the class **x_coord** has one member with the name **N**

```
X.N = 1;        // Member N is inherited from base class
```

so that the above statement is quite legal. This is the same member which the base class has. In a general case the declaration:

```
class derived : base {...};
```

means that a derived class **derived** inherits all the members of the base class **base**. This is the source of the term inheritance. But what does inheritance mean, besides the possibility of using members of the base class?

The Size of a Derived Class

When we look at the next program, you will see that the class **base** is defined which contains an array of characters with the size of 10 bytes. The size of an object of class **base** is also equal to 10 bytes. But what is the size of the class **derived**? The program's output (shown in the comments) shows that this size is also equal to 10. It becomes clear that the class **derived** inherits member **M** in the sense that it contains it in itself in the same way as if its declaration had the form:

```
class derived {char M[10]; };
```

Therefore, the colon (:) in the declaration:

```
class derived : base {};
```

serves as an indicator to the compiler "to include all members of **base** into the declaration of **derived**". This is shown in the following figure.

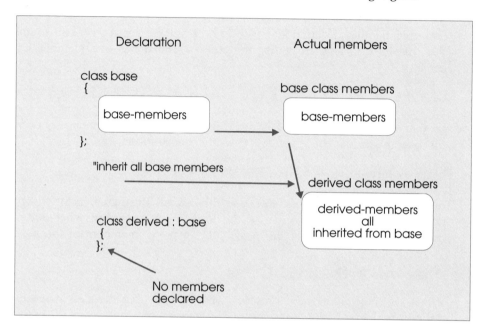

Try It Out - The Size of a Derived Class

We can now look at the program described above.

```
//      Program 13.3
//      Size of a derived class

#include <iostream.h>

class base {char M [10];};      // Base class
class derived : base  {};       // Derived class

void main ()
{
  cout << sizeof (base)      // 10
       << sizeof (derived);  // 10   <-- !
}
```

Try It Out!

Inherited and Own Members of a Derived Class

Its own member is added into the derived class in Program 13.4. As a result the class **derived** has two members with names **B** and **D**. Of course the size of the class **derived** is twice as large as the size of the class **base** from which it is derived. This is shown in a generalized form in the following figure where a derived class contains all members of the base class and also all its own members declared in its declaration.

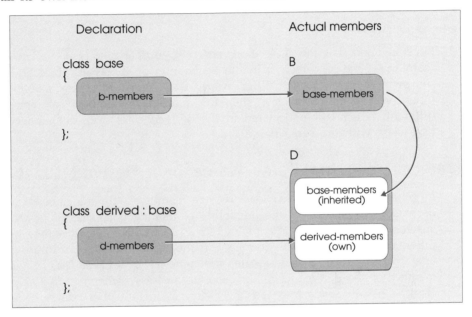

Try It Out - Adding Data Members to a Derived Class

Let's see how this works in the example.

```
//  Program 13.4
//  Adding data member to derived class

#include <iostream.h>

struct base                        // 1 member:  B
{
    int B;
};

struct derived : base              // 2 members: D and B
{
    int D;
};
```

Try It Out!

```
void main ()
{
  base  B;          // Definition
  derived  D;

  B.B = 1;
  D.D = sizeof (D) / sizeof (B);
  D.B = 3;
  cout << B.B << D.D << D.B;      // 123
}
```

How It Works

Keep in mind that the class **derived** has two data members - **B**, inherited from **base**, and **D**, which is in the declaration of **derived**. Since addressing "its own" member doesn't differ in any way from addressing a member inherited from the base class, then the question arises: how can you differentiate a member declared in the derived class from a member of the base class with the same name?

Members With the Same Name in a Derived Class

In general, it is not a good idea to have members with the same name in a derived class, because of the possibility of making mistakes. However, the answer to this question is contained in Program 13.5 which shows how to differentiate members with the same name using the scope resolution operator. Note that **D.M** designates the same as **D.derived::M**, i.e. "its own" member of the derived class. In order to address a member of the base class with the same name, it is necessary to include the base class name as a prefix to the member name:

```
D.base::M
```

Try It Out - Name Hiding

Now we can try the whole program.

```
//   Program 13.5
//   Name hiding

#include <iostream.h>

struct  base {int M;};
```

```
struct  derived : base {int M;};        // 2 members
                                        // with the same name M


void main ()
{
  base  B;
  derived   D;

  B.M  = 1;                             // Base member
  D.M  = sizeof(derived)/sizeof(base);  // D own member   derived::M
  D.base::M  = 3;                       // Inherited member  base::M

  cout << B.M
       << D.M                           // Implicit access
       << D.derived::M                  // Explicit access
       <<  D.base::M;                   // Only explicit access is possible
                                        //  to the hidden name

}
```

Try It Out - Adding a Member Function to a Derived Class

In order to distinguish an inherited member with the same name in the body of a member function, it is also necessary to use the scope resolution operator as is shown in Program 13.6. Here a constructor initializes both members that have the same name **M**, one of which is inherited from the base class **base**, and the other of which is a proper member of the class **derived**.

```
//  Program 13.6
//  Adding member function to derived class

#include <iostream.h>

struct base {int M;};
struct derived : base {int M;  derived();};

derived:: derived()                        // Constructor              <-- !
{
  base::M=1;  M=2;
}

void main ()
{
  derived D;                               // Constructor is called

  cout << D.base::M                        // 12
       << D.M;
}
```

Introduction to Polymorphism

Now that we have covered inheritance let's have a look at polymorphism.

Inheriting Functions

All member functions of a base class are inherited by a derived class in the same way as data members. A special case arises when a derived class contains its own member function having the same name and list of arguments as a member function of the base class. For example, you might want to do this so that calls in your program work the same way for objects of both the base and the derived class. This is illustrated in Program 13.7. Here the derived class has 2 member functions **Say()** with the same name. This is shown in the following figure.

For object **D** of the class **derived,** its own function **Say()** is called in one of two ways:

```
D.Say ();            // Derived Say()
D.derived::Say ();   // Derived Say()
```

A member function inherited from the base class may be invoked only with the use of the scope resolution operator. The name of the inherited function is hidden by the function of the derived class that has the same name.

Try It Out - Member Function Hiding

Let's look at the complete program.

```
//        Program 13.7
//        Member function hiding

#include <iostream.h>

struct base
{
  void Say() {cout << "Base Say()\n";}
};

struct derived : base                    // 2 member functions in class derived
{
  void Say() {cout << "Derived Say()\n";}
};


void main ()
{
  derived D;                             // Derived class object

  D.Say();                               // Derived Say()
  D.base::Say();                         // Base Say()
  D.derived::Say();                      // Derived Say()
}
```

Try It Out - Using a Pointer to a Derived Class

The use of a pointer for accessing a hidden member is shown in Program 13.8.

```
//        Program 13.8
//        Using a pointer to a derived class

#include <iostream.h>

struct base
{
  void Say () {cout << "Base Say()\n";}
};

struct derived : base
```

```
{
  void Say () {cout << "Derived Say()\n";}
};

void main()
{
  derived  D;              // Derived class object
  derived * pd;            // Pointer to derived

  pd = &D;                 // pd points to D
  pd->Say();               // derived::Say()

  pd->base::Say();         // base::Say()              <--
  pd->derived::Say();      // derived::Say()
}
```

How It Works

In this program, pointer **pd** has the type "pointer to **derived**" and points to
the object **D** of the class **derived**. This time its own member function can
be called in two ways

```
pd->Say();
```

and

```
pd->derived::Say();
```

```
pd->base::Say();   // base::Say()
```

The call of the hidden member function of the base class is made only with
the use of scope resolution operator .

Using a Pointer to a Base Class

In Program 13.9 there is a special case of using a pointer for calling a
member function, that plays an important role in C++.

Try It Out - Using a Pointer to a Base Class

Let's look at the example.

```
//  Program 13.9
//  Using a pointer to a base class

#include <iostream.h>
```

Try It Out!

```
struct base
{
  void Say() { cout << "Base Say()\n";}
};

struct derived : base
{
  void Say() {cout << "Derived Say()\n";}
};


void main()
{
  derived  D;              // Derived class object
  base *  pb;              // Pointer to base                    <--
  pb = &D;                 // Default conversion 'derived *' to 'base *'    <-- !
  pb->Say();               // base::Say(). Use POINTER type                 <-- !

  pb->base::Say();         // base::Say()
  //pb->derived::Say();    // Error: 'derived' is not a base class of 'base'
}
```

How It Works

```
  base *  pb;              // Pointer to base                    <--
```

The pointer **pb** is defined with the above statement. Its type is 'pointer to **base**' (in other words pointer to base class).

```
  pb = &D;                 // Default conversion 'derived *' to 'base *'   <-- !
```

But it is set to the address of an object **D** of the derived class. As a result **pb** points to object **D** just as pointer **pd** did in Program 13.8. In spite of the fact that the pointers **pd** and **pb** point to the same object the following two statements in the two programs:

```
pb->Say();
pd->Say();
```

lead to different results. In the following figure and table the use of pointers of different types in the two programs is compared.

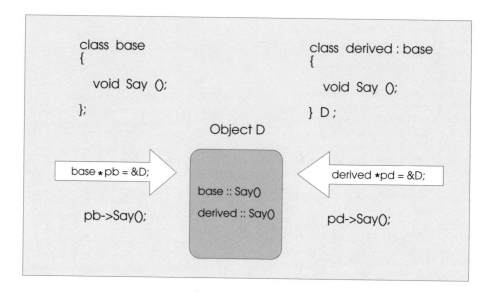

	Program 13.8	Program 13.9	
Declaration	derived * pd;	base * pb;	
Pointer type	pointer to derived	pointer to base	
Pointer Value	&D	&D	the same
Call statement	pd -> Say();	pb -> Say();	
Called function	Say() in derived	Say() in base	different

As you see, the type of pointer determines which function is to be called, when more than one of them has the same name: a pointer to a base class calls a base member function **Say()**, and a pointer to a derived class calls a derived member function **Say()**.

Note that in Program 13.9 an attempt to call **Say()** in the derived class with the help of the pointer to the class **base**:

```
pb->d::Say();  // Error
```

is considered by the compiler to be an error.

Default Pointer Conversion

```
pb = &D;      // Default conversion 'derived *' to 'base *'      <-- !
```

Let us return to the above statement from Program 13.9. Here the type of the pointer to the left of the equals sign is 'pointer to **base**', and the type of the pointer to the right of it is 'pointer to **derived**'. In C++ there is strict control of the matching of data types in expressions. In particular the assignment of pointers of different types usually is considered to be an error.

Try It Out - Errors When Converting Pointers

We can see an example of this in Program 13.10 where there are 2 such errors.

```
//        Program 13.10
//        Error: Cannot convert pointer

class base {};
class derived : base {};

void main()
{
  char C;
  int *pi=&C;           // Error: Cannot convert 'char *' to 'int *'

  base B;               // Base class object
  derived * pd=&B;      // Error: Cannot convert 'base *' to 'derived *'
}
```

How It Works

This program will not compile because of the two errors.

```
int *pi=&C;             // Error: Cannot convert 'char *' to 'int *'
```

You are not allowed to assign an address of a variable of the type **char**, to a pointer to **int**.

```
derivrd * pd=&B;        // Error: Cannot convert 'base *' to 'derivrf *'
```

It is also erroneous to assign an address of a base class object to a pointer of the type 'pointer to derived class'.

So, why doesn't the statement:

```
pb = &D;
```

in Program 13.9 generate an error? The point here is that this is a special case: in C++ it is permitted to convert (and to assign as well) a pointer of the type 'pointer to derived class', to a pointer of the type 'pointer to base class'. This is allowed because the base class is effectively a subset of the derived class, so anything you can access through a pointer to the derived class, you can also get through a base class pointer. This is called 'default pointer conversion'. However, the reverse conversion won't always be true. In the following figure admissible and inadmissible default conversions of pointers to base and derived classes are shown.

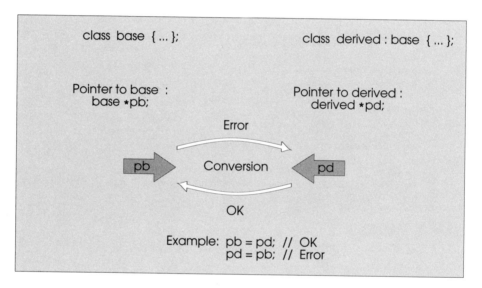

Explicit Pointer Conversion

It should be emphasized that an explicit pointer conversion is admissible in C++, but it should be avoided as serious program errors may occur which are not detected by the compiler. For example, in Program 13.11 a pointer to the class **a** is explicitly converted into a pointer to the class **c** with the help of the type cast expression **(c*)**. Calling the function **Destroy()** of the class **c**:

```
pc -> Destroy();
```

is not an error for the compiler, as it doesn't violate the C++ language rules. However, it is a dangerous error that becomes apparent during program execution. The fact is that the function **Destroy()** is called for an object **A** in which there is no member **M**. Nevertheless the assignment **M = 0** will be performed, and some data or machine instructions will be destroyed, which may lead to the failure of the program or the operating system.

> Don't use an explicit pointer conversion unless it is absolutely necessary.

Using an Explicit Pointer Conversion

Let's see the whole program, described above.

```
//        Program 13.11
//        Danger usage of an explicit pointer conversion

struct c
{
  int M;
  void Destroy()
  {
    M = 0;
  }
};

void main()
{
  c * pc;            // Pointer to c

  class a{};         // Any class
  a  A;              // Any class object

  pc = (c *) &A;     // Explicit conversion 'a *' to 'c *'

  // There is no A.M. Data will be destroyed !
  // pc->Destroy ();       <-- Don't uncomment this line !
}
```

Virtual Member Functions

Now let us look at Program 13.12. Ignoring comments, it differs from Program 13.9 by one word, **virtual**. In the statement:

```
pb->Say();        // d::Say(). Use OBJECT type                <-- !
```

the derived class member **Say()** is called, and not the base class member as it was in Program 13.9.

Try It Out - Virtual Member Functions

Let's see this program in action.

```
//        Program 13.12
//        Virtual member function

#include <iostream.h>

struct base
{
  virtual void Say()
  {
    cout << "Base Say()\n";
  }
};

struct derived : base
{
  void Say()
  {
    cout << "Derived Say()\n";
  }
};

void main ()
{
  derived   D;
  base * pb;

  pb = &D;
  pb->Say();                    // d::Say(). Use OBJECT type            <-- !

  pb->base::Say();        // b::Say()
  //pb->derived::Say(); // Error: 'd' is not a base class of 'b'
}
```

A virtual function is a member function that is called via a pointer to a public base class. The actual member function invoked is decided by the class type of the actual object that is addressed by the pointer. An example would be a **shape** class which is used as the base class for a number of different shapes - like square, rectangle, arc, ... Each of these classes can have its own show function that puts the shape on the computer screen. To create an image using several of these shapes you can create an array of pointers to all the shapes in the program with a statement like

```
shape * array[MAX];
```

If pointers are put into the array you could use a simple loop to draw your image. For example

```
for (int i = 0; i < MAX; i++)
    array[i] -> show();
```

If the pointer in **array** points to a circle, the function that draws the circle is called. But, all the different classes must be derived from the same base class and the base class member function must be virtual.

Polymorphism - A Quick Summary

Congratulations. You have reached the top of the third mountain - polymorphism with a pointer to a base class showing you the correct route.

Polymorphism in C++ means the mechanism of virtual functions. The use of derived classes and virtual functions are fundamental to object-oriented programming in C++. Therefore, it's essential to clearly understand the difference between ordinary and virtual member functions. In the following figure and table, the difference between the calls of virtual and non-virtual functions with the help of a pointer to the base class is shown.

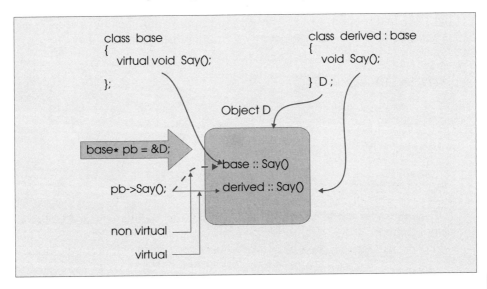

	Program 13.9	Program 13.12
Function	non-virtual	virtual
Pointed object	**D**	**D**
Call	`pd->Say();`	`pb->Say();`
Called function	`base::Say();`	`derived::Say();`

The difference between calling an ordinary member function, and a virtual function may seem small, but it represents the key to Object Oriented Programming. It provides a totally different approach to programming. The interpretation of the call of the virtual function **Say()** in the statement:

```
pb->Say();
```

depends upon the type of the object (**D**) for which it is called, not on the type of the pointer **pb**, as is the case with a non-virtual function.

Using Virtual Functions

When the exact type of an object is known at compile time, as it was in Program 13.12, the virtual function call mechanism need not be used. But the virtual mechanism must be used when a virtual function is called through a pointer or a reference.

Imagine that it is necessary to develop a function which has a pointer to an object as an argument. In addition, it is necessary that the function should take different actions depending upon the type of the object: base or derived. In Program 13.13 a typical solution without using virtual functions is presented. Here, for each type of pointer being passed there is a separate function:

```
void UseB(base * pB)
{
  pB->NV();
}

void UseD(derived * pD)
{
  pD->NV();
}
```

(Of course, you could use function overloading to give these functions the same name.)

Try It Out - Using Non-virtual Functions

Let's have a look at the program.

```
//      Program 13.13
//      Using nonvirtual functions

#include <iostream.h>

struct base {void NV(); };
struct derived : base {void NV(); };

void base::NV()
{
  cout << "Base NonVirtual \n";
}

void derived::NV()
{
  cout << "Derived NonVirtual \n";
}

void UseB(base * pB)
{
  pB->NV();
}

void UseD(derived * pD)
{
  pD->NV();
}

void main()
{
  base B;          // Base    class object
  derived D;       // Derived class object

  UseB (&B);
  UseD (&D);
}
```

Try It Out - Using Virtual Functions

When using virtual functions one can solve this problem with the help of just one function. This is defined as:

```
void Use(base * pB)
{
  pB->V();
}
```

Here the argument is a pointer to the base class. Because of the virtual function mechanism, when calling the function **Use()** in the line:

```
Use(&D);        // Default conversion 'derived *' to 'base *'
```

the required function **v()** of the class **derived** is called by the statement in the body of the function **Use()**. You should note that **Use()** is not the important function in this case. As the function **v()** is made a virtual function in the base class, it is overridden by the function **v()** in the derived class.

```
//        Program 13.14
//        Using virtual functions

#include <iostream.h>

struct base {virtual void V();};
struct derived : base { void V ();};

void base::V()
{
   cout << "Base Virtual \n";
}

void derived::V()
{
   cout << "Derived Virtual \n";
}

void Use(base * pB)
{
   pB->V();
}

void main ()
{
   base  B;         // Base class object
   derived D;       // Derived class object

   Use (&B);
   Use (&D);        // Default conversion 'derived *' to 'base *'
}
```

Try It Out - Using Virtual Functions With References

You should note that a reference can be used in the same manner as a pointer for calling a virtual function. This is shown in Program 13.15.

```
//        Program 13.15
//        Using virtual functions with references

#include <iostream.h>

struct base {virtual void V ();};
struct derived : base { void V ();};

void  base::V()
{
  cout << "Base Virtual \n";
}

void derived::V()
{
  cout << "Derived Virtual \n";
}

void Use(base & B)
{
  B.V ();
}

void main()
{
  base  B;        // Base class object
  derived D;      // Derived class object

  Use (B);
  Use (D);        // Default conversion 'derived' to 'base &'
}
```

How It Works

Here in the call of the function **Use()** in the line:

```
  Use (D);        // Default conversion 'derived' to 'base &'
```

a default reference conversion from the type **derived&**, to the type **base&** takes place, and in the body of the function **Use()**, the required call of the virtual function **V()** in class **derived** is made.

Try It Out!

It should be noted that the virtual function mechanism operates with exact matching of not only the names but the arguments of all functions as well. If any of the arguments or their types are different, then the virtual mechanism isn't invoked. We shall return to virtual functions later on in the next section when we look at multiple inheritance.

Multiple Inheritance

Until now, we have considered the simplest version of the derivation of one class from another. This is called single inheritance. This is shown graphically in the following figure. The illustration follows accepted practice where an arrow points from a derived class to a base class.

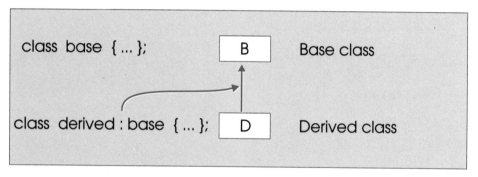

In this section we will look at the following two rules of the C++ language:

- A derived class can itself serve as a base class.
- A class may be derived from any number of base classes.

These rules and the language syntax that corresponds to them, allow you to program a wide variety inheritance connections between classes that enable you to reflect the kind of connections that exist between real objects.

A Point on a Straight Line

To illustrate multiple inheritance, let's return to our example with coordinates on the x-axis in Program 13.1 and consider a new type of data - point. The concept of point includes the idea of a coordinate, so that we can declare the type **point** as follows:

```
struct
{
  x_coord X;
};
```

If necessary, we can include such characteristics as the color of a point in this declaration:

```
struct
{
  x_coord  X;
  color  Color;
};
```

assuming the type **color** has been previously declared elsewhere.

Try It Out - Nested Classes

We can modify Program 13.1 to obtain Program 13.16, which demonstrates representing the concept point with the help of a nested structure.

```
//      Program 13.16
//      Nested classes c, x, p

#include <iostream.h>

struct coordinate{int N;};        // Coordinate
struct x_coord{coordinate C;};    // x coordinate
struct point{x_coord X;};          // Point at x axis

void main()
{
  coordinate C;                    // Define objects
  x_coord X;
  point P;

  C.N     = 1;                     // Set values
  X.C.N   = 2;
  P.X.C.N = 3;

  cout    << C.N                   // Use member N
          << X.C.N
          << P.X.C.N;
}
```

How It Works

To access the value of a point coordinate you have to apply the member selection operator (.) three times as in the line:

```
<< P.X.C.N;
```

Derived Class as a Base for Another Derived Class

Now we shall consider Program 13.17 in which a representation of the concept 'point' is implemented differently.

Try It Out - Indirect Inheritance

Let's look at the program.

```
//      Program 13.17
//      Multiple inheritance

#include <iostream.h>

struct coordinate {int N;};          // Coordinate
struct  x_coord : coordinate {};     // x coordinate
struct  point : x_coord {};          // Point

void main()
{
  coordinate C;                      // Define objects
  x_coord X;
  point P;

  C.N   = 1;                         // Set values
  X.N   = 2;
  P.N   = 3;

  cout     << C.N                    // Use member N
           << X.N
           << P.N
           << endl;

  cout     << P.N
           << P.coordinate::N
           << P.x_coord::N
           << P.point::N;
}
```

How It Works

Here the class **point** is derived from the base class **x_coord**, which in its turn, is derived from another base class **coordinate**. As a result the class **point** inherited all members of the class **x_coord**, including those which the class **x_coord** inherited from the class **coordinate**. This mechanism is still indirect inheritance. It is illustrated in the following figure.

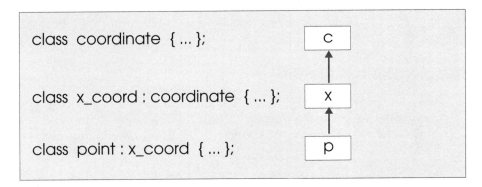

Member **N** of the class **coordinate** is inherited by the class **x_coord** and then by the class **point**. Therefore the expression:

```
P.N
```

is valid. The following figure shows that each of the classes **coordinate**, **x_coord**, and **point** contains a member with the name **N**.

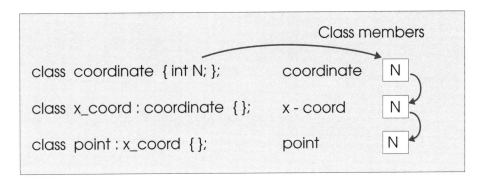

Note that you can refer to the member **N** of the object **P** using any of the following equivalent ways:

```
P.N
P.coordinate::N
P.x_coord::N
P.point::N
```

Of course, the first one is the most useful. Class **x_coord** is called a direct base for class **point**. Class **coordinate** is called an indirect base for class **point**.

Multiple Base Classes

Now let us consider the idea of 'a point on a plane'. In this case two coordinates (e.g. x and y) define it. (See the following figure). The corresponding description of the idea of 'a point on a plane' in C++, using nested structures, may have the form:

```
struct coordinate {int N;};
struct x_coord {int X;};
struct y_coord {int Y;};
struct point {int P;};
```

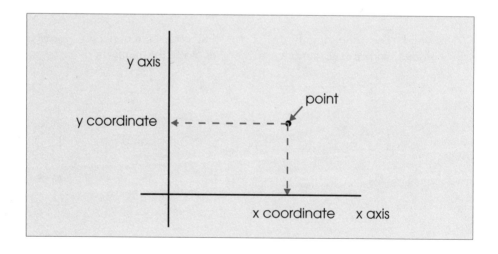

Try It Out - Two Base Classes

We can now compare this with the description in Program 13.18.

```
//        Program 13.18
//        Two base classes

#include <iostream.h>

struct coordinate {int N;};
struct x_coord : coordinate {};
struct y_coord : coordinate {};
struct point : x_coord,y_coord {};        // 2 base classes  <--
                                          // 2 members x_coord::N and
y_coord::N
void main()
{
  point P;

  P.x_coord::N  = 1;
  P.y_coord::N  = 2;

  cout      << P.x_coord::N
            << P.y_coord::N
//          << P.N                        // Error: 'N' is ambiguous in 'point'
//          << P.coordinate::N            // Error: 'c::N' is ambiguous in 'point'
            ;
}
```

How It Works

```
struct point : x_coord,y_coord {};        // 2 base classes  <--
                                          // 2 members x_coord::N and
y_coord::N
```

Here the class **point** is derived from two base classes - **x_coord** and **y_coord**, that is shown by comma delimiter. An appropriate inheritance diagram is presented in the following figure. This mechanism is called multiple inheritance.

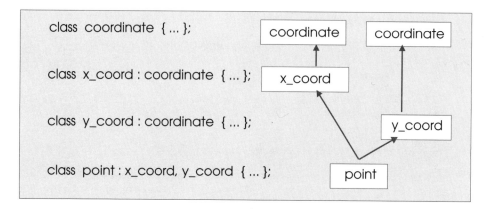

In the general case, the syntax of the declaration of a derived class **d** has the form:

```
class  d : <base-list>  {...};
```

where a base-list is a list of direct base classes separated by commas. A base class cannot be repeated in the list.

Class **point** inherited all the members of class **x_coord**, and all the members of class **y_coord**. As a result, in the class **point** there are two members with the same name, **N**. This is shown in the next figure.

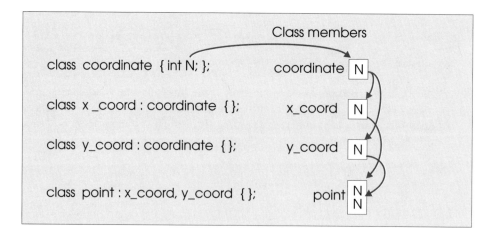

Now the expression **P.N** is not allowed. It is ambiguous, as it is not known which of the two members with the name N is meant. In order to remove the ambiguity it is obligatory to use the scope resolution operator as we did in the lines:

```
P.x_coord::N  = 1;
P.y_coord::N  = 2;
```

Multiple Inheritance of Virtual Functions

Now we want to look at how the virtual function mechanism operates in the case of multiple inheritance. To show this, a virtual function **Say()** is added to each class declared in Program 13.17.

Try It Out - Multiple Inheritance and Virtual Functions

The result is presented in the following program.

```
//      Program 13.19
//      Multiple inheritance and virtual functions

#include <iostream.h>

struct coordinate {int N; virtual void Say(); };
struct x_coord : coordinate {void Say(); };
struct point : x_coord {void Say(); };

void coordinate::Say() { cout << N << " coordinate::N\n"; }
void x_coord::Say() { cout << N << " x_coord::N\n"; }
void point::Say() { cout << N << " point::N\n"; }

void Say(coordinate & C) { C.Say(); }

void main()
{
   coordinate C;                          // Define objects
   x_coord X;
   point P;

   C.N    = 1;                            // Set values
   X.N    = 2;
   P.N    = 3;

   Say(C);                                // Display N
   Say (X);
   Say (P);
```

```
//        Any derived class with Say() function
  struct any : point { void Say() {cout << N << " any::N\n";} };

  any A;                              // Define object of new derived class

  A.N    = 4;
  Say(A);                            // Ok
}
```

How It Works

The members of each class are shown in the following figure.

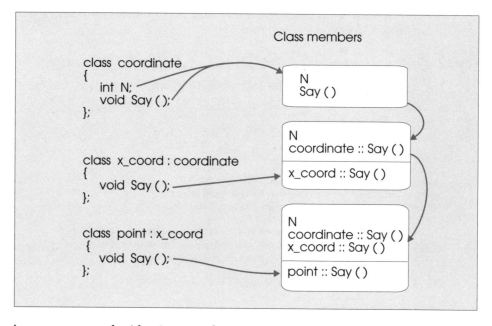

As you can see, besides its own function **Say()**, the class **point** has a "rich" inheritance - three members:

```
coordinate::N
coordinate::Say()
x_coord::Say()
```

In Program 13.19, a global non-member function **Say()** serves to process objects of various types **coordinate**, **x_coord**, **point**, though in its declaration in the line:

```
void Say(coordinate & C) { C.Say(); }
```

its argument is a 'reference to **coordinate**'. Due to the virtual function feature, in the body of the global function **Say()** the function **Say()** is called which is a member function of the same class as the object which is passed as an argument. For example, if **Say()** is called with an argument **P**, then **Say()** in the class **point** is called. This is confirmed by the output from the program, which has the form:

```
1 coordinate::N
2 x_coord::N
3 point::N
4 any::N
```

You can try discarding the one word "virtual" in the declaration of the class **coordinate** in Program 13.19. Make certain that in the absence of a virtual function mechanism, in all three calls of **Say()** the version corresponding to class **coordinate** will be called (in accordance with the type of the argument **coordinate&**), and the output of the program will be:

```
1 coordinate::N
2 coordinate::N
3 coordinate::N
4 coordinate::N
```

What is most impressive about the virtual function mechanism is that if you extend the hierarchy of derived classes, you need not change the general function for processing, which in our example is the global function **Say()**.

The last example shows that it is sufficient in a new derived class **a**:

```
struct any : point { void Say() {cout << N << " any::N\n";} };
```

to introduce the necessary virtual function **Say()**, and it will be called automatically by:

```
Say(A);
```

Designing a Program

Before we reach the end of the chapter let's write another program that links together what we have learnt.

Problem

The problem we are going to solve is two-fold. Firstly, we'll write a program that uses a class to sum a set of data. Then, we'll amend the program so that the average is calculated as well.

Analysis

1 Define a class to store the sum and provide a means of entering the data and displaying the result.

2 Write the appropriate member functions.

3 Put the class into a program and test that it works.

4 Define another class that will perform the same operations as our original class but that will additionally record the number of data items input so that the average can be calculated.

5 Write the appropriate member functions.

6 Put the class into a program and test that it works.

Solution

1 The first thing we must do is define our class.

```
class sum
{
public:
  sum();
  void get_data( double num);
  void say();

protected:
  double total;
};
```

We'll call the class **sum** as it represents what we want to do. We'll need a constructor which can initialize the data member total to 0.0. Additionally we want two member functions, one which can be used to input the data and the other to display the results.

As we want to output the sum, or total, of a list of data we can call our data member **total**.

2   We can now write the appropriate member functions.

```
class sum
{
public:
  sum() { total = 0.0;}
  void get_data( double num);
  void say() { cout << "The sum is " << total << endl;}

protected:
  double total;
};

void sum::get_data(double num)
{
  total += num;
}
```

The constructor simply initializes the data member to 0.0

The function **say()** is similar in concept to similar named functions we have used throughout this book. It's purpose is to display a short message and the sum.

The function **get_data()** keeps a running total of the data entered. It's a very simple function as you can see.

3   We can now write put our class and functions into a program and test that it works.

```
// sum.cpp
// create a class to sum numbers

#include <iostream.h>
```

```
class sum
{
public:
  sum() { total = 0.0;}
  void get_data( double num);
  void say() { cout << "The sum is " << total << endl;}

protected:
  double total;
};

void sum::get_data(double num)
{
  total += num;
}
```

```
void main()
{
  sum number;                    //declare a variable of our class

  number.get_data(1.1);          //enter sample data
  number.get_data(2.2);
  number.get_data(3.3);
  number.get_data(4.4);
  number.get_data(5.5);
  number.get_data(6.6);
  number.get_data(7.7);
  number.get_data(8.8);
  number.get_data(9.9);

  number.say();                  //output the sum
}
```

The output looks like this:

```
The sum is 49.5
```

4   We can now define our next class. As this class needs to do the same as **sum** we can create a derived class. Let's call this new class **average**.

As before, we want the class **sum**.

```
     class sum
{
public:
  sum() { total = 0.0;}
  void get_data( double num);
  void say() { cout << "The sum is " << total << endl;}
```

```
protected:
  double total;
};
```

```
class average : public sum
{
public:
  average();
  void get_data( double num);
  void say();

private:
  int count;
};
```

5   We can now write the appropriate member functions. These are very similar to the functions you saw previously.

```
class sum
{
public:
  sum() { total = 0.0;}
  void get_data( double num);
  void say() { cout << "The sum is " << total << endl;}

protected:
  double total;
};

class average : public sum
{
public:
  average() {count = 0;}
  void get_data( double num);
  void say() { sum::say(); cout << endl << "The average is "
                                      << total / count;}

private:
  int count;
};

void sum::get_data(double num)
{
  total += num;
}

void average::get_data(double num)
{
  sum::get_data(num);
  count++;
}
```

6 We can now write put our class and functions into a program and test that it works.

```
// average.cpp
// create a class to calculate mean

#include <iostream.h>

class sum
{
public:
  sum() { total = 0.0;}
  void get_data( double num);
  void say() { cout << "The sum is " << total << endl;}

protected:
  double total;
};

class average : public sum
{
public:
  average() {count = 0;}
  void get_data( double num);
  void say() { sum::say(); cout << endl << "The average is " << total /
count;}

private:
  int count;
};

void sum::get_data(double num)
{
  total += num;
}

void average::get_data(double num)
{
  sum::get_data(num);
  count++;
}

void main()
{
  average number;

  number.get_data(1.1);
  number.get_data(2.2);
  number.get_data(3.3);
  number.get_data(4.4);
```

```
    number.get_data(5.5);
    number.get_data(6.6);
    number.get_data(7.7);
    number.get_data(8.8);
    number.get_data(9.9);

    number.say();
}
```

The output looks like this:

```
The sum is 49.5

The average is 5.5
```

Summary

Well, we have reached the end of another chapter. We've covered quite of lot in this chapter and you may have to go over it again. The concepts we've discussed in the chapter are important if you want to feel comfortable with object-oriented programming.

We've looked at inheritance, multiple inheritance and polymorphism in this chapter. Don't be put off by the terms. In the next chapter we will continue to look at inheritance and encapsulation to finish off our exploration of OOP. We'll then conclude the chapter by looking at dynamic memory allocation and templates.

CHAPTER
14

Inheritance And Encapsulation

In this chapter we will continue our look at object oriented programming. We will continue looking at inheritance and encapsulation and will finish by looking at some additional C++ features.

In this chapter you will:

▶ Examine access specifiers

▶ Look at dynamic memory allocation using the operators **new** and **delete**

▶ Have a look at function and class templates

▶ Write a program that uses a function template to raise numbers to a power (for example, 2^2)

Inheritance and Encapsulation

Up until now, when considering inheritance we have said little about the attributes for accessing members: private, and public. These attributes in C++ are component parts of the mechanism for hiding information, which is as important in OOP as the two others: inheritance and polymorphism. Now we shall consider how the attributes for accessing members from functions are transferred and modified during inheritance.

Access Specifier for the Base Class

In the majority of programs in the previous chapter, we deliberately used the keyword **struct** in the declaration of classes, so that we might avoid some complications connected with accessing members which arise when using the keyword **class**. As you know, members of structures by default have the access attribute **public**, and are accessible from any other functions.

On the other hand members of classes derived with the keyword **class**, by default are **private,** and are inaccessible from non-member functions. You would expect that if we put the keyword **class** in Program 13.2 instead of **struct**, and explicitly added the attribute public as is done in the line:

```
class coordinate  {public: int N;};     // Public  member N
```

in Program 14.1, we would end up with the equivalent of Program 13.2. However, this isn't the case.

Try It Out - Public Members

The complete code looks like this.

```
//        Program 14.1
//        Error: no access to public member ?!

#include <iostream.h>

class coordinate
{
public:
  int N;                          // Public  member N
};

class x_coord : coordinate {}; // Private member N

void main()
{
  x_coord X;
```

```
  X.N     = 1;       // Error: 'coordinate::N' is not accessible in x_coord

  coordinate C;
  C.N     = 1;                // Ok. N is accessible in coordinate
}
```

How It Works

Program 14.1 generates a compilation error. Member **N** appears not to be accessible in the class **x_coord**, even though in the class **coordinate** it can be accessed. Why?

The fact is that inheritance can be accompanied by changes to the access attributes, so that inherited members can have different access attributes in a derived class than those that they have in a base class. Explicitly indicating how attributes should be passed from a base class to a derived class, is done as follows:

```
class derived : <access-specifier> base
{
  ...
};
```

where the access-specifier can assume one of two values: **public** or **private**, or be absent. If it's absent then it's assumed by default. If you use the keyword **struct** the default value is **public**, and if you use the keyword **class** the default value is **private**. This distinction is reflected in the following table.

Declaration	The same with explicit access specifier

`struct derived : base`
`{`
`  ...`
`};`
	`struct derived : public base`
	`{`
	`  ...`
	`};`

`class derived : base`
`{`
`  ...`
`};`
	`class derived : private base`
	`{`
	`  ...`
	`};`

Let's summarize the position regarding access specifiers. There are three levels of visibility for classes.

A **private** member can only be used by member functions and friends of the class in which it is declared. Members of a class are **private** by default;

A **public** member can be used in any function. Members of a structure are **public** by default; and

Protected Members

There is another (third, and last) access attribute, **protected**, which is used only for the declaration of class members, for example:

```
class c
{
protected:
  int   N;
};
```

but can't be used as an access specifier for a base class in the declaration of a derived class.

The figure below shows what is meant by the following declarations:

```
class coordinate
{
public:
  int  N;
};

class x_coord : private coordinate {};
```

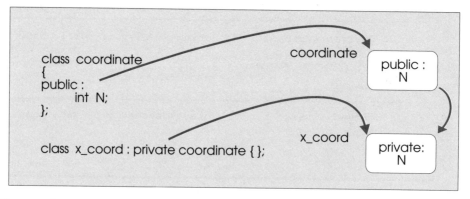

The member **N** in the base class **coordinate** is explicitly declared as **public**. So it is accessible from **main()**. The member **N** inherited in the derived class **x_coord** from the base class **coordinate**, receives a different access attribute: **private**.

Try It Out - Changing the Base Access Specifier

In order to make **N** in the derived class, accessible from **main()**, it is necessary to change the base access specifier as in Program 14.2 for the class **y_coord**:

```
//        Program 14.2
//        'private' and 'public' base class

#include <iostream.h>

class coordinate
{
public:
  int N;
};

class x_coord : private coordinate {};      // Private base (default)
class y_coord : public coordinate {};       // Public  base

void main()
{
  y_coord  Y;

  Y.N     = 1;     // Ok! 'coordinate::N' is accessible in y_coord
}
```

How It Works

The next figure shows that member **N** of the class **y_coord** now has the attribute **public**, and member **N** is accessible in **main()**, as you see in the line:

```
Y.N     = 1;     // Ok! 'coordinate::N' is accessible in y_coord
```

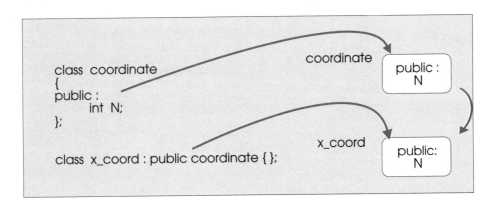

We have now seen that class member can have one of three possible access attributes:

- ▶ **private:**
- ▶ **protected:**
- ▶ **public:**

If you group members with the same attributes, then in the general case the declaration of a class will have the form shown in part A of the next figure. As you can see, the protected members have the same access properties for member and friend functions as private members, and they are inaccessible for other functions. In some of the following illustrations, we'll use the simplified picture shown as part B of the following figure as the equivalent of part A.

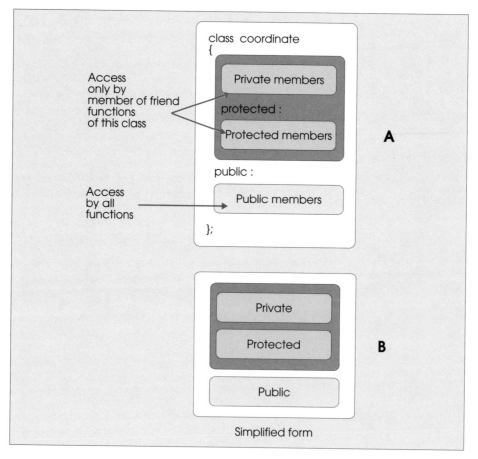

Public Base Class

The distinction between the attributes **protected** and **private** becomes apparent in inheritance as is shown in the next figure for a public access-specifier in a base list:

```
class derived : public base {...};
```

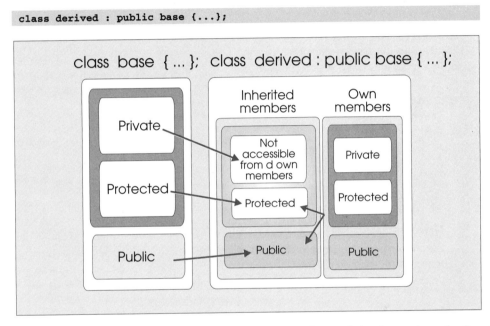

In the case shown, **private** and **protected** members of the base class don't change their attributes in the derived class. But **private** members of the base class in spite of being present in the derived class are inaccessible even for member functions of the class **derived**.

Try It Out - Public Base Class

This is demonstrated by Program 14.3. It generates compilation errors.

```
//      Program 14.3
//      Public base class. Errors.

class base                      // Base class
{
private:
  int Private;                  // Private member
protected:
  int Protected;                // Protected member
public:
  int Public;                   // Public member
```

```
};

class derived : public base    // Public base class
{
  derived()                    // Constructor
  {
    Private = 0;               // Error: not accessible
    Protected = 0;
    Public  = 0;
  }
};

void main()
{
  derived D;                   // Error: 'derived::derived()' is not
accessible

  D.Private = 1;               // Error: not accessible
  D.Protected = 1;             // Error: not accessible
  D.Public = 1 ;               // Ok!
}
```

How It Works

Here the derived class **derived** contains only one member - a constructor. In the constructor, a **private** member of the base class named **Private** is inaccessible, whereas the inherited members **Protected** and **Public** are accessible. From the function **main()**, only the member **Public** is accessible.

Access to the Inaccessible

Members that are **private** in the base class are not accessible by members that belong to the derived class. You may think that they aren't needed at all. But this isn't the case. They are still accessible for all member functions inherited from the base class. Therefore, you can obtain access to inaccessible inherited members through **protected** or **public** inherited member functions.

Try It Out - Access to Private Members of Base Class

This is demonstrated by Program 14.4 and the next figure.

```
//        Program 14.4
//        Access to private member of base class

#include <iostream.h>

class coordinate                        // Base class
{
  int  N;                               // Private
public:
```

```
   void SayC();                          // Public
};

class x_coord : public coordinate        // Public base
{
public:
  void Say();
  // void SayX() {cout << N;}            // Error: N is not accessible
};

  void coordinate::SayC() {cout << N;}
  void x_coord::Say() {coordinate::SayC();}    // Access to public SayC()

void main()
{
  x_coord X;

  X.Say();                    // Access to coordinate::N through
coordinate::SayC()
}
```

How It Works

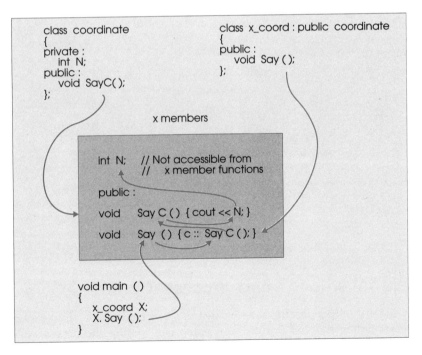

As you see, to display the "inaccessible" member **N** in class **x_coord**, we can use the public function **SayC()** from the base class which has access to **N**. Note that **N** is not initialized, therefore the program outputs a random number.

The mechanism we have just seen for access to private data of a base class that is inherited in a derived class using **public** or **protected** functions of the base class, is widely used in C++. Data is hidden by using the private access specifier, and access to it is carried out through interface functions provided by the class developer to users of the class as a base.

Private Base Class

Now let's consider the variant of a **private** base class:

```
class derived : private base {...};
```

The following figure illustrates how the access attributes change in this case: both **protected** and **public** members of the base class become **private** in the derived class.

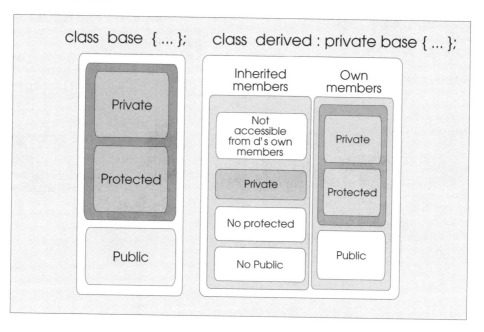

Multiple Inheritance and Access Control

Using the two rules for access attribute inheritance for single inheritance presented in the last figures, you can easily define the access attributes in any case of multiple inheritance.

Constructing Derived Class Objects

As you know, when you define a class object a special member function known as a constructor is called. In this section we will look at how constructors of base classes are used to create a derived class object.

Constructor Calls For Single Inheritance

When an object of a class derived from one base class is defined, then first a base class constructor is called, after which a derived class constructor is called. When an object of a derived class is destroyed, the destructors are called in reverse order to that of the constructors.

Try It Out - Order of Constructor and Destructor Calls

A simple test in Program 14.5 confirms this.

```
//       Program 14.5
//       Order of constructor and destructor calls

#include <iostream.h>

struct base
{
  base() {cout << "Base constructor\n";}
  ~base() {cout << "Base destructor\n";}
};

struct derived : base
{
  derived() {cout << "Derived constructor\n";}
  ~derived() {cout << "Derived destructor\n";}
};

void main()
{
  cout << "Main start\n";

  derived D;                 // Call constructors

  cout << "Main end\n";
}
```

It outputs:

```
Main start
Base constructor
Derived constructor
Main end
Derived destructor
Base destructor
```

How It Works

Here, two constructors are called successively during the definition of the derived class object **D** in the line:

```
derived D;                    // Call constructors
```

and the destructors are called for the same object after exit from **main()**.

An implicit call of a base constructor has a significant drawback - only a default base constructor (that doesn't have any arguments) can be called.

Try It Out - Compilation Errors

Look at Program 14.6 , where a base constructor has an argument (in other words, it's not a default constructor), and the default constructor is given in a comment. This program produces a compilation error.

```
//        Program 14.6
//        Error: Cannot find default base constructor base()

#include <iostream.h>

struct base
{
  base(int i) {}        // Not default constructor base(int)
  // base() {}          // Commented default constructor b()
};

struct derived : base
{
  derived() {}          // Implicit call to b()
};

void main()
{
  derived D;
}
```

You can try uncommenting the default constructor **base()** in Program 14.6 and making certain that the error disappears.

A Constructor With an Initializer List

C++ provides a special syntax for writing a constructor that allows you to specify which base constructor must be called. This is shown at the example of Program 14.7 in the line:

```
derived(): base(1) {}  // Explicit call to base(int)
```

Here, an explicit call of the required constructor **base(int)** is written after the colon. When it's called during the execution of the program, it outputs to the screen:

```
1 Int constructor
```

Try It Out - Constructor With Initializer List

Let's see the program in action.

```cpp
//      Program 14.7
//      Constructor with initializer list

#include <iostream.h>

struct base
{
  base(int i)
  {
    cout << i << " Int constructor\n";
  }

  base()
  {
    cout << "Default constructor\n";
  }
};

struct derived : base
{
  derived(): base (1) {}  // Explicit call to b(int)
};

void main()
{
  derived D;
}
```

In Program 14.7, try substituting an explicit call of the default constructor for the call **base(int)**:

```cpp
derived() : base(){}
```

or try using an implicit **base()** call

```cpp
derived() {}
```

Make sure that in both cases the program will output:

```
Default constructor
```

Make certain that during the definition:

```
derived()
{
  base(1);
}
```

or

```
derived() : base()
{
  base(1);
}
```

first the default constructor is called, and then **base(int)** is called from the body of **derived()**. The program's output in both cases will be:

```
Default constructor
1 Int constructor
```

Constructors Calls for Multiple Inheritance

In Program 14.8 there is an example of object initialization for the class **point** which has two base classes. The program is obtained from Program 13.17 by adding a constructor.

Try It Out - Initializer List For Two Base Classes

Let's have a look at the program.

```
//        Program 14.8
//        Initializer list for two base classes

#include <iostream.h>

struct   coordinate
{
  int N;
  coordinate(int n) {N=n;}
};

struct   x_coord : coordinate
{
  x_coord(int n) : coordinate(n) {}
};
```

```
struct  y_coord : coordinate
{
  y_coord(int n) : coordinate(n) {}
};

struct  point: x_coord,y_coord
{
  point (int nx, int ny) : x_coord(nx), y_coord(ny) {}
};

void main()
{
  point P (1,2);

  cout      << P.x_coord::N
            << P.y_coord::N;
}
```

How It Works

Note that the syntax of a class declaration is similar to the syntax of a constructor definition:

```
struct point : x_coord, y_coord {...};
point(int nx, int ny) : x_coord(nx) , y_coord(ny) {...}
```

The constructors which are required to be called are listed, separated by commas, after the colon in the constructor definition. This list of constructors is called an initializer list. Only the constructors of a direct base class can appear in it, in other words, those that are in the declaration of the current derived class (in our case these are classes **x_coord** and **y_coord**), but not the constructors of an indirect base class (in our case this is the class **coordinate**).

In Program 14.8 during the definition of the object:

```
point P (1,2);
```

the argument values for the constructor **point()** are between the parentheses. These values are then passed to the constructors **x_coord()** and **y_coord()**, which in their turn pass them to the constructor **coordinate()**. As a result **P.x_coord::N** and **P.y_coord::n** assume the values 1 and 2 which is confirmed by the program's output:

12

Initializing Members

With the help of an initializer list, you can also initialize a derived class's own members that aren't inherited from the base class. This is the only way to initialize **const** and reference members. In the following program, Program 14.9, you will see the line:

```
const int N;        // Const member
```

Here, a **const** member **N** is declared in the class **coordinate**. As indicated in the comment in the lines:

```
// Error: Cannot modify a const object N
// coordinate::coordinate() {N=1;}
```

you can't initialize a **const** member using an assignment in a constructor body. The only way is to place the name of the **const** member in the initializer list of a constructor and to specify its value in parentheses as in:

```
coordinate::coordinate() : N (1) {}       // Initializing const N member
```

Try It Out - Initializing const Member

Let's have a look at the program.

```
//        Program 14.9
//        Initializing const member

#include <iostream.h>

struct   coordinate
{
  const int N;        // Const member
  coordinate();       // Constructor
};

coordinate::coordinate() : N (1) {}        // Initializing const N member

// Error: Cannot modify a const object N
// coordinate::coordnate() {N=1;}

void main()
{
  coordinate C;

  cout << C.N;        // 1
}
```

Additional C++ features

In the concluding section of this chapter we will look at some important additional facilities in C++:

▶ Operators **new, delete**

▶ Function templates

▶ Class templates

Creating Objects Using the Operator new

In the example programs that we have looked at, all the variables have been declared in the source code. If two integer variables were required, we would have to declare two **int** variables. We have to know what variables we will need and what size the arrays should be. However, there may be times when you won't know how many variables are needed until the program is running.

Consider, for example, a program that creates a database of some kind. The records are kept in a disk file and are loaded into an array when the program starts so that the records can be manipulated in some way. As the program is used, more and more records will be added. Do we re-write the program every couple of weeks when we no longer have enough memory to load all the records?

What we need to do is create variables as we need them and de-allocate their space for use by other variables when we no longer require them.

The ability to manage memory from inside your program, to get sections of free memory to use for storing variables and then to release that memory is known as dynamic memory allocation.

The operator **new** enables you to dynamically create objects without the need for a definition. This is done by allocating memory dynamically from the memory that is unused in your computer.

The operator **delete** destroys an object created by the operator **new**. At the same time the memory is freed, and can be used again later in your program for the creation of other objects with the help of the operator **new**.

Dynamic storage allocation is used if the amount of memory required in a program is not known beforehand. For example, this would be necessary if an array is required, but the number of array elements and the array itself are input from a file. This mechanism is also used when you want to minimize the amount of memory occupied by a program.

Try It Out - Creating Objects With new and delete Operators

In Program 14.10 there is a simple illustration of the use of the operators **new** and **delete**.

```
//          Program 14.10
//          Creating objects with new and delete operators

#include <iostream.h>

void main()
{
  int * p1;
  p1 = new int;            // Allocate memory and return address
  *p1 = 1;
  int * p2 = new int (2);  // Initialize to 2

  cout << *p1 << *p2;      // Use objects through pointers to them

// Using objects don't change pointers p1 and p2 !

  cout << endl << p1;      // Display pointer value

  delete p1;               // Free memory, destroy objects
  delete p2;

  cout << endl << p1;      // The same pointer value as above

  cout << endl << *p1;     // Garbage, not 12
}
```

How It Works

```
int * p1;
```

The operator **new** acts like a function that returns an address of an object being created (in fact, **new** isn't a function name, but a keyword of the C++

language, as is **delete**). The program shows that in order to create an object of the type **int**, you need to perform three operations. The first is to define a pointer to an object of the type **int**.

```
p1 = new int;          // Allocate memory and return address
```

Next, this pointer has to be initialized with the address value returned by the operator **new**.

```
*p1 = 1;
```

Finally, the object created needs to be initialized with an appropriate value.

```
int * p2 = new int (2); // Initialize to 2
```

The above statement shows that all these three steps can be combined into one. The initializing value (2) is placed in parentheses.

```
delete p1;             // Free memory, destroy objects
delete p2;
```

To remove an object you simply specify the object address received from the operator **new**, in the operator **delete**.

A simplified syntax for the operators **new** and **delete** is:

```
<pointer_to_object> = new <object_type>;
delete <pointer_to_object>;
```

where **object_type** is the type of the object being created. Here a **pointer_to_object** should have the type 'pointer to **object_type**'.

Don't forget that writing:

```
delete  p1;
```

means the destruction of the object to which **p1** points, but it doesn't mean removing (or changing the value of) pointer **p1**. This pointer retains its value after **delete**, as you can see from the program output, which on our computer was the following:

```
12
0x27140004
0x27140004
10004
```

In the first line the values of the objects (1 and 2) are displayed. In the second and the third lines, two identical values of the pointer **p1** (before and after **delete**) are shown and in the fourth the "value" of the first object (pointed to by **p1**) after its destruction is displayed. It is a good idea to always set a pointer to NULL after deleting the object at which it was pointing; in this way, problems caused by accessing 'garbage' through invalid pointers can be avoided.

Creating Arrays of New Mountains

The use of the operators **new** and **delete** while operating with arrays is demonstrated by Program 14.11. The number of elements in the array to be created is indicated in square brackets in the line:

```
mountain * pM = new mountain [N];          // Call constructor
```

Try It Out - Creating Arrays

Let's see the program in action.

```
//          Program 14.11
//          Call constructor for new mountain array

#include <iostream.h>

struct  mountain
{
  char   Name [21];
  int    Height;
  mountain() {cout << "Constructor is working\n";}
  ~mountain() {cout << "Destructor is working\n";}
};

void main()
{
  int  N = 3;                                // Number of elements

  cout << "Creating " << N << " new mountains\n";
  mountain * pM = new mountain [N];          // Call constructor

  cout << "Deleting " << N << " mountains\n";
  delete [N] pM;                             // Call destructor
}
```

How It Works

The program shows an important feature of the operator **new** - it automatically calls a constructor for the class object being created. This is seen from the program's output:

```
Creating 3 new mountains
Constructor is working
Constructor is working
Constructor is working
Deleting 3 mountains
Destructor is working
Destructor is working
Destructor is working
```

In the same way the operator **delete** calls a destructor. From the program's output it is seen that the constructor is called several times - once for each array element.

Out of Memory

There may be times when there isn't enough memory required to create an object. In such a case, the operator **new** returns 0. It can be used for analyzing whether it's possible to continue the program operation as is shown in Program 14.12. You should always check the pointers returned by **new** to ensure the operation was successful. Note that the size of a **mountain** structure is set to be large (1000). The operator **new** is called in the **for** statement. The address of each **mountain** is retained in an element of a pointer array **pM[i]**. If a value returned by **new** is equal to 0, then further processing is senseless and the operator **break** exits from the loop.

Try It Out - Out of Memory

We can now look at the program in full.

```
//        Program 14.12
//        Out of memory

#include <iostream.h>

struct mountain
{
   char  Name [1000];                      // Big size      <--
};
```

```
void main()
{
  const int N = 1000;                     // Number of mountains

  cout << "Creating " << N << " big mountains\n";

  mountain * pM [N];                      // Array of pointers

  for (int i=0; i < N; i++)
  {
    pM [i] = new mountain;                // Create one mountain
    if (! pM [i])
    {
      // new returns 0 - out of memory
      cout << "Out of memory\n";
      break;                              // Exit loop
    }
  }
  cout << "Only " << i << " mountains were created.\n"
       << "Deleting them\n";

  for (int j=0; j < i; j++)
    delete pM [j];
}
```

How It Works

The value of **i** after the exit from the loop is equal to the number of **mountain** objects created successfully. This value is then used in the loop with another index **j** in the line:

```
for (int j=0; j < i; j++)
  delete pM [j];
```

to remove all objects that were created, and to free the occupied memory. If on your computer the message "Out of memory" isn't produced and all **N = 1000** mountains are created, then you can increase **N** until the message is produced.

Templates

Templates are new constructions in C++ which were introduced in recent versions of the language. They allow you to construct a family of related functions or classes.

Function Templates

Let us consider a function **Say()**, which is to output the values of variables of different types to the screen with a new line. One approach is to write a set of overloaded functions with the same name and different types of arguments (see Program 7.4). A second approach is to use a template as shown in Program 14.13. Here you see the template declaration:

```
template <class  type>
void  Say(type Obj)
{
  cout << endl << Obj;
};
```

Here the words **template** and **class** are keywords, and the word **type** can be any C++ data type. We have chosen the word **type**, in order to emphasize its connection with the idea of an object type. Note that the angle brackets are also syntax components here. Writing in the form of two lines rather than one line is purely for convenience. It isn't an actual requirement of the syntax of a template declaration. The definition of **Say()** has the word **type** applied as a parameter. For this reason templates are also called parameterized (or generic) types.

Try It Out - The Say() Function Template

Let's look at how this works in practice.

```
//        Program 14.13
//        Say () function template

#include <iostream.h>

//        Template declaration

template <class  type>
void Say(type Obj)
{
  cout << endl << Obj;
};

void main()
{
  Say ('1');
  Say ( 2 );
  Say ("3");
```

```
class c
{
    int N;
} C;

// Error: Illegal structure operation in function Say(c)
// Say (C);
}
```

How It Works

```
Say ('1');
Say ( 2 );
Say ("3");
```

Now look at the three calls of the function **Say()**. In each call the type of the argument is different. Nevertheless the appropriate function is called, having been generated through the template mechanism. Therefore, the template declaration allows a whole set of function definitions to be generated by substituting any of the types for which the operator << is defined.

If the operation << isn't defined for some class, such as the class **c** for example:

```
class c
{
    int N;
} C;
```

then the compiler generates an error message and it's necessary to define a friend function **operator<<()** in class **c**.

Class Templates

A class template enables you to define a pattern for a set of class declarations. Let's consider the following declaration of the class **PointInt** as an ordinary example:

```
class PointInt
{
    int x;
    int y;
};
```

This type can be used for the representation of integer coordinates. If coordinates are fractional numbers then you need to use another class such as:

```
class PointFloat
{
  float X;
  float Y;
};
```

Try It Out - Class Templates

Program 14.14 shows how one template declaration of the class **Point** replaces these two declarations and also a number of others (for types **long double** and so on). A class template declaration has the same form as a function template:

```
template <class T> class-declaration
```

here **T** - is a name defined by you, and **class-declaration** is an ordinary declaration in which the name **T** can be used as a parameter.

```
//        Program 14.14
//        Class template - Point

#include <iostream.h>

//        Template declaration

template <class T>
class  Point
{
  T   X;                  // Two members of type T
  T   Y;
public:
  void  Set(T x,T y);  // Set X, Y values
  void  Say() {cout << "\nX = " << X << "\nY = " << Y;}
};

template <class T>
void Point<T>::Set (T x,T y)
{
//      Set point coordinates
  X=x;
  Y=y;
}

void main()
{
  Point<int>  pi;       // Point integer
```

Try It Out!

```
    pi.Set (1,2);
    pi.Say ();

    Point<float>  pf;        // Point float

    pf.Set (1.1, 2.2);
    pf.Say ();
}
```

How It Works

In the class declaration in Program 14.14, the parameter **T** is used instead of the data type (**int**, **float**).

```
template <class T>
void  Point<T>::Set (T x,T y)
{
//        Set point coordinates
   X=x;
   Y=y;
}
```

The syntax of the external definition of the member function statement **Set()** is interesting. The first line coincides with the first line of the class template declaration **template <class T>**. You can also see that the name of the parameter **T** in angle brackets is added to the class name **Point**. This parameter may be used in an argument list and in the body of a function. The rest of the function definition is quite normal.

Now look how the name of a type is written in the definition of an object:

```
    Point<int>  pi;
```

Here **int** in angle brackets is a real value of the parameter **T**, in other words **int** replaces **T** everywhere in the template class declaration. The name:

```
    Point<int>
```

is the full name of the type in which the **int** type is used for **x** and **y**.

In a similar way:

```
    Point<float>  pf;
```

defines an object **pf** in which **x** and **y** have the type **float**. So, one template class declaration replaces a number of declarations of similar, but nevertheless different types.

Designing a Program

Before we reach the end of the chapter let's write another program.

Problem

We are going to write a program, using a function template, that raises a value to a power, for example $2^2 = 4$, $3^2 = 9$, and $2^3 = 8$.

Analysis

1   We need to decide on a suitable name for our function and produce a function prototype.

2   The next step is to define the function.

3   The function should then be tested in a suitable program.

Solution

1   The first thing we must do is choose a suitable name and produce a function prototype. Let's call the function power and pass it two arguments: the number that we will raise to the power, and the power to which the number will be raised.

```
// power.cpp
// program to demonstrate function templates

#include <iostream.h>

template<class T>
T power(T number, int pow);

void main()
{

}
```

```
template<class T>
T power(T number, int pow)
{

}
```

2   We must now define the function. If the power to which we will raise the number is 0, the answer is 1. We can code this as:

```
if (pow == 0)
   return (T) 1;
```

If the power is less that 0 the answer can become slightly complicated. From a mathematical point of view:

$$4^2 = 16,$$
$$4^{1/2} = \sqrt{4} = 2,$$
$$4^0 = 1,$$
$$4^{-2} = 1/16 = 0.0625$$

If the number is less than 0, we are dealing with the inverse of the power, but if the number is also fractional we are dealing with roots of the number as well.

```
if (pow < 0)
   return (T) 0;
```

So how will we calculate our power? A square is simply a number multiplied by a number. A cube is a number multiplied by a number, multiplied by a number... It sounds as if a **for** loop could be used.

```
for(int i = 0; i < pow; i++)
   result  *= number;
```

```
// power.cpp
// program to demonstrate function templates

#include <iostream.h>

template<class T>
T power(T number, int pow);

void main()
{

}
```

```
template<class T>
T power(T number, int pow)
{
  T result = 1;

  if (pow == 0)
    return (T) 1;

  if (pow < 0)
    return (T) 0;

  for(int i = 0; i < pow; i++)
    result  *= number;

  return(result);
}
```

3   We must now test our function in a suitable program:

```
// power.cpp
// program to demonstrate function templates

#include <iostream.h>

template<class T>
T power(T number, int pow);

void main()
{
  int num1 = 5, ans1, exp1 = 2, exp2 = 3;
  float num2 = 5.5, ans2;
  double num3 = 12.75, ans3;

  ans1 = power(num1, exp1);
  cout << "5 squared is " << ans1 << endl;

  ans1 = power(num1, exp2);
  cout << "5 cubed is " << ans1 << endl;

  ans2 = power(num2, exp1);
  cout << "5.5 squared is " << ans2 << endl;

  ans3 = power(num3, exp2);
  cout << "12.75 cubed is " << ans3 << endl;
}

template<class T>
T power(T number, int pow)
{
  T result = 1;
```

```
    if (pow == 0)
      return (T) 1;

    if (pow < 0)
      return (T) 0;

    for(int i = 0; i < pow; i++)
      result  *= number;

    return(result);
  }
```

The output from the program looks like this:

```
5 squared is 25
5 cubed is 125
5.5 squared is 30.25
12.75 cubed is 2072.671875
```

Summary

In this chapter we completed our exploration of object oriented programming. You have now learnt the central concepts of the C++ language that define its strength and power: inheritance, encapsulation and polymorphism. You have also learnt the mechanism of inheritance that allows you to create hierarchical structures of classes, the mechanism of virtual functions, and the passing of access attributes during inheritance.

The last part of the chapter looked at the method of dynamically creating objects "on the fly" using the operator **new**, and functions and class templates recently introduced into C++.

CHAPTER 15

Using Preprocessing Directives

In this chapter the preprocessing directives are considered. One of these directives:

```
#include <iostream.h>
```

is well known to you. The fact that it is met in almost every program shows how important preprocessing directives are. However neither the character '#' nor the word 'include' are part of the C++ language. The preprocessing directives form a special language. This language cannot be used by itself for writing programs, but constructions in this language are used to augment and modify C++ programs.

The aim of this chapter is not to go into the details of the preprocessor language. Examples of the practical use of preprocessor directives will be explored for: including header files, conditional compilation and the creation of macros. Part of this chapter is devoted to discussing general methods of C++ program debugging using preprocessor directives.

In this chapter you will:

- Understand what preprocessing is
- Learn about including files
- Learn about conditional compilation
- Learn how to create macros

What is Preprocessing?

The origin of the term 'preprocessing' is connected with an implementation of the first C language compilers. In these compilers the process of converting a source program text into object (executable) form was composed of two steps as is shown in the following figure.

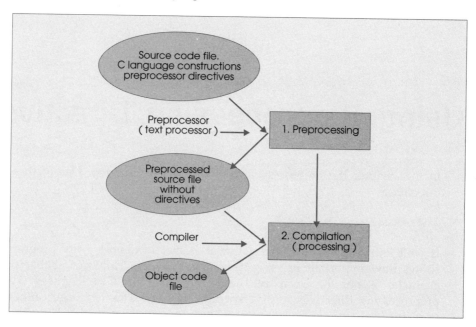

Since compilation, which is the main processing phase, was performed during the second step, the previous first step was naturally called **preprocessing**. In this step a program separate from the compiler, and called a preprocessor was used. It operated as a text processor, converting a source code file which contained preprocessing directives into an output text file that did not contain such directives, and which served as a source file for the compiler.

The preprocessor scanned the source program text searching for directives beginning with the character **#**. Having found such a directive the preprocessor executed it (for example, it inserted the file indicated in an **#include** directive in place of the directive). As each directive was processed by the preprocessor it was removed from the text of the program, and so the preprocessed output file contained only C language statements.

If a source code file that contained preprocessor directives was compiled, omitting the preprocessing phase, then all these directives would be flagged by the compiler as errors since the preprocessor directives were not permissible constructions in C. However, this was true only for the early compilers. Modern compilers usually contain built-in facilities for preprocessing and perform preprocessing handling in parallel with compilation in a single step as shown in the next figure.

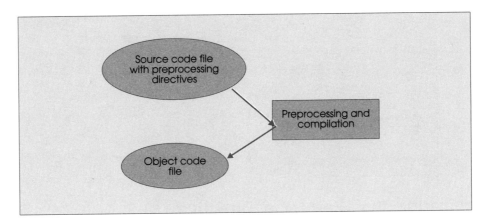

As a result, the word preprocessing has lost its original meaning. Nevertheless, it still means that first the compiler interprets the preprocessor directives, replacing them with C++ language constructions, and only then does it compile these C++ constructions.

Including Files

The preprocessing directive:

```
#include <file>
```

enables you to include a file with the name 'file' in your program text. The directive itself is removed and in place of it, the entire contents of the file specified is inserted, as shown in the figure on the following page.

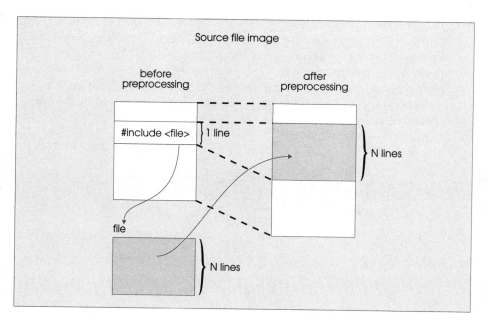

Source file image

Indicating the Start of a Directive

The character '**#**' at the beginning of a line indicates a directive (not just **#include**, but any other preprocessing directive as well). This symbol must be the first in the line ignoring blanks and tab characters. There can be blanks or tabs after the character '**#**', so all the following forms of writing the directive are equivalent:

```
#include
  #include
  #  include
```

Positioning #include in a File

The **#include** directive may be located anywhere in a source file, not just at the beginning. For example, in Program 15.1, it's in the body of the function **main()**. The included file:

```
//      P15-01.inc
//      Including file for program P15-01.c

  cout << "Included statement is working\n";
```

contains comments and one C++ statement. The program outputs:

```
Included statement is working
```

Try It Out - Positioning #include in a File

Let's see how the program looks in full.

```
//  Program 15.1
//  Including file

#include <iostream.h>

void main()
{
  #include "P15-01.inc"

// Error: Illegal character '#'
// cout << "Error"; #include "P15-01.inc"

}
```

Each directive must begin on a new line. An attempt to write a directive after a C++ statement in the same line will result in an error.

You can try writing two directives in Program 15.1 in succession on one line:

```
#include "P15-01.inc"   #include "P15-01.inc"
```

Confirm that the output from the program hasn't changed. This means that the second directive is ignored. You should just follow the simple rule of beginning each directive with a new line.

Searching For an Included File

Note that in Program 15.1 the name of the file to be included is put in double quotes:

```
#include "P15-01.inc"
```

not in brackets as with:

```
#include <iostream.h>
```

The two ways of writing the file to be included:

```
#include <file>
#include "file"
```

differ in the way the file is retrieved. This procedure is implementation dependent. You can read more about it in your compiler documentation. Writing the file name in angled brackets means that the file is to be searched for in a set sequence of standard directories, and writing it in double quotes means that the file is to be searched for first in the directory of the original source file, and then as in the previous case.

The first form is normally used to include standard system header files, which are looked for in set directories.

Try substituting brackets for double quotes in the include directive in Program 15.1. Does the compiler find the file **P15.01.INC**? Our compiler didn't.

Nested #include and Rescanning

An included file can contain arbitrary statements in C++. It can also contain other preprocessing directives including **#include** as shown in Program 15.2 and in the following figure.

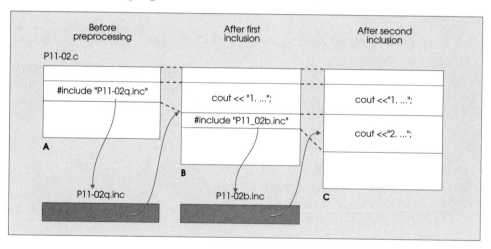

In such a case, an intermediate program text (designated by letter B in the figure above) is obtained after preprocessing:

```
#include "P15-02a.inc"
```

The result is rescanned for directives. When the directive:

```
#include "P15-02b.inc"
```

is found it is executed and the file specified is included. As a consequence, the final expanded file contains the two statements:

```
cout << "1. First  including\n";
cout << "2. Second including\n";
```

and the program outputs:

```
1. First  including
2. Second including
```

```
//   Program 15.2
//   Nested including

#include <iostream.h>

void main()
{
  #include "P15-02a.inc"
}
```

The contents of the file **P15-02A.INC** is:

```
//   File P15-02a.inc
//   Include file for Program 15.2

  cout << "1. First  including\n";
  #include "P15-02b.inc"
```

The contents of the file **P15-02B.INC** is:

```
//   File P15-02b.inc
//   Including file for Program 15.2

  cout << "2. Second including\n";
```

The illustration shown in the previous figure doesn't mean that the compiler creates files B and C, but the final result looks as if these were created.

Using #include for Headers

Most often, the **#include** directive is used at the beginning of a program for the inclusion of header files. A header file usually contains function prototypes (not definitions), type declarations (classes, structures, enumerated types), and global data definitions. These is no need for special examples of header files, since the ANSI standard makes a set of standard header files, such as **IOSTREAM.H**, available.

The separation of function and type declarations into a separate header file makes sense, even when the program is located in one file. Its improves the program's clarity and readability. If the program consists of many files that use common user-defined types and functions, then the separation of type and function declarations into a separate header file becomes a necessity. Program 6.11 demonstrated this.

Using Conditional Compilation

In this section we will consider the directives that allow parts of the source code to be omitted from the compilation process, depending upon the conditions you specify. This is called conditional compilation.

The #if Directive

The two directives **#if** and **#endif** are always used in a pair. Each **#if** directive must be paired with a following **#endif** directive. These directives can be nested, for example:

```
#if
  ...
  #if
    ...
  #endif
  ...
#endif
```

Try It Out - Using the #if Directive

Program 15.3 illustrates the use of the **#if** directive.

```
//   Program 15.3
//   Conditional compilation with #if directive
```

604

```
#include <iostream.h>

void main()
{
  const int Condition = 1;

  cout << "Working...";

  # if Condition
    cout << " on condition";
  # endif
}
```

How It Works

```
  # if Condition
    cout << " on condition";
  # endif
```

These statements resemble an `if` statement:

```
if (Condition)
{
  cout << " on condition";
}
```

But if the `if` statement affects the program's operation, then the `#if` directive affects the process of compilation, as shown in the following figure.

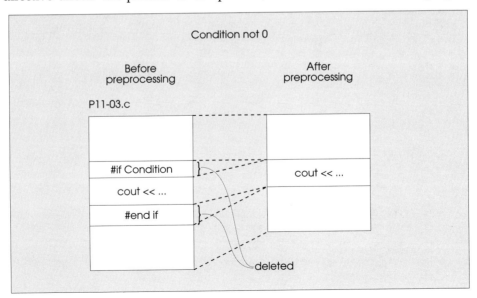

During preprocessing, the two lines containing **#if** and **#endif** are deleted, and the lines appearing between them (in this case there is one, but there can be as many as you need) remain in place, since the constant **Condition** is not equal to zero. You can use any constant expression that has a known value during compilation, instead of this constant.

Try deleting the **const** specifier from the definition in Program 15.3:

```
int Condition = 1;
```

The compiler will generate an error in the **#if** statement, showing the need for a constant expression after the directive **#if**.

Try It Out - Using the #if Directive Again

If **Condition** is equal to 0 as it is in Program 15.4, then the lines containing the **#if** and **#endif** directives, and also all the lines placed between them, are omitted from the text of the program. This is shown in the following figure.

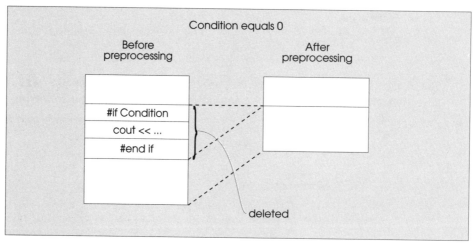

The program only outputs:

```
Working...
```

```
//   Program 15.4
//   Conditional compilation with #if directive

#include <iostream.h>

const int Condition = 0;
```

```
void main()
{
  cout << "Working...";

  # if Condition
    cout << " on condition";
  # endif
}
```

Differences Between #if and if

You can use an **if** statement:

```
if (constant-expression)
{
    ...
}
```

instead of a conditional expression:

```
#if constant-expression
    ...
#endif
```

Here you will obtain a program working in just the same way, but it will contain superfluous machine instructions for the condition test so it will operate a bit slower, and if the value of the constant expression is equal to 0, then it will contain code that is located in the block after the **if** that can never be executed. The version of the program using **#if** won't contain code that cannot be executed, and it will be shorter. The difference will be more apparent, the more lines there are affected by the **#if**.

Using Conditional Compilation for Debugging

The directive **#if** is often used for writing the text of a program, that allows you to create one of two versions: a debugging version and a working version (without a debugging code). For this purpose a global constant is defined in the program, for example:

```
const int Debug = 1;
```

and the debugging statements (for example, statements that contain the output of the intermediate variable values) are placed at required places in the source code in the form of:

```
#if Debug
   // One or more debugging statements
#endif
```

In order to get the debugging version of a program, it is compiled with the value of **Debug** set to 1, and in order to get the short working version - with the value of **Debug** set to 0.

The #else Directive

The directive **#else** is paired with **#if** just like in an **if else** statement:

```
#if constant-expression
   //  if-group of lines
#else
   //  else-group of lines
#endif
```

As a result of preprocessing, one of the two groups of statements is omitted from the compilation process. If the constant expression is not equal to 0, then the **else** group of lines is omitted. Otherwise the **if** group of lines is omitted. This is shown in the following figures.

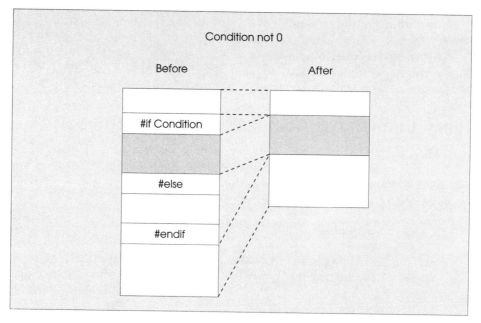

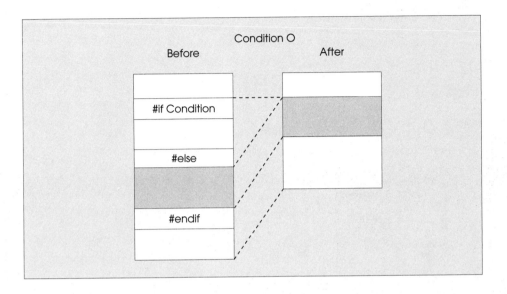

Try It Out - The #else Directive

You can check this by compiling Program 15.5 once with a value of the constant **Version** equal to 1, and the second time with any other value.

```
//  Program 15.5
//  #else directive

#include <iostream.h>

  const int Version = 1;

void main()
{
  #if Version == 1
    cout << "Version 1 large amount of code";
  #else
    cout << "Version 2 large amount of code";
  #endif
}
```

The #ifdef Directive

One more directive, **#ifdef**, is used for conditional compilation as shown in Program 15.6. It differs from **#if** in that you use a name formed under the rules of C++ in **#ifdef**, instead of a constant expression:

```
#ifdef <name>
```

This directive is read as "if name is defined". The output of the Program 15.6

```
Name Debug is not defined
```

shows that the name **Debug** isn't defined.

Try It Out - Using the #ifdef Directive

Let's look at the program.

```
//   Program 15.6
//   #ifdef directive

#include <iostream.h>

void main()
{
  #ifdef Debug
    cout << "Name Debug is defined";
  #else
    cout << "Name Debug is not defined";
  #endif
}
```

The #define Directive

There is a special directive for defining names:

```
#define<name>
```

Try It Out - Using the #define Directive

In Program 15.7, the name **Debug** is already defined and the program confirms this by its output:

```
Name Debug is defined
```

Note that the name **Debug** is not the name of a C++ variable. This is a name defined and used by the preprocessor.

```
//  Program 15.7
//  #define directive

#include <iostream.h>

#define Debug

void main()
{
  #ifdef Debug
    cout << "Name Debug is defined";
  #else
    cout << "Name Debug is not defined";
  #endif
}
```

Including the Same File Twice

You may think that you won't often need to include the same file into a program twice, in which case the subject of this section won't seem very important. But in reality this situation often happens during multiple inclusions of files, similar to multiple inheritance for classes. For example, the next figure shows that the file with the name 'p' includes 2 files: 'x' and 'y', each including the same file 'c'. After preprocessing, the file 'p' will contain two copies of the file 'c'.

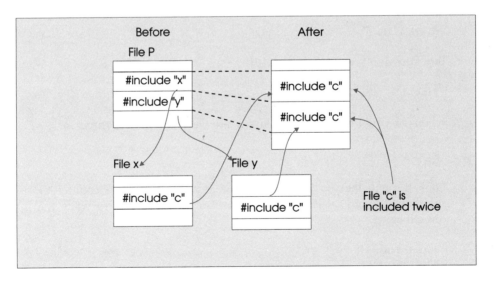

Try It Out - Including the Same File Twice

Program 15.8 will show you that multiple inclusions of the same file will lead to a compilation error. Here the class **c** is declared twice, and so you get a compilation error.

```
// Program 15.8
// Including the same file twice. Error.

#include <iostream.h>
#include <iostream.h>

#include "P15-08.inc"

// Error: Multiple declaration for 'c'
// # include "P15-08.inc"

void main()
{
  // ...
}
```

How It Works

The file to be included contains:

```
// P15-08.inc
// Including file for program P15-08.c

class c {};
```

But you don't get an error with:

```
#include <iostream.h>
```

when as you know several classes are declared in **IOSTREAM.H**.

The #ifndef Directive

Look through the file **IOSTREAM.H** (or any other system header file), and you see that to avoid multiple inclusions of a file you have to write the directives:

```
#ifndef <name>
#define <name>
```

at the very beginning of the file (not taking into account the comments), and at the very end - the directive:

```
#endif.
```

Here the new directive **#ifndef** is read as "if not defined". This directive means the opposite to the directive **#ifdef**. How does the protection mechanism work after the inclusion of the second file?

When the file is included for the first time, **<name>** is not defined. Therefore, the whole file is included and at the same time the directive:

```
#define <name>
```

is executed. The name **<name>** becomes defined, so that in all subsequent inclusions of this file, the condition:

```
#ifndef <name>
```

is no longer true. As a result the file is not included on the second and all subsequent occasions. You can verify that Program 15.9 compiles without an error with the help of this mechanism.

```
//  Program 15.9
//  Including the same file twice using #ifndef

#include "P15-09.inc"
#include "P15-09.inc"

void main()
{
   // ...
}
```

The include file **P15-09.INC** should contain:

```
//  P15-09.inc
//  Including file for program P15-08.c

#ifndef p15_09
#define p15_09

class c {};

#endif
```

The Directive Operator Defined

Instead of the **#ifdef** and **#ifndef** directives, you can use the **#if** directive with the operator **defined**. The directives:

```
#ifdef <name>
#ifndef<name>
```

are equivalent to the following directives:

```
#if   defined    (name)
#if   !defined   (name)
```

Here the character **!** is the logical negation (not) operator of C++.

The advantage of using the operator **defined** is that it can be used in a constant-expression together with other C++ operators, for example:

```
#if defined (A) && defined (B)
```

Using Macros

The **#define** directive has wider application than simply to define a name (defined or not defined). It permits the definition of a macro name. In this section we will look at macros in more detail.

Defining a Simple Macro

In a simple case, a macro specifies a name that that is to be replaced by a constant. In Program 15.10 the macro **N** is defined in the line:

```
#define N 1    // Macro name N
```

Try It Out - Defining a Simple Macro

Let's look at the program.

```
//   Program 15.10
//   Defining simple macro

#include <iostream.h>

#define N 1    // Macro name N
```

```
void main()
{
                    // Macro
                    // expansion    Output
    cout << N       // 1            1
         << N + 1   // 1 + 1        2
         << N / N;  // 1 / 1        1
}
```

How It Works

This definition results in the symbol 1 being substituted for the symbol **N** during pre-processing. This type of replacement is known as a macro expansion. After a macro expansion of the statement:

```
    cout << N       // 1            1
         << N + 1   // 1 + 1        2
         << N / N;  // 1 / 1        1
```

you get the statement:

```
    cout << 1
         << 1 + 1
         << 1 / 1;
```

This doesn't contain the macro name **N**. This last statement is compiled along with the rest of the program and the program's output has the form:

```
121
```

Using a Macro Constant

Macro constants are used so that you can use names instead of numbers in your program, making it more easily understood. Another advantage of using a macro constant becomes apparent when you need to modify a constant value. If you don't use a macro, then a modification like this would have to be performed throughout the whole program's text everywhere that the constant appears. If you use a macro, the value of the constant is modified only in one place - in the macro definition.

In C++ you usually use named constants instead of macro constants, for example:

```
const int  N = 1;
```

instead of:

```
#defineN 1
```

The qualifier **const** is preferred because the **#define** directive does not specify a data type and this can lead to program bugs.

Note that you mustn't terminate the directive **#define** with a semi-colon, as you do in a C++ statement.

Try putting a semi-colon at the end of the directive in Program 15.10:

```
#define N 1;
```

and see how difficult it can be to understand the cause of a compiler error message!

Macro Substitution and Tokens

Not every inclusion of the macro name **N** is substituted by 1. This is evident from Program 15.11 which outputs **NN** instead of the expected 11.

Try It Out - Macro Substitution

The program looks like this.

```
//    Program 15.11
//    No macro expansion

#include <iostream.h>

#define  N   1

void main()
{
                    // Output
  cout << 'N'       // N
       << " N ";    // N

  //cout << N1;     // Error: Undefined symbol 'N1'
  //cout << 1N;     // Error: Expression syntax
  //cout << N.N;    // Error: Field identifier expected
}
```

How It Works

Macro names in strings and symbol constants are not subjected to macro expansion, but remain as they were. In Program 15.11, other examples also appear in which a macro expansion doesn't take place, thus 11 does not replace **N1** and **1N**, and **N.N** is not converted to 1.1. Why is this the case?

The point is that is not just occurrences of the symbol **N** that are subjected to a substitution, but what are called "tokens". A token is a syntactic element that consists of an elementary part of a program text. There are five kinds of tokens: identifiers, keywords, literals, operators and other separators.

In our example, **N1** is an identifier kind of token. Since the two characters **N** and 1 are written here adjacent to each other, the compiler considers them to be one token **N1**, and not as two tokens: the name **N** and the constant 1. If there were a space between **N** and 1, then it would be two tokens.

We shall not go into detail of how a program is divided into tokens. But note that a name delimited by blanks, which is not included in a string literal or a comment, always creates a token, and therefore is subjected to a macro expansion.

Defining Expressions

A macro definition has the form:

```
#define <macro-name> <macro-body>
```

Here **macro-body** is any sequence of symbols that give correct C++ code after a macro expansion. For example, a macro-body can contain a C++ expression, as shown in Program 15.12.

Try It Out - Defining Expressions

Let's look at an example.

```
//  Program 15.12
//  Defining expressions: 2*2=3 !

#include "iostream.h"

#define Exp 1+1                          // Define expression
```

```
void main()
{
                        // Output
  cout << Exp         // 2
       << Exp*Exp;     // 3              1+1*1+1

  #undef  Exp                           // Undefine name
  #define Exp (1+1)                      // Redefine name

  cout << Exp*Exp;    // 4              (1+1)*(1+1)
}
```

How It Works

It's easy to be trapped when applying these kinds of macros. For example, if the value of **Exp** is equal to 2:

```
<< Exp*Exp;   // 3                 1+1*1+1
```

for some reason you get 3.

The reason the answer is given as 3 is because the value of **Exp** is not equal to 2! **Exp** expands to **1+1**. Therefore **Exp*Exp** expands to **1+1 * 1+1**, which equals 3. This is because of the rules of precedence. The precedence of ***** is higher than **+**. Therefore, the multiplication is performed first, which results in the expression **1 + (1 * 1) + 1**, which equals 3.

In order to use complex macros correctly, you must make sure you really understand the result of a macro substitution. Beginners are better off using functions instead of macros.

The #undef Directive

```
#undef  Exp                        // Undefine name
```

In Program 15.12, the use of another directive **#undef** is demonstrated. The name specified in the directive becomes undefined, and you can redefine the macro with a new body:

```
#define Exp (1+1)
```

By using parentheses in a macro body, you can avoid the error that arose earlier, and get the correct result (4) for **Exp * Exp**.

Try commenting the directive **#undef** in Program 15.12. The compiler will output a message about a repeated definition of the name **Exp**.

Using a Long Macro

When you have a long macro body, you will need to continue it on a new line. Unlike C++, continuing preprocessor directives on a new line can only be done by using a backslash, after which no further characters must appear on the same line.

Try It Out - Using a Long Macro

Program 15.13 contains an example of a long macro which carries over to the next line.

```
//   Program 15.13
//   Using a long macro

#include <iostream.h>

#define LongMacro        "This is the body of the very long \
macro"

void main()
{
    cout << LongMacro;
}
```

Try changing Program 15.13 by inserting something after the backslash, for example, a period (full-stop) at the end of the line. If you compile the program you will see that errors appear. Then try doing the same with spaces or tabs instead of a period. (The result may depend upon your text processor. Some processors remove the final blanks in lines, regardless of how many you insert).

Function-like Macros

There is a special form of syntax for the **#define** directive, that enables you to create a macro with parameters. Program 15.14 illustrates this.

Try It Out!

Try It Out - Using Function-like Macros

A peculiarity of the syntax is that the left bracket opening the parameter list must follow the name of the macro directly, without intervening blanks.

```
//   Program 15.14
//   Function-like macro

#include <iostream.h>

#define Say(m)   {cout << m;}                    // No blank between Say and (

void main()
{
  Say (1);
  Say (2)
  Say (3; cout << " Ok!";)
}
```

How It Works

The first statement written in the function **main()** is:

```
Say (1);
```

This looks like a function call, but in reality it is a macro with parameters. When preprocessing takes place, the body of the macro replaces this "call", in which, instead of the parameter **m**, its value is inserted. In our case:

```
{cout << 1;};
```

replaces:

```
Say(1);
```

As you see the whole body of the macro including braces is inserted in place of **Say(1)**. Then the obtained macro expansion is compiled.

```
Say (2)
```

Now look at the second use of the macro. Here, the usual semi-colon at the end of the statement is absent. Nevertheless this compiles normally, since after preprocessing it is converted into the form:

```
{cout << 2;}
```

and this is a legal construction (a block) in C++, after which a semi-colon isn't required.

In the next use of the macro, the parameter looks strange. However, this expression also works, because after the macro expansion it gives:

```
{cout << 3; cout << " Ok!";}
```

in other words, a legal C++ statement.

Try substituting parentheses for the braces in Program 15.14:

```
#define Say(m)   (cout << m;)
```

Confirm that this produces some errors. Now delete the parentheses:

```
#define Say(m)   cout << m;
```

Verify that the program compiles normally.

Insert a blank between the name of the macro and the list of parameters in Program 15.14:

```
#define Say  (m)   cout << m;
```

Verify that the number of errors arising doesn't match the number of blanks inserted, but don't attempt to find out the real reason for the compiler error messages by yourself.

Functions and Macros

The use of function-like macros results in the possibility of errors that are difficult to detect. That's why you should always use functions rather than macros wherever possible. However, the information we have given in this chapter relating to function-like macros, will be useful to you if you have to examine the source code of someone else's program written using macros.

Summary

Preprocessing directives are not part of the C++ language. Nevertheless, they have an important role in C++ programs. The **#include** directive frees the programmer from having to repeat function and type declarations by locating these declarations in a header file.

Directives for conditional compilation (**#if**, **#ifdef**, **#ifndef** and so on) provide a simple mechanism that allows you to include or omit parts of your program code that contain several program versions, or debugging statements.

CHAPTER 16

Using C++

In this final chapter we will write a complete application, using the tools you have learnt in the last 15 chapters. We are going to create a tutor program which you can use not only to demonstrate how C++ can be applied, but also can teach you to touch-type, if you can't already do so.

To write this program we have used the Turbo C++ programming system library files, that allow you to control key-strokes, keep track of time, and emit sound. To create a graphical color image we have used the library **GRAPHICS.LIB**. We will describe the methods of operation with this library function.

In order to compile and run the program in this chapter, you will need an IBM compatible PC running DOS, and the Borland Turbo C++ programming system, version 1 or later.

We have included this to show you how you can create really professional programs. Spend some time picking through the code to see how it all fits together. If you type it in, you should get some exciting results.

The Typing Tutor Program - Version 1

Professional typists use all their fingers and don't look at a keyboard. Their fingers automatically press the right keys, because they know where the keys are. Many computer users have to input a lot of text. If they use one finger, or even two fingers, they waste a lot of time. If you learn how to use all your fingers (even if you peep at the keyboard occasionally), then the time you will save will justify the time you spend.

Program 16.1 in this section can be used for learning how to touch type. This is the simplified first version. We provide an improved second version at the end of the chapter.

Starting the Game

If you type in the code in Program 16.1 and compile it, it will begin to output a single character that "runs" to the right. The character will run up to the middle of the screen, then the running character will start again on the next line. Your job is to press the key corresponding to the running character. The earlier you manage to do it, the more points you will score. If you are not quick enough, or you press the wrong key, then the score will decrease. The program is terminated after 20 lines have been output to the screen. To interrupt its operation, press the *Esc* key. The output of the program is similar to the following:

```
FFFFFFFFFFFFFFFFFFFFF
FFFFFFFFFFFF
JJJJJJJJJJJJJJJJJJJJJJJJJ
FFFFFFFFFFFFF
```

and so on.

You can try playing the game in two ways. First, press the keys using the same finger of one hand. You will have to look first at the screen, and then at the keyboard, and it won't be easy to keep up with letters that run quickly. Next, put the forefinger of your left hand on the F key, and the forefinger of your right hand - on the J key.

Then try only looking at the screen and pressing the required key. After a little practice you will undoubtedly find that you do better with the second method than the first.

Playing with More Characters

The data file **P16-01.DAT** should be set up with a text editor to contain:

```
fj
dfjk
sdfjkl
asdfjkl;
asdffjjkl;
```

The program operates with the letters in the first line of the file. Once you are adept with F and J, delete the first line in the file so the program operates with:

```
dfjk
```

You should press the keys D and K using your middle fingers. Having played using four keys, try the next line using your ring-fingers for the keys S and L, and then using your little fingers for keys A and ;. Now, the four fingers of your left hand should be on the keys ASDF, and the four fingers of your right hand on JKL;. These are the home keys for your fingers. At the same time the first line of the file **P16-01.DAT** should be:

```
asdfjkl;
```

Fingers and the Keyboard

If you are wondering which fingers should be used for pressing the other keys, the following figure should help. As you see the forefingers and the right little fingers do the major part of the work. In addition, the little fingers operate the *Shift* key, and the thumb operates the spacebar. You should move your fingers back to the home keys after each key operation. For example, having pressed the Y key using the forefinger of your right hand, return the finger to the location above the J key.

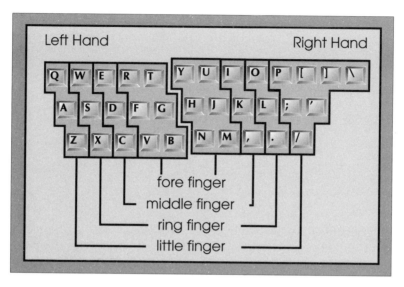

Implementation

We can now see how the game is implemented in Program 16.1. At the beginning, you see some **#include** directives which are commented to show the names of the functions and data which are supplied by that file. Many of these functions are absent in the standard ANSI library definitions. They expand your programming options to a considerable extent, but they mean you lose some portability in your programs.

```
//   Program 16.1
//   Playing with C++. Version 1 (text mode)

#include <iostream.h>          // cout
#include <ctype.h>             // toupper()
#include <conio.h>             // getch(),kbhit()
#include <stdlib.h>            // random(),randomize()
#include <dos.h>               // sound(),nosound(),delay()
#include <stdio.h>             // FILE,EOF,fopen(),fgetc(),fclose()

//     Global data

const int MaxKey  = 20;        // Stop after MaxKey times
const int Delay   = 30;        // More delay - slower playing
const int MaxChar = 40;        // Number of running characters

const int Esc     = 27;        // Escape key code - for exit
```

```
//     Types

enum  beep {BeepAtt,BeepErr};

//     Function declarations

int InputKeySet(char * KeySet, int & NKeys);
int Run(char Char, int & Key);
void Sound(beep Tone);

int main()
{
  int Score   = 0;              // Game score
  int Key     = 0;              // Last key pressed
  int KeyNum  = 0;              // Number of keys pressed

  char Char;                    // Running character
  char KeySet[1000];            // Key set, used for playing
  int  NKeys;                   // Actual number of used keys

  NKeys = sizeof KeySet;
  if (InputKeySet(KeySet,NKeys)) // Input key set from file,
                                 //   set actual NKeys
    return 1;                    // Return on file open error

  cout << "Press any key to start...\n";
  getch ();                     // Wait for key pressed
  randomize ();                 // For a random start key

  while (KeyNum++ < MaxKey)     // Main loop <= MaxKey times
  {
    Char=KeySet[random(NKeys)]; // Get random character
    Sound (BeepAtt);            // Attention beep
    Score += Run (Char,Key=0);  // Run character, get Key
    if (Key == Esc)             // Exit if Esc was pressed
      break;
    if (Key != Char)
      Sound (BeepErr);          // Error beep
  }

//    Display score

  cout << "\nScore " << (Score > 0 ? Score : 0);
  return 0;
}

int  InputKeySet(char * KeySet, int & NKeys)
{
  /*    Input key set
        from the first line of the file P16-01.dat
        to the array of characters KeySet
        Reset NKeys to the actual number of imputed keys
```

```
        Return
          0 - on success
          1 - on error
  */

  FILE *  pFILE;                      // Pointer to FILE structure

  pFILE=fopen ("P16-01.dat","rt");// Open data file
  if (! pFILE)
    return 1;                         // Return 1 on open error

  int i = 0;
  while (i < NKeys)                   // Loop <= sizeof(KeySet) times
  {
    int Key = fgetc (pFILE);          // Get character from a file
    Key = toupper (Key);              // Uppercase it
    if (Key == EOF)
      break;                          // Exit on end of file
    if (Key == '\n')
      break;                          // Exit on end of LINE  <--
    if (Key == ' ')
      continue;                       // Ignore blanks
    KeySet[i++] = (char) Key;         // Initialize KeySet
  }
  NKeys = i;                          // Number of inputted keys

  fclose (pFILE);                     // Close data file
    return 0;
}


int  Run(char Char, int & Key)
{
  for (int i = 0; i < MaxChar; i++)  // Running character loop
  {
    cout << Char;                     // Output a character
    delay(Delay);                     // Delay to slow speed
    if (kbhit() )                     // Test for key pressed
    {
      Key = toupper (getch ());       // Get key from the keyboard
      if (! Key)
        getch();                      // If not ASCII character
      break;                          // Exit loop
    }
  }
  cout << endl;                       // Go to new line

  int Score;

  if (i == MaxChar)
    Score = -MaxChar;
```

```
   else
     if (Char != Key)
       Score = -MaxChar/4;
     else
       Score =  MaxChar - i;

   return Score;
}

void Sound(beep Tone)
{
   int Freq=0;                          // Frequency, Hz
   int Delay=0;                         // Time (milliseconds)

   const int AttFreq  = 110;            // Hz
   const int ErrFreq  = 440;            // Hz
   const int AttDelay = 50;             // msec
   const int ErrDelay = 200;            // msec

   switch (Tone)
   {
     case BeepAtt:
       Freq=AttFreq;
       Delay=AttDelay;
       break;
     case BeepErr:
       Freq=ErrFreq;
       Delay=ErrDelay;
       break;
   }
   sound (Freq);
   delay (Delay);
   nosound ();
   delay (Delay);
}
```

Global Data

```
const int MaxKey  = 20;     // Stop after MaxKey times
const int Delay   = 30;     // More delay - slower playing
const int MaxChar = 40;     // Number of running characters
```

Three constants are defined which are used as set-up parameters. The constant **Delay** determines the speed of a running character. Its value is set in milliseconds. The smaller the value of **Delay**, the faster the character moves. The constant **MaxChar** determines the maximum number of characters in a line. The constant **MaxKey** determines the number of key strokes necessary to terminate the program.

```
const   int Esc    = 27;                      // Escape key code - for exit
```

The constant **Esc** defines the ASCII code of the key which interrupts the program.

The Program Algorithm

The program is written in such a way that its algorithm can be seen from **main()**.

In the function **InputKeySet()**, the characters that are used in the game are read from the file **P16-01.DAT** and are stored in the array **KeySet**. In the loop, which is repeated **MaxKey** times, the function **random()** is used to select one of the characters from the array.

```
Char=KeySet[random(NKeys) ];          // Get random character
```

The function **Run()** is used to display the character as a running line until the correct key is pressed and returns the points for that letter which are summed in the variable **Score**.

```
if (Key == Esc)
   break;
```

If the *Esc* key is pressed the program terminates.

```
if (Key != Char)
   Sound (BeepErr);
```

If an incorrect key is pressed a sound is emitted by the computer.

Now let's consider some details of the implementation.

Using the Data File

The function **InputKeySet()** reads a sequence of characters from the file **P16-01.DAT**. The file is set up to contain:

```
fj
dfjk
sdfjkl
asdfjkl;
asdffjjkl;
```

But only the characters in the first line are read, since the condition:

```
if (Key == '\n')
   break;
```

interrupts the input process when the end of the line is reached. The characters read are placed in the array **KeySet**, and the number of characters read is returned in the variable **Nkey**.

File Handling

If you look at the function **InputKeySet()** you will notice the file handling is done in a different way to the one we examined in Chapter 8. The methods we showed you in that chapter are specific to C++. The original C language also has methods for file handling and we are going to take this opportunity to introduce you to some of these features.

The functions that we will be using are contained in the header file **STDIO.H**. This header file contains a number of functions which are based on the ANSI standard.

A list of some of these ANSI C++ standard functions for operations with file streams is given in the following table.

Name	Action
fopen	Opens a stream
fclose	Closes a stream
fgetc	Gets a character from a stream
fputc	Puts a character on a stream
feof	Detects the end-of-file on a stream
ferror	Detects errors on a stream
fgets	Gets a string from a stream
fputs	Outputs a string on a stream
fread	Reads data from a stream
fwrite	Writes to a stream
fseek	Repositions a file pointer on a stream
ftell	Returns a current file pointer

Opening a File Stream

In order to use a stream with the functions indicated in the previous table, you must first declare it with the help of the statement:

```
FILE * pFILE;
```

Here **FILE** is a type associated with file streams. All the letters here must be upper-case. This type is defined in **STDIO.H**. It isn't necessary to go into the details of this type's definition. You can assume that the type **FILE** is just an additional data type. The asterisk in this declaration indicates that this is a declaration of a pointer to an object of the type **FILE**.

The file is opened using the function **fopen()** whose declaration is as follows:

```
FILE * fopen (char * FileName, char * Mode);
```

Here, the argument **FileName** is a literal string or name of a character array that contains the file name which is to be opened, in other words connect the file with the stream. The argument **Mode** is also a character string which determines the mode in which the stream will be used.

We said that the second argument to **fopen()** is a character string which specifies what you want to do with the file. As you would expect, this covers a whole range of possibilities.

"w"   open file for write operations
"a"   open file for append operations (for example, adding to the end of the file)
"r"   open file for read operations

Text mode is generally the default mode of the operations, but you can specifically select this mode if you want to. You do this by adding a **t** at the end of the existing specifiers. This gives us mode specifiers **"wt"**, **"rt"**, and **"at"** in addition to the original three. We can also open a file for update, that is for both reading and writing, using the specifier **"r+"**. If you wanted the mode to be specified explicitly as a text operation, it would become **"r+t"** or **"rt+"**. You can also specify the mode **"w+"** if you want to both read and write a file. To specify text mode explicitly, this would become **"wt+"** or **"w+t"**.

Binary mode is specified by appending a **b** to the basic mode specifiers, giving us the additional specifiers **"wb"** for writing a binary file, **"rb"** to read a binary file, **"ab"** to append data to the end of a binary file, and **"rb+"** to enable reading and writing of a binary file.

File Opening Error

An object of the type **FILE** is created dynamically during program execution; its creation depends upon conditions which are external to the program, in other words, upon the availability of a file on disk. If the file, whose name is indicated as the first argument of **fopen()**, is absent, then the object of the type **FILE** and the stream which corresponds to it cannot be created by the function **fopen()**. In this case it returns a pointer with the value 0. This is designated by a symbolic constant, **NULL**. It's impossible to use a pointer with the value 0. Therefore, you should always test the value **pFILE** returned by **fopen()**, as is done in the function:

```
    if (! pFILE)
        return 1;                    // Return 1 on open error
```

If **pFILE** is equal to 0 then **!pFILE** is 1 and this statement quits the program.

Closing a File Stream

If the stream is no longer required, then it is good programming practice to close it. This is done using the function **fclose()**, which takes as an argument the pointer to a stream opened earlier. This is shown below:

```
    fclose (pFILE);                  // Close data file
```

After this operation it is not possible to perform any other operations with the stream previously addressed by **pFILE**, though the value of the variable **pFILE** remains the same.

Having closed the stream, you can open another using the same pointer **pFILE**, or another pointer declared specially to do so. If, before the end of the program, you don't close a stream, then it will be closed automatically. That's why the call of the function **fclose()** isn't obligatory, although explicitly closing a stream as soon as the program no longer needs it, is still preferable, especially if the number of streams opened simultaneously is great and approaches the limit of the operating system.

Getting a Character From a File Stream

After successfully opening a file, characters can be read from it.

```
int Key = fgetc (pFILE);        // Get character from a file
```

The argument of the function `fgetc()` is a pointer to `FILE`, and the function returns a character which is stored in the variable of type `int`. Type `int` is used in order to allow the value `EOF (-1)` to be returned when the end of the file is reached. By testing the value returned by `fgetc()` you can provide an exit from the loop.

It's probably worth reading your compiler documentation regarding the other functions that can be used for file operations.

Using Random Numbers

The function `random()` generates random numbers. Each time it's called with a similar argument it returns different values. Here the probability of each value is equal. For example, `random(2)` returns either 0 or 1 during repeated calls. But it doesn't mean that the values 0 and 1 are alternated. They are scattered in a random manner as the output of Program 16.2 shows:

```
1011001000011110011111010110011000100100
20+20=40
Probabilities: 0.5 + 0.5 = 1
```

```
//  Program 16.2
//  Random number generation


#include <iostream.h>
#include <stdlib.h>        // random(),randomize()

void main()
{
   long N  = 40;           // Number of random() calls
   long N0 = 0;            // Number of returned 0 values
   long N1 = 0;            // Number of returned 1 values
   long Ret;               // Value returned by random()

   randomize();            // For random start value

   for (long i = 0; i < N; i++)
   {
```

```
    Ret = random (2);
    cout << Ret;
    if (Ret == 0)
      N0++;
    if (Ret == 1)
      N1++;
 }

 cout << endl << N0 << "+" << N1 << "=" << N << endl;

 float F0 = 1. * N0 / N;
 float   F1 = 1. * N1 / N;

 cout << F0 << " + " << F1 << " = " << 1;
}
```

You see that the probabilities of the appearance of 0 and 1, in 40 calls of the function **random(2)**, are close. In the same way the function **random(10)** will return one of the numbers 0, 1, 2, ... 9 with a probability of 1/10 for each one.

Try compiling and executing Program 16.2 for **N=10** and **N=1000**. Compare the difference in the probabilities of the appearance of 0 and 1.

Replace **random(2)** by **random(10)** and confirm that the probabilities of 0 and 1 appearing have become close to 0.1.

The function **randomize()** uses the current time (from the computer clock) for the initialization of a random number generator. As a result it generates different sequences on each occasion when the program is run. Execute Program 16.2 several times in succession to see that it outputs different sets of 0 and 1 each time.

Comment or delete the line in Program 16.2 that contains **randomize()**. By running the program several times confirm that each time it outputs the same series of 0 and 1.

Using Random Numbers in the Typing Tutor Program

Let us return to Program 16.1. Here in the line:

```
    Char = KeySet[random(NKeys)];
```

one character is extracted from the array **KeySet**. The index of the element is a random number from 0 to **Nkey-1**. The probability of each element is

1/Nkey. Repeating a character in the first line of the file **P16-01.DAT** two or three times, as is done in the last line of the file, alters the rate of appearance of this character. Note that the sequence of characters doesn't affect the rate of their appearance.

Testing Key Depressions

Let's see how pressing a key in **Run()** stops the loop outputting the running character:

```
for (int i=0; i<MaxChar; i++)
{
  cout << Char;
  delay (Delay);
  if (kbhit ())
  {
    Key = toupper (getch ());
    if (! Key) getch ();
    break;
  }
}
```

Once the character is displayed on the screen, the program is delayed for **Delay** milliseconds, due to the call to **delay(Delay)**.

The function **kbhit()** determines if a key has been pressed. This function doesn't wait for a key to be pressed (as **getch()** does). It only checks whether a key was pressed earlier. If no key was pressed, then **kbhit()** returns 0 and the **for** loop continues to be executed, and the character continues "to run". If a key was pressed then **kbhit()** will not return 0 and the block following will be executed. Here the function **getch()** will return the character pressed, the **break** statement will interrupt the **for** loop, and the running character will cease.

After the loop finishes the value of the loop index, **i**, is used to determine when the key was pressed. If **i** is equal to **MaxChar** then the key wasn't pressed at all. At the same time a negative value (penalty) is summed in the variable **Score**. If the key pressed coincides with that running character then:

```
Score =  MaxChar - i;
```

The earlier the key is pressed the higher the score because the value of **i** will be lower. A penalty is applied for pressing the wrong key.

Simple Sounds

Sounds in a program can be used to attract the user's attention. Two sound signals are used which are declared as enumeration constants:

```
enum beep {BeepAtt,BeepErr};
```

The sound **BeepAtt** is output before the beginning of the next running character. The sound **BeepErr** is output if you press the wrong key, or if you don't press any key. Look at how simple sounds are made in the function **Sound()** using library functions.

```
sound (Freq);
delay (Delay);
nosound ();
```

The function **sound(Freq)** produces a tone with a frequency, **Freq**, measured in Hertz. This tone will continue to sound until the function **nosound()** is called. The function **delay()** is used to determine the duration of the tone. The additional call of **delay()** after the call to **nosound()** is not obligatory, but without it there won't be a pause between the signal for an error, and the signal indicating the next running character.

Using Upper-case Characters

The function **toupper()** converts the letters into upper-case. It's used during character entry in **Run()** and during the input of characters from the data file in **InputKeySet()**. Therefore, you can put characters in the data file without worrying about the case of the letters.

The Conditional Operator

Once the game has finished and before the program terminates the total score is output:

```
cout << "\nScore " << (Score > 0 ? Score : 0);
```

The expression:

```
(Score > 0 ? Score : 0)
```

means if **Score** is greater than 0 output **Score**, else output 0 (instead of a negative value for **Score**). Here, the conditional operator is used which has the following form:

```
cond-expression ? expression1 : expression2
```

If **cond-expression** is not equal to 0 then the value of the **expression1** is used, otherwise the value of **expression2** is used.

The User's View of a Program

We have discussed the algorithm that was used in Program 16.1 together with its implementation. This was a view of the program from a programmer's point of view. Though useful improvements could be made, it achieves the main objective to teach someone how to touch-type.

If we look at this program from a user's point of view, then its appearance is far from perfect. It resembles a car that has an excellent engine, but can't be steered, is rusty inside and doesn't have a windscreen. However, before we proceed with "renovating" the program we need to master the facilities available for this. This will be done in the next section, and then we will return to Program 16.1 in order to improve the human-to-computer interface.

Using the Borland Graphics Interface

In this section you will learn how to create graphical representations on your computer screen, made up of separate dots or pixels. Such representations are widely used in computer games and in commercial programs.

We will need a short introduction to the tools in the Borland Graphics Interface (BGI). These tools are part of the Borland Turbo C++ programming system. They are designed for use in programs working under DOS on an IBM compatible PC.

Using graphics.lib

The main component of the BGI is a library of graphics functions contained in the file **GRAPHICS.LIB**. It contains a large number of functions designed to use the graphics capabilities of your computer. In order to take advantage of these functions you need to point to the library while compiling your program. For example, to compile a file **PROGRAM.CPP**, that uses graphics functions you should use the command:

```
BCC  -P -c program.cpp  graphics.lib
```

The file, **PROGRAM.CPP**, must contain the directive:

```
#include <graphics.h>
```

The header file **GRAPHICS.H** contains graphics function declarations, and all the data required for their use.

Using BGI Drivers and Fonts

Besides the library, **GRAPHICS.LIB**, there is a set of program-drivers for various types of graphics adapters (files with the extension **BGI**), and a set of fonts (files with extension **CHR**). To execute the programs appearing in this chapter you need to ensure that all files of both types are in the same directory as the compiled and linked program.

Initializing the Graphics System

Before calling graphics functions you must initialize the graphics adapter in your PC using the function **initgraph()**. Program 16.3 shows how this should be done.

```
    int Driver=DETECT;          // Driver to be used (autodetect it)
    int Mode;                   // Screen mode (returned)
    char *  Path = "";          // Path to driver (current directory)

    initgraph(&Driver, &Mode, Path);
```

It's possible to specify the values to **initgraph()** yourself, but it's probably better to let the system handle it as we have done here. You should enter the path to the directory containing your **BGI** files between the **""**.

```
// Program 16.3
// Initialize graphics system

#include <iostream.h>
#include <graphics.h>              // Graphics functions
and data
```

```
#include <conio.h>                                    // getch()

int main()
{
//      Initialize graphics system (autodetect)
//      Load BGI driver and set graphics mode

  int Driver=DETECT;             // Driver to be used (autodetect it)
  int Mode;                      // Screen mode (returned)
  char * Path = "";              // Path to driver (current directory)
                                 // Enter the path to your BGI directory
  initgraph (&Driver, &Mode, Path);

  int InitRes;

  InitRes = graphresult();       // Get result of initialization
  if (InitRes != grOk)
  {
    cout  << "Graphics Error: " << grapherrormsg (InitRes);
    return 1;
  }

  cout << "Hello, Programmer!" << "\n\nThe graphics driver "
                            << getdrivername ()
       << "\nand graphics mode " << getmodename (Mode)
       << "\nare used.\n\nPress any key...";

  getch ();                      // Wait for key pressed

  closegraph ();                 // Restore previous screen mode
}
```

If you leave **Path** initialized with an empty string the function **initgraph()** will look in the current directory for the necessary driver (a file with an extension **.BGI**). The driver found is loaded into memory.

The function **initgraph()** doesn't return any value. To find out if the initialization was successful you have to use the function **graphresult()** which returns an integer. If this value is the same as the constant **grOk**, then the initialization is successful, otherwise, an error has occurred. If an error has occurred, a call to function **grapherrormsg()** returns a pointer to the text of an error message.

If the initialization is successful then you can use the other functions of the library. Program 16.3 shows, for example, how using the functions **getdrivername()** and **getmodename()** you can get the names of a driver and the graphics mode that has been set. Both these functions return a pointer to a message text.

When you run Program 16.3 a message will appear on the screen indicating the type of graphics adapter your computer has and the current graphics mode. If the program terminates with an error, then one of the possible causes is that the required *.BGI file isn't in the current directory.

Closing the Graphics System

When you have finished working with the graphics system, you should call the function closegraph(), which performs all necessary closing operations and sets the graphics mode back to what it was before the function initgraph() was called.

Screen Coordinates

To specify a location on the screen the functions of BGI use two coordinates x and y as shown in the following figure.

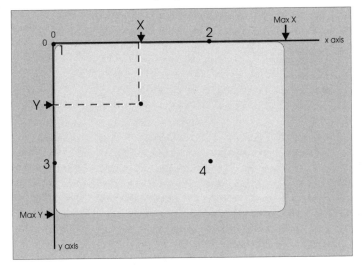

The maximum possible value of each coordinate depends upon the mode set, and may be determined using the functions getmaxx() and getmaxy() as is shown in Program 16.4:

```
const int   MaxX = getmaxx ();
const int   MaxY = getmaxy ();
```

Displaying a Pixel

A dot on the screen is called a pixel. To display a pixel you can use the function `putpixel()`:

```
putpixel (X,Y,C);
```

It has three arguments - coordinates `X`, `Y` and the color `C`. Let's look how four pixels are displayed in Program 16.4, which are marked in the previous figure by the numbers 1, 2, 3, and 4. Once the pixel is displayed the program waits for you to press a key, so you can see where each pixel is displayed. First, the pixel 1 with coordinates 0,0 is displayed, then pixel 2, with coordinates `X=MaxX/2` and `Y=0`, and so on.

```
//   Program 16.4
//   Displaying dot (pixel)

#include "P16-04.h"

int main()
{
  if (! Init ())                   // Initialize graphics system
    return 1;                      // Exit on error

//      Maximum x, y coordinates and color values
  const int MaxX     = getmaxx ();
  const int MaxY     = getmaxy ();
  const int MaxColor = getmaxcolor ();

  cout << "\n Max X     = " << MaxX << "\n Max Y     = " << MaxY
       << "\n Max Color = " << MaxColor;

  Pause();                         // Wait for key to be pressed

  // putpixel ()
  cleardevice ();                  // Clear screen

  int X=0, Y=0;                    // x, y coordinates
  int C = MaxColor;                // Color

  putpixel (X,Y,C);                // Pixel 1 at the left top corner
  Pause ();

  X = MaxX/2; Y=0;
  putpixel (X,Y,C);                // Pixel 2 at the center top
  Pause ();

  X=0;
```

```
    Y=MaxY/2;
    putpixel (X,Y,C);              // Pixel 3 at the left center
    Pause ();

    X=MaxX/2;
    Y=MaxY/2;
    putpixel (X,Y,C);              // Pixel 4 at the screen center
    Pause ();

    closegraph ();
}
```

In Program 16.4 the function `cleardevice()` is used, to clear the screen.

Two functions `Init()` and `Pause()` are put into a header file `P16-04.H`. They will be used in the following examples. The function `Pause()` waits for you to press any key. The function `Init()` is derived from Program 16.3 and initializes the graphics screen. Pay attention to the fact that it returns 0 during a successful initialization. This is done so that the statement:

```
    if (! Init())
        return 1;
```

might be read more naturally: "if not initialized, then exit".

The header file `P16-04.H` is shown below:

```
#include <iostream.h>
#include <conio.h>
#include <graphics.h>

int Init()
{
//  Initialize graphics system (autodetect)
//  Load BGI driver and set graphics mode

  int Driver=DETECT;   // Driver to be used (autodetect it)
  int Mode;            // Screen mode (returned)
  char *  Path = "I:\\TC\\BGI";      // Path to driver (current directory)

  initgraph (&Driver, &Mode, Path);

  int InitRes;

  InitRes=graphresult();  // Get result of initialization
  if (InitRes != grOk)
  {
```

```
      cout  << "Graphics Error: " << grapherrormsg (InitRes);
      return 0;
   }
   return 1;
}

int Pause()
{
   int key = getch();
   if (!key)
      getch();
   return key;
}
```

With the help of the function **putpixel()** you can draw any image. However, there are special functions for drawing simple figures.

Drawing a Line

The function **line()** is used for drawing lines. An example of its use is given in Program 16.5.

```
//   Program 16.5
//   Draw line, filled polygon

#include "P16-04.h"

int main()
{
   if (! Init ())            // Initialize graphics system
      return 1;              // Exit on error

   const int MaxX    = getmaxx ();
   const int MaxY    = getmaxy ();
   const int MaxColor = getmaxcolor ();

//      Line between two points: line ()

   int Color  = MaxColor, X1 = 0, Y1 = 0, X2 = MaxX, Y2 = MaxY;

   setcolor (Color);         // Set draw color
   line (X1,Y1, X2,Y2);      // Diagonal line from left top
   Pause ();                 //    to right bottom screen corner

//      Move current position (CP): moveto ()

   cleardevice ();

   cout    << "\n Before moveto ()" << "\n Current X = " << getx ()
```

```
                << "\n Current Y = " << gety ();

  moveto (MaxX,MaxY);                              // Move CP

  cout     << "\n After moveto (MaxX,MaxY)" << "\n Current X = " << getx ()
           << "\n Current Y = " << gety ();
  Pause ();

//      Line from current position: lineto ()

  int X=MaxX/6, Y=MaxY/6;

  cleardevice ();
  setcolor (Color);          // Set draw color

  moveto (  0,Y*5);          // Go to new CP
                             // Two peak mountain ( /\/\ )
  lineto (X*2,Y*1);          // Line 1
  lineto (X*3,Y*2);          // Line 2
  lineto (X*4,Y*1);          // Line 3
  lineto (X*6,Y*5);          // Line 4
  lineto (  0,Y*5);          // Line 5
  Pause ();

//      Fill bounded region: floodfill ()

  int FillColor   = Color;
  int BorderColor = Color;

  setcolor (Color);                          // Set draw color
  setfillstyle (SOLID_FILL,FillColor);       // Set fill color
  floodfill (MaxX/2,MaxY/2,BorderColor);     // Fill enclosed area Pause ();

//      Fill polygon: fillpoly ()

  int Shape [] = { 0,16, 3,14, 6,10, 8,6, 10,8, 12,4, 16,12, 20,16 };
  int NPoints = sizeof Shape / sizeof (int) / 2;
  int     i,j;

  for (i=j=0; i<NPoints; i++,j+=2)
  {
    Shape[j]   = Shape[j] * MaxX / 20;
    Shape[j+1] = Shape[j+1] * MaxY / 20;
  }

  cleardevice ();
  setcolor (Color);                          // Set draw color
  FillColor = Color;
  setfillstyle (SOLID_FILL,FillColor);       // Set fill color
  fillpoly (NPoints,Shape);                  // Draw and fill
  Pause ();
```

```
    closegraph ();
}
```

Here **X1**, **Y1**, **X2**, **Y2** are the coordinates of two points which will be connected by a line. The color of a line is fixed by a separate function:

```
    setcolor (Color);
```

The function **lineto()** was also used in the last program:

```
    moveto (   0,Y*5);

    lineto (X*2,Y*1);        // Line 1
    lineto (X*3,Y*2);        // Line 2
    lineto (X*4,Y*1);        // Line 3
    lineto (X*6,Y*5);        // Line 4
    lineto (   0,Y*5);       // Line 5
```

Two mountain peaks were drawn in the form of the letter M with the help of these 5 lines. The result, an enclosed area, was obtained and is shown in the following figure.

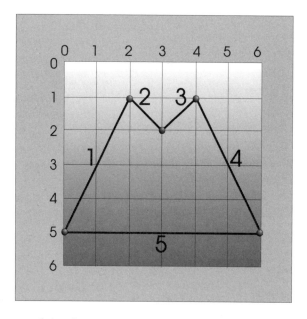

In the figure and in the program comments, the lines that were drawn are marked by numbers.

Filling-in the Bounded Region

The enclosed area obtained with `lineto()` can be filled with color using the function:

```
floodfill (MaxX/2, MaxY/2, BorderColor);
```

The first two arguments set an arbitrary point inside an enclosed area (in our case it is the screen center). The third argument sets the color of the border. The color which fill in an area is set by a separate function:

```
setfillstyle (SOLID_FILL, FillColor);
```

The constant **SOLID_FILL** indicates the type of filling.

However, this method is relatively slow. To fill in a polygon you can use the function `fillpoly()` which operates quicker. Program 16.5 also used `fillpoly()` and the result is shown in the following figure.

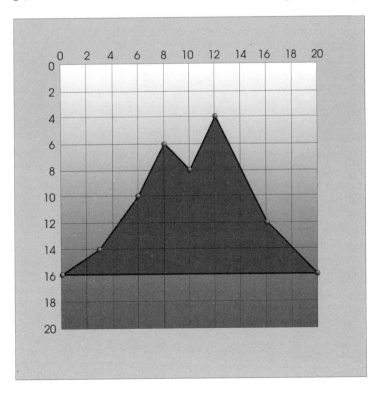

A call to **fillpoly()** has the form:

```
fillpoly (NPoints, Shape);
```

where **NPoints** is the number of points in the polygon. In our case these are 8. The argument **Shape** is an array of 8 integer pairs which correspond to pairs of X, Y coordinates. The function **fillpoly()** draws a polygon with a color that can be set by **setcolor()**, and the fill is set by **setfillstyle()**.

Drawing a Bar

Program 16.6 demonstrates three methods of drawing a bar. The first method uses the function **putpixel()**. This is a very slow method. The second method uses **line()**. This way is quicker but the fastest way is to use **bar()**. The function **bar()** uses four arguments which set the top left and bottom right coordinates. The fill style is set by **setfillstyle()**.

The function **getbkcolor()** returns the current background color and is used in the program. The background color can be set by **setbkcolor()**.

```cpp
// Program 16.6
// Draw bar

#include "P16-04.h"

int main()
{
  if (! Init ())          // Initialize graphics system
    return 1;             // Exit on error

  const int MaxX    = getmaxx();
  const int MaxY    = getmaxy();
  const int MaxColor = getmaxcolor();

//      Draw bar with putpixel ()

  int Color = MaxColor,
      X, Y = 0,            // Loop variables
      X1=0, Y1=0,          // Left top corner
      X2=MaxX, Y2=MaxY;    // Right bottom corner

  for  ( X = X1; X <= X2; X++)
    for (Y = Y1; Y <= Y2; Y++)
      putpixel (X,Y,Color);      // Output dot at X,Y
  Pause ();
```

```
//      Draw bar with line ()

  setcolor(getbkcolor());           // Set background color

  X1+=5;
  Y1+=5;                            // Adjust bar
  X2-=5;
  Y2-=5;

  for  ( X = X1; X <= X2; X++)
    line (X,Y1,X,Y2);               // Draw vertical line
  Pause ();

//      Draw bar with bar ()

  X1+=5;
  Y1+=5;                            // Adjust bar
  X2-=5;
  Y2-=5;

  int FillColor = Color;

  setfillstyle (SOLID_FILL,FillColor);    // Set fill color
  bar (X1,Y1,X2,Y2);                // Draw bar (not outlined)
  Pause ();

  closegraph ();
}
```

Outputting Text

Text can be output onto the graphics screen using the function **outtext()**.
Program 16.7 demonstrates how this function works.

```
//   Program 16.7
//   Draw text

#include "P16-04.h"

int main()
{
  if (! Init ())          // Initialize graphics system
    return 1;             // Exit on error

  const int MaxX    = getmaxx ();
  const int MaxY    = getmaxy ();
  const int MaxColor = getmaxcolor ();

//      Output text
```

```
  int X, Y, Color = MaxColor;

  setcolor(Color);          // Set draw color
  outtext ("A");            // Output text at CP (0,0)
  Pause ();
  outtext ("B");            // Output 'B' after 'A'
  Pause ();

  X=MaxX/4, Y=MaxY/4;
  outtextxy (X,Y,"of");     // Output text at X,Y
  Pause ();

  outtext ("C");            // Output 'C' after 'B', not after 'of'
  Pause ();

//      Change font

  int Font = TRIPLEX_FONT, Direction = HORIZ_DIR, Size = 1;

  X=MaxX/2, Y=MaxY/2;                    // Move CP to the
  moveto (X,Y);                          // screen center

  settextstyle (Font,Direction,Size);

  outtext ("BGI text output");
  Pause ();

//      Clear text

  Color = getbkcolor();
  setcolor(Color);                   // Set background draw color moveto (X,Y);
  outtext("BGI text output");    // Clear
  Pause ();

//      New text at the same place

  setcolor (MaxColor);
  outtextxy (X,Y,"C++");
  Pause ();

  closegraph ();
}
```

Run the program. The pauses let you see how the program operates. The program outputs the letter 'A' into an upper left corner of the screen. This is a result of the statement:

```
  outtext ("A");
```

The color of the text is set by **setcolor()**. Press a key and the letter B will appear to the right of 'A'. This is a result of the statement:

```
outtext ("B");
```

After the next key press the text "of" will appear

```
outtextxy (X,Y,"of");
```

at the location specified by the coordinates **x** and **y**. Press the key once again and the letter C is displayed by the call to **outtext()**. The letter C appears not after "of", but after "AB". This is because **outtext()** outputs text relative to the current position. The function **outtextxy()** doesn't move the current position.

After a graphics screen has been initialized and after a call to **cleardevice()**, the current position is set to 0,0.

Using Fonts

The BGI include a set of fonts and a font is selected by using **settextstyle()**. In Program 16.7 its call has the form:

```
settextstyle (Font, Direction, Size);
```

The first argument **Font** is a number that determines a font. The enumeration type **font_names** defined in **GRAPHICS.H** provides names of constants for admissible values of **Font**. One of these enumeration constants **TRIPLEX_FONT** is used in Program 16.7. The second argument **Direction** can take two values: **HORIZ_DIR** and **VERT_DIR**. They designate an output direction - horizontal (from left to right) or vertical one (upwards). The third argument, an integer, is used for setting the font size. It may take any value from 0 to 10.

The function **settextstyle()** operates by looking for the file with the extension **CHR,** from the set of BGI files, which corresponds to the font type requested. If the file isn't found the change of the font won't take place.

```
int     Font      = TRIPLEX_FONT,
        Direction = HORIZ_DIR,
        Size      = 1;

X=MaxX/2, Y=MaxY/2;
moveto (X,Y);
settextstyle (Font,Direction,Size);
outtext ("BGI text output");
```

The previous statements result in text being output from left to right from the center of the screen. At the same time the font will be changed.

```
Color = getbkcolor ();
setcolor (Color);
moveto (X,Y);
outtext ("BGI text output");
```

These statements show how text can be erased (it is not the only way to do this) so that more text may be put in its place. As a result the appearance of the screen will be as shown in the following figure.

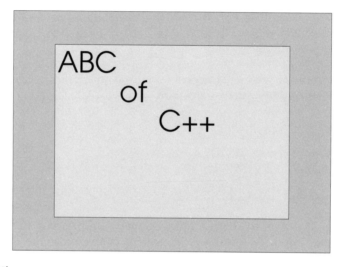

Text Justification

Program 16.8 demonstrates text justification. The function **settextjustify()** is used to position the text.

```
//   Program 16.8
//   Text justification and size

#include "P16-04.h"

void DrawCP();

int main()
{
  if (! Init ())            // Initialize graphics system
     return 1;              // Exit on error

  const int MaxX    = getmaxx ();
  const int MaxY    = getmaxy ();
```

```
    const int MaxColor= getmaxcolor ();

//      Text justification

    int Color = MaxColor, HorizJust = CENTER_TEXT, VertJust  = CENTER_TEXT;

    setcolor (Color);
    moveto (MaxX/2,MaxY/2);
    DrawCP();                                  // Draw +  at the CP

    settextstyle (TRIPLEX_FONT,HORIZ_DIR,1);
    settextjustify (HorizJust,VertJust);
    outtext ("C     +");                       // Centered text

    settextstyle (TRIPLEX_FONT,VERT_DIR,1);
    outtext ("C     +");                       // Vertical text
    Pause ();

//      9 justification styles

    struct  Justification
    {
      int  Horizontal;
      int  Vertical;
      char * Text;
    };

    settextstyle (TRIPLEX_FONT,HORIZ_DIR,1);

    Justification J [] = {
                     LEFT_TEXT,    BOTTOM_TEXT, "LEFT_TEXT    BOTTOM_TEXT",
                     LEFT_TEXT,    CENTER_TEXT, "LEFT_TEXT    CENTER_TEXT",
                     LEFT_TEXT,    TOP_TEXT,    "LEFT_TEXT    TOP_TEXT",
                     CENTER_TEXT,  BOTTOM_TEXT, "CENTER_TEXT BOTTOM_TEXT",
                     CENTER_TEXT,  CENTER_TEXT, "CENTER_TEXT CENTER_TEXT",
                     CENTER_TEXT,  TOP_TEXT,    "CENTER_TEXT TOP_TEXT",
                     RIGHT_TEXT,   BOTTOM_TEXT, "RIGHT_TEXT   BOTTOM_TEXT",
                     RIGHT_TEXT,   CENTER_TEXT, "RIGHT_TEXT   CENTER_TEXT",
                     RIGHT_TEXT,   TOP_TEXT,    "RIGHT_TEXT   TOP_TEXT"
                       };

    for (int i=0; i<9; i++)
    {
      cleardevice ();
      setcolor (Color);
      settextjustify (J[i].Horizontal,J[i].Vertical);

      moveto (MaxX/2,MaxY/2);
      DrawCP ();                          // Draw +  at the CP
      outtext (J[i].Text);
      Pause ();
    }
```

```
//      Text size

  cleardevice ();
  setcolor (Color);
  moveto (MaxX/2,MaxY/2);
  settextjustify (CENTER_TEXT,CENTER_TEXT);
  settextstyle (TRIPLEX_FONT,HORIZ_DIR, 4 );
  outtext ("Hello, C++ Programmer !");                // Large text Pause ();

  closegraph ();
}

void  DrawCP()
{
//      Draw + at current position

  int X = getx ();
  int Y = gety ();

  line(X-10, Y,    X+10, Y);     // Horizontal line
  line(X,    Y-10, X,    Y+10);  // Vertical line
}
```

When you run Program 16.8 you will see how the text is aligned in each of the 9 possible combinations. The current position is located at the cross in the center of the screen.

In conclusion, the program outputs in an enlarge size:

```
Hello, C++ Programmer !
```

The font size is increased 4 times by the call to

```
settextstyle (TRIPLEX_FONT, HORIZ_DIR, 4 );
```

Unfortunately, we have only had time for a brief introduction to the BGI. We advise you to look at your documentation. However, this taste will allow us to consider how we can apply the BGI to the original program, Program 16.1, to improve the interface.

Typing Tutor Program - Version 2

Now let's consider the program **P.CPP** which is a modification of Program 16.1. Run it and you will see a mountain with two peaks appear on your screen. Press any key to start a game. A signal will sound and above one of the mountains peaks a character appears.

You should press the key that corresponds to the character shown. A skier will descend the mountain indicating how much time has passed since the character appeared. You should try to press the key before the skier descends to the foot of the mountain. If you don't your score will decrease. The earlier you press a key the higher your score.

If the character appears above the left peak then the corresponding key is located in the left part of the keyboard. It should be pressed by a finger of the left hand as indicated in the first figure in this chapter. If the character appears above the right peak then you should use your right hand. A vertical bar in the center gradually shortens to show how much time there is before the end of the game at its current level. When the bar disappears the game will start again with a new set of keys. The Error indicator shows the percentage of erroneous key presses relative to total number of pressed keys.

To pause the game press the *Esc* key. In order to exit from the game press *Esc* once again, and in order to continue press any other key.

As you can see the human-computer interface has become much better due to the graphical capabilities of the computer. Again, there is room for improvement but you will need a better understanding of the graphical capabilities of the computer and you will have to write additional functions.

The following figure shows the game in play.

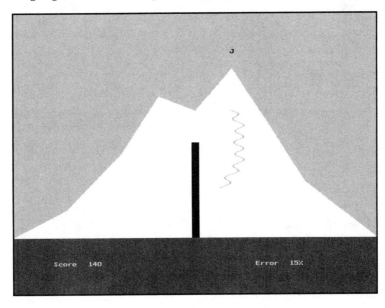

Implementation

Let us consider the text of program **P.CPP**. What alterations are put into it in comparison with Program 16.1?

First, we have a header file containing class definitions and global data:

```
// Header File for Program P.CPP

// P.h
// Header file for P.cpp
// Copyright (c) 1994 Oleg Yarosh

#include <graphics.h>          // Graphics functions

#include <stdio.h>             // FILE,EOF,fgetc(),sprintf()
#include <dos.h>               // sound(), clock()
#include <stdlib.h>            // random(), randomize()
#include <time.h>              // randomize(), CLK_TCK
#include <ctype.h>             // toupper()
#include <conio.h>             // getch()
#include <math.h>              // sin()
#include <iostream.h>          // cout


//-------------------------------------------------------------
//   Global data
//-------------------------------------------------------------

class par                      // Global parameters
{
public:                        // Public members
  static const int MaxKey;     // Stop after this number of keys
  static const int Delay;      // More delay - slower playing
};

const int par::MaxKey = 20;    // Keys to be pressed
const int par::Delay  = 10;    // Time delay (millisecomds)

const int MaxAmp = 20;         // Max trace x amplitude
const int MinAmp = 10;         // Min trace x amplitude

const int Esc   = 27;          // Key to exit (escape)

const int XStep = 20;          // Grid step
const int YStep = 20;


//-------------------------------------------------------------
//   Enumerations
//-------------------------------------------------------------

enum {
        SkyColor   = LIGHTCYAN,
        CharColor  = BLUE,
```

```
        TraceColor = LIGHTCYAN,
        SnowColor  = WHITE,
        TextColor  = YELLOW,
        ValueColor = YELLOW,
        GroundColor= GREEN,
        BarColor   = BLUE
};

enum  beep  {BeepAtt,BeepErr};

//---------------------------------------------------------------
//  Class key
//---------------------------------------------------------------

class   key                     // Class declaration
{
private:                        // Private members
  FILE *pFILE;                  // Pointer to FILE structure
  enum hand {Left,Right};       // Local enum type
  hand Hand;                    // Hand for key

  char *Set;                    // Character set to display
  int Len;                      // Its length

  int Init();                   // Initialize graphics system
  void WhatHand();              // Key for what hand?

public:                         // Public members
  key();                        // Constructor
  ~key();                       // Destructor
  char Char;                    // Displaing character
  int Input();                  // Input key set from file
  void Get();                   // Get next random char
  void Draw();
  void Clear();                 // Clear keyboard
  int Trace (int & Key);        // Display trace, get key
};

//---------------------------------------------------------------
//  Class key object definition
//
//  Call constructor to initialize graphics system before main()
//  Call destructor to close graphics system after main()
//---------------------------------------------------------------

key K;

//---------------------------------------------------------------
//  Class point
//---------------------------------------------------------------

struct point
{
```

```
  int X;
  int Y;
  point () { X=0; Y=0; }
  point (float x,float y);
};

//---------------------------------------------------------------
//  Points on the screen (must be defined after K object)
//---------------------------------------------------------------

point LeftPeak     (8,     6),   // Mountain peak
      RightPeak    (12,    4),
      LeftChar     (8,     5),   // Character
      RightChar    (12,    3),
      LeftStart    (8,     7),   // Trace start
      RightStart   (12,    7),
      LeftFinish   (8,     16),  // Trace finish
      RightFinish  (12,    16),
      TopBar       (9.8,   7),   // Moving bar
      BottomBar    (10.2,  16),
      ScoreText    (3,     18),
      ErrorText    (14,    18);

//---------------------------------------------------------------
//  Functions
//---------------------------------------------------------------

void Play ();
int  Pause ();
void Sound (beep Tone);
void DrawPicture ();
void DisplayScore (int Score);
void DisplayErr (int ErrNum);
void DisplayBar (int Count);
void GameOver ();
```

And now, the main program code:

```
/*      P.cpp
        Playing with C++

        This game program teaches you to type using all fingers

        Program uses the data file  P.dat

        containing a list of keys. Blanks in file are ignored.
         Every new line contains key set for the next level.
          Duplicate keys in line means proportionally
        increased probability for such key.

        To pause game press Esc key.
        To exit game press Esc key once more.
*/
```

```
#include "P.h"                    // Data and functions

//------------------------------------------------------------
// main() - program entry point
//------------------------------------------------------------

void main()
{
  // Play until the data file has been read, or the player has quit
  while (K.Input ())
    Play ();
}

//------------------------------------------------------------
// Play() - game loop. Accepts input from player until maximum
// number of characters has been entered, or Esc has been
// pressed.
//------------------------------------------------------------

void Play()
{
  int    Score   = 0;              // Game score
  int    Key     = 0;              // Last key pressed
  int    KeyNum  = 0;              // Number of keys pressed
  int    ErrNum  = 0;              // Number of error keys pressed

  DrawPicture ();                  // Draw static picture
  Pause ();                        // Press any key to start
  delay (1000);                    // Time to prepare (msec)

  while (KeyNum++ < par::MaxKey)   // Main loop MaxKey times
  {
    K.Get ();                      // Wait for random character to start
    K.Clear ();                    // Clear keyboard buffer
    Sound (BeepAtt);               // Beep to alert user
    K.Draw ();                     // Draw random character
    Score += K.Trace (Key=0);      // Display trace, get Key

    if (Key == Esc)                // Pause when Esc is pressed
      if (Pause()==Esc)
        exit(0);                   // Exit program if it is pressed again

    if (Key != K.Char)             // User didn't hit correct key...
    {
      Sound (BeepErr);             // Error beep
      DisplayErr (++ErrNum);       // Display error count
    }

    DisplayScore (Score);          // Display the user's score
    DisplayBar    (KeyNum);        // Display progress bar
  }
  Pause();
}
```

```
//-------------------------------------------------------------
// key::Input() - gets the next character to be displayed from
// the data file. Returns 1 if successful, or 0 if EOF has been
// reached.
//-------------------------------------------------------------

int key::Input ()
{
  int i = 0;
  while (1)
  {
    int   Char;
    Char = fgetc (pFILE);          // Get char from file
    if ( Char == EOF ) return 0;   // Return on end of file
    if ( Char == '\n') break;      // Exit on end of LINE
    if ( Char == ' ') continue;    // Ignore blank
    Set [i++] = (char) Char;       // Initialize key::Set
  }
  Len = i;                         // Initialize key::Len

  return 1;
}


//-------------------------------------------------------------
// key::key() - constructor for the 'key' class. This routine
// performs the following actions:
// (a) opens the data file, exiting if it can't
// (b) calls Init to initialise the graphics library
// (c) sets the screen font
//-------------------------------------------------------------

key::key ()
{
  pFILE=fopen ("P.dat","rt");      // Open data file
  if ( ! pFILE ) exit (1);         // Exit on error

  if (! Init ())                   // Initialize graphics system
   exit (2);                       // Exit on error

  randomize ();                    // For random start char

  // Set text font, size and justification

  int TextSize = 4;
  settextstyle (TRIPLEX_FONT, HORIZ_DIR, TextSize);
  settextjustify (CENTER_TEXT,BOTTOM_TEXT);
}

//-------------------------------------------------------------
// key::Init() - initialises the graphics library, loading the
// Borland graphics screen driver, and setting the graphics
// mode. It returns 1 if successful, and 0 on error.
//-------------------------------------------------------------
```

```
int key::Init()
{
  int     Driver=DETECT;  // Driver to be used (autodetect it)
  int     Mode;           // Screen mode (returned)
  char *  Path = "";      // Path to driver (current directory)

  initgraph (&Driver, &Mode, Path);

  int InitRes = graphresult();
  if (InitRes != grOk)
  {
    cout  << "Graphics Error: " << grapherrormsg (InitRes);
    return 0;
  }

  return 1;
}

//------------------------------------------------------------
// key::~key() - destructor for the 'key' class.  This routine
// tidies up by closing the data file, telling the user that the
// game is over, and closing the graphics system.
//------------------------------------------------------------

key::~key ()                  // Destructor
{
  fclose (pFILE);             // Close data file
  GameOver ();                // "Game over" message
  closegraph ();              // Close graphics system
}

//------------------------------------------------------------
// DrawPicture() draws the screen display - mountains, snow,
// text, etc.
//------------------------------------------------------------

void DrawPicture()
{
  int MaxX = getmaxx(),
      MaxY = getmaxy();

  //      Clear screen

  setfillstyle (SOLID_FILL, SkyColor);
  bar (0,0, MaxX,MaxY);

  //      Draw mountain

  int Shape [] = {
        0,16, 3,14, 6,10,
        8,6,                    // Left peak
        10,7,
        12,4,                   // Right peak
```

```
        16,12, 20,16
   };
   int NPoints = sizeof Shape / sizeof (int) / 2;
   int i,j;

   for (i=j=0; i<NPoints; i++,j+=2)
   {
     Shape [j]   = Shape [j]   * getmaxx() / XStep;
     Shape [j+1] = Shape [j+1] * getmaxy() / YStep;
   }

   setcolor (SnowColor);
   setfillstyle (SOLID_FILL, SnowColor);
   fillpoly (NPoints,Shape);          // Draw and fill polygon

   // Draw bottom bar

   setfillstyle (SOLID_FILL, GroundColor);
   bar (Shape[0],Shape[1],MaxX,MaxY);

   // Display score text

   setcolor (TextColor);
   outtextxy (ScoreText.X,ScoreText.Y,"Score ");

   // Display Error text

   outtextxy (ErrorText.X,ErrorText.Y,"Error ");

   DisplayScore (0);
   DisplayErr (0);

   // Display bar

   setfillstyle (SOLID_FILL,BarColor);
   bar (TopBar.X, TopBar.Y, BottomBar.X, BottomBar.Y-1);
}

//----------------------------------------------------------------
void key::Get ()
{
  Char = toupper (Set [random (Len)]);
  WhatHand ();
}

//----------------------------------------------------------------
// key::WhatHand() determines which hand, right or left, should
// be used to press a given key.
//----------------------------------------------------------------

void key::WhatHand ()
{
  static char LeftKeys [] =
```

```
          "123456" "!@#$%^"
          "QWERT"
          "ASDFG"
          "ZXCVB";
    int i;

    // Is the character a left-hand key?
    for (i=0; i < sizeof LeftKeys; i++)
      if (LeftKeys [i] == Char)
      {
        Hand = Left;
        return;
      }

    // If not, it must be a right-hand one.
    Hand = Right;
    return;
}

//-----------------------------------------------------------
// key::Clear() - clear the keyboard buffer.
//-----------------------------------------------------------

void key::Clear ()
{
    while (kbhit ())
      getch ();
}

//-----------------------------------------------------------
// Sound() - sound a tone
//-----------------------------------------------------------

void Sound (beep Tone)
{
    int Freq=0;                    // Frequency, Hz
    int Delay=0;                   // Time (milliseconds)

    const int AttFreq = 110;  // Hz
    const int ErrFreq = 440;  // Hz
    const int AttDelay= 50;   // msec
    const int ErrDelay= 200;  // msec

    switch (Tone)
    {
     case BeepAtt:
       Freq=AttFreq;
       Delay=AttDelay;
       break;
     case BeepErr:
       Freq=ErrFreq;
       Delay=ErrDelay;
       break;
```

```
     }
   sound (Freq);
   delay (Delay);
   nosound ();
   delay (Delay);
}

//-----------------------------------------------------------
// key::Draw() - output the character that the user has to
// press, above the right or left mountain.
//-----------------------------------------------------------

void key::Draw ()
{
   static int X = 0;              // Declared static in order to
   static int Y = 0;              // previous values
   static char Buf [2] = "";

   // Clear previous character
   setcolor(SkyColor); outtextxy (X,Y,Buf);

   // Set position for left or right hand character
   if (Hand == Left)
   {
     X=LeftChar.X;
     Y = LeftChar.Y;
   }
   else
   {
     X=RightChar.X;
     Y = RightChar.Y;
   }

   Buf[0] = Char;                 // Place new char into Buf

   // Output new char
   setcolor(CharColor); outtextxy (X,Y,Buf);
}

//-----------------------------------------------------------
// key::Trace() - displays the 'ski trace' from the top of the
// appropriate mountain, until the user presses a key, or the
// trace reaches the bottom. The routine returns the amount to
// be added to the user's score.
//-----------------------------------------------------------

int key::Trace (int & Key)
{
   // Display ski trace, get key pressed, count score

   int X, Y,                      // Current trace coordinates
       X0, Y0,                    // Trace start
       Finish,                    // Y coordinate of finish
```

```
      Amp,Amp2,Amp3;              // Trace amplitudes
                                  // Use global constants
Amp  = MinAmp + random (MaxAmp - MinAmp);
Amp2 = Amp/4;
Amp3 = Amp/2;

static const double PI = asin (1.) * 2.;
double Freq, Freq2, Freq3;       // Trace frequency

// Set start and finish points

if (Hand == Left)
{
  X0      = LeftStart.X;
  Y0      = LeftStart.Y;
  Finish = LeftFinish.Y;
}
else
{
  X0      = RightStart.X;
  Y0      = RightStart.Y;
  Finish = RightFinish.Y;
}

// Set frequencies for sin()

Freq  = 2*PI/(Finish - Y0);
Freq2 = Freq * 3;
Freq3 = Freq * 11;

clock_t StartTime = clock ();    // Get start time

// Calculate and draw ski trace

for (X = X0, Y = Y0; Y < Finish; Y++)
{
  int   C = TraceColor;

  X = X0 + Amp   * sin (Freq *(Y-Y0))
         + Amp2 * sin (Freq2*(Y-Y0))
         + Amp3 * sin (Freq3*(Y-Y0));

  putpixel (X,   Y,C);
  putpixel (X-1,Y,C);
  putpixel (X+1,Y,C);
  delay (par::Delay);
  if ( kbhit () )                // Test for key pressed
  {
    Key = toupper (getch ());    // Get key from keyboard
    if ( ! Key ) getch ();       // Not ASCII char
    break;                       // Exit on key pressed
  }
}
```

```cpp
    clock_t KeyTime = clock ();        // Set key pressed time

  // clock() returns the time in 'ticks', so to get it in seconds, we
divide
  // by the number of ticks per second, which is defined as a constant in
time.h
    float Time = (KeyTime - StartTime) / CLK_TCK;

    int Add;                           // Add to score
    if (Y == Finish)
      Add = 50;  // Key not pressed
    else if (Key != Char)
      Add = 10;  // Err key pressed
    else if (Time < 1.0)
      Add =100;  // Time < 1 sec
    else if (Time < 1.5)
      Add = 50;
    else if (Time < 2.0)
      Add = 20;
    else
      Add = 10;

    //      Clear ski trace

    for (X = X0, Y = Y0; Y < Finish; Y++)
    {
      int C = SnowColor;

      X = X0 + Amp  * sin (Freq *(Y-Y0))
            + Amp2 * sin (Freq2*(Y-Y0))
            + Amp3 * sin (Freq3*(Y-Y0));

      putpixel (X,  Y,C);
      putpixel (X-1,Y,C);
      putpixel (X+1,Y,C);
    }

    return Add;                        // Add to Score
}
//---------------------------------------------------------------
// Pause() - wait for a key to be pressed, and return its
// value.
//---------------------------------------------------------------

int Pause ()
{
  int Key = getch ();
  if (! Key)
    getch ();

  return Key;
}
```

```cpp
//---------------------------------------------------------------
// DisplayScore() - display the score value
//---------------------------------------------------------------

void DisplayScore (int Score)
{
  static char Buf[10] = "";

  // Clear previous value
  setcolor (GroundColor);
  outtextxy (ScoreText.X+textwidth("Score "),ScoreText.Y,Buf);

  sprintf (Buf, "%d", Score > 0 ? Score : 0);
  setcolor (ValueColor);
  outtextxy (ScoreText.X+textwidth("Score "),ScoreText.Y,Buf);
}

//---------------------------------------------------------------
// DisplayErr() - display the number of errors the user has
// made
//---------------------------------------------------------------

void DisplayErr (int ErrNum)
{
  // Display number of errors
  static  char    Buf [10] = "";

  // Clear previous value
  setcolor (GroundColor);
  outtextxy (ErrorText.X+textwidth("Error "),ErrorText.Y,Buf);

  sprintf (Buf, "%2.0f%%", 100.*ErrNum/par::MaxKey);
  setcolor (ValueColor);
  outtextxy (ErrorText.X+textwidth("Error "),ErrorText.Y,Buf);
}

//---------------------------------------------------------------
// DisplayBar() - display the progress bar
//---------------------------------------------------------------
void DisplayBar (int N)
{
  // Decrease bar
  int Y = TopBar.Y + (BottomBar.Y - TopBar.Y) * N/par::MaxKey;

  setfillstyle (SOLID_FILL, SnowColor);
  bar (TopBar.X, TopBar.Y, BottomBar.X, Y-1);
}

//---------------------------------------------------------------
// GameOver() - display the 'Game Over' message
//---------------------------------------------------------------
void GameOver ()
```

```
{
   int TextSize = 8;
   settextstyle (TRIPLEX_FONT, HORIZ_DIR, TextSize);
   settextjustify (CENTER_TEXT,CENTER_TEXT);
   setcolor(BLACK);
   outtextxy (getmaxx()/2,getmaxy()/2,"Game over ");
   Pause();
}

//---------------------------------------------------------------
// point:point() - constructor for a 'point' object
//---------------------------------------------------------------
point::point (float x,float y)
{
   // Constructor
   // x and y are relative coordinates

   X = x * getmaxx() / XStep;
   Y = y * getmaxy() / YStep;
}
```

Algorithm

The program's algorithm has only been slightly changed. The loop in `main()` causes:

```
while (K.Input ())
   Play ();
```

the next line to be read in the file **P.DAT**, where the letters used in the game are stored. The loop is terminated when we reach the end-of-file marker for **P.DAT**.

We have added functions for keyboard buffer clearance (**K.Clear()**), display of scores (**DisplayScore()**), a progress bar (**DisplayBar()**), and error rates (**DisplayErr()**).

Data

Significant changes have taken place in data description. The class **key** is introduced and a global object **K** of type **key** is defined (see header file **P.H**). Data and functions are hidden in the class **key**. Some functions that process the data are declared as public.

Functions

You should note that the opening of the data file and the initialization of the graphics is carried out in the constructor of our new class, **key**. The graphics screen is reset to a text one in the destructor.

The function **key::Draw()** outputs the letters to the screen.

In the function **key:: Trace()** (which is substituted for the original function **Run()**) the calculation of the **Score** is different. Now a library function **clock()** is used, which returns the current time according to the computer clock, expressed in ticks (a tick is a period with a duration of about 55 milliseconds). The value of **Score** depends upon the time (in seconds) elapsing from the moment the letter appears until the key is pressed.

A skier skis down with the help of the function **sin()** and **putpixel()**.

The functions **key::Init()**, **Pause()**, **Sound()** are familiar to you from the other programs. The functions **DrawPicture()**, **DisplayScore()**, **DisplayErr()**, **DisplayBar()** make use of the BGI.

What Next?

Program **P.CPP** is far from complete. There are lots of improvements that you could make. For example you could try to change the program to:

- Display the game level (possibly from the line number in the data file).
- Count the total **Score** for the whole game.
- Adjust the program's speed before the game starts coupled to a corresponding change of **Score** calculation.
- Retain the ten highest scores in a disc file.
- Turn the sound on and off by using a key press.
- Output a message if the game is paused.

Summary

You have now successfully reached the end of the book. You have covered C++ thoroughly and have written some useful and interesting programs. Learning to program is really only completed by sitting at a the computer and writing programs. We have shown you the tools and how to use them. You may want to go over some of the chapters again to make sure it's all clear, but this is now your chance to start experimenting with C++. That's the really fun and exciting part! Good luck.

Reserved Words in C++

The following list of words are C++ keywords and may not indeed, cannot be used as variable names or for any other purpose.

__asm	__es	interrupt	short
_asm	_es	__interrupt	signed
asm	__except	_interrupt	sizeof
auto	__export	__loadds	__ss
break	_export	_loadds	_ss
case	extern	long	static
catch	far	near	__stdcall
__cdecl	__far	_near	_stdcall
_cdecl	_far	__near	struct
cdecl	__fastcall	new	switch
char	_fastcall	operator	template
class	__finally	__pascal	this
const	float	_pascal	__thread
continue	for	pascal	throw
__cs	friend	private	__try
_cs	goto	protected	try
default	huge	public	typedef
delete	__huge	register	union
do	_huge	return	unsigned
double	if	__rtti	virtual
__ds	__import	__saveregs	void
_ds	_import	_saveregs	volatile
else	inline	__seg	while
enum	int	_seg	

Changes to the C++ language

Authors of good books on C++ have a particularly difficult task because the language is still considered to be under development. During the process of standardizing C++, numerous minor problems surface that need fixing. Most of these fixes involve a more precise definition that will increase reliability and remove ambiguity in code. Some changes just make something possible that was not previously allowed. Changes to a language operation are carefully considered by national and international panels and committees. Extensive discussions and tests are monitored within the programming industry before any alterations are implemented.

An example of such a change is the one that allows explicit template function instantiation. This means that future compilers will support a wider range of template function definitions.

Note that it takes time for compiler writers to catch up with changes, even when they are members of either ANSI X3J16 (the US committee on standardizing C++ - membership open to non-US nationals/companies) or their own national committee for C++ standardization (such as the UK C++ panel).

The problem is made worse by the existence of a number of talented compiler developers who are not members of any C++ standardization committee. Without such membership they assume that the 'Annotated Reference Manual ' defines C++ .It doesn't!

This same problem is faced by many authors. Some are either members of X3J16 or have access through their employers. Most have to rely on whatever they can find published in journals such as 'The Journal of C Translation' and 'C++ Report'.

Minor Changes

There are some changes, fortunately very few, that are correcting aspects of the language as a result of experience and programmer demand. Arguably, only two of these will impact most ordinary C++ programmers (as opposed to specialist library designers, or those involved in large projects using very advanced idioms).

1 The change in the scope rule for a variable declared in the **init** clause of a **for** statement. The new scope rule specifies that such a variable goes out of scope on exit from the body of the **for** statement. When compilers implement this change, they will have to issue a warning in a situation such as:

```
int i =0;
void fn(){
  for(int i=0;i<10;i++){ // whatever
  }
  cout<<i; // required warning, i is outer scope version
}
```

There are further enhancements that allow other declarations in iterations, but this is the only one that affects existing code. Fixing the code is easy, just move the declaration to immediately before the **for** statement.

2 The specification for an **enum** has been tightened up. The range of valid values for an **enum** is now effectively from the minimum to the maximum value of the specified set. Actually, it is slightly larger because it's specified in terms of the minimum bit-field that can represent that range (possible as offsets from a value). This means that existing uses of **enums** to provide named bit values will work correctly. Values outside the required range are undefined.

3 Explicit conversion to an **enum** is now legal (it wasn't before!) and an attempt to convert an integral value outside the **enum**'s range is undefined (i.e. an error that the compiler is not required to diagnose).

If you want to provide operators for your **enums** you can do so as long as the relevant operator is not restricted to definition in a class scope (assignment is, so you can only use default assignment, with explicit conversion if needed)

Major Changes

The original mandate handed to the X3J16 and WG21 groups (the ISO committee working in parallel with X3J16) included templates and exception handling.

1 The fuller specification for templates is unlikely to affect existing code, it largely better defines the facilities and extends them.

2 Exception handling is far more problematic as it impacts on all existing code. Once an exception can be thrown, there are substantial implications. Resource management in an EH environment needs care, to ensure that resources are not lost when an exception is thrown. Of course, if no exception is thrown you might reasonably expect your code to function as previously. This is NOT true because of changes that have resulted from re-specifying the new operators. (See below.)

3 More recent experience has caused the introduction of **RTTI** (run time type information) because existing practice was resulting in a multitude of vendor or library specific tools to support some form of RTTI functionality. The only impact RTTI has on existing code is that some could be re-written to use it.

4 A fourth major extension is the introduction of something called **'namespace'** to resolve the growing problem of name clashes between different vendor libraries. This has a minor impact on existing code - don't use the global scope operator unless it is needed to resolve an ambiguity.

Some authors have recommended use of the global scope operator. This is simply to make explicit that a function, used in the definition of a member function, is not itself a member function. This use of the global scope operator is now suspect, and might cause errors in future compilations of code using it. There might be a remote possibility that it would change the meaning of the code.

The Impact of EH and new

ANSI X3J16/WG21 determined that the dynamic memory assignment operators (**new, new[]**) will give an "out of memory exception" if insufficient memory is available.

Despite considerable discussion, no acceptable way has yet been found to support both the original and the new mechanisms for handling out-of-memory. The conclusion, is that programs (and program idioms) that rely on **new** and **new[]** returning a null-pointer, will not function correctly in the future.

Attempts to fix this via the **new_handler** only make matters worse, as it hijacks the use of the **new_handler** mechanism in a way that is likely to introduce further inconsistencies. It's true that you can restore the return of a null-pointer by such a mechanism (if the compiler supports it) but you cannot, in addition, provide your own handlers in the traditional way.

In simple terms, the effects of introducing exception handling (which was required by the mandate for standardization) coupled with a requirement that **new** and **new[]** operators should throw an exception if there's insufficient memory, breaks all existing code.

There are many positive aspects to this change (and the introduction of a specific operator **new[]** which can now be replaced by an in-class version) but the transitional stage will cause problems to both programmers and authors.

New Keywords

The following are currently reserved as keywords (note that a keyword is more than a reserved word, it is a word that has significance to the parser) in addition to those listed in the ARM.

bool	const_cast	dynamic_cast	false
mutable	namespace	reinterpret_cast	static_cast
true	typeid	using	wchar_t

Note that both **bool** and **wchar_t** are full built-in types and not provided as **typedef**s.

As a result of deliberations concerning problems incurred by certain national character sets, the following have also effective keyword status:

bitand   **and**   **bitor**

or   **xor**   **compl**

and_eq   **or_eq**   **xor_eq**

not   **not_eq**

The use of a double underscore in an identifier is reserved to implementors for support of name-mangling algorithms. Otherwise its use should be avoided - although a compiler is not required to diagnose it.

The following digraphs are also provided for use by those with nationally restricted character sets:

```
<%  %>  <:  :>  %:
```

(in the same manner as %:% is used as a preprocessing token equivalent to ##)

INDEX

Symbols

! 143, 174
!= 87
#define directive 46
% 38
& 249
&& 108, 173
( ) 18
dereference op 251
*= 150
++ 57, 121
-- 133
/* 17, 70
// 16, 70
: 106
< 75
redirection symbol 312
<< 17, 19, 188
  using with arrays 189
  using with strings 184
= 52, 54
== 75
> 75, 87

>= 87
>> 63, 191
  using 310
  outputting blanks 311
[ ] 18
\ 167
\0 169
\a 168
\n 168
\r 168
\t 167
{ } 18
{} 84
|| 157, 173

A

access specifier 432-
    436, 455, 568, 569, 571-573, 576
addition
  operator+() member function 499
address operator (&) 249
addresses 43
  finding values 251

P

T

tab character 167
tellg() 342
tellp() 342
templates 588, 589
  class 590, 592
text files
  appending to 333
  processing 318
  reading 329
  writing 331
text lines 36
type casting 154
type conversion 155, 164
type modifiers 60
types
  enumerated 457
  floating point 67
  of numbers 43
  of variables 51, 125, 254
    memory required for 123
  reference 386

U

uninitialized
  arrays 183
unions 382-385, 457
unsigned 152, 154

V

variables 50, 245
  addresses of 249
  assigning values to 52, 88
  declaring 50
  global 241, 243, 246
  in arithmetic calculations 65
  initializing 54
  local 240, 243
  maximum values 57, 149, 152
  memory required for 123

naming 60, 243
pointers 254
reusing names 244
scope 239, 243, 426
scope within blocks 248
static 246
types of 51, 125
using 52
values 52
void 17, 228
  return type 216

W

while 131, 186
  using do/while 188
whitespace 69
  extracting whitespace characters 312
words
  counting 323
write() 335
writing
  text files 331

C++ is widely taught as a first programming

language because of its power and simplicity.

This book provides wide coverage of the

language and is aimed squarely at the

beginner to C++.

Author: Ian Wilks   Price $19.95   ISBN 1-874416-29-X

INSTANT....................

Designed as a rapid introduction to the programming

language, these books deliver fundamental, essential

knowledge in an entertaining, painless way. These

books are ideal for students looking for a swift

grounding, or indeed for anyone wanting to make a

quick breakthrough into programming proficiency

The Book

Author: Ben Ezzell (Includes disk)
Price $39.95 ISBN 1-874416-22-2

The Revolutionary Guide to Visual C ++   provides the reader with a

comprehensive understanding of objects, thus making Windows programming with the MFC an easier

task to accomplish. Section One allows the C programmer to quickly get to terms with the difference

between C and C++, including the concepts involved in object oriented design and programming. In

Sections Two and Three, you are guided through the various steps required to produce complete

Windows applications.

The Series

REVOLUTIONARY GUIDE TO ....

Learn the programming techniques of the industry experts with the Revolutionary Guides. This series guides

you through the latest technology to bring your skills right up to date. Example applications are used to

illustrate new concepts and to give you practical experience in the language.

The Book

Author: L.Romanovskaya   Price $29.95   ISBN 1-874416-27-3

The Beginner's Guide To OOP in C++

leads you from the standard world of C into today's most popular Object Oriented language, C++.

Following through the development of a typical Object Oriented program, you will learn the

fundamental concepts of both C++ and the Object Oriented approach to programming.

The Series

BEGINNER'S GUIDE TO ....

These guides are designed for beginners to the particular language or to

programming in general. The style is friendly and the emphasis is on

learning by doing. The chapters focus on useful examples that illustrate

important areas of the language. The wealth of examples and figures

help make the transition from beginner to programmer

both easy and successful

Authors: Various Price: $44.99 ISBN 1-874416-34-6

The Book

Assembly Language Master Class covers the 386,

486 and Pentium processors. This guide gives

aspiring experts a tutorial covering subjects such as

direct SVGA access, serial communications, device

drivers, protected mode and Windows, and virus   ....*MASTER CLASS*

protection secrets.

The aim of this series is to bring together the ideas of a

number of the leading edge experts in one indispensable

book. Each chapter has a defined objective built around

the key application areas of the language.

The Series

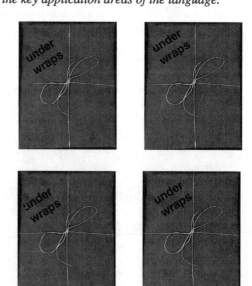